THIS
THING
CALLED
THE
WORLD

THIS THING CALLED THE WORLD

The Contemporary Novel as Global Form

DEBJANI GANGULY

Duke University Press   Durham and London   2016

Printed in the United States of America on acid-free paper ∞
Designed by Courtney Leigh Baker
Typeset in Arno Pro by Graphic Composition, Inc., Bogart, Georgia
Library of Congress Cataloging-in-Publication Data
Names: Ganguly, Debjani, author.
Title: This thing called the world : the contemporary novel as global form /
Debjani Ganguly.
Description: Durham : Duke University Press, 2016. | Includes bibliographical references
and index.
Identifiers: LCCN 2016004520 (print) | LCCN 2016006127 (e-book)
ISBN 9780822361374 (hardcover : alk. paper)
ISBN 9780822361565 (pbk. : alk. paper)
ISBN 9780822374244 (e-book)
Subjects: LCSH: English fiction—21st century—History and criticism. | English fiction—
20th century—History and criticism.
Classification: LCC PR889.G36 2016 (print) | LCC PR889 (e-book) | DDC 823/.9209dc23
LC record available at http://lccn.loc.gov/2016004520

COVER ART: Ann Hamilton (lineament · book/ball), 1994. Ball wound from strips of text,
book, wood, and glass vitrine, Edition 15 with 4 Artist's Proofs, 12½ × 28½ × 5½ inches /
31.8 × 72.4 × 14 cm (vitrine). Courtesy Ann Hamilton Studio.

To my family
&
In memory of
Srinivas Aravamudan
(1962–2016)

Contents

Acknowledgments

I have carried within me a book on the novel for as long as I can remember. It is gratifying to have finally written it. Even as my friends in school were rapidly abandoning the novel for television, I refused to give up the pleasure of losing myself in its printed pages. This habit has stayed with me right through the evolution of the multimedia and the digital age. The sense of marvel at the alchemy of words turning into gold, the magic of transport to worlds distant and different, and my capacity to enter into the lives of myriad fictional characters, none of these pleasurable experiences has diminished over a lifetime. In some senses, then, my first debt of gratitude is to the shelves of books that adorned by parental home and to my late father, who urged me to discover the pleasures of reading. A good book, he used to say, will never let you down.

I owe a world of debt to many friends and interlocutors who have given so generously of their time and thoughts to the making of this book. Srinivas Aravamudan, Ian Baucom, James Chandler, Joseph Slaughter, Tom Ford, Ned Curthoys, Desmond Manderson, Fiona Jenkins, Ankhi Mukherjee, Shameem Black, and Gillian Whitlock read early drafts of various chapters and helped shape my arguments in important ways. I am very grateful to them. Joseph Slaughter's *Human Rights Inc.* and Ian Baucom's *Specters of the Atlantic* were foundational triggers for this book. At a later stage James Chandler's *An Archaeology of Sympathy* mattered significantly. I thank them all for their inspiration. Joseph and I were on a panel on the global novel at a conference at Cambridge University in 2011 at the invitation of Mary Jacobus, the director at that time of the Centre for Research in Arts, Social Sciences and Humanities. Our exchanges were productive and timely during that trepidation-filled, midway stage of the first draft that most authors will recognize with some empathy.

Over the years conversations with Mary Jacobus, Ato Quayson, Neil Ten Kortenaar, David Damrosch, Anthony Cascardi, Simon Schaffer, Vilashini Cooppan, Rochona Majumdar, Dipesh Chakrabarty, Simon During, Michael Steinberg, Daniel Herwitz, Leela Gandhi, Lauren Berlant, Ranjana Khanna, Kachig Tololyan, Jon Mee, Stuart Elden, Christopher Wise, Alex Houen, Saikat Majumdar, Vanessa Agnew, Kader Konuk, Ronit Ricci, Sara Guyer, Caroline Turner, Gillian Russell, Neil Ramsey, Monique Rooney, Hamish Dalley, and Rosanne Kennedy helped crystallize many of the ideas in the book. Ranjana Khanna's skepticism about world literature in particular, which she expressed at the dinner table in her elegant Durham home one evening in early 2012, catalyzed thoughts about the postcolonial provenance of world-making. "Where is the postcolonial in all this talk about the global and the world?" she asked with some impatience. The novelist Amitav Ghosh participated in our conversation, as did Srinivas Aravamudan, and together we talked long into the night after an invigorating day at the Duke University conference Novel Worlds. I am grateful to Nancy Armstrong and her team for inviting me to convene a panel at that event.

Parts of this book were presented as talks at various universities: Goldsmiths, Warwick, Leeds, Cambridge, Oxford, Duke, Berkeley, Toronto, Michigan, Wisconsin–Madison, British Columbia, Stellenbosch, Sydney, Melbourne, and Queensland. I thank my hosts at these institutions: Sanjay Seth, Neil Lazarus, Rashmi Varma, Jon Mee, Graham Huggan, Mary Jacobus, Ankhi Mukherjee, Elleke Boehmer, Nancy Armstrong, Penny Edwards, Ato Quayson, Daniel Herwitz, Sara Guyer, Phillippa Kelly, Liam Semler, and Lisa O'Connell. Few books can be written without assistance from fellowships and grants. A three-year Australian Research Council Discovery grant helped me plunge into the research for this book, and fellowships at the University of Chicago in 2010 and the University of Cambridge in 2013 provided the essential time to write. The British Library, the Bodleian, the University Library at Cambridge, the Regenstein in Chicago, the National Library of Australia, and the Chifley and Menzies libraries at Australian National University were havens of discovery. My place of work from 2007 to 2014, the Humanities Research Centre at ANU, has also been a wonderful venue for scholarly replenishment. I thank my colleagues, fellows, and students for their generosity and insights. Without my two smart and energetic graduate students, Elen Turner and Nonie Tuxen, to assist me in my research, this book would have taken longer to complete. I am truly grateful for their help.

Excerpts from previous versions of chapters 7 and 8 were published in *Postcolonial Studies* 11, no. 1 (2008) and *Cambridge Journal of Postcolonial Literary Inquiry* 1, no. 1 (2014). Arguments from an earlier draft of the introduction were published in *Angelaki* 16, no. 4 (2011) and in *What Was the Human?*, edited by Liam Semler et al. (Melbourne: Australian Scholarly Publishing, 2012). Excerpts from the introduction and chapter 4 were published in *Cambridge Companion to the Postcolonial Novel*, edited by Ato Quayson (Cambridge: Cambridge University Press, 2015). Excerpts from an earlier draft of the coda were published in *Humanities Research* 15, no. 2 (2007). Excerpts from chapter 2 were published in *Edward Said: The Legacy of a Public Intellectual*, edited by Debjani Ganguly and Ned Curthoys (Melbourne: Melbourne University Press, 2007), and *The Values in Literary Studies*, edited by Ronan McDonald (Cambridge: Cambridge University Press, 2015).

I thank the two anonymous readers of Duke University Press whose invaluable comments helped me craft the book into the shape you see here. One of them reminded me of my tough high school teacher in India who invariably managed to bring out the best in me after first ensuring that I had my back to the wall. I can only hope that the magic has worked this time. Ken Wissoker's editorial keenness to see this book through has never wavered. An admixture of warmth and toughness in just the right measure, his approach to this project has done me a world of good. Thank you, Ken. Elizabeth Ault and Susan Albury shepherded the manuscript with a generous efficiency through its various stages of production. I am grateful for their editorial help.

Rana has been privy to my thoughts about this "global" thing for years now, as have our children. This book has seen our son, Ritwik, grow into an advanced-year undergraduate student and our daughter, Geetanjali, into a graduate scholar of human rights and climate law. They have lived with my novelistic obsessions with great love and have even ventured to read some of the works in this book. I dedicate this book to them, to my parents, and to the late Srinivas Aravamudan, who tragically left this world while the book was in production.

Introduction

A Nonsynchronous Contemporaneity

On the eve of the 2003 Iraq War, Henry Perowne, the neurosurgeon protagonist of Ian McEwan's novel *Saturday*, ponders the pervading sense of anxiety
and vulnerability in the world, a feeling aggravated by incessant exposure to
images of violent global flashpoints: "He takes a step towards the CD player,
then changes his mind for he's feeling the pull, like gravity, of the approaching TV news. It's *the condition of the times, this compulsion to hear how it stands
with the world,* and be joined to a generality, to a community of anxiety. . . .
The television networks stand ready to deliver, and their audiences wait. Big-
ger, grosser, next time. Please don't let it happen. But let me see it all the
same, as it's happening and from every angle, and let me be among the first
to know."[1] *Saturday* is a symptomatic case study for this book on the "condition of the times," a zeitgeist marked by our "compulsion" to be world-
oriented in the aftermath of the cold war and the geopolitics of violence that
we have been witness to. This spectatorial, world-making sensibility, mediated by a flow of images that iconicize terror-inducing devastation as a sign
of our times, produces the distinctive literary formation that is the primary
focus of this study: the contemporary world novel. My primary thesis is that
around the historically significant threshold of 1989, a new kind of novel as a
global literary form emerged at the conjuncture of three critical phenomena:
the geopolitics of war and violence since the end of the cold war; hyperconnectivity through advances in information technology; and the emergence of
a new humanitarian sensibility in a context where suffering has a presence in
everyday life through the immediacy of digital images.

This novel form is a distinct product of the age of informational capitalism in the sense that its capacity to be world-oriented is inextricably linked to the capacity of a global informational economy to work as "a unit in real time on a planetary scale."[2] This does not mean that it encompasses the world as a whole in its spatial and affective orientation. It means rather that the novel now evinces a capacity, predominantly through a global informational infrastructure, to imagine the human condition on a scale larger than ever before in history and certainly beyond national and regional configurations, which have traditionally marked both its conditions of possibility and its limits. If the industrial age saw the rise of the novel as a genre representing a new space-time configuration enabled by print capitalism that then created the conditions under which the "nation" could be imagined (as Benedict Anderson has taught us), the radical spatiotemporal shifts generated by the information age produce the global novel that helps imagine the new chronotope "world." The information age, of course, began long before 1989. Yet the age of informational capitalism that saw the rise of the Internet, the World Wide Web, and various forms of social media under a largely capitalist world system became a powerful phenomenological horizon after 1989.

The comparison with the rise of the novel in the age of industrial and early commercial capitalism advances the larger frame of my study. I seek to understand the emergence of this global fictional form and its world-oriented sensibility by revisiting a narrative grammar of the "human" and "humanitarianism" that constituted the foundations of the novel in the eighteenth century. The twin ideas of Sovereignty and Sympathy constituted the parameters of this novelistic grammar. These were critically shaped by the moral imperatives of the new commercial society that was itself on the threshold of multiple technological revolutions.[3] What happens to this novelistic grammar in the age of informational capitalism when the literary imagination confronts ever more expansive and rapidly mutating territorial, infrastructural, social, and cultural frontiers? In bringing the eighteenth-century English novel into a comparative frame with the contemporary world Anglophone novel, this study seeks to excavate a genealogy of this aesthetic form that is remarkably apposite for our times. Such an approach is informed by uncanny homologies between the conditions that gave rise to the novel in eighteenth-century England and those that have produced the contemporary world novel. The grounds of comparison are constituted by several salient circumstances: shifts in life-forms and the moral imagination enabled by technologies of capitalism in both eras; the emergence of ideas of cosmopolitan world-making through heightened connectivity by trade and information flows; colonization and occupation of lands and peoples distant and different; formulations and mutations of the idea of rights that were critical to the novelization of the collective imaginary in both eras, through the discourse of the sentimental and the sympathetic spectator in the eighteenth century and the politics of witnessing in our era; and radical epistemological shifts in the ideas of truth, value, virtue, and freedom that transformed and amplified the generic range of literary production in both eras. A careful calibration of these homologies urges a closer examination of the intensification of and ruptures with eighteenth-century literary and cultural forms in the contemporary global novel, a task that this book undertakes in the unfolding chapters.

In arguing for the nonsynchronous contemporaneity of my literary archive after 1989, however, I do not wish to suggest that it is nothing but a ghostly revisitation of the long eighteenth century. The neoromanticist, postmodern rhetoric of specters, memorialization, and even musealization cannot begin to capture the sheer novelty—hence novelization—of our era.[4] The world historical dimensions of our era are scarcely just an extension and expansion of the European world of industrial modernity. As any number of scholars have argued, including Giovanni Arrighi in his provocatively entitled book *Adam Smith in Beijing*, the history of capital is now global in ways that comprehensively exceed and thoroughly complicate its beginnings in the eighteenth-century transatlantic world.[5] What, then, do I propose to achieve with such a genealogical analysis? The novel more than any other genre is future-oriented and semantically open-ended, ready to absorb within its polymorphous, heteroglossic ambit the indeterminacy of the present; it is a genre that, in Mikhail Bakhtin's words, has a "living contact with the unfinished, still evolving contemporary reality."[6] As theoretical work on the genre attests, the modern novel is also an irrefutable product of capitalist lifeworlds.[7] So what I am urging with this analytical gaze across the chasm of two centuries is a renewed critical attention to the very conditions of the novel's possibility and, more important, to conditions that fortify the realization of its full potential as a genre of an indeterminate, evolving present par excellence of the mutating lifeworlds of global capitalism. Two key historical moments in that mutation, the second half of the eighteenth century and the world after 1989, are astonishingly apposite and homologous. They both constitute definitive ruptures in the evolution of capitalist lifeworlds and the politicocultural ideologies that have shaped them. Information technology is to this revolution what new sources of energy were to the successive industrial revolutions, from the steam engine to electricity, fossil fuels, and nuclear power. The two periods bookend the ascension and decline of liberalism, the ideological cornerstone of much of the modern world and a powerful shaping force of the novel in the modern age. In an age when print medium is in serious competition with multiple other media generated by information and communication technologies, the novel more than any other print literary genre has flourished due to its robust accommodation of and adaptation to new worlds in the making much as Bakhtin had predicted nearly a century ago. To translate my approach into a Jamesonian reading of genre made famous in *The Political Unconscious*, the world Anglophone novel after 1989, while not a mere reiteration of the eighteenth-century English novel, does carry within itself the substrate of the early capitalist world and its competing ideologies that founded the novel in that period. What happens to this substrate as it is radically globalized in our times is a primary concern of this book.

Around 1989

To come back to where we started: the compulsion that McEwan's anxious neurosurgeon feels in the aftermath of 9/11 and on the eve of the Iraq War to understand where he stands with the *world*, a nervous compulsion born out of a habit to turn to the too accessible information networks he is surrounded by, networks that feed his absorption with global violence that threatens to engulf *his* world, a compulsion to *visualize* his condition on a hitherto unprecedented scale—with no less than the *world* as its measure—marks our protagonist as a quintessential character of novelistic worlds after 1989. I am aware that in choosing 1989 as a temporal horizon for the emergence of a new kind of novel, I am going against the grain of some recent scholarly literature on the importance of this date for literary studies. Amy Hungerford, for instance, in her essay "On the Period Formerly Known as Contemporary," says quite categorically, "Political watersheds are one thing, but cultural or aesthetic ones quite another, and it was not immediately clear—nor is it clear now—that . . . literature changed, even if the world did, on or about 9 November 1989."[8] Hungerford's analysis focuses on the novel, and at first blush her caution does appear sensible. After all, transformations in literary worlds and genres hardly occur in cataclysmic ways. And yet, as this book will gradually make clear, by 2008 (the year of Hungerford's publication) visible changes were indeed evident in novels emerging from different parts of the world in the wake of 1989, and even within the American canon, on which Hungerford focuses. Interestingly, what Hungerford saw

transformed after 1989 was not the novel but its extradiegetic domain—the
world that, according to her, had launched into the "age of multicultural-
ism, or more negatively, sectarianism."⁹ In other words, her American *world*
now had more differences to contend with than just communist worldviews.
The bipolar fractures had become multipolar. It is as if the 1968 student and
civil rights movements, the decolonization of large swaths of Asia and Africa
through the 1950s and 1960s, and their concomitant "multiculturalization" of
global public spheres had simply passed America by. This, as we well know, is
not the case even within American academia: the U.S. academy did not have
to wait until the 1989 watershed to become "multicultural." But such a quar-
rel is beside the point here and not one that I wish to pursue in this book.
More pertinent for my purposes is Hungerford's insistence that the period
around 1989 and after has not transformed the novel in any significant way.
This position is affirmed in Amir Eshel's *Futurity: Contemporary Literature
and the Quest for the Past* (2012), despite its focus on a significant novelistic
corpus—works by Coetzee, Sebald, McEwan, Ishiguro—around 1989: "As
Amy Hungerford has noted, 1989 hardly signaled a new chapter in the history of the novel. None of the works I turn to . . . depict 1989 directly or formally [as] signal[ing] the dawn of a new literary age. Rather, they consider
what the future may mean in view of the political realities and subsequent intellectual discussion that emerged after 1989."¹⁰ Eshel's modesty is surprising,
for his book is a rich study on the hermeneutics of precisely this futurity in
the contemporary novel, as well as a sharp and salutary revision of the "end
of temporality" thesis that has informed so much philosophical and literary
theoretical scholarship on late modernity in the past few decades. The proliferation of the prefix *post-* annexed to a range of metaconcepts has often been
cited as a symptom of our cultural incapacity to imagine a meaningful future
in the wake of the catastrophes of the twentieth century. Eshel's close readings of some of the most powerful contemporary novels from German, He-
brew, and Anglophone worlds challenge this theoretical worldview.

While I broadly concur with his futurity thesis about the novel after 1989,
in this book I wish to make a much stronger claim than Eshel about the
provenance of the world novel and its transformations after 1989. In doing
so I draw upon the force of the distinction that Frank Kermode once posited between *chronos* and *kairos*. The former connotes the successive repetition of the same, the latter on happenings of hypertemporal significance,
those that intensify and create anew a literary world in a particular stretch of
time.¹¹ The phrase *around 1989* features in my literary analysis with the force
of kairos, not chronos, and I do mean it to signal a significant shift in the evo-

lution of the novel. I evoke the period around 1989 as a critical threshold of the "contemporary" that contains within its intensified temporality developments from the 1960s to the present. These include an accelerated growth in information and communication technologies, globalization of a human rights culture, the rise of new forms of warfare and insurgencies, and their increasing visibility in new media forms, culminating in the spectacle of 9/11. In conceiving of the period around 1989 in this manner, I draw on the force of recent theorizations of the contemporary not as an epochal term in the sense of being fixated on ideas of the "new" and the "revolutionary" like the term *modernity*, but rather as a structure of temporality that illuminates the present through a remediation of the recent past and that conceives of modernity itself as already becoming historical.[12] The idea of the contemporary is in many respects the apposite temporal descriptor of our media-saturated age, enfolding both ruptures and continuities with past forms, much like new media genres.[13]

The kairos of 1989 is germane to my literary archive in ways that urge immediate elaboration. In what may come as a surprise, 1989 in my analyses is not limited to a postcommunist historical horizon. Nor is this book a study of literary worlds from either Eastern Europe or the erstwhile Soviet Union. The year features instead as a temporal horizon around which more things ended and began than just communism and the capitalist unification of the world. On the largest scale I am talking here of a different though related historiography, one that is far more intimately linked to the rise of the modern novel—that of the two hundred years of geocultural hegemony from 1789 to 1989 of the ideology of liberalism that Immanuel Wallerstein saw coming to an end right through what he called our "transitional present" from 1968 to 1989.[14] *Liberalism*, as I use it here, is shorthand for a modern political imaginary that, at least since the 1789 French Declaration of the Rights of Man and Citizen, established an international system of sovereign nation-states governed by the principles of individual liberty, private property, and equality before the law. Rights within such a paradigm have meant an idealized inviolability of the rights of citizens within the parameters of state sovereignty. Extrapolated onto literary history, the novel since the late eighteenth century has been the classic forbear of this liberal ethos of bourgeois individuality and also the prime modality along with newsprint of cultural imaginings of this international system of nation-states.

The years around 1989 and after feature in this book as a threshold of criticality, of a mode of addressing through the genre of the world novel the cracks in the two-hundred-year-old global liberal consensus that began to be visible in the spring of 1968 and grew exponentially until 1989, after which it was even more rapidly fractured by the excesses of a neoliberal world order that culminated in the U.S. occupation of Iraq in 2003. If liberalism dominated European worlds (and their colonies) from, say, 1789 with the French Declaration of the Rights of Man and Citizen until 1914, the postwar period from 1945 to 1970 (the cold war notwithstanding) saw the ideology becoming all but global under the aegis of the United States. Much of this was due to the decolonization of the erstwhile colonies in Asia, Africa, and Latin America and the reconfiguration of this zone into the Third World largely under a liberal consensus that packaged the ideals of universal suffrage, the welfare state, national identity, and economic development as a fourfold guarantor of progress. The 1968 movement was the first world revolution that challenged this liberal consensus. A plethora of crises generated precisely by this packaged liberalism in both the core and the peripheries of the world system led to a series of student-led uprisings across the globe. The 1968 revolution rejected both the old liberal and the old left legacies of the capitalist world system. Inserting itself as a geocultural force at the interstices of the bipolar cold war conflict, on the one hand, and the emergent postcolonial nation-making forces in Asia, Africa, and Latin America, on the other, it generated a heat, albeit tremulously at first, that for a while threatened the cold, calculated, détente-oriented politics of the more visible bipolar world order. The Vietnam War and the concomitant civil rights movement were the definitive beginnings of the fraying of liberal politics. It was in this earlier moment as well that the ideals of human rights and humanitarianism began to appear in rejuvenated registers around various global governmental and nongovernmental constituencies, which have had a bearing on the emergence of the new world novel. But it was not until 1989 and the U.S. triumphalism in that moment that the global liberal consensus seriously dissolved even as neoliberalism paradoxically gained an ominously inflated currency in the rhetoric of the free market and a democratic world order.[15] The Persian Gulf War of 1990–91 was the first tellingly violent spectacle to emerge in the wake of this dissolution.

"The year of miracles," Bruno Latour wryly called 1989, as he watched in equal dismay the comprehensive defeat of communism and the triumphalism of the cold war victors. Not that he was an apologist for communism. His first words of rebuke were directed at the excesses of the socialist regimes that had immeasurably multiplied man's exploitation of man in the name of ending such exploitation. But their dismantling was as dismaying, for "the voracious elites that were to have been dispensed with return[ed] at full strength to take up their old work of exploitation in banks, businesses and factories."[16] While Latour's 1991 treatise *We Have Never Been Modern* began in a semi-elegiac mode about the imminent devastation of the natural world and multiple lifeworlds around the globe with this unequivocal triumph of capital, yet another 1991 book heralded with evangelical zeal the same iconic event. This was Francis Fukuyama's neo-Hegelian treatise, *The End of History and the Last Man*. Backed by generous philosophical doses of an improvised Kojève, the book's crowing rhetoric about the triumphant marriage of liberal democracy and the free market was quickly challenged, and not least by Jacques Derrida in *Specters of Marx* (1993). "At a time when a new world order is attempting to install its neo-capitalism and neo-liberalism, no disavowal has managed to rid itself of all of Marx's ghosts," Derrida warned.[17] Fukuyama, he grimly pointed out, was in truth the harbinger of no promised land but of a world that was in dangerous disarray.[18] Derrida's nine-point inventory of the "plagues" of the advanced capitalist world system definitively heralds the demise of liberal aspirations around 1989. It includes the following: employment crises; exclusionary zones for noncitizens; economic wars; push and pull of the free market; foreign debt, especially of the developing world; global arms trade; proliferation of nuclear technology for military purposes; rise of phantom states run by the mafia and drug cartels; and not least, the globalization of interethnic wars.[19]

This last—the global state war—has been a topic of extensive deliberation among scholars of the post-1989 world and is of central significance to this book.[20] Many of the novels that constitute the archival bulwark of my analysis were written under the shadow of the wars that followed the triumphalism of 1989. The first of these was waged within nine months of the announcement by the East German government that GDR citizens could visit West Germany. In August 1990 the internecine warfare between the Kurds and the Iraqis escalated into the first Gulf War when the sole superpower of the post–cold war world thought fit to push through an alliance of thirty-four states to intervene in this ethnic conflict and declare war on the state of Iraq. Operation Desert Storm was the first war to be staged live on global media. The old Heideggerian idea of the world picture had sprung ominously to life through the display of the sole superpower's technological prowess that now seemed to encompass the entire planet. In some senses, with CNN's beaming of Operation Desert Storm, the interpellation of *Homo spectator* seemed to continue unabated from the days of the iconic demolition of the Berlin Wall, which Guy Debord, in a revised edition of his *Society of the Spectacle*, described as the ultimate triumph of a spectatorial capitalism wherein image and commodity united in a seamless spectacle for repeated consumption. Had Debord lived beyond 1994, he would no doubt have had much to say about the hypervisualization of many a war that followed in the wake of the spectacles of 1989 and 1991. The wars in Yugoslavia were among the most visualized ethnic wars of the century. They began in 1991 with the first conflict in Slovenia and lasted until 1999 and the NATO bombing of Kosovo. The genocidal horrors that global publics witnessed during much of this Balkan crisis were repeated in Rwanda, but these were soon eclipsed by the spectacular horror of 9/11 and the global "War on Terror" that followed, including the wars in Afghanistan and Iraq. This last was the most recent symbol of both the comprehensive defeat of liberal political ideology and a replay of 1989 U.S. triumphalism. As Michael Cox, an international relations expert at the London School of Economics, noted in his 2008 essay, "Who Won the Cold War in Europe?," "Iraq is the by-product of an American mindset that never for once questioned the assertion that the United States—and the United States alone—won the Cold War a decade and a half earlier."[21]

Crucial for grasping this contemporary wartime inventory is an understanding of the transformation in the very nature of warfare. Phrases such as *new wars, perpetual wars,* and *everywhere wars* have been frequently used, as has the phrase *humanitarian wars* due to the magnitude of humanitarian crises these have unleashed.[22] In brief, these new wars are characterized by transnational forms of violence that occur at the interface of conventional warfare between sovereign states, organized crime, and state-sponsored violations of human rights through population displacement and genocide.[23] Predominantly fuelled by fragmented ethnic and identity politics as opposed to the bipolar ideological divide of the cold war, the new wars have the globe as their battleground. They are peopled with mercenary troops and diasporic volunteers adept at using insurgency techniques aimed at mass-scale destabilization, generation of fear, and perpetuation of a state of emergency. More than in any other kind of war in human history, civilians are the largest casualties in these new wars. These transformations in the nature of political violence have in turn amplified the scale of operation of a global humanitarian industry made up of media reporters, NGO workers, and international human rights networks. Rapid advances in information and communications technology have further transformed the nature of wars in this era, in terms of both their execution and their impact.[24] These constitute the definitive features of what I call "deathworlds" of our contemporary era. The liberal romance with the idea of sovereignty, of both the state and the individual, as the right to life, liberty, and equality before the law, is here transformed into the right to kill, to spread death. As Achille Mbembe puts it, this is a sovereignty that is necropolitical in that it oversees "the generalized instrumentalization of human existence and the material destruction of human bodies and populations."[25] The obverse of this necropolitical sovereignty is the cult of death embodied in the sacrificial political act of suicide bombers. "We love death the way you love life," declared Shehzad Tanweer, one of the 2005 London suicide bombers, in a video he left behind to be played on the first anniversary of this event.[26]

In the past two and a half decades a critical mass of novels has creatively captured and transfigured shifts in sensibility triggered by radical phenomenological transformations in the apprehension of war and violence. These include McEwan's *Saturday*, Andrew Miller's *The Optimists*, Tom Keneally's *The Tyrant's Novel*, Salman Rushdie's *Shalimar the Clown*, David Mitchell's *Ghostwritten*, Michael Ondaatje's *Anil's Ghost*, Gil Courtemanche's *A Sunday at the Pool in Kigali*, Richard Flanagan's *The Unknown Terrorist*, John Updike's *The Terrorist*, Janette Turner Hospital's *Orpheus Lost*, Don DeLillo's *Falling Man*, Mohsin Hamid's *The Reluctant Fundamentalist*, Nadeem Aslam's *A Wasted Vigil*, Kevin Powers's *Yellow Birds*, and Joe Sacco's *Footnotes in Gaza*. Many of these novels are inflected with an acknowledgment of crisis—the mass of stateless people, the plight of refugees, the experience of war and terror, genocidal reprisals. Written at the cusp of what has been a horrific century of wars and ethnic carnage and a new millennium that does not augur much better, such works express a new kind of humanitarian ethic, a new internationalism built on a shared dread of human capacity for evil coupled with a deep awareness of the ambiguities of sharing grief across large expanses of ravaged deathworlds.

In conjunction with the global proliferation of war and violence that marks a profound decline of liberal ideological hegemony, two other global developments, hitherto only briefly mentioned, have a significant bearing on the emergence of these new world novels. One is the growing visibility in the geopolitical arena since the 1970s of the idea of human rights and, hitched to it, a rejuvenated politics of humanitarianism that has gained ground with the proliferation of the ever more visible war-ravaged deathworlds after 1989. The second is the stupendous transformation wrought by the digital revolution on our everyday worlds of political engagement and sociability, which, in turn, has amplified the infrastructural potential for humanitarian connectivity on a global scale. It is worth considering these two developments in turn. The idea of human rights, as Samuel Moyn has recently argued, far from being the natural sibling of the early modern idea of natural rights, and despite its UN enshrinement in 1948, actually became a force in world history after the late 1970s as late modernity's "last utopia," when all other emancipatory models appeared to descend into chaotic nonfulfillment: socialism, postcolonial nationalisms, liberalism.[27] How, one might well ask, can one talk of the simultaneous decline of liberalism and the emerging visibility of the discourse of human rights? Isn't the notion of "right" the cornerstone of liberal ideology? Here it is worth noting that there is a fundamental difference between the liberal conception of rights as it has politically manifested itself in the past two hundred years and the postliberal horizon of human rights. The notion of right that comes down to us from the 1789 Declaration of the Rights of Man and Citizen is the right of a polity to be incorporated into a sovereign state that in turn protects its citizens who are the bearers of such right. The idea of human rights, on the other hand, is conceived as an international covenant that questions the violence of a sovereign nation-state's regulation of the rights of its polity. It breaks with the secular sanctity of the inviolable link between rights, state sovereignty, and citizenship that has been the cornerstone of liberalism. To that extent, human rights are a postliberal phenomenon. Hence, as Moyn avers, previous attempts by scholars such as Lynn Hunt to trace a seamless genealogy of human rights from the early modern articulation of natural rights to their revolutionary recasting in the eighteenth century as political rights under a sovereign nation-state are based on a critical misunderstanding of the countervailing forces of our postwar times that have effected this radical disjunction.[28]

The distinction between a revolutionary model of rights (the cornerstone of early liberal thought) and a postliberal ameliorative model as manifested in the idea of human rights is fundamental to grasping the mutation of the rights discourse in our times. Crucially Moyn's analysis emphasizes a shift in the global imaginary toward the utopian horizon of human rights rather than emphasizing the actual performance of human rights as an international instrument of transformation.[29] He is scarcely unaware of the myriad failures of the human rights system, but he is more interested in tracing the ideological ascendancy of human rights through the 1970s and into the present—a historiographic exercise that, in its focus on the imaginary, is critical to understanding the emergence of contemporary literary forms such as the world novel and the humanitarian life narrative.

By the early 1970s the world was beginning to be disillusioned by the existing ideologies—liberalism, socialism, postcolonial nationalism, developmentalism—and their institutional forms that since the end of the Second World War had promised to transform the international world order into one that was relatively stable, the cold war notwithstanding. The United Nations may have enshrined the Universal Declaration of Human Rights in 1948, but it was in effect controlled "by a concert of great powers that refused to break in principle with either sovereignty or empire." To that extent, in a world focused on postwar reconstruction and decolonization on the basis of positivist legal systems circumscribed by the nation-state, the UN was "as responsible for the irrelevance of human rights as for their itemization as a list of entitlements."[30] Nor were the postcolonial states morally invested in a transnational vision of rights over their own ability to reinforce a positivist regime of constitutional and other rights for their new citizens. The right of self-determination that they avidly advocated—and which they often conflated with the notion of human rights—was in truth the right of collective autonomy from colonial forms of governance.

Minimal visibility began to be accorded to human rights in the early 1970s with the persecution of dissidents in the Eastern European and Soviet blocs. The desire for a new European identity among these dissidents outside the cold war context, coupled with the rise of dissidents from authoritarian Latin American states, catalyzed a gradual shift in U.S. liberal policy toward an internationalist human rights vision. The defeat in Vietnam was an added impetus for the Carter administration to recuperate, through a human rights discourse, the moral and missionary stature of the United States as a force of good in the world. Carter's words at a commencement address at the University of Notre Dame in 1977 marked this shift in U.S. government policy toward taking human rights seriously, albeit in a collective national context:

> For too many years, we've been willing to adopt the flawed and erroneous principles and tactics of our adversaries, sometimes abandoning our own values for theirs. We've fought fire with fire, never thinking that fire is better quenched with water. This approach failed, with Vietnam the best example of its intellectual and moral poverty. But through failure we have now found our way back to our own principles and values, and we have regained our lost confidence. . . .
>
> The Vietnamese war produced a profound moral crisis, sapping worldwide faith in our own policy and our system of life, a crisis of confidence made even more grave by the covert pessimism of some of our leaders.[31]

To highlight U.S. foreign policy interest in human rights after Vietnam is by no means to suggest that the United States was the prime initiator of a shift toward a human rights–oriented world. Carter's statement in fact was symptomatic of a shift that had already begun to gain momentum in different parts of the world. I have already noted the significance of the 1968 movements as symptomatic of the decline of the political hegemony of the North Atlantic brand of liberalism. The Helsinki accord finalized in July and August 1975 as the culmination of the Conference on Security and Cooperation in Europe contained "respect for human rights" as one of its ten points of agreement. The series of meetings that led to the final accord was oriented toward a rapprochement between the communist bloc and the Western powers. Dissidents from the communist bloc, such as the Bulgarian intellectual Julia Kristeva, were already making their voices heard, and a nongovernmental group called Helsinki Watch, funded by the Ford Foundation, was set up in 1977 with the United States as a central node. This group later morphed into Human Rights Watch. The Ford Foundation also funded the world's first center for the study of human rights, at Columbia University.[32] In France philosophers such as André Glucksmann and Bernard-Henri Lévy poured vitriol over the failures of the Soviet experiment and the catastrophic interventions of the capitalist alliance in Indochina. The arch Soviet dissident, Alexander Solzhenitsyn, became Lévy's hero in an ethical worldview that championed human rights over existing political systems.[33] At the onset of the Soviet occupation of Afghanistan in 1979, Lévy cofounded with a group of French philosophers, intellectuals, journalists, and activists a humanitarian organization called Action Contre la Faim (Action against Hunger) to focus on war-generated destitution, and especially malnutrition.[34] ACF's mission statement declares that its primary goal is "saving lives via the prevention, detection and treatment of malnutrition, in particular during and following disasters and conflicts."[35] Soon several other NGOs were founded, also focused on humanitarian relief in war-torn regions of the world. Not surprisingly Didier Fassin calls this period "the second age of humanitarianism," characterized by the emergence of the "witness."[36] The Cambodian genocide that lasted from 1975 to 1978 was also significant in the rejuvenation of the 1948 drafting of the Universal Declaration of Human Rights. But it was the ethnic cleansing in Yugoslavia and Rwanda in the 1990s that made genocide prevention one of the main pillars of the contemporary human rights movement—half a century too late and a lamentable irony given that the primary impetus for the 1948 declaration was the experience of the Nazi Holocaust.

For the purposes of my analysis the year 1989 is important in the expanding ideological reach of human rights. The years after 1989 saw a decisive shift from human rights as a global language that addressed the persecution of cold war dissidents to human rights as a worldview that encompassed a humanitarian orientation to mass-scale suffering at the hands of myriad political regimes around the world. This conjunction of humanitarianism with human rights is unprecedented in the history of rights. Never the historical cousin of any notion of "right" in modernity, humanitarianism has for too long been a shadow of its moral self that was honed in eighteenth-century debates on abolitionism and the period's philosophy of "moral sentiments," to partially cite the title of Adam Smith's tract. Seen for much of the nineteenth and twentieth centuries as the domain of soft and sentimental activism for its sensitivity to "distant suffering," or at worst as a patronizing form of pity that often morphed into cruelty, humanitarianism has witnessed a robust resurgence since the end of the cold war. It has accorded human rights a visibility and an affective reach that is now well-nigh maximal, a phenomenon I explore in more detail as I trace its impact on the evolution of the world novel.

Related to these momentous shifts in global humanitarian sensibilities is the emergence of the idea of transitional justice in the 1990s as a cathartic ethicolegal space for coming to terms with the trauma of long-standing political vivisections within a nation or a multiethnic congregation. Transitional justice is primarily oriented toward healing a community after a mass atrocity and prolonged internal armed conflict. In 2001 a global community for this new kind of human rights advocacy founded the International Centre for Transitional Justice (ICTJ), which describes the infrastructure of transitional justice in these terms: "Transitional Justice refers to the set of judicial and non-judicial measures that have been implemented by different countries in order to redress the legacies of massive human rights abuses. These measures include criminal prosecutions, truth commissions, reparation programs and various kinds of institutional reforms."[37] Even before the formation of the ICTJ, however, transitional justice had attained a most vivid legibility in the work of the Truth and Reconciliation Commission after the end of apartheid in South Africa. The importance given to individual testimonies in this juridical process and the consequent proliferation of the testimonial genres in our humanitarian era have had a powerful impact on contemporary literary worlds, especially on the form of the world novel.

No less significant for my story than the global state of war and the maximalism of a human rights culture is the digital revolution. In my analysis 1989 is a technological threshold in respect to one revolutionary event: the discovery of the World Wide Web by Sir Tim Berners-Lee, who put forward a proposal to the Geneva firm CERN in March 1989 to create a service feature on the Internet that, for the first time in human history, would enable informational connectivity on a global scale. Manuel Castells's deployment of the term *network society* can be dated to these developments. These transformations have been marked by the convergence of the Internet, the World Wide Web, and wireless communication services to radically amplify the breadth of human connectivity. In the 1970s and 1980s two other phenomena converged to catapult information technology onto the global stage: entrepreneurial tapping of its potential for wider use and countercultural movements that exploited its potential for social change. This was the period that saw the emergence of Bill Gates's Microsoft and Steve Jobs's Apple, not as giant conglomerates at first but as modest enterprises. The revolution proper, however, happened after 1989, with the explosion of wireless communication through rapid advances in the distributive capacity of opto-electronics and the convergence of wireless capabilities with the versatile processing and networking capacity of the Internet and the World Wide Web, respectively. The pervasive effects of these developments are evident in our world today. On the macro side these developments have revolutionized manufacturing, communication, finance, transport, infrastructure, medical applications, security and military operations, and the very foundations of our knowledge economy. On the micro side, for millions of people around the world the social, cultural, and communicative fabric of their lives is now critically linked to digital networks. The integration of various modes of communication—written, oral, visual, and aural—into an interactive network has revolutionized the very intellectual and social foundations of human existence.

The implications of the informational technology revolution on the thematics of war and humanitarianism are hard to recount in any exhaustive way in an introduction. Nor are they the core preoccupation of this book, except as they illuminate my theorization of the world novel. Suffice it to say that the hypermediation of wars in our times, like the unprecedented reach of a global human rights culture, would not have been possible without the digital revolution. These phenomena in turn are deeply relevant to my efforts to recalibrate for our times the interplay between distant suffering, technology, and humanitarian witnessing that has historically constituted the conditions of possibility for the rise of the early novel in the eighteenth century and that critically informs the framework of my theorization of the world novel after 1989. For novel studies today the charge of this affective formulation has multiplied beyond measure in our era of saturated visualization of geopolitical carnage. Since the first Gulf War, and more so in the rhetoric presaging the wars in Iraq and Afghanistan, we have come to accept that there is very little difference between the technologies used to wage war and those used to visualize it.[38] Pertinent in this context is an exploration of the transitive affectivity of new visual media in the emergence of novelistic genres of our times. Such mediated deathworlds, I argue, have critically transformed the novel form.

So far I have attended to the significance of the temporal framing of this book around 1989 and have delineated in detail the various vectors—political, cultural, ethical, technological—that converge to generate a world picture of deep relevance to my theorization of the contemporary world novel. I have also argued for the relevance of attending to the substrate of this literary genre as it transforms itself from the era of early capitalism to our informational era. In what follows I briefly examine the import of our mediated and hypervisual overexposure to worlds of war for my theorization of the idea of the "world" in the contemporary novel, and conclude with an analysis of the narrative grammar of the "human" as it constitutes the substrate of novel worlds from the eighteenth century to our times.

Neovisuality and Archives of the Sensible

The intensification of the visual appears to have become an ubiquitous feature of contemporary warfare.[39] The phenomenon ranges from exorbitant visualization of the field of war to the viral circulation of war images. The period after 1989 is particularly significant in this regard, for that is when the world witnessed an unprecedented intensification of a necropolitical mode of visuality in war tactics.[40] One example is the increasing use of unmanned aerial vehicles (UAVs)—drones, in common parlance—to target insurgents who are seen to infect the global body politic. Unlike field visualization in wars of previous eras, visualization in the use of UAVs, as Nicholas Mirzoeff notes, need be aware of no specific "cultural or governmental environment." It solely targets people to be killed.[41] Aligned with this necropolitical visual economy of the military imaginary is another phenomenon Derek Gregory calls "vanishing points"—those sites that operate as politicolegal gray zones or nonplaces where prisoners of the war on terror are ghosted away, spaces "of both constructed and *constricted* visibility.... Most of what happens there continues to be shielded from public gaze."[42]

At the other end of the spectrum of neovisuality is the unprecedented multimedia presence in global public spheres of deathworlds after 1989. How else could the 1994 genocide in a tiny central African republic, Rwanda, evoke such unprecedented global outrage and generate such a plethora of creative responses? These responses in turn have attracted charges of voyeuristic obscenity and atrocity tourism. The televisual assault on global publics during the two Gulf wars has been commented on so extensively, and in some cases with such near-farcical criticality,[43] that it has since become a commonplace to read media coverage of global states of war as an extension of twenty-first-century warfare itself. As the character Huw in David Mitchell's novel *Ghostwritten* remarks sardonically, "Preemptive strike must mean not declaring war until your cameras are in position."[44] Two other infamous sites of post-1989 war and violence, the visually sublime and spectacular horror of 9/11 and the digitally captured shame of the Abu Ghraib torture, both had instantaneous global reach and became an indelible part of the psychic life of the everyday for millions of spectators around the world. This overdose of war and death spectacles within our everyday spaces has led to "compassion fatigue," as many a scholar has argued.[45] Serious moral questions have also been raised about the constructed nature of global responses to war and terror, of the way dominant news and other media regulate what we *see* and how we *feel* about the massification of carnage all around us.[46]

If the "excruciations of war have devolved into a nightly banality," as Susan Sontag avers,[47] how may we characterize the dramatic rise in novelistic works on the depredations of war and violence in our time? To see such works as but symptoms of an impotent and voyeuristic sensibility, or of disproportionately regulated media imaginaries, would, I contend, close off avenues of analysis that could register their strong attunement to our precarious times, that could read them as melancholic witnesses urgently, compulsively propelled to find out, in the manner of Henry Perowne, how they "stand with the world." In their preoccupation with multiple civil wars across the globe, the problem of religious fundamentalism, the ravages of extreme capitalist pursuits, the shared feeling of vulnerability, and the everyday human dimensions of incessant global insecurity, these novels excavate traumatic traces of worlds around 1989; they are narratives that preserve for history a radical transformation of sensibilities, an expansion of the moral imagination due to instant and incessant media exposure to distant suffering. The circuits of affect these novels traverse—from fear to extreme dread, despair, anxiety, grief, sympathy, and hope—lend eminently to their conceptualization as archives of the "sensible" as against archives of the "insensible" theorized by Allen Feldman in the context of the war on terror as those "supplemental, artificed devices that support, repeat and preserve memory in prosthetic media."[48] Instances include nuclear weapon reserves, robotic projectiles that miss their mark, digitized replays in the Pentagon of the impact of the "shock and awe" doctrine, and even the burned stumps of the Twin Towers. It is also interesting to contemplate how these novels capture in their narrative flow the phenomenology of mediatized witnessing in our time, as it is to explore the work of genre, trope, rhetoric, and narrative as these transact with new media environments. A comparative frame would be the work of many modernist scholars who studied the changes in the novel form with the emergence of cinema in the early twentieth century or, for that matter, the emergence of photography in the nineteenth century.[49]

Further, the late eighteenth-century historiographical lens through which this analysis is filtered allows one to argue for the impact of the *visual* on one's moral imagination in ways that complicate the desensitization thesis. Here I cite one small example. During the 1806 parliamentary debate that eventually led to the termination of British participation in the transatlantic slave trade, William Wilberforce, in a powerful indictment of the few remaining apologists for slavery, invoked precisely the power of the *visual* in generating sympathy: "If the members of this House could actually *see* one thousandth part of the evils of that practice . . . they would not suffer the Slave Trade to exist for another year." "But it is because," Wilberforce angrily lamented, "they do not *see* . . . because *the objects, as they actually exist, are not allowed to obtrude upon their vision.*" "It is *for these reasons*," he concluded his powerful tirade, "that arguments such as we constantly hear, in favour of the continuance of the Slave Trade are heard at all."[50] What made early abolitionists like Wilberforce "see" the horrors of the slave trade? What stood in for *visual* evidence? Literature, it appears. Historians and literary scholars of the abolitionist movement find that the expectations placed on literary narratives of slavery carry the burden of making people *visualize* the evils of the slave trade to generate sympathy through their graphically "factual fictions," to cite the eponymous title of Lennard J. Davis's work on the origins of the English novel.[51] The inaugural World Anti-Slavery Convention in 1840 passed a resolution to this effect, in the words of Henry B. Stanton, the president of the American Anti-Slavery Society: "The abolitionists are feeble in number but strong in moral power. . . . Therefore is it that we fall back for assistance upon the enlightened sentiments of the civilized world. *One influence which we desire to bring to bear for this purpose is the literature of the world. We are in America a reading people. . . . We come to England and say give us an anti-slave literature. . . . We fall back for assistance upon British sentiment, upon English literature.*"[52] Literature and its melancholy realism thus stood in for the visual stimulus that we take for granted today. Literature made the abolitionists *see* and hence *feel* the horrific violence of the transatlantic slave trade. Conversely, in our era of global wars, I submit, the exorbitant visual stimulus *generates* the melancholic realism of the world novel. This is not to say that the visual now has primacy over the novelistic, but rather that many contemporary novels are now self-consciously intermedial in that they actively work into their formal structures and modes of address phenomenologies of apperception that far exceed the medium specificity of print.

The term *melancholic realism* has its origins in Romantic theories of documenting loss, of bearing witness to what has been disavowed or not been witnessed so as to render the unseen and unacknowledged suffering visible and, in the final analysis, humanized through shared sympathy. In its testamentary logic the term has been recuperated by Ian Baucom in his book *Specters of the Atlantic* as a countercategory to what he calls actuarial or speculative realism, whose logic is not the singular occurrence of loss and pain but the average type, the aggregate event, the nominal rather than the real value of suffering. Baucom describes the epistemological context in which this distinction arises:

> The history of the English novel comprises not only a history of the rise of fiction, but a continuing history of the vicissitudes of what constitutes and counts as fact. Through the middle of the eighteenth century ... the novelistic labour of constituting fictional facts is broadly consistent with ... the theoretical realism of speculative culture. ...
> The facts its fictions generate are not only compatible with but foundational to ... an actuarial historicism, a historicism whose key figure is the average, the aggregate, and abstract type. Such types operate by abstracting, from the manifold of observed, recorded or categorizable persons, events, or things, average representations of those persons, events or things.[53]

What, then, of the epistemological context of the rise of melancholy realism? It is the same as that of speculative realism, except that its object is the singular person, event, or thing that has been *lost* in the scramble for an actuarial or speculative mode of knowledge making. The melancholy witnessing of such loss brings it to light and life, and the factual fictions of the time were as much invested in such recuperation as in representing the abstract type. This distinction between melancholy and speculative realism—the former resisting the abstract logic of capital and its principle of general equivalence, and the latter very much embedded in the principle of exchange value—is one I wish to map onto my use of the term *world* and its complex relation to the term *global*.

Thus far I have used the term *world* rather unreflectively to connote an expansion of scale in the novelistic horizon of the present. It is time now to attend to its deeper conceptual purchase for this book. Woven into my analysis of novel worlds after 1989 are recent philosophical inflections on the idea of the world that are in deep tension with contemporary geopolitical understandings of globalization as a realigning of the globe with a new capitalist world order since the end of the cold war. While one hears the term *world* often enough in literary critical circles now,[54] and in ways that mark our global current conjuncture as perhaps the most apposite historical *moment* for its circulation, *world* as a concept has carried considerable philosophical and literary weight in intellectual history. Let us start with an apposite *postcolonial* usage, for it is in postcolonial literary theory that one finds some of the most compelling arguments in recent decades for a more global and worldly perspective on literary texts. Over three decades ago, in his celebrated work *The World, the Text and the Critic*, Edward Said questioned the insulation of canonical texts of English literature from the world historical imperatives of their times. His historical frame was the period of high European imperialism from the mid-eighteenth century until the end of the Second World War. The task of the critic, he said, was to prize open the "worldliness" of the literary text, to situate it as a product of its material allegiances and historical affiliations. At the time of Said's writing, the category *world* in relation to literature did not circulate with the charge it does today. The noisy, strident presence of globalization as an intellectual exchange alley was still a decade away, as were ways of imagining the world as maximal connectivity through information technology—all of which give the idea of world literature and the world in literature today an inflection not exactly available to Said's protean intellect and imagination in the late 1970s and early 1980s.

The most trenchant attacks on the category today are a throwback to a neomaterialist idiom that characterized the rise of postcolonial literary studies in the 1970s. *World* and *worlding* in the early postcolonial disciplinary context categorically meant an orientation to the material reality outside the literary text, and often even a position of radical anti-aestheticism that denounced any intellectual gesture that hinted at literary and cultural autonomy from the realm of imperial interest. In *Culture and Imperialism* Said wrote, "Cultural experience or indeed every cultural form is radically, quintessentially hybrid, and if it has been the practice in the West since Immanuel Kant to isolate cultural and aesthetic realms from the worldly domain, it is now time to rejoin them."[55] This polarization between "cultural materialism" and "cultural immunity," to use Leela Gandhi's terms,[56] often led literary studies down an antiliterary path, as if the only legitimate way to read a text produced during the period of high European colonization was to unmask its aesthetic features as signs of imperial intent. This is not to suggest that there were no rich literary critical studies produced under this rubric or that the discipline as a whole was afflicted by a materialist determinism. It is rather to draw a point of comparison with current circulations of the idea of world in literary productions of our globalized era and the contentions that the category has generated. The world for Said, as it is for scholars currently deeply critical of globalization's cultural hegemony, was primarily the material domain of economic and political interests.

My reading of the relationship between the world and the novel stands at significant variance from Said's for it resists his overwhelming emphasis on the novel's extradiegetic dimensions and his "one-world" mimetic argument about the role of the critic in evaluating the novel. I will have much more to say about this in part I; here I only briefly sketch the lineaments of my larger argument. The human in the novel, both Bakhtin and György Lukács remind us, is a surplus, an entity that signifies modes of world-making irreducible to empirical truths: "The dissonance special to the novel, the refusal of the immanence of being to enter into empirical life, produces a problem of form."[57] The novel, in other words, is the one standout genre in which form and content are "radically heterogeneous."[58] Its relationship to its extradiegetic worlds is extremely complex. To follow this logic through, one could say that the world novel of our times, while being a product of our global age, is not reducible to the *realism* of globalization. The global, I contend, is an empirical category in the Saidian sense; it is the domain of territorial and material expansion. The novelistic world can be conceptually distinguished from the globe by a phenomenological apprehension of the work of the human in making worlds through language and through an orientation critically attuned to the *surplus* of humanness.

Such an understanding of the world as *related to but not synonymous with its material and chronotopical coordinates* has an exciting genealogy, going back to Leibniz and his idea of possible worlds in the analytic philosophy tradition and the existential thought of Heidegger, Arendt, Eugene Fink, and more recently Jean-Luc Nancy. To explicate this rich body of thought in any detail is not feasible in an introduction. In brief, I take from Leibniz a minimalist reading of *world* as a linguistically finite set of entities and relations marked off by worlds made up of other finite sets of entities and relations. The novel in such a reading is a world-enclosing total system, and its various degrees of *realism* derive primarily not from its correspondence with the *actual* world out there but from the ways the entities within its demarcated set relate plausibly to each other, or as Leibniz put it, are "compossible" with each other.[59] The actual world is but one of the conditions of possibility for the creation of the fictional world, and not the sole determinant of its *realism*. A recent parallel iteration of this point can be found in literary theorizations of the world-systems model in the works of Franco Moretti and Pascale Casanova. For them the world is not the actual world of material and territorial expansion but a world-constituting system of literary production and consumption whose myriad patterns can be grasped only by a system of analysis that scales up way beyond an individual text, author, nation, and region. Further, such literary world-systems operate at a remove from political and economic ones. Such an approach invests in a fundamental difference between *ontological* and *ontic* understandings of the world, a distinction that Eric Hayot in *On Literary Worlds* usefully highlights. It is important, he suggests, to "clarify the difference between the ontological status of worlds in world-systems and their material or ontic ground with respect to the planet (rendered as globe). World systems *are* worlds in the sense they constitute a self-organizing, self-enclosed, and self-referential totality, but they are not to be confused with *the* actual world which—though it is also, of course, a world—is the only world whose geographical scope coincides exactly with that of the Earth."[60]

This distinction between the ontic and the ontological is, of course, quintessentially Heideggerian, and his celebrated difference between the earth and world is the source of much writing on the *world* in recent times. From this rich existential tradition I take the idea of the world and the human as mutually enclosing and disclosing each other through language. A stone is world poor, as Heidegger famously said, while the human is world rich. Technology objectifies the world, while the human dwells "in" the world through language.[61] The distinction that Heidegger poses between *worldmaking* in art and *picturing* the world that modern science enables—that is, the placing of the world "before us" to be "looked at," which for him is what distinguishes "the essence of the modern technological age"—actually weaves together two complementary ideas of the world that add immense value to my argument. In reading the world as I do in literary works that critically manifest a global humanitarian sensibility digitally mediated through the power of *visually* witnessing sites of violence, I subscribe to *both* Heidegger's invocation of aesthetics as the most powerful ground of world creation *and* his idea of the force of "world picturing" in our modern era. Not that

Heidegger had much to say about the actual status of the picture or visual stimuli of any kind in his philosophical work, but the charge of his idea of "world picture" can scarcely be underestimated in our image-saturated age. Technological wizardry as coextensive with our habitation as also the one powerful source of disembodied rapture is precisely what DeLillo's neocapitalist tycoon protagonist, Eric Packer, experiences in a cyborgian moment of illumination in *Cosmopolis* as he is about to be assassinated. His subliminal mind functions "as data, in whirl, in radiant spin, a consciousness saved from void. The technology was imminent or not, It was semimythical. It was the natural next step ... an evolutionary advance that needed only the practical mapping of the nervous system onto digital memory. It would be the master thrust of cyber-capital, to extend the human experience toward infinity as a medium for corporate growth and investment, for the accumulation of profits and vigorous reinvestment."[62]

The modern human's predilection to *picture* the world as object is now also intimately tied—precisely through the digital surround—to a saturated consciousness of the world as a zone of immanence. It is precisely this immanent dimension of the world, as opposed to an object-like globe, that Jean-Luc Nancy highlights in his recent exposition of the tension between globalization and world-making. Nancy plays on the availability of the term *mondialization* in French and its semantic range that captures both ideas. In his reading *world* escapes all horizons of speculation and calculability; it is immanence itself, containing every expansive potential of human creativity and empathetic connection beyond the abstract, speculative calculus of finance capital and its political coordinates. He defines the death drive of contemporary globalization as "the conjunction of an unlimited process of eco-technological enframing and a vanishing of forms of life and/or of common ground." The logic of this quest for a life-imbued "commons"—a singularity—is the obverse of the principle of general equivalence that characterizes the space-time continuum of late capitalism. As Nancy explains, the French term *monde*, "by keeping the horizon of a 'world' as a space for possible meaning for the whole of human relations ... gives a different indication than that [given by the globe] of an enclosure in the undifferentiated sphere of totality."[63]

The meaning of *world* I invoke in this book—a world of hyperconnected humans sensitized as witnesses to the depredations of gruesome global violence and the excesses of a liquid capitalism—has substantial affinities with Nancy's in that it is invested with an aesthetic and normative capacity to enter into yet another compact with humankind in this era of violent wars and intense connectivity, a kind of relationality that is informed but not over-determined by the economic and political systems of globalization. The contemporary world novel, I argue, is a significant cultural corpus that captures this disjunction. The following brief example of the difference between market understandings of the term *world literature* and the way the term features in this study illustrates this point. As a market category, world literature has signified cultural productions predominantly from the putative non-West, and also from non-Anglophone regions of Europe. The idea of world literature here is congruent with the flows of globalization and a space-time compression that David Harvey has talked of.[64] Conventionally these generate a constituency of tastes across global commodity circuits such that only certain kinds of literary works—often a niche of foreign or translated novels that are prize-friendly and translation-happy—make it into the category of world literature. My conceptualization of *world* through the genre of the novel is not disconnected from the world-making possibilities enabled by the new technologies of globalization. But it resists the space-time compression of global flows and opens up the category *world* to emergent literary sensibilities not overdetermined by spatial and regional configurations of capital accumulation but informed rather by a constellation of aesthetic, affective, and ethical forces generated by the conflicts of a post-1989 world. This enables me to bring a mainstream British novelist, Ian McEwan, into the same analytical frame as the Afghani British author Nadeem Aslam, the American novelist Don DeLillo, the Sri Lankan writer Michael Ondaatje, the French Canadian author Gil Courtemanche, and the Iraqi blog novelist Riverbend. What I am arguing for is not a simple convergence of a diverse novelistic corpus on a thematic plane but an opportunity to demonstrate ways of literary world-making that are apposite for our times but not reducible to the space-time continuum generated by the speculative flows of late capitalism. "What," I ask through this literary corpus, and with Nancy, "is the world as the product of *human beings*, and what is the human being in so far as it is *in the world* and as it *works* this world?"[65]

The articulation of the problematics of being human with that of making or working in the world in our hyperconnected global era is, then, what underlies my theorization of the grounds of emergence of the new world novel. It envisions the post-1989 world of violence through the new media technologies that enable instantaneous broadcasting of this violence, and that, in turn, constitutes the condition of possibility for the emergence of an amplified global infrastructure of sympathy and witnessing of extreme human suffering. This literary capture of the dilations and complexities of a hypermediated humanitarian orientation appears to be radically at odds with the narratives of "muscular" or "military" humanitarianism of the neoliberal apparatus of global governance after 1989 and its many interventions in the name of order, democracy, justice, and peace in parts of the non-Anglophone world, such as Kosovo, Somalia, Afghanistan, and Iraq. In recent years critical legal theorists have painstakingly traced out the narrative architecture of this interventionist humanitarianism. Anne Orford, for instance, identifies a teleological pattern ending with the victory of the "good" invading forces over the "evils" of disorder, violence, and powerlessness of the invaded dysfunctional polities. One of the narratives she identifies, Brian Urquhart's "Learning from the Gulf," begins with a frightening inventory of threats to the established world order in the wake of 1989: "The world is entering a period of great instability, characterized by long-standing international rivalries and resentments, intense ethnic and religious turmoil, a vast flow of arms and military technology, domestic disintegration, poverty and deep economic inequalities, instantaneous communication throughout the world, population pressures, natural and ecological disasters, the scarcity of vital resources, and huge movements of population."[66] Such a litany is almost invariably followed by a statement of responsibility that rests on the shoulders of the global law enforcers to restore order. In 1995 the U.S. secretary of state Madeleine Albright wrote, "We are privileged to live at a time when the enforcement of international standards of behaviour through the actions of the Security Council is more possible, widespread, and varied than it has ever been. It is also perhaps more necessary than it has ever been. Although we are opposed by no superpower, threats and conflicts continue to arise that engage our interests, even when they do not endanger directly our territory or citizens. We live in an unsettled age, beset by squabbles, wars, unsatisfied ambitions, and weapons that are more deadly and more widely available than ever in history."[67] Other accounts take the moral high ground and highlight the inevitability of intervention in "hard cases." The law here becomes dispensable as the perceived crisis escalates and urges immediate action. Thus Bruno Simma writes, "The lesson which can be drawn from [the use of force by NATO in the Bosnian war] is that unfortunately there do occur 'hard cases' in which terrible dilemmas must be faced, and imperative political and moral considerations may appear to leave no choice but to act outside the law."[68] Another advocate of "security over law" writes that the NATO action transformed the sitting U.S. president "from Clinton to Clint [Eastwood]" for he "took matters in his own hands to protect the common good."[69]

Such humanitarian intervention narratives are invariably populated by a composite of knights in white armor, heroic characters who embody the international values of democracy, peace, security, order, and freedom. These are usually the UN Security Council, the NATO forces, the large contingent of humanitarian foot soldiers, and of course the United States and its allies. These agents of peace and freedom are on a mission to rescue the helpless and powerless from a swath of rogue states and ruthless dictatorial regimes cutting through Eastern Europe, the Middle East, and Central Asia. The narrative progresses from crisis to resolution through the "punishment, sacrifice and salvation of the target state," the liberation of abject victims, and the reestablishment of the international order. Security or intervention texts regularly produce images of the people in states targeted for intervention as starving, powerless, suffering, abused, or helpless victims, often women and children in need of rescue or salvation.[70] The entanglement of humanitarianism, sovereignty, and security within a necropolitical mesh of actors and practices is a familiar global scenario.

The novels of this period tend to offer trenchant critiques of the redemption projects of this international security and humanitarian assemblage. As the serial post–cold war security crises repeatedly reveal, such redemption is almost always carried out over the bodies of others. Further, the massive civilian casualties caused by aerial bombings and targeted infrastructural warfare of the knights are dismissed in such texts as collateral damage, inevitable if unfortunate side effects of the noble project of restoring order. Incessant media projections of such strategic justification of unlawful wars and military occupations enable the latter to enter into the domain of everyday common sense, often through absurd metaphors of domestic conjugality, as when one commentator noted that the first Gulf war "finally consummated the marriage between the UN and the one power whose backing is a precondition for any collective security system."[71] The contemporary world is in constant danger of seeing the dictum of "just war" naturalized as ordinary wisdom.

The power of the strongest literary works I consider in this study lies in their ability to cut through this miasma of received political truth. The humanitarian imagination of the novel after 1989 is also, of course, inescapably mediatized, as in McEwan's *Saturday*. But far from being image brokers of the dominant neoliberal narrative of powerful international do-gooders and right-less victims, these novels navigate multiple registers and genres of humanitarianism that circulate in global public spheres. Importantly their focus on the very singularity of suffering bodies foregrounds the inextricability of an economy of vulnerability with that of an economy of militarized protection. The figure of the human in human rights–based interventionist talk marks the suture between absolute rightlessness and the logic of sovereign exception—a suture that the novels under study bring graphically to the fore.[72] More specifically these novels navigate complex affective fields generated by the instantaneous availability of spectacles of war, violence, and suffering in digital media. To the extent that these novels resist an aggregative and abstract approach to the idea of humanitarian suffering and the human—the cornerstone of just war theories as also that of actuarial or speculative realisms of a globalized economy of exchange—they operate, in their melancholic mode, less as agents of the normalization of the "international human rights person," as Joseph Slaughter might urge us to imagine, than as affective scripts that disturb such normalization. While Slaughter attempts to show "the mutuality, complementarity, and complicity of literature and law as they cooperate in mundane, but important, ways to universalize and naturalize the normative image of the human in human rights,"[73] I urge an understanding of the relationship between the world novel and law that is aporetic and disjunctive—one that illuminates the dangerous violence of projecting an abstracted image of the international human rights person, and also one that exposes the radical vulnerability of being human in our times. The relationship I invoke here between the novel, the human, distant suffering, technologies of mediation, and the emergence of a humanitarian sensibility has a rich intellectual genealogy to which I now turn.

The Novel and the (In)Human: An Eighteenth-Century Genealogy

In literary history one finds close links between the emergence of the novel in the eighteenth century and the emergence of a particular narrative grammar of the human. Two aspects of this narrative grammar are especially pertinent to my analysis of the novel's industrial-era roots and their purchase in our information age. One stems from theories of sensibility and moral sentiments informed predominantly by the works of the Scottish Enlightenment philosophers Adam Smith and David Hume. The other originates from the 1789 French Declaration of the Rights of Man and Citizen, a discursive framework that has subsequently informed the shape of rights-based liberal polities in modernity. I use the terms *sympathy* and *sovereignty* as shorthand to characterize these two eighteenth-century discursive rubrics. Bookended by sympathy and sovereignty, this narrative grammar of the human shaped the evolution of the novel as a genre manifesting a capacity to respond sympathetically to distant suffering due to the emergence of new conventions of moral responsibility and a new sense of self generated by the rise of a new commercial society in the wake of technological advancements of early capitalism.[74] Let us first attend to the lineaments of these literary developments through a brief engagement with Thomas Haskell's essay "Capitalism and the Origins of Humanitarian Sensibility." Haskell argues that the ability of the human to feel the suffering of others remote and distant—what we now call the humanitarian sensibility—did not just exist in a timeless, transcendental domain of moral choice but can be historically accounted for by the emergence of certain forms of life, certain changes in cognitive and social styles wrought by the demands of the market during the era of capitalism. These by no means determined the emergence of the humanitarian sensibility, but they constituted its enabling preconditions. One of these was the relation of technology to distance, so that the more distance technology covered, the less remote the rest of the world seemed. Accordingly the threshold of responsibility toward others shifted too. Two others included "promise keeping as a form of life"—for markets could not function without the contractual imperative—and responsibility for the remote consequences of one's actions, for in the market one is a node in a "long chain of wills."[75] Together these created certain conventions of moral responsibility that coalesced to give momentum to the antislavery movement during the latter half of the eighteenth century.

In light of this it is scarcely a coincidence that the rise of the sentimental novel in the eighteenth century occurred in tandem with the emergence of the idea of humanitarian sensibility that culminated in the rise of abolitionism in the United States and England.[76] The narrative code of the eighteenth-century sentimental novel, like that of humanitarian sensibility, begins with one primal scene: "a spectacle of suffering that solicits the spectator's sympathy."[77] Likewise the narrative code of the Bildungsroman tracks the emergence of the sovereign self from given relations based on status, custom, or tradition and its right to make its own destiny, albeit within a framework of incorporation into an emerging capitalist world order. This self as a free and fully developed person is but an abstraction of "common modalities of the human being's extension into the civil and social order" and is intrinsically linked to what Lynn Festa has referred to as "the affective work of the sentimental novel" in the eighteenth century.[78] For only such a self could recognize that a distant subject of suffering was also a subject with full rights despite vast cultural and political differences. This brief analysis of the work of sympathy and sovereignty is not to suggest that novels of the period or the protagonists in them unfailingly sympathized with suffering at a distance. In fact there are enough instances that demonstrate the acuity of Hume's observation that it is not irrational to care more for one's finger than for the deaths of millions of Chinese.[79]

What I foreground instead is the emergence of a new infrastructure of sympathy in the eighteenth century that enabled novels to deploy narrative techniques oriented toward a commitment to the *reality* of human suffering elsewhere. The grammar qua thematics argument is significant for my book as a whole: when I talk of sympathy and sovereignty as the narrative grammar of the human, I by no means propose that they are necessarily expounded in the novels under study in any thematically explicit way. There is one other significant aspect of this historical discussion that bears mention. In talking about the *infrastructure* of sympathy, one needs to reckon with the fact that sympathy and the sentimental, as the terms were used in the eighteenth-century literary context, were more than just feelings or emotions. In a recent monumental study on the architectonics of the sentimental in literature and cinema, James Chandler takes great pains to retrieve a visual and virtual substrate of sympathy that flourished in novels of the eighteenth and nineteenth centuries and that subsequently formed the bulwark of the early Hollywood cinema of D. W. Griffith and Frank Capra. The sentimental in Chandler's reading is multilayered both historically and formally. Its structuring principle can be cryptically stated in the author's own words: "a relay of regards virtualized in a medium." Drawing on the fictional works of Laurence Sterne, the philosophy of spectatorship of Adam Smith, and the journalistic repertoire of Addison and Steele, Chandler highlights the importance of sightlines—the gaze or regard—in the phenomenon of sympathetic recognition. The sentimental in the literary text is a triangulated ensemble "that elaborate[s] a system of looking at lookers looking—even or especially when all this looking is taking place in the virtual space of the printed page."[80] The resonance of such a reading in our hypervisual and multimedia age can scarcely be underestimated.

Apart from the market and technology, two other coordinates of the cultural and intellectual history under discussion bear particular mention here. Tom Laqueur calls them "bodies" and "details."[81] The first is an allusion to the impact of growth of medicinal science and forensic pathology on heightened sensitivities to the suffering body. The second refers to the impact of the empiricist legacy of the seventeenth century and the spawning of multiple genres of fact-finding, of which the autopsy and case history are key examples. The increasing reliance on detail as a sign of truth and on minute corporeal dissection as a demonstration of human suffering had a direct bearing on the genesis of the eighteenth-century novel. The body in pain was the locus of the humanitarian narrative, and the more forensic science was able to factualize a matrix of cause and effect through extensive autopsy reports, the more effective was its impact on the capacity to make palpable the reality of human suffering. The early novels drew extensively on these fact-finding genres and this conjoining of *fact* and *feeling* to create an architectonics of proximity to diverse forms of human experience, including that of distant suffering. The excruciatingly detailed realism of Daniel Defoe's novels to create a verisimilitude of the factual and the use of the epistolary mode by Samuel Richardson and Henry Fielding to generate a sense of intimacy—to close the distance, as it were—between the reader and the protagonists are apt illustrations of this point. Romance or sentimental abolitionist fiction from the late eighteenth to early nineteenth century, such as Dorothy Kilner's *The Rotchfords* (1786), Robert Bage's *Man As He Is* (1792), William Earle's *Obi, or the History of the Three-Fingered Jack* (1800), and Maria Edgeworth's "The Grateful Negro" from *Popular Tales* (1804), are other instances that attest to the power of factual genres in generating a humanitarian sensibility.[82]

Sympathy and Sovereignty in the Contemporary World Novel

Thus far I have argued that realism at the service of humanitarianism, and humanitarianism as the conjugation of sympathy and sovereignty, broadly defined the narrative frame of the eighteenth-century English novel. Over the years, where literary theory is concerned, there has been a disaggregation of sympathy from sovereignty, with the humanitarian strand in the form of sympathy and the sentimental as structuring principles woven into the novelistic genre not faring particularly well, especially in the robust theorizations of Ian Watt on the rise of the novel as a realist genre par excellence and subsequently in the works of Fredric Jameson, who eulogizes the "first great realisms" of Balzac and Stendhal.[83] The sentimental (and its poor cousin, melodrama) was seen as either a relic of medieval romance or gothic genres or as a feminine, idiosyncratic, second-order narrative strain that the novel successfully overcame, at least in Watt's analysis, with the publication of Fielding's *Tom Jones*.[84] Sovereignty, as the narrative twin, has fared better, for the notion of individual autonomy feeds well into the discourse of rights that has been so fundamental to the evolution of the Bildungsroman, the novelistic subgenre that is the literary correlate of the bourgeois public sphere and one most amenable to a canonized aesthetics of a robust, even masculinist realism. Dubbed by Margaret Cohen "the novel of a young man with great expectations," the early Bildungsroman features a protagonist who is an abstraction of two phenomena that marked the emergence of the individual self in early industrial capitalism: mobility and interiority.[85] Embedded in this symbolic human is the idea of autonomy theorized in Hegel's tripartite history of right as the second phase, the right of the bourgeoisie marked by the formal logic of equivalence or, in terms referred to earlier, the speculative, actuarial logic of the market. Slaughter's brilliant exposition in *Human Rights, Inc.: The World Novel, Narrative Form and International Law* of the novel's capacious ability to make legible the emergence of the human as a subject of rights in postcolonial and global contexts is a powerful recent iteration of this critical strain in historical theorizations of the novel.

Given the deservedly strong influence that Slaughter's work has had on contemporary scholarship on the world novel and the discourse of rights, a productive intervention would not be amiss here. I wish briefly to point to Slaughter's aversion to a sentimental invocation of human rights and the absence in his theoretical framework of any engagement with the long philosophical tradition of sympathy that played such a critical part in intellectual formulations of the idea of humanitarianism in capitalist modernity. Slaughter is highly critical of what he calls the sentimentalizing of human rights discourses by liberal pragmatists like Richard Rorty and militaristic humanitarians like George W. Bush. In his 1993 Oxford Amnesty lecture, "Human Rights, Rationality and Sentimentality," Rorty suggested that literature is a far more powerful medium of internationalization of human rights than any rational legislative measures for it enables us to "see similarities between ourselves and people very unlike us as outweighing the differences" and to give a sense that "anyone could assume the role of the subject endowed with rights."[86] More than a decade later President Bush implored the American public to listen to "stories" of "young girls going to school in Afghanistan," for "we like stories, expect stories, of young girls going to school in Afghanistan." "It is," he continues in a self-congratulatory manner befitting his benevolent view of the Afghan invasion, "our country's pleasure and honor to be involved with the future of this country."[87]

Slaughter is of course right to be repulsed by both Rorty's "cosmopolitan solipsism" and Bush's "humanitarian interventionist sentimentality."[88] But the point I wish to make is something else. Such has been the devaluation of the idea of sympathy in theorizations of the novel that Slaughter cannot read the sentimental except in terms of a reductive First World benevolence manifested by either Rorty's pragmatic liberalism or the militaristic humanitarianism of Bush. The fact that our hyperconnected world may have enabled the emergence of a new global infrastructure of sympathy beyond the benevolent and the militaristic is not something that Slaughter addresses in his otherwise fine account of the evolution of the Bildungsroman for our late modern times. This is the gap I propose to address. What, *pace* Slaughter, is the purchase of the human beyond the abstract, speculative logic of rights in our times? What of its sentimental other—the domain of melancholic as opposed to actuarial fact—that disturbs the principle of general equivalence found in benevolent liberalisms of our time and that resists the militarization of human rights and the hijacking of humanitarian discourses by contemporary global regimes in the name of law and order? In other words, what of facts that *world* the human in the sense discussed earlier in relation to the work of Nancy and the world literature corpus that is the focus of this book? What insights can the now obscured sympathy-sovereignty dyad of eighteenth-century realism offer here? And what of the pertinence for our hypermediated age of the visual and virtual structures of the sentimental?

What changes, I ask in this context, are being wrought on the narrative grammar of the human in the novel form in this era of spectatorial capitalism, when the capacity to respond to distant suffering has increased greatly with advances in information technology? What happens to the humanitarian narrative when compassion has as its object not just a singular body in pain or at the threshold of death but a network of affects generated by horrific media spectacles of war and violence? What are the ethical limits of a panoptic aesthetic in representing traumatic human experience in distant parts of the world? What indeed is the epistemological purchase of fact and evidence in this era of exorbitant witnessing and scopophilic omniscience, and how do these novels configure genres of truth making tropologically and narratively? How is sovereignty coded in novels after 1989, works that track the inhuman force field of global capitalism and its war machines? Figures of sovereignty in these works appear to invest not so much in the idea of freedom and autonomy as in the will and capacity to incarcerate, maim, humiliate, and kill in order to live.[89] Politics as the work of death transforms fraught geopolitical spaces into states of exception with their own elaborate architectures of enmity.

Questions arise about this modality of literary worlding in the globe's dominant language, English. Philological wisdom about the inextricable links between the lifeworlds and language worlds rings warning bells about the dangers of an Anglo-globalism flattening out and remaking the world in its own image. A recent blog in the *New York Review of Books* does indeed warn about the dangers of a "dull new global novel" as writers tailor their foreign lexicon to enable felicitous translations into world languages.[90] Further, what are the stakes in aligning the temporal frame of my literary analysis with the synchronic time of global capital—the world after 1989? There is also the problem of the "authoritarian" spectatorial gaze that Luc Boltanski addresses in *Distant Suffering*, a problem that arises in relation to the theatrics of the sovereign self's sympathetic and impartial visualization of suffering. Are these world-making novels inflected with the supposition that all agency lies with the sympathetic viewer—the omniscient author or narrator—and that the suffering multitudes can do nothing beyond appealing to our compassion?

Three caveats may be in order here. First, while the warning about the flattening effect of global translations is salutary, it is worth noting in the Anglophone context of this book that English is also a world language that is heavily inflected by the diversity of lifeworlds and that it has spawned multiple literary and aesthetic worlds. If, on the one hand, the field of Anglophone literature incorporates novels such as Iain Banks's *The Business* (1999), replete with the Anglophone mediaspeak of global capitalism, it is also required to grapple with the "rotten English" of Ken Saro-Wiwa's *Sozaboy* (1995) that illuminates a disturbing aesthetics of capitalist marauding and environmental degradation in postcolonial Nigeria. The second highlights the deep temporality of world-making and world literature that through history have not exactly submitted to circumscription and shrinkage by the geopolitical and economic pressures of its times.[91] The ecumenical imaginary is not invariably complicit with imaginaries of world political domination, as Timothy Brennan, Djelal Kadir, and others might insist in the context of contemporary debates on world literature and globalization.[92] This is what I anticipate my study of the deep structure of the novelistic genres of our era will illuminate. The third caveat alerts us to the techniques through which this corpus of contemporary novels allegorizes anxieties evident in recent critiques of global humanitarianism and the international human rights regime as cosmopolitan largesse that the advanced capitalist world metes out to the suffering multitudes elsewhere. As Jacques Rancière notes, documents such as the Universal Declaration of Human Rights have become redundant for those who already enjoy such rights. The result is, "you do the same as charitable people do with their old clothes. You give them to the poor. Those rights that appear to be useless in their place are sent abroad, along with medicine and clothes, to people deprived of medicine, clothes and rights."[93] This disjunction between the legibility of human rights and their redundancy except under conditions of extreme *rightlessness* is also what marks the aporia of the human in our times, at once a speculative abstraction and a melancholy fact.

The Book's Plan

The three rubrics under which I have organized the chapters are "World," "War," and "Witness," In chapter 1, "Real Virtualities and the Undead Genre," I trace the provenance of the novel in our hypervisual age. Drawing on the rhetorical trope of *ekphrasis* as an intermedial space between narrative and image, I make a case for the transformation of the novel in our time into a dynamic morphological space-time entity in which text and image interpenetrate in unprecedented ways. These mutual articulations of the verbal and the visual not only bring to the fore formal innovations in the shape and structure of the novel but also highlight a new structure of address and a new infrastructure of responsibility toward a wider circuit of mediating publics. The deathworlds after 1989 bring into our everyday informational circuits worlds of excessive otherness: suicide bombings, genocide, terrorist attacks, carceral zones of uncertain legality, ghost prisoners, and war refugees. These are hypervisualized excesses, the remaindered zones of otherness that cannot be made sense of within a generalized exchange economy of rights or value. And yet they exist in deep phenomenological intimacy with the global publics. The ekphrastic mode, notes W. J. T. Mitchell, is the bridge that traverses from the semiotic to the phenomenological in the apprehension of *otherness*. The defamiliarization of both text and image in the movement from one to the other lies not so much in any experience of semantic dissonance (both can mean the same thing) as in semiotic difference: "sign-types, forms, materials of representation, and institutional traditions." This experience of semiotic difference crosses over into the phenomenological.[94] Extrapolating from this entwining of the semiotic and the phenomenological in the human apprehension of otherness, I read novel worlds of our time as ekphrastic texts that carry the burden of making legible to our myriad virtual publics the melancholic, visually excessive remainders of our capitalist deathworlds.

Under the rubric *world*, whose capaciousness Hannah Arendt captured half a century ago as the zone of immanence between "human subjectivity" and "nature's sublime indifference,"[95] and whose theoretical provenance as the analogue of the global has recently come under intense scrutiny, I undertake three tasks. First, I excavate a literary genealogy of the idea of world and examine its valence for thinking about world literature in our global age. Second, I examine the relevance of the philosophical literature on "possible worlds" to my conception of the world novel. The complex relation between the empirical world picture around 1989 and the novel worlds I have chosen to study offers a challenge to our conception of the *literary* in these global times, which, I argue, needs attending to if we wish to rescue the value of the literary from a sociological and materialist determinism. Third, I analyze two case studies that illustrate the makings of the contemporary world novel: David Mitchell's *Ghostwritten* and Salman Rushdie's *Shalimar the Clown*.

The global state of war in our time, I noted earlier, is the grim horizon of the novelistic works that feature in this study. While visualization has long been acknowledged as critical to a war imaginary—especially the perception of enemy positions in battle—the wars of our time saturate our everyday visual fields in unprecedented ways. Whether as evidence or as retribution, or even as a quest for justice, pictures and images in accelerated motion and across a wider topological spectrum have become ubiquitous in any contemplation of war in our times. The second part of the book under the rubric of *war* begins with a chapter that traces the conjoining of human rights, technology, and media activism in confronting the ubiquity of contemporary wars and argues for their impact on the novelistic imagination. I then excavate a literary genealogy of the experience of wartime from the Napoleonic era to our hypermediated age, and in the process illuminate the aesthetic purchase of war (and its technologies) as a shaper of distinct literary imaginaries: the sentimental, the humanitarian, the panoptic, and the spectacular. All of these are at play in the contemporary world novel. Chapter 6 is a contemplation, using DeLillo's *Falling Man*, of the sublime cruelty of the 9/11 spectacle—a supramediated phenomenon and a defining icon of the twenty-first century. Disaggregating my analysis from that of performance scholars who foreground the imagistic horror of the burning towers as an aesthetic tableau par excellence, I offer a reading of *Falling Man* as a counter-memory of that spectacular terrorist performance, a novel that resists the mediated thrill of the event in its somber contemplation of the inchoate horror of falling bodies.

The third part—in some sense the heart of the book—is devoted to the overarching theme of *witness*. Central to the humanitarian imagination is the trope of witnessing. The chapters under this rubric uncover the trope's aesthetic manifestations and ethical valence. Here eighteenth-century accounts of the spectator—split between the actuarial logic of impersonal detachment and the melancholic logic of interestedness—provide fertile ground for reprising Adam Smith's views on spectatorship and tracing its intensification as the trope of witnessing in our time. To put it telegraphically, witnessing the suffering of others is for Smith an act not of unmediated and instant compassion but of mimetic reflection on what it would feel like to suffer if one changed places with the other. Sympathy is thus affective cognition, a union of feeling, imagination, and reflection. In Smith the generation of sentiment and the regulation of sentiment are mutually imbricated, as befits the civilizational ethos of a commercial society. This provides an interesting opening for the theorization of the Smithian spectator as an entity split between "interestedness" and "disinterestedness," or what Baucom in his Derridean reading of Smith calls the "supplementary splendor" of spectatorship "in the fullness of its self-relating difference as both the *melancholy* and *disinterested judge of humanity,* as both a *creature of interest* and a *model of detachment.*"[96] Derrida and Agamben, both writing in the wake of the Holocaust, address at length this twining of disinterested and interested witnessing and its implication for our times.[97] Agamben is particularly apposite here, for he points to the disaggregation of the "politics of human rights" from the "politics of witnessing" by arguing that the former, in its investment in the human as a speculative ideal grounded in natural law, is captive to the entanglement of justice and violence—to the paradoxical production of bare life that it purports to resist—in ways that the "politics of witnessing" is not. The logic of witnessing for Agamben is not abstract but singular and interested. Its object is the real depredation, the naked abandonment, of bare life, unlike that of human rights, whose object is abstract humanity and whose politics is open to appropriation by a liberal disinterestedness that fails to oppose the sovereign production of bare life, as we saw during the occupation of Iraq in 2003. For Derrida the witness is one who *survives* the event, and the act of witnessing has a responsibility as much to the nonsurvivors— to the silent and silenced dead in extreme instances—as to unknown future victims of traumatic psychogeographies of our late capitalist world. The responsibility for such witnessing is hence infinite. Tracing the intensification of the eighteenth-century impartial spectator into the melancholic witness in our time, the chapters in this final section analyze three different novelistic modes of witnessing: that of Art Spiegelman's novelized graphics on the horror of 9/11 (*In the Shadow of No Towers*) and a mediated *Maus,* his early work on the Holocaust; of Michael Ondaatje's forensic realism in a novel about an anthropologist interring bones of war victims in her ancestral land ravaged by civil war (*Anil's Ghost*); and of Janette Turner Hospital's testimo-

nial realism in a novel allegorically replete with graphic human rights violations (*Orpheus Lost*).

In sum, this book seeks to interpret a set of contemporary literary works
through a theoretical framework informed by the history of the novel form
and its long thinking on the human, on the one hand, and on the other, the
distinctively contemporary phenomena of global violence, mediatization
of distant suffering, and the emergence of a humanitarian sensibility that
reformulate for our times the conundrum of imagining the human condition on a *world* scale. A literary study of this scale that purports to cover the
globe might appear dauntingly ambitious. Here I take my cue from Moretti,
who visualizes the problem of doing world literature not in terms of an ever-
expanding ambit of reading to encompass the globe but as a quest for "new
conceptual interconnection of problems" that can generate new theories
and methodologies.[98] The world literature study I propose here offers precisely such a "new conceptual interconnection of problems." It purports not
to undertake an exhaustive study of all world novels written after 1989 but to
select a few that manifest transformations in the narrative grammar of the
human due to the emergence of a new orientation to distant suffering, of a
late modern moral imagination mediated by informational capitalism. When
distant suffering is visually amplified and instantly vivified, it radically shifts
the ground on which conventions of moral responsibility are generated. Instant televisual and digital images of extreme duress expand the possibilities
of moral relations between strangers that go far beyond the realm of the humanitarian imagination as conceived in literary works of the early capitalist
era. This is not to suggest that the digital internationalism and the possibility
of a new humanitarian sensibility I am invoking necessarily lead to more
ameliorative action on a global scale. But they certainly create a precondition for greater global engagement with extreme human suffering—a new,
amplified infrastructure for sympathy—that the world novels under study
bring powerfully into view.

ONE
REAL VIRTUALITIES AND
THE UNDEAD GENRE

Putting the Novel in Its Place

"The novel achieved its devastating success as an upstart," writes Marthe
Robert in *The Origins of the Novel*. She is reflecting on an oft-expressed anxiety about the novel's prodigious and promiscuous adaptation of whatever
came its way and the threat of anamorphism that has hovered over this genre
in modern literary studies. Robert's breathless inventory of its many suspect
attributes is worth quoting at length:

> Graduating from a discredited sub-category to an almost unprece-
> dented Power, it now reigns more or less supreme over the world of
> literature which it influences aesthetically and which has now be-
> come economically dependent on its welfare. With the freedom of a
> conqueror who knows no law other than that of his unlimited expan-
> sion, the novel has abolished every literary caste and traditional form
> and appropriates all modes of expression. . . . And while it squanders
> an age-old literary heritage it is simultaneously intent on monopo-
> lizing ever wider provinces of human experience of which it frequently

claims an intimate knowledge. . . . Revolutionary and middle-class, democratic by choice, but with a marked tendency for totalitarian over-rulings of obstacles and frontiers, free to the point of arbitrariness or total anarchy . . . [yet it is also] strangely parasitic; for the novel is naturally compelled to subsist both on the written word and on the material world whose reality its purports to "reproduce."[1]

The novel's faults by this account are "very grave indeed," as Mr. Darcy would say to Elizabeth Bennett in response to her own breathless and angry inventory of his suspect character. A parasite, a conqueror, a commoner, an anarchist, a totalitarian persona, a thief, a shape-shifter, and an outlaw. No wonder so many writers, theorists, and critics over this past century have periodically wished the novel dead. Barring Bakhtin and Lukács, who each built complex theories of literary production around the novel, elaborate theories of emergent cultural forms and technological regimes have been propounded to hint loudly at the imminent obsolescence of this insouciant genre. The rise of photography, cinema, and television and the subsequent explosion of digital media have each been put forward as reasons why the novel may be on its last legs. A quintessential product of the print revolution, the age of the novel in such understandings broadly extends from 1830 to 1960, after which its cultural dominance diminishes in direct proportion to the rise of the media industry, especially the ensconcing of television sets, and now the personal computer, in the intimacy of the domestic sphere.[2]

The realm of the hypervisual and the spectacular in our digital age is posited as a devastating rival for the novel, often by novelists themselves. In 1991 Don DeLillo pronounced the death of the novel in the face of horrific spectacles of terror in our time. "I do think," he averred, "we can connect novelists and terrorists. . . . In a society that is filled with glut and repetition and endless consumption the act of terror may be the only meaningful act. . . . True terror is a language and a vision. There is a deep narrative structure to terrorist acts and they infiltrate and alter consciousness in ways writers used to aspire to."[3] DeLillo's anxiety about the narrative power of terror is echoed by the character Bill Gray in his novel *Mao II*. "What terrorists gain," says Gray, "novelists lose. The degree to which [terrorists] influence mass consciousness is the extent of our decline as shapers of sensibility and thought."[4] DeLillo reiterated this position after 9/11 in his powerful essay "In the Ruins of the Future": "Today again the world narrative belongs to terrorists. Terror's response is a narrative that has been developing over years, only now becoming inescapable. It is our lives and minds that are occupied now."[5]

Against this thesis of the death of the novel in the face of horrific media spectacles and the inordinate influence of visual media, I propose that we rethink the role of the novel in our hypervisual age in terms of the genre's fundamental open-endedness to new influences, including the multimedial. The novelistic trajectory is itself a phenomenon of constant accrual and renewal. In other words, I think it is worthwhile to renew an argument for what, after Bakhtin, is popularly called the *novelization* thesis—that is, a historicist understanding of the novel as having an infinite future because, by its very nature, the novel "reflects the tendencies of a new world in the making."[6] This means that rather than seeing new visual genres as competitors of the novel, we can explore the ways in which the realm of the visual itself exerts an extraordinary pull on the novelistic imagination. In light of the specific concerns of this book, for instance, we might productively explore how the novels themselves abstract the phenomenology of spectatorship and exorbitant visual witnessing in our time. In doing so we conceptualize the phenomenon of novelization not in terms of the novel's exceptionalism, which can often sound grandiose, totalizing, and ahistorical (everything is novelistic), but by attending to the shifting horizons of novelistic work in different technological eras.[7]

In the spirit of André Bazin's appeal in the age of cinema for a common ground of "technical civilization," it might be best to abjure what he called "competition and substitution" in the study of evolving forms and genres and focus instead on what kinds of enrichment—of both genres and publics—are enabled by developments in each technological era. Bazin's essay "In Defense of Mixed Cinema" was a significant intervention in the mid-twentieth century against the movement of "pure cinema," a movement intent on affirming the absolute autonomy of cinema as an art form. When he talked of some films in the late 1940s and early 1950s as a "point at which the *avant-garde* has now arrived, the making of films that dare to take their inspiration from a novel-like style one might describe as ultracinematographic," this was often interpreted as his valorization of the novel as some kind of *ur*-form to which the cinema would always be indebted.[8] True, Bazin claimed for the novel a technological longue durée for which cinema's avowed technological wizardry was no match. A close reading of the essay, however, reveals Bazin's deep insistence not on the superiority of the novel as an exemplary product of what he calls our "technical civilization" but on his critical appeal to attend to the rich aesthetic convergences that emerge as novel and cinema battle it out for the minds and imaginations of the publics. The critical point to note here is that it was Bazin who cleared the theoretical ground for asking questions that are actually attentive to the interpenetration of genres, the recursive historicity of their formal and technological evolution, and the consequently changing phenomenology of apperception.

The discussion thus far provides a rich and enabling opening from which to understand the complex habitations of the novel in our era of proliferating digital and visual genres. The imagistic and the visual are such a given that it is pointless to argue against their influence by positing the influence of the novel as a counterpoint in print. It is far more illuminating for novel scholars to understand the transformation of apperception on novel worlds of our time and to explore the ways in which the idea of the novelistic itself is in the process of being transformed by the vastly magnified spectrum of ocular and sonic stimulation that characterizes our information age. The relationship between the verbal and the visual, narrative and image, the print and the digital has never been more fraught or more charged with radical transformative possibilities than in this information-rich, war-torn age.

In this chapter I illustrate this argument in two ways. First, I trace a mode of novelistic intermediality derived from the trope of ekphrasis—the verbal description of a visual object—and argue that the novel, far from being dead, manifests a radically new mode of engagement with an ever-expanding realm of virtual publics. Second, I undertake a reading that complicates the relationship between the widespread mediatization of war-induced humanitarian crises and visualization of such crises in contemporary novels. I argue that the melancholic mode that these novels adopt operates with a dissensual force that destabilizes the visual economy of media representations of war and humanitarian suffering.

Intermediality and World-Making

In order to explicate in some detail my argument about intermediality and novelization, I begin with a reading of excerpts from Martin Amis's story "The Last Days of Muhammad Atta" and Ian McEwan's novel *Saturday*. Given the extraordinary focus on 9/11 in recent prognostications on the novel's death, that date is central to these excerpts. Together they serve as a frontispiece to my extended contemplation on the powerful provenance of the novelistic imagination in our age of endemic violence and visual witnessing. In what follows I am mindful that I am using a short story to talk about the novelistic imagination. My rationale for doing so is this: Amis is primarily a novelist, and this creative venture represents his intention not so much to consciously experiment with the *form* of the short story itself as to craft a few short and sharp descriptive vignettes of Muhammad Atta's final hours based on scattered CCTV footage, an effort he hoped would help him write a novel on the aftermath of 9/11.[9] Amis has also gone on record that he was tempted to craft his story of the last days of the lead hijacker of American Airlines Flight 11 after being repeatedly exposed to the televisual spectacle of the collapsing towers of the World Trade Center alongside the security footage of Atta's movements before his group boarded the ill-fated flight—a visual juxtaposition that stimulated his novelistic imagination. It is Amis's transcription from image to text, to fill in the gaps, as it were, that makes this piece relevant to my argument.

As he descended slowly around 8:44 a.m., he first saw the "lesser totems of Queens, like a line of defence for the tutelary godlings of the island." Then "he came clattering in over the struts and slats of Manhattan," and "there it was ahead of him and below him—*the thing which is called the World.*"[10] Thus culminates Amis's short ekphrastic narrative of the last moments of the life of Muhammad Atta, just before he crashed into the North Tower of the World Trade Center on that fatal September morning. Atta's contemplation of his target—the *thing* called the *World*—reverberates in a kind of intermedial temporal flash across millions of screens round the world that played over and over again the imagistic horror of the burning towers. Intermedial because it remains suspended between narrative and image, between Amis's literary transcoding of a gap in the report of the 9/11 Commission—the impetus for his story—and the global circulation of video footage of Atta and his suicide squad making their way through the security checkpoints at Logan Airport just before boarding the plane.

Published on the eve of the fifth anniversary of 9/11, "The Last Days of Muhammad Atta" has its origins in this sentence from the report of the 9/11 Commission, which Amis cites at the start of his story: "No physical, documentary or analytical evidence provides convincing explanation of why Atta and Omari drove to Portland, Maine, from Boston on the morning of September 10, only to return to Logan on Flight 5930 on the morning of September 11." Amis attempts to fill this evidentiary gap. His story unspools with graphic details of Atta performing his morning ablutions in his Maine hotel on the dawn of September 11. The world has been incessantly exposed to the blurry long shots of security footage of this fully clothed, squat and muscular Egyptian, here given flesh in Amis's adroit hands with a slow close-up of a stripped-down Atta, as if to magnify for the rest of the world his rancid body and soul on the day he carried out his murderous act:

Now, emitting a sigh of unqualified grimness, he crouched on the bowl. He didn't even bother with his usual scowling and straining and shuddering, partly because his head felt dangerously engorged. More saliently, he had not moved his bowels since May. In general his upper body was impressively lean, from all the hours in the gym with the "muscle" Saudis; but now there was a solemn mound where his abdominals used to be, as taut and proud as a firsttrimester pregnancy. Nor was this the only sequela. He had a feverish and unvarying ache, not in his gut but in his lower back, his pelvic saddle, and his scrotum. Every few minutes he was required to wait out an interlude of nausea, while disused gastric juices bubbled up in the sump of his throat. His breath smelled like a blighted river.

The close-up shot zooms in with excruciating detail on the terrorist's face as he scans it in the shaving mirror. But of course it is Amis's gaze that is projected onto this passage: a gaze over the shoulder of Atta that pierces the terrorist's mirror image. The mirror image becomes Amis's contemplative window as he asks, How can this man not hate his visage, the "disgusted lineaments of the mouth" and "the frank animus of the underbite?" Amis here transcodes for the reader yet another gap, this time in an image—that of the *inscrutable, forever nonvocalized,* full frontal photograph of Atta in the files of the 9/11 Commission Report. The author face-reads with an acuity that in the absence of a camera only the literary imagination can conjure. Who else but a novelist can even begin to give shape to the mutating visage of a leading member of "a peer group . . . for whom death was not death and life was not life" and who was about to embark on his monumental journey to his own Judgment Day?

The worst was yet to come: shaving. Shaving was the worst because it necessarily involved him in the contemplation of his own face. He looked downwards while he lathered his cheeks, but then the chin came up and there it was, revealed in vertical strips: the face of Muhammad Atta. Two years ago he had said goodbye to his beard, after Afghanistan. Tangled and oblong and slightly offcentre, it had had the effect of softening the disgusted lineaments of the mouth, and it had wholly concealed the frank animus of the underbite. His insides were seized, but his face was somehow incontinent, or so Muhammad Atta felt. The detestation, *the detestation of everything, was being sculpted on it, from within.*

Earlier I used the term *ekphrastic* to describe Amis's story. Ekphrasis is an age-old rhetorical device in which the essence of one form of artwork is conveyed in another medium. A painting, say, of Michelangelo's sculpted masterpiece *David* would be a good example, as would a sonic transformation of a classic literary text. In modern literary and art theory, the term has almost exclusively featured as a device for translating the visual into print medium. That is, it is a text replete with vivid description.[11] But more happens in ekphrasis than simply a secondary description of the original work of art. In a work of ekphrastic aspiration, as Mieke Bal usefully explains, the "radical, ontological difference between visual and the linguistic utterances is suspended in favour of an examination of the semiotic power of each and their relation to truthful representation. The age-old trust in the reliability of vision yields to the delicate balance of words and images in the production of *evidence*."[12] Keeping in mind Bal's emphasis on the suspension of medial difference in a quest for "truthful representation" that could produce "evidence," does it make sense to speak of the ekphrastic force of Amis's story? At first this question may appear forced. For what work of visual art does Amis's descriptive effort bring into vivid life? And yet if we shift our terms of reference from *art* to *medium* in understanding the contemporary force of this rhetorical device, we can move toward a compelling reading of the ekphrastic force of not just Amis's story but of much novelistic work that has emerged in our digitally mediated, information-rich era.

What stands out in "The Last Days of Muhammad Atta" is the vividness of the description as it probes deep into the corporeal and metaphysical unease of the terrorist as he contemplates his habitation in what he sees as an unclean world: "Adultery punished by whipping, sodomy by burial alive: this seemed about right to Muhammad Atta. He also joined in the hatred of music. And the hatred of laughter. 'Why do you never laugh?' he was sometimes asked. Ziad would answer: 'How can you laugh when people are dying in Palestine?' Muhammad Atta never laughed, not because people were dying in Palestine, but because he found nothing funny. 'The thing which is called World.' That, too, spoke to him. World had always felt like an illusion—an unreal mockery."

Here is Amis imagining for us the singular zeal that drives Atta: material and metaphysical defeat of the West: "'Purify your heart and cleanse it of stains. Forget and be oblivious of the thing which is called World.' Muhammad Atta is not religious; he was not especially political. He had allied himself with the militants because jihad was, by many magnitudes, the most charismatic idea of his generation. To unite ferocity and rectitude in a single word. . . . A peer group piously competitive about suicide, he had concluded, was a very powerful thing and the West had no equivalent to it."

And yet Amis is primarily working from just a few images of Atta as they sit secure in the files of the 9/11 Commission and the CCTV footage. Hardly works of art! He may have also seen the graphic illustrated version of *The 9/11 Report* that was published in the same year as his story and that could serve as an interesting counterpoint of mediatic normalization to Amis's ekphrastic elaboration. But, more significant, his inspiration was an unparalleled visual archive: Atta's morbid agency in generating a spectacular montage of images of planes crashing into the twin global emblems of *uber*-capitalist triumph, of near-apocalyptic televisual tableaux of billowing smoke and dust that swallow whole neighborhoods, not to mention hundred-story leaps toward certain death of all too many trapped victims.

Not that the story transcribes any of this. How could it? The temporal impossibility of the case stares the reader in the face, for Atta's perspective is extinguished at the very moment the plane hits the towers. All Amis can do is foretell the horror in a breathless buildup and strategically stop at the very moment of Atta's dissolution in this very inferno accurately timed at 8:46 a.m.: "Even as his flesh fried and his blood boiled, there was life, kissing its fingertips. Then it echoed out, and ended." Hard as he has labored until that moment to prolong Atta's final moments, Amis's words appear to fall short of the power of multimedia spectacle that followed in its wake and which the world has seen over and over again. What modal form of witnessing can Amis's one last contemplative foray into the suicidal mind of Atta offer that would be adequate to the enormity of the event?

> At 8.44 he began his descent. The core reason was, of course, all the killing—all the putting to death. Not the crew, not the passengers, not the officeworkers in the Twin Towers, not the cleaners and the caterers, not the men of the NYPD and the FDNY. He was thinking of the war, the wars, the warcycles that would flow from this day. He didn't believe in the devil, as an active force, but he did believe in death. Death, at certain times, stopped moving at its even pace and broke into a hungry, lumbering run. Here was the primordial secret. No longer closely guarded—no longer well kept. Killing was divine delight. And your suicide was just a part of the contribution you made—the massive contribution to death.

The inadequacy of these reflections in the face of what is to follow at first appears to bear out the truth of many statements made by writers themselves in the immediate aftermath of 9/11 about the defeat of the literary imagination and the transference of imaginative power from novels to world spectacles such as these.[13] Earlier we saw DeLillo declare the novel's oblivion in the face of terror as a world narrative.

The many reverberations of the idea of *world* are hard to miss in the discussion thus far. The term's objectification in Atta's gaze on the World Trade Center—this thing called the *world*—appears metamorphosed into *worlds* generated by horrific spectacles and *worlds* lost for novelists even as we as readers are urged to imagine the *world-shattering* magnitude of the catastrophe about to unfold, which only digital connectivity on a *world* scale has made real to millions of us. The Heideggerian "world picture" as something that stands *before us* in a science- and technology-driven subject-object relationship, as we have seen, can be productively extrapolated onto our image-saturated worlds. It thus appears as not just being *out there* to be *looked at*, like Atta does, but as a relationship of immanence, as something that is fundamentally constitutive of our *being-in-the-world*. The technological sublime—whether experienced in the spectacular horror of terrorist acts or in the liquid shimmer of financial wizardry—palpably unnerves the writer Bill Gray in DeLillo's *Mao II*, who sees this phenomenon as the death knell of the craft of narration. In a startlingly prescient pre-9/11 vision, Gray sees images of spectacular annihilation as the new domain of aesthetic world-making: "Beckett is the last writer to shape the way we think and see. After him, the major work involves midair explosions and crumbled buildings. This is the new tragic narrative."[14]

And yet this overwhelming focus on the potential eclipse of the significance of imaginative literature, including novels, due to the immanence of the *world*—as something no longer out there as *picture* because it has engulfed us, has *become us*—overlooks at least two important aspects of novelization in our times. One is the intermedial truth making and evidentiary function that Bal refers to in talking about ekphrasis, the narrative urge to graphically transcode for publics around the world the evidentiary gaps that the images of this mass killer moving in and out of security footage have left behind. This is a challenge to the reality of *perceptual* effect that has blinded so many into thinking that other imaginative forms of reality making, especially in words, are no longer available. There are several stories waiting to be written in the interstices of the digital spectacles with which our mediascapes are engorged. The Atta story's intermedial status moving from text to image and back to the text offers a mode of witnessing and producing evidence that can be powerfully extrapolated onto analyses of novel worlds in our times. In a later chapter I call these the forensic and testimonial functions of the world novel. Why did he travel to Maine the day before the event? Who did he meet? How did he prepare for his final journey? What generated such world-scale hatred in him, this pan-anathema that sought such a monumental scale of destruction as its measure? What may have been his final thoughts if he did not believe in religion but purely in the nihilism of will? Surely the space for such work has not been consumed by the inferno of 9/11 or the ever-escalating mediation of technoviolence around the world. Surely imaginative stimulation of the novelistic kind I have just described is not defeated by the temporary incoherence of a murderous global spectacle. In fact it cannot afford to be defeated, for what other ethical power can transcribe and make legible for future generations the full tragic humanity of this and many other war-induced catastrophes? And who better to meet this demand for new imaginative modalities than the novelist?

The second aspect that Amis's descriptive powers bring to the fore is the sheer pressure on the novelist to reckon with and bring to life worldviews and habitations of staggering incommensurability, a pressure I contend is indelibly linked to our digitally enabled connectivity on a global scale. The writer before and after 9/11 — as Amis's story and many novels generative of worlds around the temporal threshold of 1989 evince — does indeed pick up her pen and delve long and deep into material, cognitive, affective, and metaphysical lifeworlds that are very much part of our global co-belonging but that have been willed into incommensurability the more they are *seen*, not least with the help of our visual technologies, to reside at an existential distance from the rational and progressive comforts of the advanced capitalist world. Despite his evident fear and loathing of the terrorist's mind, Amis is overwhelmingly conscious of this responsibility to explicitly record this incommensurability, to allow it to speak for itself and to be heard. His portrait of the suicide squad's leader is not stuck in a time warp, and there are scarcely any cultural essentialisms at play. Atta's rapturous contemplation of jihad as the single most charismatic idea of his times is adroitly juxtaposed with aspects of the jihadist that are quite recognizably modern, even Western. Amis is at pains to emphasize that Atta is no Arab yokel, that he has two degrees in architecture and that his English and German are "excellent." Even more startling is his choice to make Atta an agnostic who "did not believe in the virgins, did not believe in the Garden. (How could he believe in such an implausibly, and dauntingly, priapic paradise?) He was an apostate: that's what he was. He didn't expect paradise. What he expected was oblivion." Where, then, is the source of his death drive? In his pan-anathema, or world-scale hatred. Amis's deft strokes suggest a deep moral repugnance for the excesses of a pleasure-driven advanced capitalist world, a repugnance that metamorphoses into a pathological self-denial, a sociopathic nihilism, and eventually a superordinate will to kill. The suicide killer for whom "life is not life and death is not death" is the single most powerful entity that sits as an irreducible singularity at the core of the capitalist system of exchange, abjuring its fundamental logics of production, circulation, and consumption. Amis's reading of the motivations of the suicide bomber will no doubt make social scientists uncomfortable.[15] To foreground suicidal mass killing as a primordial act of will and a completely internalized psychopathological reaction to the excesses of capitalist violence does not sit well with the systemic approaches of the social sciences or even with those of postcolonial trauma analysts investigating war-ravaged zones of the world. However, rather than debating this representational conundrum, I want to focus on the implications for my argument of Amis's attempt at a figural abstraction of the incommensurable *singular* through the characterization of Atta.

I suggest that Amis's approach highlights a new structure of address and a new infrastructure of responsibility toward a wider circuit of mediating publics that world novelists are compelled to confront if they are to be at all relevant in our time. "The deliverance of others," David Palumbo-Liu writes in a recent provocation on the ethical burdens of literature, is the novel's single most important calling in our global age. Deliverance not in the sense of redemption or salvation or bringing to enlightenment but in its root meaning: to deliver, to bring forth into view; of literature as a "delivery system" of *excessive* otherness that our systemic structures look to moderate or tame into a generalized system of exchange.[16] To say so is not to equate Amis's recuperation of the internal workings of a heinous killer like Atta with the poetic rendition of the humiliation of shackled prisoners in Guantánamo Bay or even to literary responses to the incessant mediation of the visual traces of dehumanized bodies of Iraqi prisoners at Abu Ghraib. It is rather to address interpretive structures that regulate our affective fields and to ask with Talal Asad, for instance, why suicide killings evoke such horror and revulsion in us when we routinely accept state-sponsored violence.[17] It is also to ask why 9/11 is such an exceptional event in our mediated domains when there have been (and continue to be) other instances of mass-scale carnage in various parts of the world. Not that novels can give us all the answers. But at least they have the imaginative wherewithal to raise such questions and to be open to the extreme discomfort of confronting otherness in a form that global publics see as monstrous—undoubtedly as much a form of *excessive* otherness as untried prisoners of the war on terror or the Palestinian teenager recruited to blow himself up in a busy spot in the occupied West Bank.

As a second illustration, and this time from a novel proper, let us examine this world-oriented compulsion of the contemporary novelist to address an ever-expanding realm of virtual publics routinely exposed to spectacles of war-induced carnage. An opening sequence from McEwan's *Saturday* serves as a powerful example. The protagonist, Henry Perowne, a highly success-ful neurosurgeon, in a moment of insomniac restlessness stands in front of his bedroom window. The scene behind him is one of comfortable domes-ticity: a double bed on which his deeply loved wife is fast asleep under her warm duvet. Saturday's dawn is still three hours away, and the evening before he had drifted into slumber after hearing the UN weapons inspector make yet another case for why the war in Iraq ought not to happen. In the liminal bluish-gray light between darkness and dawn he suddenly sees a bright object moving across the sky. It leaves a trail of bright flashing light. His im-mediate response is not panic. He thinks of his window as a lucky portal to a planetary spectacle: a meteor, and then, on closer reflection, a comet. Me-teors have a "darting, needle-like quality" and disappear in their own heat as they flash across the sky. This object appears to move "slowly, majestically" and could well be a comet, Perowne thinks, even as he wonders why the world media has not caught on to this celestial event. All at once the answer flashes up and the spectacle in the far sky takes an ominously earthly form. It is an airplane with one of its wings on fire. "The fire must be on the near-side of the wing where it joins the fuselage, or perhaps in one of the engines below. The leading edge of the fire is a flattened white sphere which trails away in a cone of yellow and red, less like a meteor or comet than an artist's lurid impression of one."[18]

Perowne's window suddenly frames more than just an unnatural bright-ness in the sky and the surreally quiet Fitzrovia neighborhood. It frames a whole world of possible catastrophes as it inevitably acquires allegorical weight in the wake of 9/11: that of the countless other imagistic portals of burning airplanes crashing into two tall towers: "It's already almost eighteen months since *half the planet watched*, and watched again the unseen captives driven through the sky to the slaughter, at which time there gathered round the innocent silhouette of any jet plane a novel association. *Everyone agrees,* airlines look different in the sky these days, predatory or doomed" (16).

McEwan's eloquent abstraction of the phenomenology of cinematic spectatorship and digitized imagistic exposure is all too evident in this sequence that lasts but a few minutes. The slow-moving shot that tracks the movement of the eye as it gazes at an object in motion gradually morphs into a close-up shot when the reality of the burning object becomes evident in the eyes of the protagonist. From there the narrative jumps technological eras as a frantic montage of familiar sounds and remediated sights in a nightmarish digital whirr shoots across the printed page: the imagined scream in the cabin of American Airlines Flight 11, "the fumbling in bags for phones and last words, the airline staff in their terror clinging to remembered fragments of procedure" (16). The amplified realm of a mediating public that the novelist perforce addresses is clear from the italicized phrases in the quote above: "half the planet watched," "everyone agrees." It is also with this global public that he shares the horror of *what one cannot see* in this experience of remediated exposure: the distance between image and experience, the classic conundrum of distant suffering and humanitarian witnessing: "Catastrophe observed from a safe distance. Watching death on a large-scale, but seeing no one die. No blood, no screams, no human figures at all, and into this emptiness, the obliging imagination set free. The fight to the death in the cockpit, a posse of brave passengers assembling before a last-hope charge against the fanatics. To escape the heat of that fire which part of the plane might you run to? The pilot's end might seem less lonely somehow. Is it pathetic folly to reach into the overhead locker for your bag, or necessary optimism?" (16).

The novelist here shares with his public the grave moral call that the mediated wars of our time make on the authorial imagination. Unlike DeLillo's Bill Gray he does not talk of the defeat of the novelistic imagination but rather of the many openings—windows, one might say—that such incessantly mediated spectacles offer the novelist. The moral conundrum arises not from an inability to imagine or write but from an excess of stimulation and the consequent pressure on the novelist to frame the "real" responsibly. The architectonics of fenestration—the view from the window—jostles here with the networked architecture of global media to generate an overabundance of imaged and imagined deathworlds. The novelist's response could be either a retreat to the aesthetic certitudes that have hitherto shaped his work or a risky leap into the vortex of the virtual.[19] Either way, real virtualities appear to have become the dominant chronotopes of the world novel. And writing itself becomes an act of endless vigil.

Amis's story, in its compressed para-novelistic energy, and McEwan's novel are powerful illustrations of our many extended reflections on the world-scale burdens of the novel after 1989. These, to recapitulate, are the burdens, first, of an open address to an affective public sphere in an ever-expanding realm of digital mediation; second, of the deployment of its generic powers of forensic and testimonial truth-making to bring into view the melancholic property of events and persons incommensurable with our generalized systems of exchange that now span the globe; and third, of confronting the poetics and terror of these world systems themselves. In the rest of this chapter I explicate these in more detail while keeping in play the modern understanding of the ekphrastic as an intermedial morphological space between print and the visual, the descriptive and the pictorial, the narrative and the image. This too is the burden of the world novel: to morph into forms that are legible to our virtual publics while drawing on all its historic resources as an ever-evolving genre of the present. I now turn to my second argument about the dissonance between representations of humanitarian crises in media and those in the novel, and the distinct figurations of the visual in each.

Melancholic Property and Humanitarian Inscription

Publics, Thomas Keenan notes in his account of the ubiquity of cameras in the Bosnian war, means *us* in our mediated exposure to others. Today the global public sphere is veritably an affective and remediated assemblage that comes *after* the image. The "society of the spectacle," Guy Debord called this assemblage nearly half a century ago, but no moment has seen its literal realization as clearly as ours. The writer reporting on a digital camera's instant capture of a scene of violence, which image is already part of the daily repertoire for public consumption—such instances of multilayered mediations are now all too common. At the time of writing Syria is the latest site of disturbing remediation. Keenan's example comes from a series of articles on the Bosnian war written by Mark Danner for the *New York Review of Books*. Keenan observes that Danner begins each piece not with graphic scenes of carnage but with people watching such scenes on television. One example is from Danner's November 20, 1997, installment: "Scarcely two years ago, during the sweltering days of July 1995, any citizen of our civilized land *could have pressed a button on a remote control and idly gazed, for an instant or an hour, into the jaws of a contemporary Hell. Taking shape upon the little screen in that concurrent universe dubbed 'real time,'* was a motley, seemingly endless caravan, bus after battered bus rolling to a stop, and disgorging scores of exhausted, dishevelled people . . . every last one a woman or a child. The men of Srebrenica had somehow disappeared."[20]

Keenan's engagement with this mediated corpus on the Bosnian war is colored by his disillusionment with what he sees as political paralysis in the face of such camera-induced humanitarianism. In such readings the public sphere has morphed from a rational and deliberative entity into a virtualized space of distributive affect. This transformation appears overwhelmingly to generate tragic stories that evoke a diffuse humanitarian response. One might call it sentimentalism, in the modern corrupted sense of the term, from which the ideas of reflection and imaginative projection that inhered in its rich eighteenth-century usage have been erased. It is precisely in this truncated sense that Susan Sontag calibrates the value of photographic and televisual evidence on the Bosnian war. "Sentiment," she writes, "is more likely to crystallize around a photograph than a verbal slogan." It transfixes and paralyzes. It does little to induce cognitive thought or robust political action.[21] Thomas Cushman and Stjepan Mestrovic's volume *This Time We Knew: Western Responses to Genocide in Bosnia* is another account of the failure of global political will in one of the most catastrophic war zones of our post-1989 world. Such a reading has undoubted provenance in an arena of activist scholarship that invests in the idea of humanitarianism as action rather than as affect generated by media images of distant suffering. On sites of genocide as they are happening, these images have very little to offer. Images of war can confront, induce, and testify, but they cannot guarantee a required political outcome. In fact, as a number of influential works have demonstrated, the overabundance of mediated awareness of this genocide appears to be in inverse proportion to the feeble, protracted action of the global powers. To that extent Bosnia is indeed an apposite site from which to call the bluff of humanitarianism and its mediated infrastructure.

But this exceptionally disillusioning example ought not to overdetermine the complex temporalities and moral purchase of the whole repertoire of visuality itself. Nor can it serve as the sole interpretive horizon for the domain of sentimental fact making and melancholic encryption that is so critical to the work of novels in our era. The conceptual path from visual exposure to humanitarian inscription is complicated. Each also has a pertinent history that bears some tracing if we are to address their interplay in the contemporary world novel.

I pause briefly here to reiterate my reasons for tracing this history. In my summary of the threefold burden of novelization in our time, I identified as its second burden the compulsion to retrieve the melancholic properties of lives and events that exist in a relationship of excessive otherness (or are incommensurable) with ways of world-making that have recognizable value within our generalized systems of exchange.[22] The term *melancholic property* is shorthand for what cannot be contained within an actuarial psychic economy. It encodes the singularity of the remaindered life, the nonfungible entity whose excessive particularity refuses to be negated by the address of either the narrative of contract or the narrative of right.[23] The suicide killer is an extreme instance, but others include untried prisoners and ghost detainees in war prisons, refugees, boatpeople, those maimed in war, and civilians rendered "disposable" through acts of forced occupation or civil war.[24]

Nadeem Aslam's novel *The Wasted Vigil* is a veritable graveyard of such disposable and remaindered lives. A lost daughter, a lost brother, a lost son, and a lost grandson bring the three protagonists—an Englishman, a Russian, and an American—together in the war-torn ruins of Afghanistan in the early years of the new millennium. Each has a connection with this unfortunate country that spans the years of its Soviet occupation, the rise of the Taliban, and its ruination since the 9/11 wars. If this makes the book sound like the opening of a post–cold war thriller, our expectations are soon crushed. Losses there are in gigantic measures, and they loom large in the formal work of the novel. A metaphorics of ruin, entombment, and palimpsest configure eons of war-induced devastation. And yet these are losses incapable of being redeemed, for how does one dig through entombments the size of the mountains of Tora Bora? "To visit certain streets was to realise that only the sky remained unchanged there," thinks Marcus as his eyes take in the rubble his town has been reduced to.[25] Marcus is the Englishman who married an Afghan doctor, Qatrina, years before the Soviet occupation and who made Afghanistan his home. He lost his daughter during the Soviet occupation and his wife during the Taliban regime. She was stoned to death after thirty-seven years of marriage because the Taliban refused to recognize their union under Sharia. Marcus's own punishment was amputation, which his wife was compelled to supervise before serving her own death sentence. Nailed into the ceiling of his home are remnants of books that he shared with his wife. The ruins of his now defunct perfume factory are all around him. The head of Buddha with eyes half closed lies buried somewhere in the rubble. A school for girls burns before his eyes, taking with it every single book in town that the Taliban ordered to be thrown into the inferno. And so the narrative lurches from loss to loss. Entire habitations are repeatedly buried even as a few barely alive inhabitants sporadically dare to become their own archaeologists. But perhaps some of the digs ought not to have been ventured. One of the most disturbing scenes in the novel is the desecration of a young Talib's grave by his friends to recover a photograph of an eye that lies buried with him. During their years of training to hate and kill as they professed undying love for Allah the boys had not seen any women, but they had a photo of a woman, which they cut into ten pieces so each could keep a fragment. "Travelling assorted distances, the fragments came together now and then to form her." Their grotesque fulfillment of a desire they are never permitted to feel is ruined without the eye. This is a palimpsest of loss terrifying in its *singularity*. To confront it, to hold on to it, and to testify on its behalf is a burden very few writers ought to have to carry in this world.

The melancholic mode *holds* loss, and a world novel like Aslam's functions as a testamentary mode that bears witness to such loss. Such a mode also occasionally brings to light "the lost news of the news of loss," to use Ian Baucom's pithy formulation.[26] Joe Sacco's graphic novel *Footnotes in Gaza* illustrates this pattern powerfully. The origins of this novel lie in an assignment Sacco was given by *Harper's* magazine to cover the effect of the Second Intifada on the Gaza Strip.[27] He and his journalist colleague decided to focus on one town, Khan Younis, where civilians had been massacred in 1956, a fact of history buried in a paragraph in a UN document, as Sacco discovered by accident. Sacco was keen to weave this grim history into his reporting, but he found no detailed documentation of it in any English-language scholarly or journalistic sources. The two journalists managed to interview a few Palestinians who remembered the massacre. One of these was Abdel El-Aziz El Rantisi, a Hamas official high up in the hierarchy. He was nine years old in 1956 and vividly remembered his uncle's death in the civilian carnage: "I still remember the wailing and the tears of my father over his brother. I couldn't sleep for many months after that. . . . It left a wound in my heart that can never heal. I'm telling you a story and I'm almost crying. This sort of action can never be forgotten. . . . [They] planted hatred in our hearts." Sacco and his colleague incorporated this 1956 footnote in their feature for *Harper's*, but the editors deleted it in the final version. "I found that galling," reports Sacco. "This episode—seemingly the greatest massacre of Palestinians on Palestinian soil, if the UN figures of 275 are to be believed—hardly deserved to be thrown back on the pile of obscurity. But there it lay, like innumerable historical tragedies over the ages that barely rate footnote status in the broad sweep of history—even though, as El Rantisi alluded, they often contain the seeds of the grief and anger that shape present-day events."[28]

Sacco's determination to document this lost history of *loss* fueled his decision to travel to Khan Younis two years later. *Footnotes in Gaza* is the novelized outcome of his quest. The work gives visual form to the intractable contours of this forgotten massacre. Frame after frame constellates faces, voices, backdrops, action, and affect as the story leads the reader slowly through a series of recursive narrative loops to the 1956 moment. But this recovered history is itself a history of erased, repressed, or distorted memories. It urges patience and waiting. It manifests itself in a throwaway line or a fragment of conversation, or even in a dark corner of a makeshift tent. It makes for a wayward journey into the labyrinths of refugee settlements and into the contortions of the Arab-Israeli conflict. The search is as agonizing as the discovered truth. This truth conjoins memory, information, imagination, and empathy. It enfolds in a graphic visual constellation unimaginable pain and suffering. The result is an aesthetic encryption cognitively unavailable to official discourse but available to those who care to *look*.[29] This is sentimental investment in visuality of another kind, not the ineffectual humanitarian gaze of the public as it glazes over the televisual screen. Sacco's brilliance lies in giving formal shape to the historical blur that the Khan Younis massacre has become in official narratives on both sides of the divide. His novel exteriorizes the opacity, the variability, and the evanescence of public memory of this traumatic event even as it exposes the terror of the regime that regulates this memory (figure 1.1).

The visualization of such lost histories of trauma are fundamentally dissonant with the visual continuum of digitally mediated wars and their imagistic excess in the public domain. If one considers the current regime of humanitarian wars, civil conflicts, and refugee regulations, one cannot fail to notice that the norms of who is less than human (in the sense of not belonging to a regime of rights or our generalized economies of exchange) more often than not arrive in visual form. There is no dearth on our screens of images of boatpeople, rows of massacred bodies, shackled suspects of terrorism, dismembered torsos of suicide bombers, and shell-shocked victims of relentless bombing. But far from being imbued with a melancholic property, these visual entities become annexed to a circulatory information economy that invents an abstract lexicon to account for them: *collateral damage, terrorist, illegal asylum seeker* (figures 1.2 and 1.3).

This brings us back to the question of the links between visual affect and humanitarian inscription. What might Sacco's work tell us? That the relationship between melancholic properties and visual economies is "dissensual," that it *makes visible* the unequal "distribution of the sensible," to cite Rancière. By "the sensible" Rancière means both sense data and the sense we make of it, that is, "a system of *a priori* forms determining what presents itself to sense experience."[30] Dissensus arises when a "division" is inserted in "common sense." It is the uncalibrated remainder of the *sensus communis*, a dispute over what is given and about the frame within which we see something as given. Thus the dissensual is not about a conflict of opinions; it is the very condition of the possibility of the political, the moment that signals the irruption of the unheard and the unseen, of subjects excluded or uncounted by a given sociopolitical order, what Rancière refers to as "the part of those who have no part," and what I have called the melancholic singularity of remaindered lives. Dissensus with visuality correspondingly means "dispute over what is visible as an element of a situation, over which visible elements belong to what is common, over the capacity of subjects to designate this common and argue for it."[31] Sacco's Palestinian witnesses in *Footnotes in Gaza* offer myriad scenarios of the 1956 massacre, none of which crystallizes into a coherent picture of what really happened. Yet they frame scenarios of unconscionable violence that tear through the official and public discourses of the Israeli-Palestinian conflict. Sacco's Israeli witnesses see the 1956 Palestinian carnage as a legitimate counterinsurgency strategy, the result of a mode of visualization of war as proper state action in the face of revolt. He abjures his adjudicating role and allows the dissensual full play in sequence after horrific sequence of visualized events.

At this juncture we are forced to confront an experience of visuality that is not just about responding to the physicality of the image or its hypertrophy in the circulatory economy of information. Sacco's *aesthesis* of visual graphics inscribes a melancholic history of Palestine that is far removed from visual tableaux of the Israeli-Palestinian conflict that we are routinely exposed to in various public media forms. Instead of lamenting the ineffectual nature of public mobilization due to media overexposure and compassion fatigue, we are urged to explore the historicity of various regimes of the visual that regulate the irruption of the dissensual in a field of unequal distribution of the sensible, that regulate in the case of Sacco's text what can or cannot be made real in the eyes of the public.

Visualization, argues Nicholas Mirzoeff in one of the most penetrating studies of this concept in recent years, has a history that began long before the consolidation of the visual as the dominant phenomenological trope of our time.[32] The slave plantations were its first domain and the overseer its primary actant. To visualize in the eighteenth-century colonial context—to once again bring into play the comparative frame of my book—was to oversee the classification and segregation of racialized bodies, to affirm as

THE GAZA STRIP

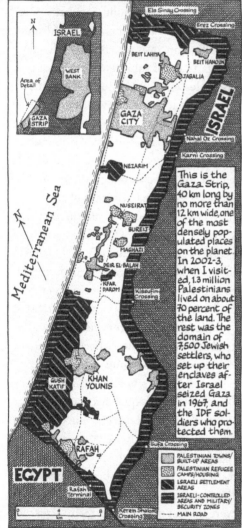

This is the Gaza Strip, 40 km long by no more than 12 km wide, one of the most densely populated places on the planet. In 2002-3, when I visited, 1.3 million Palestinians lived on about 70 percent of the land. The rest was the domain of 7,500 Jewish settlers, who set up their enclaves after Israel seized Gaza in 1967, and the IDF soldiers who protected them.

PALESTINIAN TOWNS/ BUILT-UP AREAS
PALESTINIAN REFUGEE CAMPS/HOUSING
ISRAELI SETTLEMENT AREAS
ISRAELI-CONTROLLED AREAS AND MILITARY/ SECURITY ZONES
MAIN ROAD

Among the Palestinians here, unemployment was at 50 percent. The number of people below the poverty level — living on less than $2 per day — was at 70 percent.

About two-thirds were registered refugees, the jetsam of the '48 war. Most of these lived in the eight major camps administered by the United Nations Relief and Works Agency — UNRWA (pronounced as one word).

All access to and from Gaza, for Palestinians and foreigners, was controlled and heavily restricted by the Israelis.

J. SACCO 5-06

FIGURE 1.1. The Gaza Strip.

FIGURES 1.2 AND 1.3. The Fall of Rafah.

Abed and I track down Mohammed Ismael El-Sbakhi, one of the Palestinian soldiers on the receiving end of the Israeli attack.

Rafah's defenses collapsed within hours.

"When we felt it going wrong, we entered the fields of cactus. We escaped before the road was cut."

I WAS IN THE BACK POSITIONS, IN HEAD-QUARTERS.

I COULD READ AND WRITE, WHICH WAS WHY I WAS IN HEAD-QUARTERS.

[IT] WAS CLOSE TO THE ROAD THAT LEADS TO THE EASTERN VILLAGES.

"All the high-ranking Egyptian soldiers took off their uniforms."

By mid-morning, Dayan was already on the way to his next objective.

He later wrote, "As soon as we left Rafah, the excitement and tension suddenly vanished, giving way to the same serenity I used to feel after a jump during my parachute days."

But those left in his dust felt anything but serene

169

right and proper (as aesthetic) the allocated division of work. This soon morphed into an imperial discourse that understood visualization as the power to imagine the course of history. In Thomas Carlyle's writing, where Mirzoeff claims the first reference to the term *visual* emerged, such power was available only to chosen leaders or "heroes," as Carlyle called them. This understanding of heroic visuality served as a bridge between the history of the abolition of slavery and an anxious preoccupation with the "condition of England" as a rising imperial power. Such an aristocratic understanding of visuality as foresight into the future ran counter to the Benthamite bureau-cratization of the warden's gaze in the image of the panopticon. Nevertheless both participated in a complex of visuality that could be called "imperial," for they were fundamentally invested in the idea of a centralized command of remote populations scattered across the colonies. If slave plantations de-fined the parameters of the eighteenth-century visual economy, imperial-ism marked its history in the long nineteenth century, which lasted until the middle of the twentieth with the retreat of empires after the Second World War. Interestingly the abolitionists themselves frequently used the language of visualization to challenge the visual regime of slave plantations. We saw this in Wilberforce's speech to Parliament in 1806, when he berated the few remaining apologists for the slave trade for not *seeing* its evils "because the objects, as they actually exist, are not allowed to obtrude upon their *vision*."[33] In 1840 a far more powerful visual contestation emerged in the legendary painting by J. M. W. Turner, *Slavers Throwing Overboard the Dead and the Dying: Typhoon Coming On*. The painting, now commonly referred to as *The Slave Ship*, is universally recognized as the most powerful melancholic com-memoration in a visual medium of the Zong massacre of 1781.

If the slave plantation and the imperial systems defined the parameters of visuality from the eighteenth to the mid-twentieth century, the military-industrial complex of the cold war era has dominated the horizon of visual-ization since. Since 1989—and this is of critical significance to the *kairos* of 1989, the literary historical frame of my book—this complex has become in-tensified with the revolution in informatics. What we see now is a militarized visuality that goes under the name of counterinsurgency. Visual modalities of the slave plantation, of imperialism, and of the cold war, far from being left behind, undergo greater intensification under the digital eye that now reigns supreme over a much larger terrain. "The Commander's *visualization* forms the basis for conducting . . . an operation," quotes Mirzoeff from the *U.S. Army/Marine Corps Counterinsurgency Field Manual*, one of the symp-tomatic texts of this posthuman neovisuality.[34]

In such a posthuman visual regime the commandeering agency to conduct war is no longer invested in the body of a single individual but is co-extensive with the vast information infrastructure whose digital depth and foresight far exceed that of a single commander. Since the wars in Iraq and Afghanistan, a cluster of war strategies has begun to be subsumed under the category of information operations. These are not just the use of high-tech surveillance and pilotless air attack systems to identify areas of chaos that need "managing" but the deployment of all information available in the digital sphere to generate scenarios and counterscenarios of conflict. These modalities of visualization are posthuman in another critical sense. In their finished form—a composite of global digital data generated by tens of hundreds of brains around the world—they erase the presence of the human visualizer and hence the *formal materialization of perspective* that all theories of art and visual culture claim is indispensable to visualization. "The viewer can toggle between image sets that he or she did not create, zoom in and out of an image whether by digital or optical means, and compare them to data-bases of previous imagery. The viewer is able to use satellite imagery, infrared, and other technologies to create previously unimaginable visualizations."[35]

How might the effects of this posthuman militarized regime of visuality manifest themselves? As counterinsurgency aided by a multiperspectival informatics, the whole planet potentially becomes the scene of action. For areas identified as epicenters of insurgency, a tripartite strategy of "clear, hold, and build" operates. The first involves use of military might to clear the troubled area of insurgents; the second erects barriers such as walls and barricades to keep the insurgents from infiltrating the cleared space; the third erects a neoliberal form of provisional governance with puppet leaders and outsourced building contractors to rebuild the bombed-out terrain. According to the *Counterinsurgency Field Manual*, the entire operation is intended as an exercise in helping the brutalized inhabitants visualize "a way of life of free and open societies, based on the rule of law, defeat [of] terrorist extremism and creat[ion of] a global environment inhospitable to extremists."[36] This ideal, stated without a trace of irony, is of course never realized, but it leaves in its wake a series of weak and failing states in constant need of counterinsurgency operations. The sites of counterinsurgency since the formal adoption of the Petraeus doctrine are arguably even more ridden with violence, destitution, and death than they were before the operations began. The mediated publics become witness to news cycles that perpetuate narratives of unstable regions that appear to be ever more in need of assistance from the very regimes that generated the instability in the first place.

An episode from Kevin Power's novel on the Iraq war, *The Yellow Birds*, captures in spare language the pure horror of the "clear and hold" strategy in Iraq. "Shoot the hajji fucks," Sterling commands his boys after a particularly brutal round of firing that left men dead on both sides. The U.S. troops are now in a cordoned-off area, a clearing effected by tanks and bulldozers. There are no obvious insurgents in view. Only two old people in a car dare to venture out. The narrator, Bartle, can see the old man, but his commander, Sterling, doesn't and fires a volley of bullets:

—He couldn't see them. I'll yell, I thought. I'll tell him they are old. Let them pass.

But the bullets bit at the crumbling road around the car. They punched into the sheet metal.

—I said nothing. I followed the car with my scope. The old woman ran her fingers along a string of pale beads. Her eyes were closed.

—I couldn't breathe.

—The car stopped in the middle of the road but Sterling did not stop the shooting. The bullets ripped through the car and out the other side. The holes in the car funneled light, and the smoke and dust hung in the light. The door opened and she fell from the old car. She tried to drag herself to the side of the road. She crawled. Her old blood mixed with the ash and dust. She stopped moving.

—"Holy shit, that bitch got murdered," Murph said. There was no grief, or anguish, or joy, or pity in that statement.[37]

Commanders like Sterling are the operational experts of this model of counterinsurgency, carrying out orders on behalf of the militarized visual informatics regime and ordering his battalion to stay in a state of readiness for the next lot of clearing and holding. "Get ready, motherfuckers" is his rallying refrain, even as his weary but obedient platoon haul themselves into the action yet again after having barely survived the last. The narrator, a member of Sterling's platoon, observes, "We would be tired when the mission came, but we would go, for we had no alternative. Perhaps, we'd had them once: alternatives, other paths to take. But our course was certain then, if unknown. It was going to be dark before we knew it. We had lived, Murph and me."[38]

Counterinsurgency does not look for a solution; it looks for ways to prolong the chaos and embark on yet another lethal cycle of "clear, hold, rebuild." Riverbend's blog novel, *Baghdad Burning*, and Sacco's *Footnotes in Gaza* offer graphic illustrations of this perpetuation of deliberate, chaos-induced militarization. In her blog entry of October 13, 2003, Riverbend writes of the destruction of palm groves and olive plantations in Dhuluaiya, Iraq, by U.S. security forces, a mode of "clearing" attributed to operations to flush out Shiite guerrillas believed to be hiding in the groves. These groves were the primary livelihood of the farmers who had known no other home except Dhuluaiya: "The trees are bulldozed and trampled beneath heavy machinery. We see the residents and keepers of these orchards begging the troops to spare the trees, holding up crushed branches, leaves and fruit—not yet ripe—from the ground littered with a green massacre. The faces of the farmers are crushed and amazed at the atrocity. I remember one wrinkled face holding up 4 oranges from the ground . . . and screaming at the camera—'Is this freedom? Is this democracy?!'"[39] Riverbend's astute observation of the strategic destruction of existing habitats and manufacture of crisis zones by U.S. forces is also evident in her blog post of December 29, 2006:

It's like having a big piece of hard, dry earth you are determined to break apart. You drive in the first stake in the form of an infrastructure damaged with missiles and the newest in arms technology, the first cracks begin to form. . . . The cracks slowly begin to multiply and stretch across the once solid piece of earth, reaching out towards its edges like so many skeletal hands. And you apply pressure. You surround it from all sides and push and pull. Slowly, but surely, it begins coming apart. . . . That is Iraq right now. The Americans have done a fine job of working to break it apart. This last year has nearly everyone convinced that that was the plan right from the start. There were too many blunders for them to actually have been, simply, blunders.[40]

Similar insights pervade Sacco's *Footnotes in Gaza*. In one chapter Sacco brings to visual life the tragic fall of Rafah that preceded the occupation of Gaza. The section begins with his friend Abed reading the infamous memoir of Moshe Dayan, the Israeli foreign minister, entitled *The Diary of the Sinai Campaign*, which outlines with relish the Israeli Army's plan to capture Rafah and El Arish: "If El Arish and Rafah fall to us, the Gaza strip will be isolated and unable, alone, to hold out."[41] Anticipating the counterinsurgency tactics of the U.S. occupation forces in Iraq, Dayan in 1977 allegedly described the Israeli strategy of occupation as maintaining a permanent state of emergency: "The question was not 'What is the solution?' but 'How do we live without a solution?'"[42] (See figures 1.2 and 1.3.)

In Sacco's novel the fall of Rafah is visualized through the eyes of the Palestinian victims—shell-shocked witnesses of the Israeli Army's lethal "clear and hold" tactics. Survivors Mohammad Ismael El-Sbakhi, Owda Ayesh, and an unnamed terrified Palestinian recount the horrors of the Rafah attack even as a page from Dayan's diary appears in one of the panels of the graphic novel. Inserted between four Israeli tanks, the diary entry reads, "As soon as we left Rafah, the excitement and tension vanished, giving way to the same serenity I used to feel after a jump during my parachute days." At the edge of the panel, in a cloud of dust left behind by the Israeli tanks, is a boxed entry: "But those left in his dust felt anything but serene."[43] Those left in the dust huddle together to witness through the window the shooting of a neighbor foolhardy enough to step out during curfew. They see an alleged *fiyadeen* tied to the back of a military truck and dragged away until his body begins to tear apart. Sacco's painstaking and sensitively calibrated visual capture of the survivors' memories of the Rafah massacre offers a melancholic counternarrative to the official occupation narratives of Gaza and to global media accounts of the Israel-Palestine conflict. Likewise Powers's novelistic capture of the front line in the Iraq war acquires a humanitarian depth as much in the quiet lyricism of his account of the death of Murph, the narrator's friend, as in his mournful reflections on the sheer waste of war.

The writings of Sacco, Powers, Aslam, and Riverbend bring into melancholic reckoning the terrors of our neoliberal and militarized deathworlds—terrors that our everyday dominant media representations often normalize within a visual regime of posthuman surveillance and control. In sum, the melancholic and humanitarian inscriptions in these world novels envision the ravages of our contemporary world order in ways that radically challenge and unsettle both mediatized and militarized regimes of visuality.

THIS CHAPTER HAS SOUGHT to account for the continuing relevance of the novel in an era of proliferating new media genres. Far from becoming extinct or irrelevant in our hypervisual age, novels now operate in a transmedial space and work into their formal structures and modes of address phenomenologies of apperception natural to our multimedia environment. I have also examined in some depth the global humanitarian remit of these novels, their orientation to publics and worldviews that are no longer circumscribed by national or regional limits. Given my theoretical investment in ideas of world and world-making in relation to the global orientation of these novels, I next explore the conceptual purchase, the chronotopic force, and the tropological uptakes of the world.

PART I
WORLD

TWO
WORLD-MAKING AND POSSIBLE WORLDS

Thus far, four distinct uses of the term *world* have come to the fore: the world as spatial amplification and systemic interconnection across the globe through the circuits of informational capitalism; the world as an aesthetic remainder of the globe that resists the space-time compression of global commodity circuits; the world as an ethical site of human relationality and humanitarian connectivity; and the world as a self-contained totality analogous to a Leibnizian monad whose many parts are compossible with each other and that is not reducible to the materiality of the actual world we inhabit. Together they offer a template for an exploration of literary world-making in our time. This chapter aims to unravel the richness of the cultural, ethical, and philosophical apprehensions of the world just outlined as ground, horizon, and possibility for the emergence of the idea of world literature and of the contemporary novel. The two chapters that follow offer detailed case studies of distinct types of world novel, and in the process, illuminate the heterogeneous modes—rhetorical, tropological, narratological—in which the empirical world picture of our time is made manifest.

"Our earth, the domain of *Weltliteratur*, is growing smaller and losing its diversity," wrote Eric Auerbach half a century ago. "Yet, *Weltliteratur* does not merely refer to what is generically human or common."[1] *Welt* (world) for Auerbach was emphatically not the standardized denominator of cultural diversity. But the idea of world literature (*Weltliteratur*), he averred in the era of the cold war, was in danger of flattening the philological uniqueness of the world's many literatures into two distinct geocultural domains: the European-American and the Russian-Bolshevik. Auerbach's anxiety is even more resonant in our age, when five or six world languages—English, Mandarin, Arabic, Spanish, French, and Hindi—serve as translated homes for literatures from around the world. The distinction that Auerbach posits between the idea of world (that resists philological flattening) and that of world literature (the potential site of geocultural standardization) has deep significance for this book as a whole. What is the normative purchase of the term *world* in world literature as we contemplate the sheer scale of global literary transactions in the twenty-first century?

In order to contemplate the value of world-making in global literary studies, it may help to begin with a foray into the meaning and resonance of the term *world*, both as a chronotope in literature across time and as a theoretical frame in the discipline of literary studies as it has evolved since the time Goethe first used the term *Weltliteratur* to evoke a normative horizon opened up by the unprecedented traffic of literary works from around the globe in an era of enhanced commerce and imperial adventure. The first half of this chapter undertakes this task. I excavate a poetics of the world in texts from three distinct cultural contexts and then trace the shifting frontiers of value making in conceptions of world literature through the arc of world history from 1830 to 1950—also the era of the waxing and waning of European empires. The second half turns to our contemporary age, when the charge of the term *world* in literary studies has been magnified to mirror the ubiquity of globalization as an economic and sociocultural matrix of maximal extension. What does the specificity of the *literary*—as the work of genre, rhetoric, trope, and narrative—have to offer in understanding the complex relationship between the globe and the world? Neither synonymous with nor the obverse of each other, as we saw briefly in the introduction, the two terms seem nevertheless entangled in ways that require some conceptual unraveling. What might phenomenological apprehensions of the world have to offer here? How do we calibrate *literary* value in an era that otherwise routinely annexes the phenomenon of literary globalism to the value-laden worlds of either market capitalism or cosmopolitanism? Finally, what models of value might the philosophical literature on possible and counterfactual worlds offer in understanding the special provenance of the world novel in our time? These are some of the questions that animate the second half of the chapter.

The idea of a world has long been part of the literary consciousness of many cultures. Literary contemplations on the chronotope of world abound, but the word itself has scarcely had a settled meaning in such contemplation. It has been variously understood as cosmos, as an ecumenical horizon that universalizes the human condition, as an orientation to imaginaries beyond one's immediate space and time, and even as a will to power that seeks to globally disseminate values originating in a particular tradition. The three examples that follow illustrate this semantic variability of the term, not to mention its scalar shifts. My first example is from Walt Whitman's *Leaves of Grass*. Whitman's pantheistic panegyric to his poetic self as the embodiment of the cosmos, as "an acme of things accomplish'd and an encloser of things to come," is all too famous, as are his lines about "containing multitudes" and releasing his "barbaric yawp over the roofs of the world."[2] In Whitman's poem the world is synonymous with the idea of cosmogony, which simultaneously contemplates the origins of the universe and the palpability of sentient life. Both are recast in the poet's protean self even as he celebrates his existence in mid-nineteenth-century Manhattan as the acme of evolved human habitation. The world here ranges in a scale from the singular poetic self and the enchanted geography of Manhattan to the cosmos of all sentient creatures.

A millennium earlier, and displaying a somewhat different mode of cosmo-anthropogenic contemplation, a tenth-century Sanskrit poet and literary theorist, Rajashekara, wrote a comprehensive treatise on literary cultures in South Asia entitled *Kavyamimansa* (A discourse on poetics). In response to questions about the origin of literature (Sanskrit *kavya*), he extrapolated from the *Rig Veda* allegory about the origin of the world in the Primal Being (*Purusha*) and theorized the origin of the Primal Being of Literature (*Kavyapurusha*) as being simultaneous with the origin of the world itself. Secular temporalities of the origin of the literary, those that code histories of speech patterns, scripts, genres, language groups, and grammars, scarcely find a place in this text. Instead we encounter a cosmogenic conception that is simultaneously anthropomorphic in its figuration of literary and language worlds. The mouth of this primal literary being is Sanskrit, his arms Prakrit, his groin Apabrahmsa, and his feet Paishachi. The hierarchy of languages is clearly delineated, with the godly (Sanskrit) placed well above the finely graded vernaculars. Secularizing his interpretation, the noted Sanskrit scholar Sheldon Pollock writes, "The practice of literary culture presented here is without question a universal one: while the universe it contains may be finite, it is also final, so to speak, for no other exists outside it."[3] Literature in such a conception contains the whole world even as the world contains it. Each constitutes the other's limit. The anthropogenic form (*kavyapurusha*) allegorizes the containment of both.

A final example, which foregrounds yet another distinct understanding of the world and literary world-making—one that comes closer to modern understandings of world literature as the travel of works beyond their linguistic and national remit—is Ronit Ricci's study *Islam Translated*. Here it is not the poetic self or the primal literary being that *embodies* the world; rather it is a magisterial text that *makes* one. Highlighting the genesis of a literary world— what she calls an Arabic *ecumene*—through the travels of a single magisterial work, *Book of One Thousand Questions*, across five centuries and two continents, Ricci analyzes the production of heterogeneous Islamic literary and language worlds that linked Muslims across divides of distance and culture through this single work. The text is a well-known narrative depicting a dialogue between the Prophet Muhammad and a Jewish leader that ends with the Jew's conversion to Islam. Ricci traces the dissemination and transformations of the *Book* from its tenth-century Arabic original to its adaptations into Javanese, Malay, and Tamil textual traditions between the sixteenth and the twentieth century. In tracing the diverse meanings and circumstances of translation that shaped the history of this Islamic text, she scales up her study to draw conclusions about the role of translation, linguistic change, and literary transmission in the creation of a literary cosmopolis that was distinctly non-European even as it straddled the exact five centuries—from the sixteenth to the twentieth—that marked the ascent of Western civilization.

We see here a distinct shift from world as *cosmogony* to world as *cosmopolis*. It is this latter conception of the literary world that functions in a geocultural realm beyond and at the interstices of national and continental borders, that marks the origins of the idea of world literature as a specific mode of disciplinary practice in early nineteenth-century Europe.[4] In the history of the discipline as it has evolved in the West, Goethe's 1827 letter to Sulpiz Boisserée is the widely acknowledged source for the first modern use of the term *world literature*, that is, world literature conceived in terms of enhanced commerce and reception of literary works across national frontiers, not as a classic canon of great books. The philologic-lexigraphic revolution in the world of letters from the late eighteenth to the mid-nineteenth century made many non-European works available in translation across the continent.[5] The German term *Weltliteratur* captured for Goethe the evolving cosmopolitical transformations of Europe in a post-Napoleonic era as also his own exposure to Persian and Chinese works that was enabled by the newly minted disciplines of Oriental and Indological studies in Germany.[6] Another frequently cited source is Marx and Engel's *Communist Manifesto*, which in 1848 used the term in the Goethean sense of an expanded market of ideas and books and as arising "from many national and local literatures."[7]

Other well-known figures associated with the evolution of the idea in the decades since are Hugo Meltzl, Richard Meyer, Eric Auerbach, Claudio Guillen, and Edward Said.[8] Meltzl's Transylvanian pushback against German domination in late nineteenth-century comparatist studies and his inclusion of smaller literatures in his various bibliographic and philological enterprises make him one of the first language ecologists in modernity. Without quite naming Goethe and Herder as advocates of an undesirable German cultural nationalism that eclipsed other traditions, Meltzl wrote in 1877, "Today every nation demands its own 'world literature' without quite knowing what is meant by it. . . . This unhealthy 'national principle' therefore constitutes the fundamental premise of the entire spiritual life of modern Europe. . . . Instead of giving free rein to polyglottism and reaping the fruits of the future . . . every nation today insists on the strictest monoglottism, by considering its own language superior or even destined to rule supreme."[9] At the turn of the century another German philologist and comparatist, Richard Meyer (1860–1914), published two influential works, one in 1900, "Die Weltliteratur und die Gegenwart" (World literature and the present), and another in 1913, *Die Weltliteratur im 20. Jahrhundert* (World literature in the twentieth century). Meyer's was the first systematic attempt at a definition of world literature, and an evaluative one at that. Only literary works that significantly transcended their specific historical locations and temporally determined worldviews, that awakened a wide swath of readers to humanity's genius, that activated the full spectrum of human emotions, and that captured the elusive magic of human flourishing and decay were deemed worthy of that name. World literature for Meyer was simultaneously a poetics, an ethics, a philosophical anthropology, and a universal treatise on human affect. An avowed vitalist and visionary, and surprisingly also a Nietzschean, but primarily in his antihistoricism, he categorically eschewed the progressivism of Goethe and Goethe's additive vision of an expanding global literary sphere through trade, commerce, conquest, and influence. Nor was he enamored of the rising tide of German nationalism. While he never advocated for a canon of world literature, it would not be farfetched to imagine his inventory of literary value translating into such an exercise, as indeed it did in many major research universities in Europe, Asia, and the Americas from the early years of the twentieth century. One doesn't automatically associate Auerbach's anguish-prone 1952 treatise "Philology and *Weltliteratur*" with Meyer's works; however, they did share an aversion toward the pathologies of Germanic nationalism. For Auerbach, as is well known, this meant exile to Istanbul with the rise of the Nazis and urgent advocacy of a philologically oriented approach to literatures of the world, one that would not standardize or flatten the riches on offer or be wiped out by a nihilistic bureaucratization of human difference.

Philology and the European Other

Said's own formulations on the idea of world were built on the Auerbachian linkage between literature, philology, and world history. Combining Auerbach's insights with those from Vico's *New Science* and Arabic philological traditions, Said saw the task of the critic as prizing open the "worldliness" of the literary text, first by situating it as a product of its material allegiances and historical affiliations, and subsequently by mining words philologically as repositories of human belonging through time. Said did not see his strong advocacy of Palestinian nationalism as being in any tension with his call for a philological humanism that was world-oriented. His painstaking philological analysis of Arabic terms in *Humanism and Democratic Criticism* is worth noting here. Highlighting both the disconnect between political knowledge and cultural knowledge and Islamic fundamentalism's macabre appropriation of the basic tenets of the Holy Book, Said takes us back to the origins of Islamic knowledge in a philological attention to language beginning with the Koran, a term that itself means "deep reading of the word of God." He reminds an amnesiac modern West of the hallowed tradition of Islamic jurisprudence, hermeneutics, and the science of language that existed in Arab universities of southern Europe and North Africa in the eleventh and twelfth centuries. Said sees this tradition in a continuum with the Judaic one in Andalusia and the Maghreb as well as the Christian one to emerge centuries later in Europe with Vico's *New Science* in 1744. The interactive, translational, and intercultural communicative domain of humanities scholarship that Said envisages for our age is inspired not only by the philological comparativism of Auerbach and Spitzer but also by the quintessential philological base of medieval

Islamic textual scholarship that mined words and phrases from the Koran amid a sea of existing interpretations, constituting in the process a system of interdependent readings called *isnad*. "The common goal," he writes, "is to approach the ground of the text, its principle or *usul*." The quest for usul, he adds, is inextricably tied to the notion of *ijtihad*, a term that connotes deep personal commitment to finding one's truth in reading the holy text. It valorizes individual interpretation rigorously executed but with a responsibility toward an interpretive community. Philologically the term *ijtihad* is derived from the same etymon as the much abused and reviled *jihad*, which, as Said is at pains to point out, "does not mainly mean holy war but rather . . . a spiritual exertion on behalf of truth."[10] The *ijtihadi* tradition encourages dialogue, thus enlarging the interpretative field of the Koran. Not surprisingly the orthodox segment of Islamic scholarship has regarded it with suspicion since the fourteenth century. The merit of Said's attempt to de-Westernize the realm of a philological reading, and what one may legitimately call a translational humanist reading, of world literature can hardly be underestimated in this age of war and terror, with the Arab world as the particular locus of conflict. It resonates strongly with his activism in the cause of Palestine.

Hardly mentioned in genealogical accounts of world literature are two persons who straddled the late Victorian and Edwardian eras from opposing sides of the British colonial divide: Richard Moulton (1849–1924) and Rabindranath Tagore (1861–1941). No two people could be more unlike each other. Tagore was a landed and pedigreed aristocrat in undivided India with no formal education beyond primary school. Home-schooled in the arts and letters by a superbly talented family from a very young age, he went on to become one of Bengal's and India's most celebrated writers. He won the Nobel Prize for Literature in 1913. A polymath artist, poet, painter, novelist, composer, and educationist, he founded the first experimental "world university" in the rural environs of his home in Bengal's Birbhum district, which he named Vishwabharati (translated simultaneously as The World within India and Repository of World Knowledge). Moulton was a Cambridge-educated, late Victorian champion of English civilization, a Bible scholar, and the author of *World Literature and Its Place in General Culture* (1911). He taught for a few years at the University of Chicago, where he was a professor of literary theory and interpretation. Tagore and Moulton shared strong views about the civilizational value of world literature but had diametrically opposed conceptions of it. Moulton was resolutely Eurocentric, even Anglocentric. For him the five "bibles" that constituted the world literary canon were Homer, Dante, Shakespeare, Milton, and Goethe. These were inextricable from the idea of English civilization for they had seeped into the cultural sinews of English society. Even minor writers like Swinburne and William Morris were "Homeric" in their literary aspirations. Moulton conceived of world literature as an "angle of perspective" on the whole of literature, but his "angle" was resolutely English and in strong alignment with the idea of British colonialism as a civilizational force of good in the world. In 1907, around the time that Moulton was formulating his Anglocentric theory on literary world-making, Tagore was invited by the National Council of Education in Calcutta to talk about comparative literature. The Council was set up to resist efforts by the British to legislate for the widespread introduction of English education in the three presidencies of Madras, Bombay, and Bengal and also to protest the enforced division of Bengal into east and west by the Viceroy Lord Curzon in 1905. This division was the first conscious attempt by the British to communally divide Hindu and Muslim populations across two terrains.

Crafting his protest against both these measures in tellingly unromanticized metaphors of earth, land, and linguistic belonging, Tagore claimed that he wanted to talk about "world literature" (*vishwa-sahitya*) and not comparative literature (*tulanatmak sahitya*): "I have been called upon to discuss a subject to which you have given the English name of Comparative Literature. Let me call it World-Literature in Bengali." Comparative literature perpetuated a divide between languages and regions, and he had little patience with its discriminating and differentiating methodologies. The idea of world literature, on the other hand, embodied a more unified continuum that captured a global spiritual humanism. It also captured the essence of the term *sahitya* in its etymological sense of "togetherness" and "union":

> What I am trying to say amounts to this. Just as the earth is not the sum of patches of land belonging to different people, and to know the earth as such is sheer rusticity, *so literature is not the mere total of works composed by different hands.* Most of us, however, think of literature in what I have called the manner of the rustic. From this narrow provincialism we must free ourselves; we must strive to see the work of each author as a whole, the whole as a part of man's universal creativity, and that universal spirit in its manifestations through World-Literature. Now is the time to do so.[11]

World literature for Tagore was a panacea not only for a colonially induced provincialism and divisiveness but also for nationalistic aggression. In the aftermath of World War I, when anticolonial aspirations were being articulated in India in the language of independent nation making, Tagore famously wrote, "The Nation has thrived long upon the mutilated humanity. Men, the fairest creations of God, came out of the National manufactory in huge numbers as war-making and money-making puppets. . . . Human society grew more and more into a marionette show of politicians, soldiers, manufacturers and bureaucrats, pulled by wire arrangements of wonderful efficiency." Against Moulton's English civilizational claims to world literature and in a continuing attack on the depredations of an overweening nationalism, Tagore wrote in 1916, "If you compare England with Germany and France you will find that she has produced the smallest number of scholars who have studied Indian literature and philosophy with any amount of sympathetic insight or thoroughness. This attitude of apathy and contempt is natural where the relationship is abnormal and founded upon selfishness and pride."[12] Macaulay's ghost loomed large in the English apathy for Indological studies in the high colonial era from the 1860s to 1930s.[13] What proved more useful was ethnographic and demographic knowledge for better governance. Tagore believed world literature offered a counternarrative to this utilitarian ethnography. It became an index of a civilizational connectivity that superseded artificial and aggressively enforced political barriers, something that, in his view, the English colonial rulers were incapable of understanding.

In its periodic invocations throughout history, then, the value of world literature has been perceived as a measure of enhanced cultural diversity, a mode of cultural exchange, a timeless repository of classic works, an antidote to nationalist chauvinism and cultural monoglottism, an aspiration to a cosmopolitan public sphere, a civilizational alibi for colonial expansion, a civilizational force against colonialism, a symptom of cultural anxiety, and even occasionally, as with Auerbach and Said, a necessary philological enterprise in the face of impending political and cultural catastrophe.

The World Now: Residuum, Surplus, Immanence

Not much heard in the half century between the end of World War II and the turn of the millennium, the term *world*[14] has made a spectacular reentry as a literary critical rubric in the twenty-first century. One is reminded of Walter Benjamin's phrase "the *now* of knowability," when certain historical periods offer just the right temporal traction for an idea to gain real rhetorical currency. In literary studies in this century the idea of world finally appears to have realized its true potential as the philological home of maximal extension and maximal connectivity. At first this does not seem hard to account for. The noisy presence of globalization as a conduit for intellectual exchange and unprecedented levels of connectivity of world populations through information and communication technologies are both significant enough to make literary scholars in the twenty-first century rethink the phenomenology of literary production, distribution, and consumption beyond national and regional boundaries. Literary world-making as the travel of genres and textual patterns, as the elliptical reception of texts in different regions of the globe, as translated worlds that haunt or echo other literary imaginaries, as deep time repositories of exemplary and catastrophic cultural shifts—there is no scarcity of such celebratory accounts of contemporary approaches liberated from national, nationalistic, and cold war–era geopolitical boundaries.[15] Nor, surprisingly, of contentious and skeptical accounts: world literature as a handmaiden of the forces of globalization, as a posthistorical triumphal narrative of an enforced unification of the world, as conscription of the imagination to dangerously polarized worldviews and even to an "image capitalism" that perpetuates in the name of an ecumenical vision what is in fact the "US Empire's particular national mythology."[16] Yet another body of work turns to the study of world literature as a system in the manner of the social and natural sciences. Braudel, Wallerstein, and Bourdieu are some obvious influences, as are Darwin and Mendel. One thinks here of Franco Moretti's pathbreaking use of evolutionary theory in his analysis of the genesis, evolution, and extinction of literary forms as they cut a swath through the globe, or Pascale Casanova's theorization of the world literary system as a republic of letters wherein texts and entire literary traditions accrue or lose prestige depending on their degree of separation from a Greenwich meridian of literary space-time—which, in her case, is Paris of the nineteenth century and the high modernist era.[17]

My contention, however, is that the calibration of the value of world-making in our time demands more than a grasp of this enlarged material circuitry of literature, especially if we are to establish its specific *literary* provenance and rescue it from reductionist neomaterialist readings. It demands a close engagement with mutable and shape-shifting canons; translational adventures inconceivable before the rise of digital technology; multimedial conceptions of the literary beyond print; the irrefragable proliferation of literary forms beyond the classic genres of novel, poetry, drama, and epic; and even the genetic drift of these classic genres. Each of these demands both close and distant reading: those famous polarizing categories that have done such vigorous rounds lately in methodological debates about the global literary system. Distant reading in some respects has gained ascendancy in recent years, especially with the influential works of Moretti—so much so that close reading is often bracketed off as a methodology incapable of grasping the "world" in world literature. This notwithstanding Moretti's own brilliant close reading of nineteenth-century works in his *Atlas of the European Novel* and most recently in *The Bourgeois: Between History and Literature.* These works are both data-rich and qualitatively insightful. Significantly for this book committed to the specific provenance of the *literary* and especially the novelistic over other modes of imaginative apprehension, the resurgence of world literature is also often understood symptomatically as the rescue and revitalization of the *literary* after decades of scholarly prominence accorded to theory and cultural studies.[18] But what exactly does the resurgence of the literary in relation to world-making mean in our times, and how do we study its special provenance beyond simply scaling up and studying the system as a global phenomenon? Surely there are other ways of reading the world in world literature?

I suggest that the notion of world in literary studies can be read not as synonymous with the global (as maximal extension) but as its aesthetic remainder and analogous to the philosophical mode in which Derrida talks of Husserl's world as *residuum*, one that exists as both ground and horizon, both inside and outside the empirical reality of the global.[19] Some aspects of this phenomenological apprehension of the world were discussed in the introduction in relation to the work of Heidegger and Nancy. Phenomenological not in the sense of the concrete and sensuous world of everyday experience but as what Derrida calls the "antepredicative reality," which is always already there as a "preconstituted substrate of all meaning . . . and an infinite totality of possible foundations of every judgement."[20] The resonance with Nancy's formulation of world as both the ground of infinite possibility and a negation of the proliferating and totalizing logic of the global is unmistakable here. *Mondialization* in the way Nancy imputes meaning to it is the immanent structure of the world, a "world-forming," a mode of creation that enables flourishing and is not beholden to any externalities, least of all to the totalizing technomaterial abstractions of the global: *"To create the world means: immediately without delay, reopening each possible struggle for a world, that is, for what must form the contrary of a global injustice against the background of general equivalence."*[21]

When extrapolated from these phenomenological readings, the world in literature can operate as the realm of the immanent and imagined rather than the flattened and fungible. We have an opening here to comprehend world literature not simply as coextensive with our ever-expanding sense of connection with the rest of globe due to accelerated information flows, nor merely as a category responding to the normative frame of a postcolonial consciousness that urges consideration of literatures from parts of the world not designated as the West. No doubt these are significant conditions of possibility for the reemergence of world literature as an idea suited to our globalized times. But to limit ourselves to thinking the world purely as extension—territorial, infrastructural, and cultural—does not allow us to think of a mode of value creation that is attuned to the actual work of language, narrative, form, and genre in generating literary worlds, and not just in producing vapid equivalences of social universals such as liberal inclusiveness and cosmopolitanism. Inclusiveness amplified to cover as much cultural ground as possible is ultimately an extraliterary mode of value creation, but it does little to illuminate the specific value of the *literary* itself. Further, world literature seen in terms of pure extension is often susceptible to neomaterialist, antiaestheticist critiques of complicity with global imperial networks, more so when it circulates in world languages such as English.

To turn now to a specific illustration of this argument, what if we conceived of the *world* not as a literary system analogous to an ever-expanding global market but as a critical resource to understand some value-laden ascriptions attached to specific genres—such as the novel, for instance—in our avowedly global era? In talking about the normative value of genres, and especially the novel, Thomas Pavel once noted that rather than invoking abstract, a priori rules, it was best to have a grasp of the cultural tasks a genre like the novel attempted to fulfill. It is, after all, the genre least constrained by formal rules. The normative in this case can be read more productively in terms of a generative aesthetic resolution to a representational problem.[22] Extrapolating from Pavel's reading of the novel's normative purchase, here is the specific representational problem I raise: How might we understand the complex relationship between the contemporary world novel and the empirical world picture of contemporary globalization such that the former is not reduced to a secondary reproduction of the latter? What critical tools are available to study novelistic world-making in these terms?

A short excursus into a philosophical body of work on fictional world-making will be significant in addressing this question. Long before the revival of the idea of world in relation to literary productions of our global era, a strand of analytic philosophy addressed the problem of fictional world-making through its theory of possible worlds. Drawing its logicosemantic source from Leibniz, who proposed a minimalist reading of world as a finite set of entities and relations marked off by worlds made up of other finite sets of entities and relations, possible-world theory points to modes of thinking framed by what could have been or could be. This focus not just on *existing* but *possible* states of affairs for the first time brought fiction seriously into the realm of philosophical thought. Hitherto devalued for its lack of truth-value by philosophers from Plato's time, fictional worlds in this modal approach were seen not as inconsequential, dangerous, or delusional but as coherent systems with their own narrative logic. Further, they were not exceptional in logical and semantic senses but very much part of a broader discursive field that included propositions and ways of thinking oriented toward worlds beyond what actually is. Components of this discursive field include conditionals, anticipation, projections, forecasts, wishes, memories, and myths.[23]

Events, setting, characters, points of view, and space-time configurations are the entities that make up possible worlds in fiction. Each element works with the rest to create distinct constellations. These counterfactual constellations have independent ontological status, and their referential problems are addressed in terms of their own internal coherence. This is not the same as saying that the literary text is hermetic and needs to be understood only in terms of its own world of words and images, which is the staple of formalist criticism. It is more that *the ontological legitimacy of a fictional world is not tied to a range of possibilities emerging only from an actual state of affairs in the world.* In other words, fiction can create a parallel world with little or no relation to events in the actual world and yet have its ontological status validated. This is an important distinction between possible worlds in fiction and those in other disciplinary and discursive domains, such as the natural sciences, where the theory of possible worlds has ramified powerfully in discussions of diverse scientific paradigms. Ruth Ronen marks this distinction in terms of "parallelism" and "ramification." Fiction, she says, constitutes an "independent modal structure" in that "fictional facts do not relate what could have or could not have occurred in actuality, but rather what did occur and could have occurred in fiction."[24] Possible worlds in the scientific domain, however, operate on the logic of ramification in that their range of possibilities emerges from an actual state of affairs.

Another significant dimension of possible-worlds theory is the recognition that fictional worlds, notwithstanding their ontological parallelism, have varying degrees of distance from and proximity to the actual world. In other words, these theories are also invested in "interworld" questions, which for our purposes translates into the relationship between contemporary world novels and their emplacement within larger global systems. Much of the philosophical literature on possible worlds articulates this relationship in terms of varying degrees of realism, a concept that resonates powerfully in literary scholarship on the novel. Three of these are especially pertinent to our understanding of the relation between the fictional and empirical worlds after 1989: modal realism, moderate realism, and antirealism.[25] Schematically and telegraphically speaking, for *modal realism* all possible worlds are "actual," and there is no valorization of the real world out there as the true actual. *Actual* here operates indexically to refer to any coherent set of entities and relations that are compossible in the neo-Leibnizian sense of conveying a perceptual harmony among elements of a set. David Lewis represents this position in his book *Counterfactuals*. *Moderate realism* covers a spectrum of positions, and many prominent analytic philosophers, such as Alvin Plantinga, Robert Adams, and Saul Kripke, fit under this rubric.[26] "Actualists" such as Plantinga and Adams are of the view that possible worlds exist only in relation to the real world here and now and are but "non-obtaining states" or a "set of propositions" that signal how things could be otherwise. The "actual" here, unlike in modal realism, operates referentially, not indexically, and is potentially realizable. Adams argues that it is possible to arrive at consistent and maximally complete sets of descriptions and propositions about the world, and a possible world is but a complete description of the way the world could be. Kripke, another celebrated modal language philosopher, while positioning himself as a semantic externalist who believes in a referential theory of meaning, rejects the semantic push to *describe* possible worlds maximally. Instead he recasts possible worlds as purely formal, abstract entities. Their modality, he submits, can be expressed only in the abstract terminology of mathematical logic. The push to affirm their parity with descriptors and propositions pertaining to actual worlds paradoxically detracts from their unique contribution to the semantic field.

The third position on realism is simply *antirealism*. This position denies any concrete existence to possible worlds on the following grounds: their ontological status is attributed, in the first instance, in relation to a notion of the actual world, but there is no way to ascertain the primacy and distinctiveness of the actual world logically, only metaphysically, for the actual world, *pace* Leibniz, is itself only contingently real, a product of chance rather than of any transcendental design. Can one then not logically attribute a modal existence to even the so-called actual world? See it as the accidental realization of a possible world and not the only best possible world that could have been actualized, as Leibniz maintained? And if such is the case, how can actual worlds serve as a backdrop to any coherent possible world ontology? How indeed does one distinguish between actual worlds and possible worlds? The status of both is at best relative, as Nelson Goodman, the best-known proponent of the antirealist position, maintains.

What bearing do these degrees of realism and the dual logics of parallelism and ramification have on my study of the world novel and the representational problem I posed earlier—that is, the relationship between contemporary novel worlds and the empirical world picture of globalization? The bearing is threefold. They offer a robust register with which to open up the category of world to formal and semantic plenitude. In other words, they help me resist the one-world mimetic conception of the literary and to make a case for the novels featured in my analysis as various versions of possible worlds that sit apart from and partially free from the *actual* world out there. In such a nonmimetic reading, the real world is not granted primacy over the literary world. Together these enable me to counter the tenacious hold of a sociological and materialist position that reads the categories world and world literature as invariably complicit with the imperial networks of global capitalism.[27] They also help me differentiate degrees of fictionality in the various novels—seeing them as various versions of possible worlds—so as to guard against any reductive reading that might see them as manifesting one and the same world picture. The contemporary world novel, I aver, is not a singular artifact that affirms the *globalized world* after 1989 as fictive universality; it is a genre that opens up many worlds that variously converse with, interrogate, interrupt, and even inter the forgotten histories of the world made in the image of contemporary global capital. Finally, they help articulate a mode of literary world-making that is at odds with the materialist reduction of the world to the globe and to a formalist or transcendental poetics of the world that abjures any relation with historical or cultural contexts: a position, one might say, that aspires to a fine balance between ramification and parallelism. The epistemology of the (literary) world I invoke in this book is neither wholly materialist nor purely transcendental; it straddles the empirical and phenomenological in a relationship of excess to the global.

Based on insights gleaned from the theory of possible worlds, I have two arguments to offer about the provenance and value of the *literary* that inheres in the very specific corpus I call the world novel. The first has to do with the temporal framing around 1989. In my analysis 1989 has the full chronotopical force not reducible to the contemporary geopolitics since the end of the cold war but accumulative of other temporalities and genealogies of the literary that go back to the eighteenth century and that reappear in intensified forms in our era of global wars and heightened spectatorship. This includes the virtual and visual substrate of the eighteenth-century sentimental genre as it reemerges in formal modes of hypermediated and exorbitant visual witnessing in the contemporary novel. The morphing of the figure of the impartial spectator into witness is yet another example, as is the transmutation of the rights-bearing sovereignty of the human in the eighteenth-century novel into the figure of absolute rightlessness of the human in novels of our time. Further, in the literary theoretical framework that informs this book as a whole, 1989, as we have seen, is not conceived as a revolutionary break with all that preceded it but as a *kairos* of the contemporary that contains within its intensified temporality developments from the 1960s to the present. These, to reiterate, are the information technology revolution, the proliferation of a human rights culture, new global forms of war, and their heightened visibility in new media forms. Conceived in these terms, 1989 is imbued with properties that one can only call *literary* since it is genre-based and accumulates time across centuries in ways that a nonliterary and materialist conception of 1989 does not. Its charge as a world-making chronotope becomes visible only within the phenomenology of novel worlds.

My second argument has to do with the specific constellations of war, distant suffering, technological mediation, and humanitarian imagination that these novels generate. These novel worlds, not to mention their unique configuration of plot movements, characterization, point of view, and moral vision, are by no means just mimetic constructs of constellations found in the real world. The material conditions of the world around 1989 are no doubt significant conditions of possibility for the emergence of these novels, but the relation between the two is not marked by a deterministic logic or even a logic of secondariness. These novels are carefully crafted and tightly constituted, and they generate their own creative logic and own rationale for aesthetic autonomy—even as many of their features ramify with the *real* world *out there*. To that extent each novel is a world unto itself and generates its own ontology. Collectively speaking, they do not constitute a mere secondary (literary) reproduction of our current empirical world picture. To the contrary, it is precisely the myriad novelistic world pictures that help me generate, as a literary scholar, the empirical world picture that I offer as a hermeneutic backdrop against which to interpret these novels. For me the world functions here with a phenomenological force referred to earlier in my discussion of Derrida and Nancy as an aesthetic surplus or *residuum* of the globe and its horizon of possibility.

In sum, then, the world in the contemporary world novel is not a literary simulacrum of our current geopolitical world order, nor is it bound to any serial, sequential, or compressed space-time of a single world like the nation or the globe. It is a temporal and spatial collage. It contains many worlds that travel with, haunt, layer, and disrupt other worlds even as it is informed in our present time by technologies that amplify our sense of the interconnections among these myriad possible worlds. It is also, in the context of our contemporary era as formulated through the kairos of 1989, a formal and semantic construct through which the human imagination as well as the humanitarian imagination seeks to make some sense of *and* sensitize our reading publics to the worlds of wars and violence that have become pervasive in our era. Qualitatively irreducible to the trope of maximal territorial extension—that is, the globe—the world is yet an ineffaceable aesthetic and normative horizon of our global present.

IN CHAPTERS 3 AND 4 I offer case studies of two distinct types of novels, David Mitchell's *Ghostwritten* and Salman Rushdie's *Shalimar the Clown*, that illustrate the workings of the world in terms I have just sought to conceptualize. I prize open different novelistic conventions in each and focus on their construction of nonmimetic worlds that ramify with the kairos of 1989. Using Benedict Anderson's formal categories, I demonstrate what happens to the novel form when the novelistic imagination goes global and acquires a networked orientation, when it is no longer analogous to imagining the nation. In his theorization of the novel as a formal analogue of the nation Anderson proposes three coordinates: a homogeneous space-time configuration, a shared point of view, and an assumed community of readers oriented toward recognizing the world represented.[28] Each of these, I argue, is fractured and radically reconstellated in a world novel like *Ghostwritten*. Through *Shalimar the Clown* I trace the conditions of possibility for the transformation of the postcolonial novel into the world novel. As a product of postindustrial Europe's retreat from its former colonies and the emergence of a Third World consciousness wary of the new and emergent global bifurcation of imperial power in the wake of World War II, the postcolonial novel has imagined human futures at the intersection of postwar, anticolonial, and nationalist movements across Africa, Asia, and Latin America and the social identity movements of the 1960s. Rushdie's own *Midnight's Children* is a classic text in this genre. A world novel like *Shalimar the Clown*, I argue, carries the literary, political, cultural, and theoretical energies of the postcolonial corpus into new configurations shaped by neoliberal wars, technological hyperconnectivity, the excesses of liquid capitalism, and the rise of Islamic fundamentalism. The novels of Mitchell and Rushdie are manifestly different in form, plot development, characterization, and narrative style, yet both are distinct literary products of the world after 1989 in that they evoke a collective *sensorium* of violence unleashed by the deathworlds of our time. *Ghostwritten* is a magical realist allegory of a networked society, of the *socius* as an extension of technologically linked urban nodes. The wiring of world cities through the flows of technology, finance, and immaterial labor is ingeniously captured in the novel's narrative structure. Through the careful crafting of a series of random but fateful encounters between the eight key protagonists and two spectral entities, Mitchell creates an apocalyptic phantasmagoria of our end-of-the-millennium world. The novel explores two themes that resonate with this study: that the potential for human connectivity enabled by information technology can easily degenerate into a dystopia of surveillance and control; that the globalization of cosmopolitan ways of being human and humane in the contemporary world has its obverse side: a cautious, fear-laden retreat into a limited repertoire of life possibilities and a militant intolerance of diversity. This intolerance, as we know painfully well, can degenerate into fundamentalism. Fundamentalist responses to the dizzying cultural mixedness and economic unevenness of the late capitalist world can be mapped temporally in two ways: one orients itself to the past and manifests a nostalgia for an imagined order of things in times past that worked to the benefit of all; the other is future-directed. Both contain a strong utopian strain that is often authoritarian and annihilative in its vision. *Shalimar the Clown* is an apt case study of this conundrum of the hyperconnected, postliberal, capitalist world order. The assassination of America's counterterrorism chief in broad daylight triggers yet another magical realist narrative of world historical proportions that takes the reader to the prehistory, as it were, of contemporary geopolitics: World War II, the wars of decolonization, the unresolved Kashmir problem of the partitioned subcontinent, and the ideological bifurcation of the cold war. The terrorist who is also an insurgent fighting a legitimate subnational cause is the paranormal specter that haunts our times, a global emblem of our collective fear whose origins lie in the unsavory shadows of a triumphalist world history. In the logic of martyrdom that the assassin embodies, we see the emergence of a new semiosis of life and death that overcomes the fear of mortality by asserting one's sovereign will over death such that death's futurity collapses into the now. Rushdie's graphing of the necropolitical face of global Islam in *Shalimar the Clown* is a significant literary intervention in contemporary debates on the future of liberal and postliberal world-making in the twenty-first century.

THREE
SPECTRAL WORLDS,
NETWORKED NOVEL

"There's no future in stories. . . . Stories are things of the past, things for museums. No place for stories in these market-democracy days," declares a hounded Mongolian folklorist in David Mitchell's *Ghostwritten*.[1] The folklorist's prognosis is belied by this end-of-the-millennium novel. An audacious parable of worlds shaped by market capitalism, the novel is also a phantasmagoric allegory of the rise of a network society in the wake of the penetration of information and communication technologies in our everyday world. The novel's plot is constituted by a series of intersections of nine discrete, end-of-the-millennium narratives spread across the globe. Geographically the narrative moves from east to west. Seven chapters take their name from places where the protagonists are located: Okinawa, Tokyo, Holy Mountain, Mongolia, Petersburg, London, and Clear Island. The two final chapters are set in heterotopic spaces: a radio station dominated by a caller from the world of artificial intelligence and an underground train station in Japan, the site of the release of poisonous fumes with which the novel begins. Two spectral beings, the Noncorpum and His Serendipity, are key links across these narratives. The Noncorpum could well be read as a metaphor for virtual reality, for the disembodied, modular, interoperable technological assemblages that connect us across vast distances. Mitchell ingeniously transmutes this spectral nature of networks into a literary character that transmigrates into people from all corners of the globe at will and temporarily writes their lives for them—a stunning metaphoric take on the very idea of ghostwriting and a proleptic leap into the then not-yet-existent world of simulated selves of social media. His Serendipity is the disembodied doppelganger of the religious fundamentalist, a figure of terror that haunts the advanced capitalist world. It is on his instructions that his acolyte releases the poison gas into the Japanese underground station. Mitchell's imaginative foray into the terrors of this interconnected world is manifested in a series of random but fateful interactions between the key protagonists. The bizarre interconnectivity of this world is reflected upon at one stage with these words: "Phenomena are connected regardless of distance in a holistic ocean more voodoo than Newton" (366).

Anderson Reconsidered

Given its experimentation with the classic novel form in its spectacularly radical use of time, space, characterization, plotting, and point of view, *Ghostwritten* offers a rich case study of the morphology of the contemporary world novel, the task of this chapter. One productive avenue I pursue is to explore the formal features of this world novel in the way that Benedict Anderson studied the analogous morphologies of the novel and the nation.[2] This is not simply to make the novel fit under the coordinates proposed by Anderson. Rather it is to trace the transformation these coordinates undergo when the analogue is scaled up from the *nation* to the *world*. Anderson posits a formal analogy between the space-time of the novel in the nineteenth century and that of the nation, which he sees as the dominant form of bounded community at the time. When the novel says "Meanwhile" or "Here," it is assumed that the temporal coordinates for every reader, and for the fictional characters, are the same, as would be a clearly demarcated sense of spatial location. Other aspects of this analogous relation include the structure of address that, notwithstanding the many voices in the novel, would transcend each one of them to posit a worldview that would be granted imaginative recognition by a community of readers who might otherwise be dispersed across the nation. The novel, in other words, along with other genres of print culture, especially the newspaper, manifests three formal features: a homogeneous space-time configuration, a shared point of view, and an assumed community of readers oriented toward recognizing the world represented. These create the conditions of possibility for imagining the nation. This does not mean that novels of the period necessarily thematize the emergence of the nation as a modern community. This distinction between the novel as a formal analogue of the nation and the novel as thematizing the formation of the nation is critical; as Jonathan Culler has pointed out, it is often overlooked in adapting Anderson's thesis to the study of national narratives across the globe.[3]

Interestingly, when Anderson turns his focus beyond the nation to the world at large, he does not imagine a different morphology of the community. The world is the sum of nations, each with its own quotidian universals generated by the level of its material development and the particular configuration of its bound and unbound serialities. By "unbound seriality" he means everyday universals marked by overlapping domains of demographic difference, sociocultural groupings, and occupational categories. These are typically performative. They inform the imaginary horizons of the genres of print capitalism, mainly newspapers and novels, genres that in their horizontal reach create zones of anonymous sociability and also sites of revolutionary transformation. Bound seriality is the domain of governmentality oriented toward creating finite measures to govern the populace. Census and electoral systems are instances of this. Integers, not fractions, as Anderson famously put it, are the units of bound seriality. They generate essentialist readings of ethnicity and give rise to a politics of measurement and entitlement. Each of these serialities creates standardized vocabularies that then generate a sense of a natural universality of the nation that is recognizable across the globe. In this modular way he sees nations as cohabitants of a continuous global domain unified by the communicative commonalities, if not the political economy, of capitalism. Of course, Anderson's logic of equivalence—that nations are morphologically similar across the globe—is informed by a politically nuanced comparative approach. As he writes in a later book, *The Spectre of Comparisons*, "Series of this kind are quotidian universals that seeped through and across all print languages by no means unidirectionally. . . . This does not mean exactly the same thing, but rather that from Bangkok and Birmingham two parallel series were stretching out across and seamlessly mapping a singular world."[4] In the same work he also challenges the normative prioritization of Europe as the originary site of nationalism and makes a case instead for why the Americas should be considered so. Further, some of the classic twentieth-century debates on nationalism—on majorities and minorities, on the relationship between census and identity politics, and on diasporic nationalism—were informed not by the political configurations of the North Atlantic world but by the adventures of colonialism in South and Southeast Asia. Despite this global comparative perspective, however, Anderson's morphology of the world continues to be informed by the modular logic of the nation.

There are many challenges to Anderson's "nation in the world" thesis once we turn to a world novel like *Ghostwritten*. The novel ceases to be an analogue of a limited sovereign community like the nation. Nor is *Ghostwritten* an analogue of the compressed and flattened planetary space in thrall to the powers of capitalist globalization, which, as we saw earlier, is how the idea of world is often interpreted by skeptics. A unified point of view becomes untenable for such a novel. This consequently scrambles the chronotopic assumptions of a shared space-time, which in turn fractures the sense of a coherent community of readers who would grant imaginative recognition to the worldview(s) portrayed. I look in some detail at the play of each of these in Mitchell's work: the novel's structure of address, its space-time configuration, and its interpellation of the reader.

Structure of Address

There is no omniscient narrator in *Ghostwritten*, nor is there a single privileged point of view that organically connects the various strands of the narrative. In a metafictional move, the author introduces the idea of ghostwriting in the very title to signal the ceding of authorial privilege to forces beyond his control. The motif is picked up when a character named Marco is introduced as the ghostwriter of a biography of a wartime spy, Alfred. Marco's literary agent, Tim Cavendish, takes this allusion a step further when he declares, "We're all ghostwriters, my boy. And it's not just our memories. Our actions too. We all think we're in control of our own lives, but really they're pre-ghostwritten by forces around us" (287).

In a gesture illustrating the work of forces larger than himself, the authorial voice capitulates to a networked structure of address with multiple narrative nodes that are often randomly connected. Voices of key narrators zoom in and out as the novel progresses. At one level the novel's structure of address appears to mime what Jaron Lanier has called the "hive mind" of social technomediation, a series of digital relays of fleeting connectivity that eventuates in a fragmented and dissolved sense of individuality.[5] Each of the nine chapters has a first-person narrator who does not necessarily feature in any other part of the novel, except sometimes as an allusion. Thus the narrator of chapter 3, Neal Brose, a British corporate lawyer, talks of his collapsing marriage to Katy Forbes even as he takes us through his disreputable journey in the financial and sexual netherworld of Hong Kong. Neal commits suicide at the end of the chapter, but strands from his life are picked up in chapter 7, "London," where we see his estranged wife with her casual one-night lover, Marco, who is now the narrator of this chapter. They have an exchange about the photo Marco sees on her bathroom wall:

> "Katy, I hope this isn't an impertinent question, but I saw the photo in the toilet and I wondered if I wasn't treading on anyone's turf here?"
> "Nobody's turf but mine. He was my husband. We separated, and then he went and died. . . . He was a bloody clot. He always insisted on having the last word." (260)

Soon after Katy receives a registered delivery. It's a family heirloom, an antique chair that she had shipped from Hong Kong after the divorce:

> We looked at the packing case for a moment. "Nice big present," I commented. "Is your birthday coming up?"
> "It's not a present," she said. "It's already mine. Come and give me a hand, would you? In the cupboard under the sink there's a hammer and a cold chisel, in a box with some fuses. . . . "
> We prised open the lid and the four sides fell away.
> A Queen Anne chair. (261)

Katy then disappears from the narrative because she is a one-night stand. But references to her deceased husband's shady dealings in Hong Kong continue to appear throughout the chapter, most specifically through the presence of Marco's literary agent. Marco ghostwrites the life stories of famous and infamous people and is currently writing the life of a Hungarian Jew, Alfred Kopf, who was a British intelligence agent during World War II. One night he gets a voicemail message: "Ah, Marco, sorry to bother you, this is Tim Cavendish. We're having a slight family crisis. It appears that my brother's law firm in Hong Kong has gone down the tubes. It's all a bit of a mess. . . . There's the Chinese police, asset freezing, and what not. . . . Erm, why don't you drop in middle of next week, and we'll see how this might affect my ability to run Alfred's book. . . . Erm, terribly sorry about this. Bye" (294).

Obviously the law firm Tim refers to is the one that had dealings with Neal's financial outfit. The collapse of that firm in Hong Kong has a domino effect across many parts of the world, not just on Tim's literary agency. The theft of art in St. Petersburg, Russia—the substance of chapter 6—and the money laundering that ensues across three continents has the Hong Kong firm as a chief conduit. Anticipating the domino effect of the 2008 global financial crisis, this episode can be seen as an allegory of the networked interdependencies of our global era. In a parody of such interdependencies, in chapter 4 Neal's Chinese maid, who stole secreted cash from him while seducing him every evening, returns from Hong Kong to her native village. She triumphantly flaunts her wealth by buying a hotel in the village and converting it into a haunt for rich travelers. To her great-grandmother—the narrator of chapter 4, "Holy Mountain"—she appears to be living proof of a childhood fantasy that "Hong Kong is paved with gold" (146). From her deprecating and fabricated response to her relative's fantasy, we realize that the young Chinese woman is the same maid who lived with Neal: "You can find a lot of things on Hong Kong's pavements, but not much gold. My employer died. A foreigner, a lawyer with a big company, he was extremely wealthy. He was very generous to me in his will" (146).

The shenanigans of the Hong Kong characters are again picked up in chapter 8, "Clear Island," when the Irish quantum physicist Dr. Mo Muntervary, remembers her stay at the Hong Kong apartment of her friend, Huw Llewellyn. She especially remembers his long absences: "Summer. Huw came back late most nights, to snatch a few hours of sleep before returning to his office. A securities firm has crashed, and the effects were rippling out. Sometimes a week went by and apart from noticing the toothpaste tube depleting we were barely aware of one another" (336). Huw Llewellyn is a shadowy character in the Neal Brose narrative, but as the novel progresses we see him through the eyes of other protagonists who are spread across the world—from Mongolia to St. Petersburg and eventually Ireland.

However, it is not just the networked flow of global finance that is allegorized and parodied in this novel. Other narratives of interconnectivity are less labored and allegorical. These are a matter of random adjacencies, such as the links between the Japanese narrators of chapters 1 and 2. Entitled "Okinawa" and "Tokyo," respectively, these chapters have Keisuke Tanaka, aka Quasar, and Satoru Sonada as their first-person narrators. In an interesting twist on Anderson's thesis, both are inhabitants of a single nation, yet they inhabit imaginaries that are all too far apart. One harbors fundamentalist fantasies of a new world cleansed of "impure," vermin-like humans. The other looks for a modest suburban haven in the world of music and tender love. The only thing they have in common is that they both went to the same school in Tokyo and had the same teacher. But Japan as a nation is not a common frame of reference for either. Quasar is a fanatical doomsday cultist who has just executed a poisonous gas attack in a Tokyo subway and is now in hiding in Okinawa. Just as he is about to accomplish his mission of releasing the phial of poison gas, he has a vision of a future in which the leader of his cult, His Serendipity, will rule over everything on earth:

> In those last few moments, as we pulled into the station, His Serendipity fortified me with a vision of the future. Within three short years His Serendipity is going to enter Jerusalem. In the same year Mecca is going to bow down, and the Pope and the Dalai Lama will seek conversion. The Presidents of Russia and the US petition for His Serendipity's patronage. . . . Then, in July of that year, the comet is detected by observatories all over the world. Narrowly missing Neptune, it approaches Earth. . . . The unclean rush out and welcome this latest novelty. And that will be their undoing! The Earth is bathed in microwaves from the comet, and only those with high alpha quotients will be able to insulate themselves. The unclean die, retching, scratching out their eyes, stinking of their own flesh as it cooks on their bones. The survivors begin the creation of Paradise. His Serendipity will reveal himself as His Divinity. A butterfly emerging from the chrysalis of His Body. (16–17)

In a brilliant telescoping of the lunatic prognosis found in Scientology manuals of world cleansing by extraterrestrial agents and the real-life sarin gas attack engineered by the Aum Shinrikyo cult in a Tokyo subway in 1995, the novel figuratively invests in Quasar an imaginary of a world to come that fanatically wills the destruction of Satoru and at least six other narrators.

Satoru is a young jazz aficionado who manages a nondescript music store in Tokyo. An orphan who survives on the beneficence of his disreputable relatives and friends, this teenage inhabitant of Tokyo's populous and intimidating anonymity finds the world of jazz music his only source of comfort. Every experience of his daily life is mediated through the horizon of jazz. After a call from his female guardian, Mama-san, who we deduce runs a bar and a brothel, he "felt in a Billie Holiday mood. 'Lady in Satin,' recorded at night with heroin and a bottle of gin the year before she died. A doomed, Octoberish oboe of a voice" (38). His enchantment with a visitor to his store one bored afternoon reminds him of the "beautiful" and "pure" music of Duke Pearson's "After the Rain." She becomes his sublimated obsession, and he weaves his world of jazz around the idea of her, for as he tells us, "I can't even remember accurately what she looks like. Smooth skin, highish cheekbones, narrowish eyes. Like a Chinese Empress. I didn't really think of her face when I thought of her. She was just there, a colour that didn't have a name yet. The idea of her" (47).

When they eventually fall in love, the young woman, Tomoyo, confesses that she was entranced by the music he was playing during her first visit to the store. The song was "Left Alone" by Mal Waldron, he informs her, delighted. The Satoru episode ends with yet another allusion to Hong Kong, this time not in relation to Neal Brose, who has yet to enter the novel, but as Tomoyo's home. Tokyo is her maternal abode; her father is "Hong Kong Chinese" (55). She invites Satoru to visit her sometime, and he promises to do so. The only other time we readers see this beautiful young couple is through the jaded eyes of Neal Brose at a café in Hong Kong.

The narrative has now moved to chapter 3, "Hong Kong," and Neal's is the lead voice. Satoru and Tomoyo are strangers to him. He is mulling over the ruins of his life as he casts a wistful eye in their direction. He even fantasizes about a Mephistophelian bargain that would bring him back the innocence of their love:

> This kid and his girl came in. He ordered a burger and a cola. She had a vanilla shake. . . . She was Chinese, I could tell that, but they spoke in Japanese. He had a saxophone case and a small backpack with airline tags still attached. . . . They didn't hug or cloy over each other like a lot of Chinese kids do these days. They just held hands over the table. They were so happy. Sex twitched in the air between them, which made me think that they hadn't done it yet. . . . Right at that moment, if Mephistopheles had genied his way from the greasy ketchup bottle and said, "Neal, if I let you be that kid, would you pledge your soul to the Lord of Hell for all eternity?" I'd have answered, "Like a fucking shot I will." (75–76).

The novelist's experimentation with multiple first-person points of view allows him to play smartly with perspectival surfaces and depths. We get into the characters' heads and, at the same time, are scrambling to collect and make sense of fragments from other perspectives. Few of these add up. This refractory energy of the novel's structure of address frustrates the reader's attempts to attain any full and coherent understanding of a protagonist. In the episode just narrated, for instance, the sentimental flow from the previous chapter is fleetingly allowed to wash over the murkiness of Neal's world. Does this mean that Neal is even slightly regretful of his crimes—one legal, the other social—of embezzlement and infidelity? The novelist's intention here, I maintain, is not to surreptitiously slip a moral compass into the frame so as to generate in his readers an emphatic response to the fall of Neal Brose. That would defeat the dexterous artistry with which he sets up the sheer ve-

nality of Neal's world, the spectral nature of his financial and personal dealings that would come to haunt and terrify him toward the end of his life. As
the next passage illustrates, Neal is not so much a soulful tragic hero brought
down by his own frailties as a figuration of the irreconcilable fantasies of our
global age: of endless empowerment, sustained erotic gratification, limitless
wealth, unfettered mobility. Tellingly the imagery here is not of networks
and flows that promise unpredictable and exciting pathways but of compartments that appear to entomb each fatal desire: "The key to understanding
Neal Brose is that he is a man of departments, compartments, apartments.
The maid is in one, Katy is in another, my little visitor in another. Cavendish
Hong Kong in another. Account 1390931 in another. In each one lives a Neal
Brose who operates quite independently of the neighbouring Neal Broses.
That's how I do it. My future is in another compartment, but I'm not looking
into that one. I don't think I'll like what I see" (100).

If there is a moral undercurrent here, it is one of existential claustropho-
bia. The key to the novel's mode of address is experimentation with perspective: fractured, atomized, random, hardly ever crystallizing into a stable
and rounded narrative of a character. The motif of the hyperlink has been
suggested as a way to get a handle on the novel's point of view.[6] Much like
a hyperlink on the Internet, we can metaphorically click on the name of a
random character in any of the nine chapters and find data on the person
elsewhere in the novel, but data embedded in a completely different plot.
The morphology of the web mind, oriented to jumping from hyperlink to
hyperlink in search of an ever more amplified field of information, is meta-
phorized brilliantly in the novel.

It is tempting to compare the hyperlinked strategy of *Ghostwritten* with
actual instances of hyperlinked novels and hypertext literary works on the
web. An example of the former is Geoff Ryman's *253*, an interactive web novel
that first hit cyberspace in the mid-1990s and was subsequently published on
paper in 1998.[7] Another instance is a nonrefereed hypertext version of *Pride
and Prejudice* found on a number of sites, such as The Republic of Pemberley. Run by ardent Austen fans who have created a "Pemberley World" of the
web, this site also features connectors to every allusion to a single character
or event in the body of the original text. A click on "Elizabeth Bennett" takes
us to thirty-one hyperlinks that highlight every reference to her character,
her physical appearance, and her social skills. In less than fifteen minutes the
reader can follow each of the links and have a reading experience saturated
with the presence of a single character. The unit of reading in this web version thus need not be a single chapter in any one sitting, but the world of

words that a single click of the mouse can open up. The comparison is evidently not with the actual form of the Austen novel (which possesses a very coherent structure of address) but with the way the formal features of this hypertext version fracture the narrative flow by directing the reader away from a sequential reading and a dominant authorial point of view.

Composite authorship, nonsequential ordering of plot, digressive interludes, simultaneous compression and dilation of space-time, the absence of a privileged point of view and yet the synthetic omniscience of the virtual infrastructure, all of these feature in *Ghostwritten*. In a deft metafictional move, Mitchell captures the ceding of authorial omniscience to the surveilling power of information technology by creating the character of the Zookeeper in the penultimate chapter. Entitled "The Night Train" after a talk-back radio program run by Bat Segundo for the world's insomniacs, the chapter is a heterotopic narrative space that brings together ominously familiar end-of-the-millennium narratives: early rumblings of the global wars on terror, man-made environmental catastrophes, religious fundamentalism, and technomilitarism through territorial and cyber-infrastructural invasion. Cyber-looping these dystopian imaginaries is the figure of the Zookeeper, who infiltrates the airwaves as a cyborgian guest. The radio host, Bat Segundo, is at first befuddled by the Zookeeper's lack of earthly coordinates. He is an entity without a proper name, an address, or even a credit card. When asked if he works in the Bronx Zoo, the Zoopkeeper replies, "My work takes me all over the world" (378). This response is foreshadowed by the thematics of a doomed world played out in both the title of the radio broadcast, *End of the World*, and a Bob Dylan filler, "World Gone Wrong." We gradually learn that the Zookeeper is a specter that inhabits the satellites of the world's major powers. A breakaway fragment of the U.S. military infrastructure endowed with artificial intelligence, he takes on new prosthetic life as a posthuman surveyor of the state of the world. At once a *supernumerary* entity that exceeds the sum total of the narrative and an *exorbitant* witness of global depredations—an entity who is outside the human orbit and who orbits the earth on the back of artificial satellites—the Zookeeper is a smart figuration of an artificially sutured omniscience. However, the faux-theological excess of his claims to omniscience and unfettered agency are laid bare in this excerpt from an exchange with Bat:

> Does it hurt, Zookeeper, to have your omniscience lose its omni? How could a being with your resources believe yourself to be the only non-corporeal sentient intelligence wandering the surface of creation? You have a lot to learn. . . . Ease up, Zookeeper! You've got the weight of the

world on your own shoulders? What magic wand can you wave? I believe I could do much. I stabilized stock markets; but economic surplus
was used to fuel arms races. I provided alternative energy solutions;
but the researchers sold them to oil cartels who sit on them. I froze nuclear weapons systems; but war multiplied, waged with machine guns,
scythes and pick axes. (413–16)

In the final analysis the Zookeeper as the posthuman embodiment of what
Friedrich Kittler calls "information materialism" can only parody authorial
omniscience and, in the process, embody its impossibility in a novel about
the world.[8]

Chronotopic Configurations

To continue my comparative analysis of Anderson's theory of the novel, I
turn to the space-time coordinates of this world novel and ask how world-
making through the metaphor of informatics, connectivity, and border
crossing is chronotopically configured in *Ghostwritten.* A chronotope is that
quintessentially Bakhtinian concept that brings to the fore the "fleshly" constellation of four critical coordinates of the novelistic world: space, time,
character, and historical worldview. Through the latter two "time as it were,
thickens, takes on flesh and becomes artistically visible," and "space becomes
charged and responsive to the movements of time, plot and history."[9]

The two chronotopes that are units of analysis in this section are *network* and *city*. Earlier I used the term *network* to describe Mitchell's experiments with the novel's structure of address. Here I argue that the network,
much like Bakhtin's road in picaresque novels and the Bildungsroman, or
the castle in Gothic fiction, materializes for this world novel the new workings of space-time in our age of hyperconnected globality. Likewise the city
emerges as a maximal site of cultural comingling and extranational, extrater-
ritorial, heterotemporal belonging. In manifesting a massively scaled-up interplay between technology, temporality, mobility, imaginaries, and affects,
both chronotopes serve to give flesh to the world after 1989. Both have features that are fundamentally antinomian to the three qualities that Anderson
posited for the nation and its literary analogue, the novel: they are limited,
sovereign, and manifest a horizontal sense of community.[10]

What is the morphology of the network, and how does it acquire metaphorical flesh in *Ghostwritten*? A minimal understanding of a network is that
it is a nonhierarchical, open-ended structure of interlinked nodes that can

potentially expand without limits as long as the new nodes share a minimal common code. One network can connect to multiple others through a series of interoperating switches that end up acquiring enormous power, for they are critical to keeping the networks optimally connected. In recent years digital technology has enabled almost every aspect of human societal activity—economic, political, social, cultural, and interpersonal—to acquire the shape of a network that can potentially spread across the globe. This has led to new experiences of space-time connectivity that are not bound by the calendar or the clock.[11] In the particular novelistic representation under discussion, calendar and clock time work only in the individual chapters; read as a whole, the boundedness conceived by Anderson as a prerequisite for a sequential working of clock and calendrical time is fractured. The "meanwhile" of the old woman in the Holy Mountain is not the same as that of the Irish physicist Dr. Mo Muntervary or that of Margarita Latunsky, the Russian grand dame of chapter 6. And yet the lives of each are connected by nodes that figure Hong Kong and London in particularly significant ways.

The oft-heard formulations of the phenomenology of our digital age, such as *simultaneity without contiguity* and *deterritorialized proximity*, are among many aspects of the contemporary human experience of space-time. Sociologists and geographers have hitherto conceptualized space as the material manifestation of a society's time-sharing activities.[12] The experience of simultaneity, in other words, generally goes hand in hand with spatial contiguity. The information age has ruptured this conventionally experienced correlation between time and space. For millions of people around the world who have access to information and communication networks, the experience of simultaneity no longer coincides with sharing the same latitude and longitude. Likewise the experience of proximity has been wrenched from its fixed spatial coordinates. As the proliferation of social media networks demonstrates, the massification of the experience of virtual connectivity generates modes of proximate belonging that have a tenuous connection with territorial or national location. Each of these experiences of new space-time connectivity is allegorically represented in *Ghostwritten*. The interactions between the Japanese cult leader, His Serendipity, and his acolyte, Quasar, are instances of deterritorialized proximity. Quasar hears instructions from his master no matter where he is. In one instance of virtual connection, His Serendipity manages to send a message meant only for Quasar from a live television broadcast of his arrest in the United States. Simultaneity *sans* contiguity figures in the global reverberations of the Hong Kong firm's crash.

The novel's narrative play with networked time and space also includes features such as nonsimultaneous contiguity. We see this in Mo Muntervary's recounting of her brush with death on a London street and her rescue by our London narrator, Marco, whom she does not get introduced to and whose life never intersects with hers except for that single moment. Here I use "simultaneity" in the sense of Anderson's reading of the novelistic "meanwhile": as a shared experience of time and worldview over a long stretch within a bounded space even if the people in question never meet physically. In fact in the story of this fugitive Irish physicist who, throughout the narrative, is fleeing from the menacing neo-imperial hand of the Republican U.S. regime, we see the novel's most potent figuration of the intersecting space-times of a networked social order. She is the creator of a secret mathematical formula that the U.S. defense establishment covets. She sees her creation as a recipe for global devastation and does all she can to elude the Pentagon. She cannot bear to see her "modest contribution to global enlightenment," as she puts it, "used in air-to-surface missiles to kill people who aren't white enough" (319)—a clear reference to the first Gulf War but one that uncannily evokes the specter of others we have witnessed since 2001. In her attempt to run from the Pentagon watchdogs, she zigzags through eight of the nine sites featured in the novel and has chance encounters with each of the other protagonists. In the process she weaves relay chains across several nodes, thus allegorizing the interactive connectivity of the world I have invoked chronotopically through the idea of the network.

Global connectivity through networks does not cover the entirety of human habitation on the planet. However, its activities have repercussions on a planetary scale. This morphological feature of excluded zones and elided temporalities that are nevertheless acted upon by global flows is captured in two chapters, "Holy Mountain" and "Mongolia." The first covers a period in China spanning the entire twentieth century. Through the eyes of a little girl in rural China who grows up to be the Tea-Shack Lady, we see the comings and goings of many political regimes and, most powerfully, the transformation of China's feudal agrarian hinterlands into sites of revolutionary transformation under Mao. Her tea shack is destroyed several times by these political storms, and she herself experiences unconscionable brutality as a helpless, impoverished girl and then woman in the hands of each regime. This is the same great-grandmother who welcomes her attractive young relative, Neal Brose's maid, when the young woman returns with her riches from Hong Kong.

The reassembled tea shack becomes a symbol of resilience and continuity through the cataclysmic sociopolitical changes in China. At first nothing could be more antinomian to the chronotopic configurations of the network than the tea shack. One is fixed in place and time, the other is mobile in ways unimaginable in the tea lady's world, yet both have a modular flexibility and a minimalist infrastructural base that allows for repeated reconstruction. This chronotopic juxtaposition of the tea shack with the network brings into play the two readings of "space" that Manuel Castells has suggested as apposite for our digital age. He calls them "space of places" and "space of flows."[13] The first refers to spaces with historical roots and recognized geographical coordinates; the second refers to spaces of real virtuality enabled by information and communication flows.[14] These include physical spaces too, but ones that are intricately networked and are key nodes in the contemporary global order. The space of flows is the site of action of the global elite, while the space of places tends to be marked variously by exclusion and disadvantage. The intersections between the two create our particular experience of the uneven space-times of the worlds we inhabit. It is an experience that Mitchell adroitly captures in our reading experience as we transition from Okinawa and Hong Kong to London via Holy Mountain, Ulan Bator, and St. Petersburg. In a hyperfigurative culmination of our journey into the zone of real virtuality, we find ourselves eventually inhabiting both the panoptic heights of the Zookeeper's satellite gaze and the phantasmagoria of Quasar's horrifically cleansed earth.

As will be evident by now, cities are the main sites of action in the novel. Five of the ten chapters feature cities, and the rest are connected to events that have origins in cities. Such is the energy of Mitchell's novelistic craft that the city in each chapter is vividly anthropomorphized and has as much presence as that of the first-person narrator. Hong Kong has places like the Lantau Island, where one can pretend that "the world was once beautiful" (70), and Kowloon, which has alleys "smelling of grime and piss and *dim sum*" (94). And it is in Asia, "the last wild frontier" of capitalist expansion (103). St. Petersburg is yesterday's communist concubine, covered over in its swankiest locales with faux Americana: "All these new shops, the Benetton, the Haagen Dazs shop, Nike, Burger King, a shop that sells nothing but camera film and key-rings, another that sells Swatches and Rolexes" (211). The rest of the city is saturated with vodka-soaked "sob stories, pile driven down into the mud" (211). As for London, it is anthropomorphized as "middle aged and male, respectably married but secretly gay" (281). The London Underground has multiple personalities:

Each tube has a distinct personality and range of mood swings. The Victoria Line, for example, is breezy and reliable. The Jubilee Line, the young disappointment of the family, branching out to the suburbs, eternally having extensions planned, twisting round to Greenwich, and back under the river out east somewhere. The District and Circle Line, well, even Death would rather fork out for a taxi if he's in a hurry. . . . The Northern Line is black on the maps. It's the deepest. It has the most suicides, you're most likely to get mugged on it, and its art students are most likely to be future Bond Girls. There's something doom-laden about the Northern Line. (268)

London is also a megalopolis of accumulated losses that return to haunt its inhabitants. Its collective psychosis is captured in the figure of the Hungarian Jewish ex-spy Alfred, whose autobiography the narrator, Marco, is ghostwriting. Alfred worked for British intelligence during the war but felt a misfit in London in the postwar decades: "You can imagine, I was a bit of an embarrassment in Whitehall. A Hungarian Jew from Berlin amongst the pencil sharpeners freshly down from Oxford. The crown owed me, they knew, but they no longer wanted me. So I was given an office job in Great Portland Street working with a division cracking down on black marketeers. I never got to see any action, though. I was just doing what computers and young ladies in shoulder pads do nowadays" (276).

At one point Alfred describes an experience in which he sees himself walking past a café in South Kensington: "Not a reflection, not a lookalike, not a twin brother, not a spiritual awakening, not a waxwork. . . . I saw myself, Alfred Kopf, large as life" (277). He describes in great detail his fruitless chase after this apparition. In the sequence of events he narrates for Marco's sake, this experience comes *after* Alfred meets one Professor Baker for dinner. This is the domain of the empirical, of what *actually happened* in real time. But when he finishes his narrative, he brings Marco and us readers back to where his evening began *before* he met Professor Baker: "'Oy!' I yelled, and some genteel ladies walking dogs harrumphed. 'Alfred Kopf!' I yelled, and a man dropped out of a tree with a turfy thump. My shadow didn't even turn around. Why was he running? . . . Across Kensington Road, down past the museums, *past the restaurant where I'd arranged to meet Prof Baker that evening.* A sudden gust of wind blew my hat off. I bent down to pick it up. And when I looked up, I saw my shadow disappearing" (278–79, emphasis added).

This uncanny and reiterative temporality of Alfred's experience of his spectral self along with his insistence that he sees his apparition as real, "large as life," bring to mind philosophical ruminations on the spectral in the works of Derrida and Žižek in particular.[15] As explicated by these philosophers, in the appearance of the spectral one sees a unique conjunction of event, temporality, and subjectivity that Derrida calls "hauntological." This is an experience of a past event that acquires a startling reality and visibility irreducible to facts at the moment of its actual occurrence. In Žižek's gloss on this belated calling of an event into being, it is an act of will on the part of the subject and a faithfulness to the truth of the event, the spirit of which the subject does not want to let go, that is critical to the experience of the spectral. As Žižek puts it, "We never encounter it [i.e., the specter] 'now,' since it is always recognized as such retroactively, through the act of Decision."[16] Derrida, in conceptualizing the specter as a "revenant," a promise to come, also imparts a nonempirical futurity to the experience of the hauntological. In Alfred's frantic chase after his apparition through the streets of London, Mitchell allegorically calls into being Alfred's attachment to his émigré London self that was once useful to world history. Alfred is haunted by memories of his contribution, however minor, to the triumph of the Allies in the Second World War. He was youthful, dashing, and daring. His non-Anglo ethnicity was a good cover for British intelligence, not a multicultural headache for the British state. His and London's history has since been a narrative of decline: a story of petty ethnic unrest, political irrelevance, chicanery, sexual perversion, and drug-induced stupor. In the compulsion he feels to hire Marco to ghostwrite his life story we see a novelistic invocation of the Derridean revenant, a mode of keeping alive for the future the promise contained in his eventful past life. What else, after all, does he and London have to look forward to at the end of the millennium?

Alfred's is but one side of the story of London of course. While the city may have lost its imperial dazzle, it has been reborn as one of the world's most significant nodes in our networked era. As the vast body of sociological scholarship on contemporary forms of globalization attests, world cities such as London, New York, Tokyo, and Hong Kong operate as paradigmatic sites where global connections are enacted and performed. These global networks of urban sites are less connected to hinterlands within their own nations and more to deterritorialized spaces on which mutual interests intersect. As I explained in my discussion of possible-worlds theory, however, novel worlds do not reproduce sociological realities; they generate imaginative approximations of possible worlds through a dynamic reconfiguration of the space-times of the historical or contemporary real. Their chronotopicity, to use Bakhtin's neologism, is generically manifested in two ways:

figuratively through imagistic constellations and narratively through plot-generating movements. Both are brought into relief in *Ghostwritten*. London's historicity is given literary flesh through allegory, as with Alfred, and through intricate plot movements that make the rest of the world converge, however fleetingly, on its terrain. Neal Brose, Katy Forbes, His Serendipity, Tim Cavendish, Mo Muntervary, Jerome, and Huw Llewellyn—all feature in the London narrative even as they traverse other parts of the globe.

Mitchell's narrative play makes it evident that Alfred's hauntology, his ghostwritten life, is out of joint with the new London of infinite possibilities, Marco's London:

> There are a lot of things in London that weren't here when Alfred went round his big loop chasing Alfred. All those aeroplanes flying into Heathrow and Gatwick. The Thames Barrier. The Millennium Dome. Centerpoint, that sixties pedestal ashtray, bloody hell I wish someone would come along and bomb that. Canada Tower over in Docklands, gleaming in the sunlight now, and I think of that art deco mirror in the corner of Shelley's room. . . .
>
> A city is a sea you lose things in. You only find things that other people have lost.
>
> "Wonderful, isn't it?" I say to a man walking his red setter.
>
> "Fackin' shithole innit?"
>
> Londoners slag off London because, deep down, we know we are living in the greatest city in the world. (282)

London's connectivity to the world can no longer be traced along familiar imperial routes but only through unpredictable alleys and byways that facilitate the flow of money and people. Primarily money and people, but also lost political dreams, cultural fragments, the entire ragtag collection of broken worlds looking to acquire new shape in this city of endless possibilities. Namesakes from other novelistic worlds, such as Rushdie's Gibreel from *The Satanic Verses*, make a fleeting appearance, as do "Spanish girls who pay for their English lessons by handing out leaflets for cut-price language schools around Tottenham Court Road" (282).[17] This is a new urban constellation, protruding, misshapen, straining to represent a range of intersecting worlds. The chronotopes of the network and city fracture the Andersonian idea of a homogeneous space-time continuum in the world novel. The third coordinate proposed by Anderson is a bounded community of readers with shared worldviews.

This feature more than any other has been a source of much debate in the scholarship on Anderson. The kind of <u>community</u> he imagines being addressed by the novel is "society understood as a bounded intrahistorical entity."[18] This entity has been commonly understood as the nation primarily because of Anderson's own meticulous theorization of the analogies between the two. But Anderson himself was careful in keeping the idea of the community open-ended and conceded that it could well take other forms. He also noted the fracturing of national readership in the mid-twentieth century due to the emergence of multiple subgenres of fiction, such as spy fiction and thrillers, that had a global readership. The idea that the nation was the only correlate of a bounded intrahistorical community in the nineteenth century, especially where readership was concerned, is also not borne out in studies of the novel in the colonial era. Emergent transnational studies of the novel in colonial Anglophone and Francophone literary worlds provide evidence of readership that extended to the extreme peripheries of the British and French empires.[19] The nation, as Moretti has argued, was far from a natural site of convergence of the novel's readership: "The novel didn't simply find the nation as an obvious, pre-formed fictional space: it had to wrest it from other geographical matrixes that were just as capable of generating narrative—and that indeed clashed with each other throughout the eighteenth century." However, the more the novel aligned itself to a *national* readership, the less polyphonous and more geographically circumscribed it became, for it grew increasingly dependent on a community that unequivocally shared a familiar frame of reference linguistically, politically, culturally. The common became intrinsic to the novel. In Moretti's words, "State-building requires streamlining . . . of physical barriers, and of the many jargons and dialects that are irreversibly reduced to a single national language. And the style of nineteenth century novels—informal, impersonal, 'common'—contributes to this centralization more than any other discourse."[20]

This discussion provides an interesting opening from which to consider the interpellation of the reader in the global or world novel. Anxiety about the flattening effect of the global novel has been voiced often enough in recent years, as have misgivings about the cosmopolitical elitism of such a novel's assumed readership. How do the capacious geographical frame of *Ghostwritten* and its audacious addressing of a plethora of twenty-first-century global commons—fundamentalism, terrorism, environmental degradation, asymmetric warfare, and financial networks—fare in these respects? What is the affective fraternity that this novel aspires to create? At a first glance the answer appears to be obvious: a global elite of educated English speakers with an interest in the world outside their national or regional enclaves. But the novel, I suggest, disturbs the assumption of a flat global readership. It resists offering the cosmopolitically oriented Anglophone reader a known world of otherness, one that beams into her spaces televisually or through other digital media. How does the novel enact this resistance?

Let us first consider its representation of linguistic and cultural polyphony. An Anglophone world novel is particularly vulnerable to the charge of linguistic flattening and inept carryover of "foreign" voices. *Ghostwritten* sets itself the challenge of conveying voice in at least five different non-Anglo cultural registers: Chinese, Japanese, Mongolian, Russian, and Irish. In addition it juggles multiple Englishes. The linguistic transfer of multiple cultural voices into English succeeds only in part. There is an ease and raciness to the use of idiomatic English by its native-speaking characters, Neal Brose and Marco, that is obviously missing from the non-English intonations of Quasar, Saturo, and the old tea shack woman from rural China. However, Mitchell is quite successful in effecting linguistic transfer from Japanese. Quasar's tight and measured dialogue with the unsuspecting inhabitants in Okinawa is quite in keeping with the formal speech conventions in Japan. At the same time, it serves a dual purpose: to hide his real identity and to convey a sense of distance from the worldview of the provincial Japanese people. Here, for instance, is his exchange with the receptionist at an Okinawa hotel right after he has executed the lethal gas attack in a Tokyo subway. He is traveling under an alias:

"Your profession, Mr. Kobayashi?"

"I'm a software engineer. I develop products for different companies, on a contract-by-contract basis."

She frowned. I wasn't fitting her form. "I see, no company as such, then . . ."

"Let's use the company I'm working with at the moment."

Easy. The Fellowship's technology division will arrange corroboration.

"Fine, Mr. Kobayashi. . . . Welcome to the Okinawa Garden Hotel."

"Thank you."

"Are you visiting Okinawa for business or for sight-seeing, Mr. Kobayashi?"

Was there something quizzical in her smile? Suspicion in her face?

"Partly business, partly sightseeing." I deployed my alpha control voice. (3–4)

The modulation of voice that works so well here founders a little when Quasar finds himself in the midst of an energetic discussion about the Fellowship cult and the poison gas attack. A "thin-woman," possibly a teacher, is critical of the way people cede control to cult leaders. The novelist is keen to convey the shrillness of her righteous intervention, but her voice in its linguistic transfer to English sounds contrived: "Some get a kick out of self-abasement and servitude. Some are afraid or lonely. Some crave the camaraderie of the persecuted. Some want to be big fish in a small pond. . . . They need shinier myths that'll never be soiled by becoming true. The handing over of one's will is a small price to pay, for the believers" (23). Mitchell more than makes up for this by his brilliant capture of the many voices that populate the world of the young Japanese jazz lover, Satoru, who manages a modest music store in suburban Tokyo. His exchanges with three distinctly different customers are finely modulated. These include conversations with his wayward friend, Takeshi; with a valued customer and mentor, Fujimoto; and with Tomoyo, the girl whose pure, untouched beauty he has fallen in love with. Together these episodes evoke a finely textured ethos and culture that cannot be reduced to the worldview of a global Anglophone readership.

Occasionally, however, the novelist is compelled to fall back on global stereotypes of recognizably "national" voices, such as when his Irish characters use expressions like "mornin' to the pair o'ye!" (348), or when the Russian Margarita Latunsky says, "We used to have enough nuclear bombs to make your side of the Berlin Wall glow beet-red for the next ten thousand years. . . . You could have been born with the arms of a mushroom and a bag of pus for a head" (206). At the same time, these diverse cultural voices interrupt the seamless stretch of English across the novelistic canvas and highlight the unworkability of this global tongue in some contexts. The old Chinese tea lady's characterization of her foreign guest as someone who "communicated in gestures like a monkey" (138) and of Western speech as the sound of "farting pigs" (129) are very good examples of the estrangement of English in non-Anglo worlds.

While *Ghostwritten* complicates and fractures the notion of a global readership through its polyphonous reproduction of speech from many parts of the world, there is a particular kind of composite cosmopolitan readership it does interpellate in its strong focus on a contemporary global ethics emanating from our collective experience of ethnic civil wars, religious fundamentalism, global financial meltdown, endemic global violence, and environmental catastrophe. This is a readership united in its sense of vulnerability as it witnesses the coming together of a world under conditions of extreme duress. The fault lines of the contemporary world order are all too visible to this reader. In bringing to the fore the dynamics of globalization through its representation of international financial networks, large-scale migration, and the geopolitics of terror and insecurity, the novel cautions against all triumphal narratives of the unification of the world since the cold war. The cosmopolitan worldview it espouses no doubt urges readers to think seriously about collective global agency, but the abrasive irony of its tone as it depicts the daunting scale of the world's problems and the massively fragmented nature of global public spheres leaves one in severe doubt about the transformative potential of a future-oriented cosmopolitical ethics.[21] The impossibility of a singular world or global reader of such a novel is also laid bare. Victims of the two Gulf wars will get right to the heart of the black humor that colors the novelist's view of these catastrophic military adventures, while ardent Republican voters in the United States will not be amused. Mo Muntervary's story provides the novelist an opportunity to express his views on the excesses of the U.S. neoliberal regime. Talking of the technosimulatory nature of the first Gulf War so brilliantly theorized by Baudrillard a few years ago, Mo's husband, John, comments, "Have so many films been made about high-tech war that high-tech war is now a film?" Another character declares, "Preemptive strike must mean not declaring war until your cameras are in position." Mitchell's satire on the military misadventures of the U.S. regime through the early 1990s is unrelenting:

The TV showed the night skyline of a burning city in the Gulf.

A young pilot was talking to a CNN reporter whose hair was not his own. "Yessir, the whole place was lit up like the prettiest Fourth of July I ever did see!"

"We've been hearing about the surgical precision of the missile strikes, thanks to Homer Quancog technology."

"Yessir. With the Homers you can pick your elevator shaft. The boys at mission control program in the building blueprints, and you sit back and let the missile's flight computer do the thinking for you. Just let those babies rip! Straight down the elevator shafts!"

Alain spilled some wine. "*Putain!* Next he tells us the missiles buy a stick of bread and walk the doggie."

A General wearing a torso of medals was walking in the Washington Studio. "For Americans, freedom is an inalienable right. For all. Homer Technology is revolutionizing warfare. We can hit these evil dictators hard, where it hurts, with minimum collateral damage to the civilians they tyrannize." (314–15)

Alternative geopolitical imaginaries such as China's authoritarian ethos are not spared either, even if it is historically configured through Mao's regime. As for euphoric visions of the revolutionary transformation of global public spheres through spectacular advances in information technology, the novel's penultimate chapter, "Night Train," offers a sharply dystopic view of the powers of digital and satellite communication. The novel culminates in a brilliant telescoping of the spectral presence of the Japanese cult leader, His Serendipity, and the virtuality of communication technology. Quite aptly Mitchell stages his novel's climax amid the satellite airwaves of that greatest of global cities, New York. A nighttime radio deejay's staging of an eerily prescient musical, *End of the World Special*—all before 9/11—is interrupted repeatedly by the voice of His Serendipity. His spectral presence is magnified into global proportions as he gives frightening evidence of having deployed all possible electronic wizardry to gain a top-down, polyspatial view of every corner of the globe, flitting from one to the other in a matter of seconds. His apocalyptic warning to the deluded American navigator of satellite technology encompasses the moral of this parable of late modernity: networked societies have as much potential to enhance human connectivity as to degenerate into dystopias of surveillance and control:

> "Your ignorance, Bat! It's not funny! It's agony! . . . You fanfare your 'Information Revolution,' your e-mail, your v-mail. Your vid-cons! As if information itself is thought! You have no idea what you've made! You are all lapdogs, believing your collars to be halos! Information is control. Everything you think you know, every image on every screen, every word on every phone, every digit on every VDU, who do you think has got their hands on it before it gets to you? Comet Aloysius could be on a collision course with Grand Central Station, and unless your star guest here chose to let the instruments he controls tell your scientists, you wouldn't know a thing until you woke up one morning to find no sun and a winter of five hundred years! You wouldn't recognize the end of the world if it flew up your nose and died there!" (414)

IF *GHOSTWRITTEN* HAS allowed me to analyze the form of the *world* novel against the frame of Anderson's theorization of the analogous morphologies of the novel and the *nation*, in the chapter that follows I draw on another comparative frame and analyze a subgenre of the world novel that emerged in the wake of its *postcolonial* counterpart. Salman Rushdie's *Shalimar the Clown* is my source text here. The shadow of Rushdie's first novel, *Midnight's Children*, looms so large in the world of postcolonial literary scholarship that most subsequent analyses of his corpus have been framed by this text. What happens to the postcolonial novelistic imaginary after 1989? What transformed Rushdie from a quintessential postcolonial writer to a world novelist? The following chapter offers some insights.

FOUR

FROM MIDNIGHT'S CHILD
TO CLOWN ASSASSIN

Rushdie after 1989

"Rushdie in his Manhattan retreat is no longer a Third World or postcolonial writer but a bard of the grim one world we all, in a state of some dread, inhabit."[1] So wrote John Updike in what was one of the earliest reviews of Rushdie's elegiac narrative on Kashmir, *Shalimar the Clown* (2005). This grim world of interconnected hoops of violence interlaced with the proliferation of graphic images and an emergent global culture of witnessing is what distinguishes the horizon of the new world novel after 1989 from that of its predecessors. Only in this age of informational capitalism and the global nature of conflicts could Rushdie write immediately after the release of *Shalimar the Clown*, "It used to be possible to write a novel about, say London or Kashmir or Strasbourg or California, without any sense of connection. But now it's all one story. . . . Now I feel more and more that if you're telling a story of a murder in California, you end up having to tell the story of many other places and many other times in order to make sense of that event and that place. To try to show how these stories join."[2]

Updike's reference to Rushdie's "Manhattan retreat" and Rushdie's own reference to California as an epicenter of world-historical connections may appear to play right into the hands of the critics who decry the emergent debates on world-making and ecumenical imaginaries as nothing more than the globalization of an American way of life, as yet another imperial paradigm.[3] However, in keeping with my line of argument about the complex relationship between literary world-making and the empirical world picture of globalization, I explore two critical strands in this chapter that help resist such a reading and offer alternative avenues of analysis. In the first I trace the ways *Shalimar the Clown* novelizes the psychogeography of global Islam in a melancholic mode that retrieves for world readers the forgotten history of Kashmir as one of the epicenters of global terrorism. Far from being an alibi for U.S. global dominance, the novel's allegorical structure of interconnected histories evokes many worlds in the making from World War II to the end of the millennium, so much so that the rise of the United States in this saga becomes a subplot to the novel's epic lament of the loss of Kashmir's transcendent beauty in the catastrophic vortex of world history. My second line of inquiry traces the emergence of a world-making authorial consciousness that has been radically shaped by firsthand exposure to the terrors of fundamentalist Islam. This approach is at sharp variance from sociological readings of the world literary space in which Rushdie is a globally eminent literary figure and his works traverse the conventional circuits of the world republic of letters through Booker Prizes and other markers of market value. Rushdie no doubt has been a quintessential postcolonial success story in the West since the blockbuster reception of *Midnight's Children*. But what has been the role of the Khomeini fatwa in transforming Rushdie from a successful postcolonial novelist into a world novelist? How does *Shalimar the Clown* stage Rushdie's own existential conflict in the face of a radically postliberal and nonsecular global threat to his assured world of liberal democratic and secular values?

If 1947 was the historical threshold for Rushdie's postcolonial saga, *Midnight's Children*, the chronotope of 1989 gives flesh to his world-historical allegory, *Shalimar the Clown*. The significance of this year, however, unfolds not in the political epicenter of post–cold war eruptions, the Soviet Union, but in Kashmir, the disputed Himalayan territory that India and Pakistan continue to covet at the cost of cataclysmic military upheaval on the subcontinent. As is well known to historians of South Asia, in the redistribution of Hindu- and Muslim-majority territories during the Partition, Kashmir was an anomaly. It had a Muslim majority but a Hindu king, who wanted

Kashmir to be part of India, not Pakistan. When Pakistan attacked Kashmir in 1947 with every intention of annexing it, Maharaja Hari Singh sought help from Nehru's government. The Indian Army intervened and managed to beat back the Pakistani troops to the line that now constitutes the border between Indian Kashmir and Pakistan-occupied Kashmir. The war was halted with the intervention of the United Nations. The status of Kashmir, it was resolved then, would be determined by a referendum to be undertaken by the Indian state at a future date. The referendum never took place, and Kashmir continues to be a disputed territory torn apart by skirmishes between the two partitioned nations.

What, then, of the significance of 1989 in this tale of subcontinental fractures? Unnoticed by the rest of the world too caught up in the euphoria of the fall of the Berlin Wall, the Kashmiris staged their first insurgency against both Indian and Pakistani occupation in that very year. The uprising failed comprehensively against the military might of both nations and clarified for all that an independent Kashmir was not viable.[4] Until that time the Kashmir dispute had been a regional problem: a postcolonial casualty of half-baked colonial plans and a hasty British departure. It was not until the post-1989 transformation of Soviet-era mujahideens into global warriors of Islam and their adoption of Kashmir as a site of global jihad that Kashmir appeared in the international political radar as yet another site of global battle against Islamic fundamentalism. Bernard-Henri Lévy in fact talks of Kashmir as the new Palestine in his forensic travel account of Pakistan after 9/11, *Who Killed Daniel Pearl?* It is significant that while *Midnight's Children* features Kashmir as only a small part of the narrative of the coming into being of an amorphous India, in *Shalimar the Clown* Kashmir is a whole world. Every other recognizably world-historical event in the novel exists in relation to it: the buildup to World War II, the cold war antipathy between India and America, Vietnam, the fall of the Berlin Wall, the radicalization of Islam, and the rise of diasporic networks of terrorists.

It is not farfetched to read this world novelization of the Kashmir conundrum as the literary correlate of Rushdie's criticism in 2002 of the Bush regime's foreign policy in South Asia that rarely ever reckoned with the Kashmir problem. "In the heat of dispute over Iraq strategy, South Asia will become a sideshow," wrote Rushdie in the *Washington Post*. "Pakistani-backed terrorism in Kashmir will be winked at because of Pakistan's support for the 'war against terror' on its frontier."[5] The melancholic monumentalizing of Kashmir in *Shalimar the Clown* is Rushdie's poke in the winking eye of U.S. foreign policy on Pakistan. But the year 1989 is a literary and political threshold for Rushdie in yet another way: it was the year of the fatwa against him and the first visible global eruption of an ominously *worldly* response to his controversial depiction of the Prophet in *The Satanic Verses* (1988). As more than one scholar has argued, the Khomeini fatwa was really the beginning of the rise of a visibly fundamentalist global mobilization in the name of Islam.[6] The transition of Rushdie from a postcolonial to a world novelist began not in 2005 with his Kashmir and California saga, as Updike suggests, but in 1989.

Nominalist Fancy and Tropological Excess

Each of the five sections in *Shalimar the Clown* is named after a character that allegorically bears the burden of this unusual historical conjuncture: "India," "Boonyi," "Max," "Shalimar," "Kashmira." India's story unfolds in Los Angeles at the end of the cold war. She is the illegitimate daughter of Max, a former U.S. ambassador to India, and Boonyi, a Kashmiri beauty long since dead. She is also the stepdaughter of her father's assassin, Shalimar. She not only carries the burden of a fractious nation in her name but also embodies the dismembered history of Kashmir as she witnesses in the very first pages of the novel the beheading of her beloved "French-American cosmopolitan" father on her doorstep by his Kashmiri chauffeur. Section 2 features pre-1989 Kashmir through the character of Boonyi, named after the celestial term for Kashmir's emblematic *chinar* tree. She embodies the paradisiacal allure of this Himalayan valley state and also its dangerous vulnerability to covetous forces. Her gradual degeneration and decrepitude allegorize the fate of Kashmir torn apart by vicious politics. If the first two sections *world* Kashmir's localism for a global readership, the next two, named after Max and Shalimar, narrate the circumstances of Kashmir's entry into world history, albeit through a convoluted detour through Nazi Germany, French Resistance, the postwar rise of the United States as a superpower, the creation of the United Nations, decolonization in Asia and Africa, the partition of India, cold war–era polarizations, and the rise of Islamic fundamentalism. These sections are audacious in their historical scope and manifest Rushdie's epic ambitions as a novelist. The gendered divide between the two clusters is hardly incidental: catastrophic things *happen* to the two women, but the two men *make* them happen. The final section, "Kashmira," allegorizes the emergence of a Kashmir of the future that frees itself from the cycle of violence. There is no triumphant return to History here, no heated and muscular wresting of control over territory—only a calculated plan to extinguish ghosts from the past. The eponymous figure is none other than Max and Boonyi's daughter, India, now transformed, much like an imaginary Kashmir born anew from the swirling depths of violence, into Kashmira. She is the avenging angel who destroys her father's assassin and forges bonds with Yuvraj Singh (literally, "a young Lion Prince"), a prince of the market who makes his livelihood by exporting precious Kashmiri artifacts to the West.

Rushdie's naming of characters in the novel has come up for some stringent criticism. Updike's review expresses extreme irritation, especially with the choice of Maximilian Ophuls for the French American ambassador, lover of Boonyi, and father of India: "Why, oh, why did Salman Rushdie . . . call one of his major characters Maximilian Ophuls? Max Ophuls is a highly distinctive name, well known to movie lovers as that of a German born actor and stage director who, beginning in 1930, directed films in Germany, France, Russia, Italy, the Netherlands, and after 1946, the United States. . . . Why has Rushdie attached a gaudy celebrity name to a different sort of celebrity, preventing the Ambassador from coming into sharp, living focus on his own?"[7] Likewise Supriya Chaudhuri is scathing about the naming of India/Kashmira. She finds it "reductive" and "simplistic." She also expresses unease at the historical burden Rushdie's linguistic games and allegorical conceits are compelled to carry, which she considers a sign of a failed nostalgia, for he "sacrifices the reality of loss and suffering" in being so irreverent about credible plot and character and so confident that the linguistic surplus he generates through his exuberant style will restore the truth about Kashmir.[8]

Rushdie's flamboyant conversion of history into parable no doubt compels him to be tropologically adventurous, but his strategies are by no means as stultifying as Updike suggests nor as devoid of historical credence as Chaudhuri avers. The compulsive allusions to a Kashmiri imaginary composed (at least for those within the circle of nostalgia) of the chinar tree, the Shalimar Bagh, and Dal Lake, to name only a few, are a means of translating Kashmir's melancholic history into novelistic sentiment. Such translation owes as much to the influence of the aesthetic conventions of Indian popular cinema, globally known as Bollywood, as to the purchase of Romanticism on this cinematic genre. This latter is well documented by scholars, as is the influence of a Bollywood-derived visual and cinematic language on Rushdie's novels.[9] In the introduction I discussed how powerful a melancholic or romanticist mode of realism was in countering the abstractions of what Ian Baucom calls "actuarial" or "speculative" realism. The former is a powerful, if different, mode of getting to the truth of history. It romances the news of loss and attributes value to it. Chaudhuri's anxiety that Rushdie somehow compromises the tragic historical "truth" of Kashmir by deploying an excessively allusive and imagistic style appears not to factor in this critical genealogical argument about various novelistic approaches to the "factual" in history. There is less investment in such a sentimental or melancholic mode for fine-grained factual realism. The novelistic urge instead is to deploy a range of perspectival conceits, tropes, images, and other related forms of linguistic play, including a neo-Cratylan correspondence between naming and historical agency. In my comparativist frame from the eighteenth and nineteenth centuries, these could be seen collectively as an iteration of an orientation to fancy, a category granted substantial valence in Romantic poetics. Julie Ellison explains, "Definitions of fancy catalog verbs for operations performed on images and ideas: associating, collecting, combining, embellishing, mixing. . . . Fancy enjoys mimicry, the exotic, nomadism, displacement, strangeness. . . . As a form of motion, fancy's spatial or geographical dimension connects it to the poetics of prospect."[10]

In such a reading fancy is not flighty indulgence but a mode of configuring reality in a nonactuarial frame. The truth-claims of such a poetics are romantic, interested, passionate, and, in the final analysis, testamentary. Rushdie's nostalgia for his filial origins in Kashmir,[11] combined with his promiscuous imagination and his long-standing propensity to bring into his novelistic worlds genealogical history and genealogical romance—the globally recognized precursors of both the modern novel form and Bombay cinema—propel him to craft the magnitude of the political tragedy in Kashmir in a resolutely *melancholic* mode.

Paradise Lost

Kashmir has been part of Rushdie's melancholic imaginary from the time of *Midnight's Children*. Readers will remember the early pages of the novel devoted to a spring morning in 1915, when Saleem Sinai's grandfather Aadam Aziz, freshly back with a medical degree from Germany, prays on his mat in Srinagar and hurts his nose. But he is delighted to be back and gazes around him, appreciatively noting the retreat of the harsh Himalayan winter from the valley: "The world was new again. After a winter's gestation in its eggshell of ice, the valley had beaked its way out into the open, moist and yellow. The new grass bided its time underground; the mountains were retreating to their hill-stations for the warm season. (In the winter, when the valley shrank under the ice, the mountains closed in and snarled like angry jaws around the city on the lake.)" This was Kashmir in undivided India, when "there was no army camp at the lakeside, no endless snakes of camouflaged trucks and jeeps clogged the narrow mountain roads, no soldiers hid behind the crests of the mountains past Baramulla and Gulmarg."[12] In the eyes of Aadam Aziz, the valley has changed little since the days of the Mughal Empire, apart from the Englishmen's houseboats on the lake.

It is precisely this pristine pre-Partition Kashmir, for centuries the epitome of paradise for the Mughal emperors, that Rushdie seeks to re-create on an exuberant scale in *Shalimar the Clown*. His spokesperson in the novel is the larger-than-life figure of Abdullah Noman, father of Shalimar and chief of the village of Pachigam. This is a village of itinerant performers and cooks, the best in the entire province and untouched by the corruption of the modern industrial world. The novel in fact gets its title from Shalimar's performance in these troupes as a tightrope-walker and a clown, though the clown persona eventually acquires ominous overtones. Abdullah represents the spirit of Kashmir in his embrace of its religious, caste, and communal differences. "To be Kashmiri," he thinks to himself as he sets about planning his village's participation in the royal Dassehra celebration in the Shalimar Bagh, "to have received so incomparable a gift, was to value what was shared far more highly than what divided." The significance of the Shalimar Bagh celebrations is played up as the apogee of the Kashmiri way of life, the very last performance of communal amity before the catastrophe of Partition. The sequence of events leading to the royal festivities in this Garden of Gardens is replete with symbolism. The Hindu maharajah of Kashmir invites performers from every village to celebrate the tenth day of the Hindu Navratri festival, Dassehra, also the day the epic hero Rama vanquished the demon king, Ravana. That same night the mostly Muslim performers also stage *Budshah*, the tale of a benign Muslim sultan. As Boonyi's Hindu Pandit father notes joyfully, "Today our Muslim village, in the service of our Hindu Maharaja, will cook and act in a Mughal—that is to say Muslim—garden, to celebrate the anniversary of the day on which Ram marched against Ravan to rescue Sita. What is more, two plays are to be performed: our traditional *Ram Leela* and also *Budshah*, the tale of a Muslim sultan. Who tonight are the Hindus? Who are the Muslims? Here in Kashmir our stories sit happily side by side on the same double bill, we eat from the same dishes, we laugh at the same jokes."[13]

As the site of these celebrations the Shalimar Garden itself is an emblem of the valley's Edenic past. Situated on the far end of the legendary Dal Lake, it has a history that goes back to the first century AD, when the Hindu king Pravarsena II built a luxurious abode adorned with gardens on the banks of the lake. He named it Shalimar, the Abode of Love, and often used it as a resting place while visiting his spiritual mentor in a neighboring village. The abode did not survive the onslaught of time, but a village named Shalimar developed around it. In 1619 the Mughal emperor Jehangir reclaimed this spot and commissioned a garden to be built for his queen Noorjahan's pleasure. One of the best-known stories about Kashmir is the emperor's ecstatic response when he first glimpsed the beauty of the valley. Legend has it that he caught his breath and poetically exclaimed in Persian, "Gar bar-ru-e-zamin ast, hamin ast, hamin ast, hamin ast!" (If there is paradise on earth, it is here, it is here, it is here!). The magnificence of Shalimar's architectural layout and landscaping, complete with cascading fountains and waterfalls, was a metonym for Kashmir's heavenly beauty for generations since.

Rushdie takes these Edenic associations to new geocultural heights by making the garden not only the setting for the celebration of Kashmir's prelapsarian ethos of communal coexistence but also, in true Bollywood style, the site of the birth of the two Kashmiri protagonists, Shalimar and Boonyi, one a Muslim, the other a Hindu. The future perfect temporality of this plot movement is worth noting. Rushdie is interested in novelistically translating not just what Kashmir *is* but *what it will have been* had the world of Shalimar and Boonyi not been shattered by the insidious forces of history. One of the stock motifs in Bombay films, especially since the Partition, is the birth of siblings or lovers in different communal households due to the vagaries of their circumstances. The films almost always end in their eventual reunion and an affirmation of the secular, inclusive nature of the subcontinent's communal ethos. Rushdie deploys this heavy Bombay cinematic vernacular of symbolic births and deaths throughout his novelistic oeuvre, and it makes its appearance here in the sentimentality of the narrative when we hear that the mothers of Shalimar and Boonyi "fantasized about the future lifelong friendship of their unborn children," a fantasy that takes a worldly shape when the two are indeed bonded in passion from their early adulthood. A further analogy with Adam and Eve, and eventually the serpent in the form of Max, is admittedly labored. In fact Rushdie is barely able to modulate his excessively tropological oscillation between his extrahistorical elevation of Kashmir to Paradise incarnate and his obsession with the geopolitical Real. In the light of this it is interesting to note that he does not recast his vision of Shalimar and Boonyi's union in terms of a *national* imaginary, as he would have been inclined to do in his early novels. He mourns not pre-Partition India, but pre-Independence Kashmir—timeless, pristine, but not without the promise of seductive allure.

The fecund, life-giving splendor of his beloved valley is distilled in the figure of Boonyi. With green eyes, black hair, a rose complexion, and a Greek nose that sometimes stares down haughtily at the world and often raises itself perkily to smell new adventures, Boonyi, much like Eve, is born womanly. Premonitions of her eventual corruption by the world appear in the narrative quite early, when we are told of her reinterpretation of Sita's abduction in the *Ramayana*:

> What strange meaning that would give to the old story—that women's folly undid men's magic, that heroes had to fight and die because of the vanity that had made a pretty woman act like a dunce. That didn't feel right. The dignity, the moral strength, the intelligence of Sita was beyond doubt and could not so trivially be set aside. Boonyi gave the story a different interpretation. However much Sita's family members sought to protect her, Boonyi thought, the demon king still existed, was hopelessly besotted by her, and would have to be faced sooner or later. A woman's demons were out there, like her lovers, and she could only be coddled for so long. (50)

We encounter her erotic orientation to the world quite early on when we see her getting ready for her first sexual encounter with Shalimar barely two years after she enters puberty. Rushdie stages this in a style reminiscent of the ancient and medieval Sanskrit bardic traditions celebrating the erotic play between Krishna and his consort Radha. Typically these narrate the elaborate *shringara* of Radha, that is, her beautification, as she prepares for her rendezvous with Krishna in the moonless dark of the night in forests beside the riverbank. Rushdie describes how Boonyi enhances her allure by oiling her body and dressing her hair with a long decorative kerchief in quintessential Kashmiri fashion. She wears a full-length dark embroidered *phiran* over a long shirt, but no "other garments or undergarments" (54). The scent of peach and apple blossom makes her eyelids heavy. They are to meet by the river in Khelmarg on a moonless night. Shalimar climbs "the wooded hill to Khelmarg and listens to the river flow" as he waits for her: "He wanted the world to remain frozen just as it was in this moment, when he was filled with hope and longing, when he was young and in love and nobody had disappointed him and nobody he loved had died" (58). There is a distinct *before* and *after* in the narrative of Boonyi's erotic universe, one that maps onto the novel's representation of Kashmir before and after the Partition. The building up to the Radha-like mythological iteration of a timeless erotic bond with Shalimar is unquestionably the before: an indelible part of the mythology of

Kashmir as unspoiled paradise. The after is Boonyi's fatal encounter with Max as she dances to a completely different mythical tune, this time Bollywood inspired and mired in the vicissitudes of human passion. The political ravaging of Kashmir occurs in parallel with this melodramatic encounter.

Rushdie's artistry in the depiction of Boonyi, however, is not devoid of his trademark irony and deprecation. He appears to demystify the romance of Boonyi and Kashmir almost while mythologizing it. Thus Boonyi is not just the exquisite Kashmiri belle who tiptoes across the valley on a moonless night and modestly offers herself to her lover. At the touch of the novelist's wand she is transformed into a modern-day seeker of sexual adventure. Quite uncharacteristically she calls out to Shalimar in a voice hoarse from smoking pot, or *charas*. Ready for an encounter intoxicating on more than one level, she boldly berates Shalimar for his qualms about taking advantage of her in her drugged state. When he suggests that they could make love but not consummate their passion, she proceeds brazenly to shed her clothes, declaring contemptuously, "You think I went through all this trouble just for a kiddie-style session of lick and suck?" (60). In the aftermath of their orgiastic experience, she exclaims, "God, and *that's* what you *didn't* want to do?" (61). This complete abdication of realism effect, this defamiliarization of expected norms of credible characterization in fiction, will be familiar to Rushdie scholars.

Kashmir in the World

Boonyi's eventual fall and that of Kashmir are not local developments tucked away in the northernmost corner of India. They are world events through the allegorical power of Rushdie's most flamboyant characterization to date, Maximilian Ophuls. If Saleem Sinai in *Midnight's Children* embodied India's amorphous and fragmented postcolonial self, Max Ophuls is the grand vehicle of twentieth-century world history. At every stage in the novel we are made aware of his unique destiny as a world figure, "a living flying ace and giant of the Resistance, a man of movie-star good looks and polymathic accomplishment. . . . In addition he had moved to the United States, choosing the burnished attractions of the New World over the damaged gentility of the Old" (161). His shape-shifting, mobile self appears at the conjuncture of every significant geopolitical event since the rise of Hitler. When he first encounters Boonyi, he is in his sixties and has already been "the brilliant young economist, lawyer and student of international relations, the master forger of the Resistance, the ace pilot, the Jewish survivor, the genius of Bretton

Woods, the best-selling author, and the American ambassador cocooned in the house of power" (179). Vietnam has already somewhat diminished the superpower's postwar moral gloss, and this loss of global stature is paralleled by Max's subsequent dishonor.

Boonyi's performance as the erstwhile courtesan Anarkali at a special function organized in his honor as ambassador to India is Max's undoing. His desire for her overcomes all diplomatic scruples, and he arranges to have her ensconced as his mistress in Delhi. She willingly abandons her marital home and her acrobat husband, Shalimar, to make her life as a dancer in the wider world. Rushdie's crafting of the scandal is saturated with motifs from popular performance and cinematic cultures. The story of the dancing girl Anarkali and her doomed romance with a Mughal prince has been immortalized in India's public culture in two blockbuster films, *Anarkali* and *Mughal-e-Azam*.[14] Directed by the legendary K. Asif, *Mughal-e-Azam* is unanimously hailed as a Bollywood classic for its glittering sets, sublime music, and elevated performances by three of India's greatest actors: Dilip Kumar, Madhubala, and Prithviraj Kapoor. The infatuation of Prince Jehangir, son of the Mughal emperor Akbar, with Anarkali is part of popular Persian lore in India.[15] Rushdie re-creates the choreographed romance of the Anarkali legend with as much narrative flamboyance as Asif's cinematic masterpiece. Max's passion and Boonyi's allurements are garbed in not-so-subtle Bollywood-speak:

> Then Boonyi Kaul Noman came out to dance and Max realized that his Indian destiny would have little to do with politics, diplomacy and arms sales, and everything to do with the far more ancient imperatives of desire. . . . Her eyes met his and blazed their answer and the point of no return was passed. . . . She put the palms of her hands together, touched her fingertips to her chin, gazed at and then bowed her head before the great man of power, and had the feeling as she left his presence that she wasn't leaving the stage but making an entrance on the greatest stage she had ever been allowed to walk upon. (181)

Max's subsequent Pygmalion-like grooming of the rustic Boonyi in their Delhi love nest and his sheer inability to relate to her in any other way except through their mutual desire have geopolitical parallels in his inability to grasp the complexities of the militarized Indo-Pak stalemate over Kashmir. As the U.S. ambassador he is all goodwill toward India. He introduces the ambitious Ophuls Plan to facilitate friendly collaboration between the two enemy states. Interdependency rather than conflict is what he aims to achieve through cooperation over hydroelectric, irrigation, and energy projects. While Max is lauded back home and by the UN, his plan fails abysmally in containing the military stand-off between the two enemies. His ignorance about the subcontinental sensitivities over this Himalayan territory is evident even as it exposes the failures of U.S. foreign policy in South Asia during the cold war. He soon overreaches by allowing his judgment on Kashmir to be subtended by his passion for Boonyi. His various public statements on the oppression of Kashmiris bring his diplomatic career to an end: "Newspaper editorials lambasted him. Here, they said, beneath all the phoney Indiaphile posturing, was just another cheap 'cigarette' (this was a slang term meaning a Pak-American, an American with Pakistani sympathies, a play on the name of the Pak-American Tobacco Company), just another uncomprehending gringo. America was trampling over southeast Asia, *Vietnamese children's bodies were burning with unquenchable napalm fire, and yet the American ambassador had the gall to speak of oppression.* 'America should put its own house in order,' thundered India's editorial writers, 'and stop telling us how to take care of our own land'" (198, emphasis added).

As is obvious from the reference to Vietnam, Rushdie makes every effort to scale up the Kashmir conflict as a world event. Two significant authorial moves stand out in this regard. One is his juxtaposition of the various historical instances of insurgency across the globe with the one in Kashmir. The second is his global dispersal of Kashmiri history across a terrain that extends from the subcontinent and the Philippines in the East to California in the West. Max was a Resistance hero during the Nazi occupation of France. His role as an insurgent, constantly on the run and donning new personalities to evade capture, becomes innate to him as he subsequently morphs into various roles demanded by the world-historical circumstances of his time. "Entering the Resistance," he writes in his memoirs, "was, for me, a kind of flying. . . . One took leave of one's name, one's past, one's future, one lifted oneself away from one's life and existed only in the continuum of the work, borne aloft by necessity and fatalism. Yes, a sort of soaring feeling possessed me at times, tempered by the perpetual knowledge that one could crash or be shot down at any moment, without warning, and die in the dirt like a dog" (167). With Boonyi's abandonment and Max's violation of his marital home, not to mention the climate of radicalization exacerbated by Indian military occupation, Shalimar likewise becomes an insurgent on the run. He trains in Pakistan, travels among Muslim insurgents in the Philippines, and eventually journeys to California via Seattle and Vancouver. Like Max the Resistance hero, Shalimar assumes a chameleon-like persona at different sites; he "had passports in five names, and had learned good Arabic, ordinary French and bad English, and had opened routes for himself . . . in the invisible world." Shalimar's lethal exploits, like Max's, are described as "flying": "He remembered his father teaching him to walk the tightrope, and realized that travelling the secret routes of the invisible world was exactly the same. The routes were gathered air. Once you had learned to use them you felt as if you were flying, as if the illusory world in which most people lived was vanishing and you were flying across the skies without even needing to get on board a plane" (275).

The metaphorical equivalence posited between the heroic acts of the French Resistance and terrorizing strategies of Islamic insurgency is deliberate on Rushdie's part. Even as his liberal self is repulsed by the militant excesses of global Islam,[16] he deploys what one can only call a *world* perspective in forcing the reader to confront the discomfort of seeing the heroism of the French Resistance mirrored in contemporary acts of global terrorism. For readers in the West this is an avowedly repugnant juxtaposition. Aren't the two world-historical events of unequal moral valence in the global scheme of things? However, *to world* is also to seek startling points of connection between distant and disparate realities. As Geoffrey Barraclough once put it, "World history cuts into reality at a different angle from other types of history; and because its angle is different, it cuts across the lines they have traced."[17] Two spatially and temporally distant instances of insurgency against forced occupation—the French and the Islamic—have generated a linguistic repertoire replete with moral ambiguities: *insurgent, terrorist, freedom fighter*. Rushdie himself clarifies his literary juxtaposition of two different histories of insurgency in these words: "In *Shalimar*, the character of Max Ophuls is a resistance hero during World War II. The resistance which we think of as heroic, is what we could now call an insurgency in a time of occupation. Now we live in a time where there are other insurgencies that we don't call heroic—that we call terrorist. . . . I wanted to say: That happened then, this is happening now, this story includes both those things, just look how they sit together."[18]

This splicing together of historically and geopolitically disparate terrains and bringing them into reckoning with the global present is what distinguishes Rushdie the world novelist from Rushdie the postcolonial novelist. It is not that the postcolonial novel does not juxtapose multiple and disparate temporalities, but allegorizing *disjunctive* temporalities is its forte. Its chronotopes, so to say, rarely reckon with planetary *convergence*, with a cotemporality that is global. That is the special provenance of the world novel. We especially see this world-making force at work in the second feature I identified earlier: the global dispersal of Kashmiri history, the juxtaposition of multiple visions of *Kashmiriyat* in the novel, and the convergence of its melancholic history with the global war on terror. Deliberately blown out of the continuum of Indian nationalist history and the postcolonial conundrum of Partition, Kashmir in the novel functions as an emblematic site of the traumas of the post–cold war global present. It is no longer just a casualty of postcolonial Partition. The violation of Boonyi symbolizes the violence of U.S. cold war foreign policy in both Vietnam and the subcontinent. Boonyi's eventual physical degeneration and abandonment by Max are mirrored in the increasing insurgent activism from across the border and the subsequent military occupation of Kashmir by Indian armed forces. These are militant forces—*mujahideens*—armed by the United States in its stand-off with the Soviets. Even as Boonyi's world disintegrates, Kashmir becomes a war zone, a casualty of U.S. cold war policy in the region.

Three figures allegorize this transformation of Kashmir from a national to a global site of conflict: the Indian general Hammir Kachawa, Shalimar the Clown, and, most significant, India/Kashmira, the illegitimate daughter of Boonyi and Max. Each allegorical juncture at the same time becomes a world of its own, highlighting the sheer impossibility of a single, geopolitically recognizable Kashmir. Kashmir's entry into a traumatic world history is preceded by a short, secular fight for liberation from both India and Pakistan. Rushdie's monumentalizing of this fleeting historical moment and what it irrevocably lost is worth quoting at some length:

> In those days before the crazies got into the act the liberation front was reasonably popular and azadi was the universal cry. Freedom! A tiny valley of no more than five million souls, landlocked, preindustrial, resource rich but cash poor, perched thousands of feet up in the mountains, like a tasty green sweetmeat caught in a giant's teeth, wanted to be free. Its inhabitants had come to the conclusion that they didn't much like India and didn't care much for the sound of Pakistan. So: freedom! Freedom to be meat-eating Brahmins or saint-worshipping Muslims, to make pilgrimages to the ice-lingam high in the melting snows or to bow down before the Prophet's hair in a lakeside Mosque, to listen to the santoor and drink salty tea, to dream of Alexander's army and to choose never to see an army again, to make honey and carve walnut into animal and boat shapes and to watch the mountains push their way, inch by inch, century by century, further up into the sky. Freedom to choose folly over greatness, but to be nobody's fools. Azadi! Paradise wanted to be free. (253)

The genocidal stampede of the Indian armed forces combined with militant incursions from Pakistan quickly puts paid to this dream of an independent Kashmir. Rushdie reserves his vitriol for the sadistic Indian general Hammirdev Suryavansh Kachawa. Nicknamed "the Hammer of Kashmir," the army general symbolizes the viciousness of the Indian military occupation of Kashmir after 1989. The army's cordon-and-search crackdown without prior notice is colloquially referred to as "fuck the enemy in the crack." Rushdie captures the nihilism of Kachawa's militaristic worldview in the chilling rhetoric of administrative pseudo-reasoning: "Kashmir was an integral part of India. An integer is a whole and India was an integer and fractions were illegal. Fractions caused fractures in the integer and were thus not integral" (96). The general finds the aspiration for Kashmir independence "pathetic . . . an old fairy tale" and clearly interprets the militancy across the border as part of "Islamist terror international." The rhetoric of Indian occupation accordingly shifts to a more global register eerily familiar to those living in the era of the "Global War on Terror": "Every Muslim in Kashmir should be considered a militant. The bullet was the only solution." The relish of killing, evoked in the register of the sublime, worlds an obscene genocidal imaginary: "The idea of violence had a velvet softness now. One took off one's gloves and smelled the sweet fragrance of necessity. Bullets entered flesh like music, the pounding of clubs was the rhythm of life, and then there was the sexual dimension to consider, the demoralization of the population through the violation of its women. In that dimension, every colour was bright and tasted good. He closed his eyes and averted his head. What must be, must be." The razing of Pachigam, the village home of the families of Boonyi and Shalimar, marks the apotheosis of the Hammer's genocidal lust. Spurned by Boonyi a few years earlier, and now wearing the accoutrements of absolute power, General Kachawa directs his final crackdown on the village that for generations nurtured a syncretic, authentically Kashmiri world. An entire way of life is destroyed in the rage of a single night. Language falters in this deathworld. From an inchoate, anguished torrent it tapers into the hush of a solitary sentence: "The beautiful village of Pachigam still exists" (291). We move here into the realm of melancholic time.

Melancholic Time and Heritage-Speak

But in what form does Pachigam still exist? Or, for that matter, Kashmir? How indeed is melancholic time represented in this contemporary novel? The novel enters into the realm of heritage-speak, the transplanted circuit of lost organic pasts that accrue cultural value in global markets. Yuvraj Singh, the admirer of Max and Boonyi's daughter, is the salesperson of this packaged Kashmir. The valley's beauty is distilled in the arts and crafts that he peddles to customers for a handsome profit. For him Kashmir's soul ramifies in its exquisite rugs and shawls. He becomes the passionate scribe of this aesthetic history that stretches back to the glorious days of the Silk Route trade: "He spoke about the origins of the craft of numdah rug making in Central Asia, in Yarkand and Sinkiang, in the days of the old Silk Route, and the words *Samarkand* and *Tashkent* made his eyes shine with ancient glory" (358–59). This spiritual archaeologist of Kashmir digs deep into the origins of papier-mâché as an art practice. It was, he discovers, perfected by a fifteenth-century Kashmiri prince in the jails of Samarkand, once the glorious epicenter of Central Asian lifeworlds. His eloquence on the marvels of Kashmiri embroidery is limitless: "He told her [Kashmira] about the *sozni* embroidery techniques, which could be so skillful that the same motif would appear on both sides of the shawl in different colours, about satin-stitch and *ari* work and the hair of the ibex goat and the legendary *jamewar* shawls" (359). It is not farfetched to read in Rushdie's portrayal of Yuvraj Singh the literary correlate of contemporary scholarship on the import of heritage in a globalizing age. Minimally speaking, heritage is the past packaged as culture and rendered fungible in the global market. The result is often a thin cultural preservation at the cost of substantive local erosion. At the same time, inhering in the practice of heritage is a desire to render a dispossessed legacy visible beyond a local or regional terrain, an aspiration to participate in a global conversation about civilizational value. The heritage object acquires an attributive motion wherein the soul of the past is transported to the present. Heritage becomes part of national and cultural self-making in the global age, a modality of holding onto what has been lost and of *presencing* the trauma of that civilizational loss. Its thin, alienable form may render it fungible in the global marketplace, but the aura of heritage transcends the objects that circulate in its name. This auratic excess generated by the transport of the soul of the past thickens the temporality of the global present and renders it irreducible to the compressed space-time of the market. Is this vehicularity of heritage what Rushdie points to in his poetic capture of Yuvraj's aesthetic knowledge? Surely he is aware that the relation of heritage to the postcolony is more complex than this.

To rehearse but a few insights from the scholarly literature that are of relevance to Rushdie's transmutation of Kashmir's pristine past into Yuvraj's artifacts, the colonies have long suffered an inverted heritage syndrome wherein their lived experiences were routinely museumized by the colonial powers. In Daniel Herwitz's bracing words, "Mortified as monstrous, primitive, incapable of modernization, colonialism turned the precolonial past into a mark of inferiority, then stuck it in a museum to be gazed at like a nude alabaster Venus missing an arm and a leg."[19] The postcolonial gesture of retrieving this mortified and mutilated past through the language of heritage and making it materially visible in the global marketplace may appear to be a mark of continuing servitude. And yet isn't postcolonial appropriation of any kind primarily invested in disturbing the balance of representative power, of wresting the capacity to render valuable what has hitherto been devalued? Repetition but with a difference is the all too well-known mantra of postcolonial world-making. We encounter a narrative impasse at this juncture as Rushdie struggles to vest Kashmir's civilizational value alternately in Yuvraj and Kashmira. Pre-Partition Kashmir has been pillaged, desecrated, and aesthetically brutalized for over half a century by the combined imperial forces of British India, post-Partition India, Pakistan, and the United States at the height of the cold war. Is Yuvraj's artifactual, aestheticized, and globally accessible Kashmir adequate to carrying the allegorical weight of this traumatic history? I suggest that Rushdie eventually settles the conundrum about heritage's entry onto the world stage in favor of Kashmira. It is significant that despite allowing herself to be courted by Yuvraj, she is not enamored by his profession. When he arrives at her doorstep in Los Angeles with flowers in a papier-mâché vase and a range of other Kashmiri handicrafts, her first comment is, "You look like a walking flea market" (391).

Rushdie's virtualized Pachigam transmigrates into the deterritorialized psychogeography of Kashmira's world, which in turn becomes the live-action heritage of Kashmir in the novel.[20] The battle over the soul of Kashmir is internalized in the flesh-and-blood, Los Angeles–based love child of Max and Boonyi, Kashmira (or India, as she is first named). She is the living embodiment of Boonyi's and consequently Pachigam's destruction and also the medium of their resurrection in a deterritorialized form. But *live-action heritage* also refers to Rushdie's crafting of Kashmira's emergence in the filmic lineaments of the Bollywood revenge drama. Bollywood is arguably contemporary India's most powerful connective cultural tissue. In its blockbusters one truly does find India's live, action-filled heritage. Rushdie's deployment of its many formal features in his novels is hardly incidental. Furthermore, distant and improbable as California might appear as a site from which to craft the drama of Kashmir's memorialization, it is also home to the most globally influential film industry in the world and Bollywood's constant inspiration and interlocutor. Through an admixture of these two grand filmic traditions, India's transformation into Kashmira is predicted right at the start of the novel, when she witnesses her father's assassination by her mother's husband, Shalimar, on the doorstep of her Los Angeles home. On the arrest of Shalimar and at the urging of Yuvraj, she decides to journey to the land of her mother's birth. Her painful psychic journey compels her to reject both her father's grand vision of the post–cold war world and Shalimar's hate-filled Islamic radicalization. By the time she arrives at her mother's graveside she has already consciously morphed from India to Kashmira: "There is no India, she thought. There is only Kashmira. There is only Kashmir. She would not be India in India. She would be her mother's child" (356). Much like the melodramatic transformation of Bollywood protagonists into avengers of past wrongs, Kashmira is transformed into an avenging angel as she registers the many humiliations her mother suffered before she died: "The man who killed her father had killed her mother too. The man who killed her father had been her mother's husband. He killed her mother too. The cold weight of the information lay like ice upon her heart and the thing got into her and made her capable of anything" (367). On her return to the United States she enters a strict regimen of fitness and martial arts training; she also trains in boxing and archery. Echoes of *Charlie's Angels* are unmistakable here. She closely follows the court trial of Shalimar. Its drama is staged much like the court scenes in Bollywood, not to mention the popular crime and justice dramas on global television. There is a long passionate defense of Shalimar's psychopathology in the language that contemporary America understands—the language of terrorism:

> His village was destroyed by the Indian army. Then his mother was raped and killed and his father was also slain. And then they killed his wife, his beloved wife, the greatest dancer in the village and the greatest beauty in all Kashmir.... This is exactly the kind of person the terrorist puppet masters seek out.... This is a man against whose whole community blood crime was committed that he could not avenge, a blood crime that drove him out of his mind. When a man is out of his mind other forces can enter that mind and shape it. They took that avenging spirit and pointed it in the direction they required, not at India, but here. At America. At their real enemy. At us. (358)

But it is Kashmira's words that eventually unmake the defense's case and convict Shalimar: "That wasn't how my mother was killed. My mother died because that man, who also killed my father, cut off her beautiful head"

(386). Much like the overly long screen dramas of Bollywood, Rushdie cannot let his novel conclude at this juncture. After all, he has to make Kashmira the heroine of her own revenge drama. Shalimar's ingenious escape from his high-security prison and his infiltration of Kashmira's fortress-like mansion have all the ingredients of a second-rate thriller. The novel ends with Kashmira taking her destiny into her own hands. She avenges her parents' deaths and that of beautiful Kashmir by aiming a perfectly timed arrow at Shalimar's heart as he approaches her dressing chamber: "The golden bow was drawn back as far as it would go. . . . There was no possibility she would miss. There was no second chance. There was no India. There was only Kashmira, and Shalimar the clown" (398).

Global Islam and the Postliberal Conundrum

What might one make of Rushdie's melancholic worlding of Kashmir through this register of live-action heritage? Why does he, in the final instance, diminish the import of global Islam as a planetary force and recast it as a stylized family melodrama about dishonor and revenge? No doubt he is keen to foreground the singularity of the Kashmir tragedy and to grieve for it in a language deliberately removed from the geopolitical lexicon of the U.S. war on terror.[21] Kashmira squirms at the "alien cadences of American speech" at the trial of Shalimar. It is her personalization of his heinous act that eventually convicts him. Rushdie himself provides a related explanation in an interview he gave after the publication of the novel. Just as he is skeptical of the U.S. political rhetoric on the war on terror, he also rejects the existence of something called global Islam. He suggests instead that we attend to local particularities to understand the form that Islamist movements take in different parts of the world. "There is a tendency," he says, "to look at the jihadist movement as a monolith globally. The only real global idea they have is this laughable fantasy of the 'return of the Caliphate.' Inevitably they are disappointed that this doesn't happen, and thus there is more resentment."[22] No doubt Rushdie's caution about attentiveness to local contexts is salutary. But I have another argument to make about his skeptical stance on global Islam in *Shalimar the Clown*.

Rushdie's sense of personal injury at the hands of this global Islam during his ten long years in hiding comes significantly into play in crafting *Shalimar the Clown*. He deliberately decenters the role of global Islam in the novel because his liberal self is reluctant to confront a new kind of postliberal political rationality that global Islam now represents precisely in the language that he finds laughable. He refuses to bestow a credible literary form on this new political imaginary even as he did so successfully on the fractures of post-colonial liberal politics of India in *Midnight's Children*. Ironically his liberal self cannot comprehend a collective politics of injury that a previous novel of his had unleashed in Muslim public spheres. This public face of Islam cannot be unproblematically equated with either the brutality of the Taliban or the murderous exploits of Al Qaeda and ISIS or even the fatwa-ridden world of the erstwhile Iranian ayatollah. Semiotically speaking, of course, these are undoubtedly the most powerful projections of Islam's extremism on the world stage, but the public face of global Islam that periodically erupts in multiple media in cases such as the 1988 Bradford protests over *The Satanic Verses* is by no means the face of ISIS or the Taliban. The periodic public manifestation of Islamic collectivity has no geopolitical ends in mind. It is more an assertion of an alternative mode of cultural world-making, one that feels under threat from the forces of Westernization.

Earlier I noted the importance of the year 1989, the year of Khomeini's fatwa, in the transformation of Rushdie from a postcolonial to a world novelist. The event was preceded by media spectacles of worldwide protest against *The Satanic Verses*. While local and regional sites of Islamic insurgencies existed long before 1989, it was really the Rushdie affair that galvanized Muslim publics globally and made visible to the rest of the world the phenomenon of Islam as a powerful geocultural force. We saw it erupt again during the controversy around the representation of the Prophet in the Danish cartoons in 2006. This global Islam is a postliberal phenomenon, a mode of cultural politics that is no longer tied to the rights and responsibilities of citizens in a nation-state. Like human rights and the environmental movement, it appeals to the idea of humanity, a category that has never had institutional visibility in the political sense,[23] hence its amorphous and fragmented nature. Various Islamic subnational and transregional political groups have no doubt periodically given a frightening face to this global Islam, such as Al Qaeda, the Taliban in Afghanistan, and more recently the macabre ISIS. But none on its own quite embodies Islam's suprapolitical aura, its orientation toward a destiny that awaits humanity once the value of the various sacrifices made in its name is truly realized. In fact in recent years Muslims around the world have denounced the hijacking of their worldviews by these extremist groups. In one of the most astute analyses in recent years of the postliberal nature of this Islamic mobilization, Faisal Devji notes that the periodic global eruptions in the name of Islam are more about a politics of injury than a politics of interest. There is no systemic attempt to create a new state or political infrastructure that would give it any institutional base at a global level, except perhaps the very recent ISIS mobilization in the name of a caliphate. But even in the case of ISIS the focus is on killing as many people as possible rather than a systematic negotiation with the international system of states for more power and leverage. To that extent the reference to the lost caliphate is clearly the rhetoric of perceived collective injury from past injustice instead of an attempt at building a future for the world's Muslims. Further, collective action in the name of global Islam is primarily a product of our digital era, a phenomenon I have clearly identified as a major vector in the generation of postliberal imaginaries since 1989. About the protests in the wake of the 2006 Danish cartoons controversy, Devji writes:

> Muslim protestors did not represent some religious tradition that needs to be schooled in the lessons of modern citizenship. Rather their protests brought into being a hyper-modern global community whose connections occur by way of mass media alone. From the Philippines to Niger, these men and women communicated with each other only directly, neither by plan nor by organization, but through the media itself. . . . Most Muslims were hurt not by the offending item . . . but by its global circulation as a media report. *Yet it was this very circulation of the offending item as news that also allowed Muslims to represent themselves as a global community in, through, and as the news.*[24]

The liberal appeal to the tenets of freedom of expression does not quite hold water in such a postliberal scenario for such sites are by nature postnational. Freedoms, on the other hand, are politically protected only within the confines of a nation-state. To be sure, Rushdie was offered police protection by the United Kingdom, but the global politics of injury made it impossible for him to seek recompense for the violation of his freedom of expression or to travel beyond the United Kingdom without being open to the risk of death. It is this personal history of being exposed to the dangers of a postliberal politics of injury that makes Rushdie the novelist wary of giving credible literary form to the newfound expressionism of global Islam.

There is one other aspect of this postliberal politics that Rushdie finds hard to countenance. This is the idea of politics as sacrifice, most evident in the phenomenon of suicide bombing and other acts of suicidal terror. *Shalimar the Clown* clearly manifests this unease. It is significant that despite years of training in terrorist camps, Shalimar rejects the indoctrination of fundamentalist leaders like Bulbul Fakh. He resolves to break with the ranks of the trainees and flee. He finds suicide bombing unmanly and cowardly: "The business of finding young boys and even young girls who are ready to blow themselves up felt demeaning to Shalimar the clown who therefore decided to make a break with the iron mullah" (318). Rushdie himself claims as much in an interview: "Fighting is manly, suicide bombing is cheap." The masculine code of war in Shalimar's world is honor. Rushdie's understanding of the psychology of terrorism is couched in the language of dishonor: "The most essential characteristic of the person who commits terror of this kind is the idea of dishonored manhood. I try to show this in my novel. The character Shalimar picks up the gun not just because his heart gets broken, but because his pride and honor get broken by losing the woman he loves to a worldly man of greater consequence and power. Somehow he has to rebuild his sense of manliness. This is what leads him down the path to slashing an American ambassador's throat."[25] This total discounting of terrorist indoctrination in favor of a psychological reading of Shalimar's murderous mind-set is symptomatic of Rushdie's retreat from an engagement with the charismatic power of Islam's globally mediated abstractions.

The politics of sacrifice that suicide killing manifests is, in the final analysis, suprapolitical, for the humanity of the suicide killer, Devji writes, "no longer resides in biology or jurisprudence, but rather in the virtues of courage and sacrifice that he manifests, existential virtues whose production completely overpowers the statistical logic of equivalence."[26] Yes, suicide killing can be used to further the subnationalist cause, as we have seen with the Tamil Tigers and the fedayeen in Palestine. But the dissolution of the killer along with the victim ultimately renders void a politics of interest that is so central to the liberal imaginary. In rejecting the ideology of suicide bombing, Shalimar stands for this remnant of the liberal self, one that Rushdie is keen to hold onto in the face of the growing threat from a postliberal global Islam.

IN THE FOREGOING CHAPTERS I have explored in detail the singularly powerful literary provenance of the idea of the world. I have also extensively examined the transformations of the novel form in our era of global wars and the mass uptake of information and communication technology networks. In the case of Rushdie in particular I have traced the making of a world novelist in the shadow of postliberal wars and a global Islamic militancy. I now move to part II to focus on wartime as a world-making force in contemporary literature.

PART II
WAR

FIVE
VISUALIZING WARTIME:
A LITERARY GENEALOGY

The War Works Hard

In the aftermath of the First Gulf War, the exiled Iraqi poet Dunya Mikhail published a poem entitled "The War Works Hard." Here is an excerpt that invokes war's industriousness:

> The war continues working day and night
> It inspires tyrants
> to deliver long speeches
> award medals to generals
> and themes to poets.
> It contributes to the industry
> of artificial limbs
> provides food for flies
> adds pages to the history books,
> achieves equality
> between killer and killed,
> teaches lovers to write letters,

accustoms young women to waiting,
fills the newspapers
with articles and pictures,
builds new houses
for the orphans,
invigorates the coffin makers,
gives grave diggers
a pat on the back
and paints a smile on the leader's face.
The war works with unparalleled diligence!
Yet no one gives it a word of praise.[1]

Mikhail's poem captures war's permeability from battlefields to civilian domains. This experience of wartime as an everyday horizon of living—as a condition and not an event—is quintessentially modern, as many a scholar has noted.[2] What Mikhail does not mention in this inventory of the work of war at the turn of the twenty-first century is the prolific industry of image making and mediation generated by the explosive conjunction of digital technology, the World Wide Web, and social media. Writing in 1991, when the world had only just begun to wake up to the transmedial spectacle of smart bombing and antiwar protests had yet to progress from tarred streets to the fiber-optic highways of our networked globe, the young Mikhail could scarcely imagine the work of war in informatic terms.

The exponential increase in the quantity and velocity of imagistic exposure on a daily basis translates into a saturated global experience of endemic war and violence.[3] The viral nature of the circulation of Jason Russell's video of March 2012 urging the world at large to help capture the Ugandan warlord Kony is one recent instance. Despite his horrific crimes against children, such as enlisting prepubescent boys as child soldiers and turning young girls into sex slaves, Kony has eluded capture for thirty years. In fact, other than the inhabitants of Uganda and a handful of specialists in African studies, very few had even heard of this war criminal until the unleashing of Russell's video in cyberspace. Within a week of its release on YouTube and Vimeo, *Kony 2012* was viewed by over 70 million people. By the end of the month the number exceeded 100 million. Thousands of dollars poured in globally on the very first day of its release as people bought the "Catch Kony" kit.[4] Twitter and Facebook experienced serious overload in the first few days of the video's circulation. Invisible Children Inc., an NGO cofounded by Russell that produced the video, issued a year-long action plan to nab the war criminal. On April 20, Hitler's birthday, people across the globe were mobilized in a "Cover the Night" campaign to put up "Catch Kony" posters on walls across several cities to make the chief of the Lord's Resistance Army (LRA) famous. Few people before this campaign knew what Kony looks like, even though he continues to top the International Criminal Court's list of war criminals. The campaign aimed at making him one of the most recognizable living war criminals. The online production spiraled into the celebrity circuit, with leading actors, policy makers, legal experts, and political leaders lending their voices. These included Bill Clinton, George W. Bush, Condoleezza Rice, Angelina Jolie, Oprah Winfrey, George Clooney, and even the chief prosecutor at the International Criminal Court, Luis Moreno Ocampo. The unprecedented success of this social media campaign reached an apogee of sorts when President Barack Obama sanctioned the deployment of a hundred elite troops to assist Ugandan forces in hunting down Kony.[5] The *New York Times* reported that the commander of U.S. forces in Africa, Gen. Carter F. Ham, has a *Kony 2012* poster on his office door. "Let's be honest," one U.S. official said, "there was some constituent pressure here. Did *Kony 2012* have something to do with this? Absolutely."[6]

My focus in this chapter is on this phenomenon of humanitarian mobilization enabled by the wizardry of web technology. A hypermediated humanitarian imaginary constitutes one of the key features in my conception of the world novel. This necessitates a foray into the nature of contemporary warfare, also the temporal and thematic horizon of my book. The first part of this chapter will be devoted to these concerns. Given the larger frame of this study, which examines the intensification in our times of literary forms from the late eighteenth century, it would be useful to compare our era of viral witnessing to the representations of war that the prephotographic decades of Napoleonic conflict brought into the realm of the everyday. The idea of the modern experience of war as a phenomenon that infiltrates the everyday worlds of noncombatants is widely understood as having its origins in the Franco-British wars after the French Revolution.[7] War's "infernal tendency to escape," as Sylvère Lotringer puts it,[8] to invade domains outside its physical strategic parameters such that wartime becomes a condition of the mind and of living itself, affects us as much as it did the people of the Napoleonic era. What this comparative frame offers our understanding of the relationship among war, visualization, and literary representations today is the focus of the second part of this chapter. The final part traces the specific texts and contexts—technological, cultural, and aesthetic—of war making from the time of the cold war to the end of the twentieth century. Together these three strands of inquiry are critical not just in providing a theoretical and historical template for my literary analysis of contemporary wartime but also in generating the world picture around 1989, a chronotope informed as much by the intensification of cultural and literary forms from the eighteenth century as by those from the 1960s.

The Pixar of Human Rights Stories

Questions about the transmediality of warfare and its refractions across an array of virtual fields came seriously into the public domain from the 1991 Iraq War. Grafted onto the dizzying pace of technological and communications advancement since CNN first aired the Iraq War in the virtual medium, such questions have transformed the topology of humanitarian consciousness. It is in this context that *Kony 2012* needs to be understood. Jason Russell, who generated the *Kony 2012* phenomenon, calls his film the "Pixar of human rights stories." His words aim to distinguish his humanitarian venture from the conventional script of cultural work on human rights, "the boring documentary on Africa," as he calls it. They also inject a generational shift in attitudes to distant suffering. The Pixar reference, evoking the digital virtuosity of Steve Jobs in superanimating the animation film genre, points not just to a possible aesthetic enhancement of the documentary film through new media technologies but more significantly to a fundamental shift in the perceptual field within which the genre of the nonfiction film on humanitarian crisis operates in the age of social media. The allusion is to a vastly expanded audience networked daily into a circulatory informational economy. This global audience is exposed to a range of storytelling genres in which lines of authorship and spectatorship crisscross constantly. The "boring" documentary is not exactly a good fit in such an interactive cultural economy. In its transgeneric mutation into a thirty-minute YouTube video, *Kony 2012* comes across as a mélange of visual and narrative forms that belong in a globally recognized field of aesthetic intelligibility: the news story, the documentary, the blog, the advertisement, the sentimental soap, the televised debate with a panel of experts, narrative updates on Facebook. Prominent in its aesthetic mediation is humanitarian affect amplified across the entire globe.

The video begins with an image of our blue and green planet and quickly identifies its core audience as the multimillion social media users who appear as glowworms on the surface. "Right now," Russell's voice-over informs us, "there are more people on Facebook than there were people on the planet two hundred years ago." Russell's appeal to this vast mesh of humanity to help nab Kony, the criminal recruiter of child soldiers and under-age sex slaves, is effected in several ways. In a series of quick montages, familiar screens and vocabulary from our digital experience flash into view, along with recent political events attributed to digital connectivity, such as the Arab Spring. Various news clips about governmental attempts to contain the damage of widespread humanitarian crises across the world are also featured. The screen-within-a-screen technique is deployed throughout the film to capture the depth of virtualization of our global entanglements. The idea of humanitarian connectivity is ripe for realization, the video implies in no unsubtle terms, as Victor Hugo's hyperimprovised post-Napoleonic era observation, "Nothing is more powerful than an idea whose time has come," flashes across the screen against a red background. Having established its ethical investment in an idea—humanitarianism—whose time has finally come thanks to a radically hyperconnected world, the video quickly moves into its core narrative.

The privileged upbringing of the filmmaker's son in suburban America is juxtaposed with the story of a fugitive child soldier, Jacob Acaye, whom Russell befriended during his nine-year sojourn in Central Africa. Jacob witnessed his own brother being killed by Kony's Lord's Resistance Army and for years lived in fear of meeting the same fate. In the film we see him at various stages—as the frightened prospective child soldier fleeing Kony, as a depressed teenager unable to come to terms with life in a shelter, and, finally, as a surprisingly evolved young adult joining Russell and Invisible Children Inc. in advocacy against the war criminal. Jacob becomes the singular case around which the passion of this humanitarian war film revolves. Entangled with this passion is a pledge for action that flashes across the screen toward the end:

> Following the launch of KONY 2012, the United Nations and African Union announced an ambitious new plan to arrest Joseph Kony, protect civilians, and restore communities affected by LRA violence. But it will only work if world leaders choose to follow through by declaring their support and providing the necessary resources. Specifically, we are calling on world leaders to:
>
> - Expand communications networks and other programs that help warn communities of LRA threats and provide opportunities for LRA abductees to escape and return safely to their families.
> - Provide the African Union effort with the logistical support needed to arrest Joseph Kony and his top commanders and protect civilians.

- Engage directly with African governments to ensure Kony and his LRA forces cannot exploit remote areas or political discord to find safe haven anywhere in the region.

This June, the UN will meet to discuss their strategy, and we'll be there to deliver your signatures.[9]

Kony 2012 is crudely produced, but prominent in its aesthetic mediation is humanitarian affect amplified across the entire globe. The question of whether the film realized its ultimate goal of nabbing Kony by the end of 2012 should not be used as a barometer of its true impact for its unprecedented impact was in some sense written into the very medium it chose.[10] For the purposes of my analysis the fact that it managed to elicit a global response in ways that decades of documentation and written works on the depredations of war economies in Central Africa were unable to is a telling feature of this era of humanitarian wars.

Ours is an age of viral witnessing with ever more humans infected by the immanence of violence and hence ever more oriented as an audience to the phenomenon of humanitarian crisis. *Witnessing publics* is Meg McLagan's term for people hailed into existence by a growing visual repertoire of testimonial genres.[11] This repertoire brings to the fore an important distinction Giorgio Agamben once posited between the "politics of human rights" and the "politics of witness."[12] Agamben placed the "politics of human rights" in opposition to the "politics of witness." The first reinforces the sovereign power over bare life, while the second testifies to the excesses of such power even as it acknowledges the limits of witnessing.[13] Extrapolated onto my exploration of the actuarial and the melancholic literary modes of apprehending distant suffering, one could say that the "politics of human rights" connotes the preeminence of a legalistic and actuarial imaginary, while the "politics of witness" foregrounds an affective orientation that is more singular and hence also more transitive in its empathetic reach. In the former the suffering bodies represent the human as aggregate, as the abstract bearer of rights. In the latter the human is the singular and melancholic bearer of embodied suffering. Again extrapolating from Agamben, this time temporally, the decades after the Second World War (with the UN Declaration of Human Rights) could arguably be called the "age of human rights," while our age of hypermediated humanitarianism (especially the first two decades of the twenty-first century) could be designated the age of witnessing. This is not to say that one succeeds the other or that the politics of human rights has been completely subsumed by the politics of witness.[14] Rather, and this is the crux of my argument, the term *age of witnessing* signals an increasing inflection of the sensorial and the affective in the juridical and the transformation in the global imaginary of rights from idea to sensorium.[15] More demands are made on the visibility, legibility, and transitive affectivity of human rights in the concrete, everyday, somatic spheres of conflict than ever before. This shift, I suggest, arises from the changed nature of warfare itself since the end of the cold war, as more noncombatants than ever are corporeally and materially affected by war. It is within this sphere of amplified human casualties and heightened extrajuridical witnessing that novelistic work on the new wars finds its provenance.

In our era of humanitarian wars the unit of conflict is not (or not only) individual nation-states but various nonstate human groupings that are not recognized as legal combatants. The term *humanitarian war* itself captures the scaled-up and vastly different nature of warfare in our times. It has at least three features that distinguish it from conventional warfare. First, it is a composite of state-sponsored violence, civil and interethnic conflicts, guerrilla warfare, and organized crime. These are less interested in unseating governments in other states than in territorial capture within their own nations through large-scale displacement of populations and even genocide of targeted groups. September 11 demonstrated that in some cases even territorial capture is not a motivation; spreading terror through massive infrastructural and human damage appears to be the prime goal. Second, the largest number of casualties is among civilians, especially refugees and those maimed in war by indiscriminate targeting. "At the turn of the twentieth century," notes Mary Kaldor, "the ratio of military to civilian casualties in wars was 8:1. Today this has been almost exactly reversed; in the wars of the 1990s, the ratio of military to civilian casualties is approximately 1:8. . . . Behaviour that was proscribed according to the classical rules of warfare and codified in the laws of war in the late nineteenth century and early twentieth century, such as atrocities against non-combatants, sieges, destruction of historic monuments, etc. constitute an essential component of the strategies of this new mode of warfare."[16] The third significant feature of these new wars is the amplification of the scale of operations of the global humanitarian industry to help cope with the volume of casualties. A veritable army of international aid agencies and nongovernmental human rights networks, including Oxfam, Save the Children, the International Red Cross, Human Rights Watch, and Médecins sans Frontières, are ubiquitous fixtures in such wars. The many arms of the UN, including its peacekeeping force and the United Nations High Commissioner for Refugees, have been at work in ways scarcely envisioned in the immediate aftermath of the 1948 UN Declaration of Human Rights.[17]

Of particular significance to my analysis is the communication infrastructure of this global humanitarian and human rights industry. One hears all too much about how information technology and infrastructures of the visual have become imperative in *waging* war but relatively less about how they are used to *alleviate* the effects of war. Visual documentation via digital technology has become the primary means through which human rights advocacy functions in our era. In the past two decades there has been a massive increase in the use of visible documentation of war crimes and large-scale human rights violations. Human rights work is now unthinkable without the ubiquitous digital camera. Armies of activists trained to use a Sony handycam are as much in the front line of humanitarian wars as are journalists and official combatants. There are actually special human rights groups whose primary focus is on providing training in visual technology to aspiring human rights activists. One such group is Witness, cofounded in 1992 by the human rights advocate Peter Gabriel, along with two other NGOs, Human Rights First and Reebok Human Rights Foundation. The catalyst for the establishment of Witness was the videotaped beating of Rodney King by the Los Angeles Police. Beginning with the aim of giving "cameras to human rights activists around the world," its activities gradually extended to video advocacy and video training. Its mission statement says, "We bridge the worlds of human rights, media and technology by incorporating cutting-edge innovations into traditional approaches to advocacy. WITNESS' unique contribution to the human rights community is *to serve as global authority on best practices in the use of video for human rights purposes and a frontline resource for training and expertise.*" By its own estimates, in twenty years of work Witness "has partnered with more than 300 human rights groups in over 80 countries, [and] trained over 3,000 human rights defenders."[18] The group has developed video tool kits specially suited to human rights work and now has a dedicated online platform for human rights media called Hub.

The imagistic dependency and technological transformation of the humanitarian industry has made it impossible for any state to engage or intervene in civil or international conflict without the effects being visible globally. In fact a state's very preparedness for war or humanitarian intervention has often been provided by the informational infrastructure of news media and human rights groups. This feature more than any other—where a state has been compelled by the media networks of the global humanitarian industry to send troops to mitigate the violence of civil war—appears to mark a clear break from the politics of the cold war. The resonance of this temporal shift for my book is hard to miss. One military deployment in Mogadishu in 1992 as part of Operation Restore Hope drew the ire of one of America's towering cold war architects, George Kennan. In an op-ed piece in the *New York Times*, Kennan wrote in dismay at seeing U.S. troops land on the beaches of Mogadishu, an event that television outlets captured with great zeal. It signaled for him the end of his era: "If American policy from here on out, particularly policy involving the use of our armed forces abroad, is to be controlled by popular emotional impulses, and particularly ones provoked by the commercial television industry, then there is no place—not only for myself, but for what have traditionally been regarded as the responsible deliberative organs of our government, in both executive and legislative branches." Significantly for Kennan it is this perception of the evisceration of rational deliberation by experts behind closed doors in an age of media activism that truly marks the end of the cold war era, not "the fall of the Berlin Wall and the reunification of Europe, nor . . . the great borderless coalition and its triumph in the Gulf War."[19] Kennan's fear was to some extent overstated, of course, for the pressure of mediated public opinion has not exactly rendered redundant the need for state-level strategic deliberations. But this encroachment of "popular emotional impulses" unleashed by the globalization of the humanitarian media industry has undoubtedly transformed the terrain of contemporary war making. The architect of the theory of containment would understandably be unsettled by the proliferation of war zones in our times and the contamination of state agency by the extralegislative and extrajuridical force of a mediatized humanitarian industry.

Interestingly Kennan's anxiety that a televisually and digitally mobilized field of politics would see a dangerous ascendancy of passion echoes a recent intervention by one of the participants in precisely the new war visual politics that Kennan warns against. In a workshop hosted by New York University's Center for Religion and Media in 2003–4, the program manager of Witness, Sam Gregory, gave a personal account of his involvement with a group working on behalf of indigenous peoples in a remote island in the Philippines. Apart from emphasizing the intractable challenges of localizing human rights discourse, Gregory cautions against the enthusiasm for immediate impact that circulating video footage generally evokes when perpetrators are caught in the act of violence. The emotive rush of imagistic witnessing, he suggests, accords a dangerous shrillness to advocacy work and often hampers the possibility of considered, meaningful dialogue in the short run. The model of *broadcasting* to undifferentiated masses across the globe flattens the impact of the footage to a simplistic tale of unmitigated violation and victimization. In its stead, and as an antidote to mass televisual broadcast, Gregory advocates smart *narrowcasting*, where the story and footage are carefully edited and tailored according to the needs of different constituencies, what he calls a "contextualized, embedded video advocacy strategy."[20] His NGO currently undertakes precisely this mode of nuanced, deliberative video advocacy sensitive to place and issue.

Another instance of this shift in perception about the emotive efficacy of conventional documentary visibility and mass-scale televisual broadcast of the ravages of war can be seen in the work of Just Vision, a nongovernmental group run by Ronit Avni to promote Israeli-Palestinian peace efforts in the civic domain rather than aggressive human rights monitoring of the conflict. The Israeli-Palestinian conflict is perhaps the world's most documented conflict. "Yet," Avni legitimately observes, "with all network and satellite television cameras trained on this sliver of land, and with numerous human rights organizations issuing reports, petitions, photographs, documentaries and more, it is difficult to gauge whether the scale and scope of abuses have decreased in any measurable way." Naming and shaming can go only so far.[21]

The group's visual documentary projects expressly reject the conventional human rights script of a clear demarcation between "violation, violator and remedy." Such a script, Avni avers, is as ineffective in mitigating the effects of violence as is the global televisual script that predominantly broadcasts the West Bank and Gaza as war zones populated by suicide bombers, maimed populations, barricades, and armed militia. The conflict is no doubt real, but, she maintains, so are the civic efforts that work across the bitter divide. What exactly are her terms of engagement? One of the projects involves conducting in-depth interviews of about 180 Palestinians and Israelis who have functioned as civic leaders rather than militants. These participants come from a wide spectrum of professional and social groups. The interview plan does not pit a personal story from the Israeli side with one from the Palestinian side. Instead all participants are asked to name up to "ten historical events and up to four personal events that have shaped their understanding of the conflict and inspired them to take action."[22] The results are aggregated and annotated with the aid of digital technology to produce an immensely complex narrative that resists annexation by either the polarizing news byte of televisual interpretation or films that represent the occupied territories as zones of unmitigated violence. In this regard Avni's and Gregory's efforts come close to the dissensual mode in the graphic novels of Joe Sacco, a mode that consciously sets out to challenge the visual repertoire of dominant media representations.

The work of Gregory and Avni helps us trace the transition from an enthusiasm for transparent image-based human rights advocacy (something akin to the shock-and-awe phenomenon heralded by CNN in the First Gulf War) to a more nuanced understanding of the role of the technologies of visual witnessing of conflict. It is precisely this shift from a transparent capture of atrocities through storytelling and direct video footage to a complex grasp of the multiple perceptual and affective fields within which witnessing occurs that offers a critical point of entry into the phenomenon of novelization in wartime. The significance of novelization in this era of humanitarian wars lies not just in the increasing use of storytelling and testimonial documentation to generate a diffuse global empathy and outrage at the ever-escalating ravages of war. It lies critically in *offering multiple fields of perception*—points of view, as theorists of the novel might put it—through both the conventional novel and other multimedia forms of expressivity. If by novelization we understand the shifting horizons, both formal and ideological, of literary fiction in different technological eras as well as the adoption of the generic conventions of the novel by other media forms, then Gregory's and Avni's attempts to inject perspectival and characterological depth into their videos on human rights violations can be seen as novelistic in their orientation.

Modern War as Idea, Sensorium, and Literary Form

The French revolutionary and Napoleonic wars at the end of the long eighteenth century provide a productive point of entry in considering the role that media technologies play in making war permeate the public sphere. Gillian Russell, a Romanticist scholar specializing in the theaters of war of that era, writes that "the status of twenty-first century wars as complex multimedia events has a precedent in the way . . . eighteenth century print culture configured the wars of that era as reading experiences, imaginatively connecting the coffee houses or drawing rooms of Britain with the bloody fields of Malplaquet or Waterloo."[23] Just as the revolution in print culture brought wars into the homes of countless Britons and Europeans, so also the penetration of information and communication technologies into our everyday lives makes our twenty-first-century wars a thoroughly mediated yet intimate experience for large masses across the world. War in both eras becomes an indelible part of public consciousness, though the jury may still be out on whether our digital era makes the experience of wartime more palpable than the print capitalist era of Romanticism. In her study of war in the Romantic era, Mary Favret questions assumptions about the correlation between technological advancement and an incremental increase in the *felt* experience of war as proximate and immediate. She takes particular issue with modernist writers like Virginia Woolf for dismissing two whole centuries of literary production on the experience of war. That the First World War was felt far more acutely than the Napoleonic wars due to advances in radio communication technology, and the Second World War even more acutely, is something that Woolf made much of when writing about the generation of Jane Austen and its presumed immunity from the realities of war:

> In 1815 England was at war, as England is now. And it is natural to ask, how did their war—the Napoleonic war—affect them?.... The answer is a very strange one. The Napoleonic wars did not affect the great majority of those writers at all. The proof of that is to be found in the work of two great novelists—Jane Austen and Walter Scott. Each lived through the Napoleonic wars, each wrote through them, neither of them in all their novels mentioned the Napoleonic wars.... Wars were then remote.... The rumours of battle took a long time to reach England.... Compare that with our state today. Today we hear the gunfire in the Channel. We turn on the wireless; we hear an airman telling us how this very afternoon he shot down a raider; his machine caught fire; he plunged into the sea; the light turned green and then black; he rose to the top and was greeted by a trawler. Scott never saw sailors drowning at Trafalgar; Jane Austen never heard the cannon roar at Waterloo. Neither of them heard Napoleon's voice as we hear Hitler's.... That immunity from war lasted all through the nineteenth century.[24]

Favret objects to Woolf's refusal to distinguish between the actual scene of war and its mediation through the wireless: "Her war was brought to her by the wireless radio, by disembodied voices in the air.... Has she actually witnessed sailors drowning? Planes crashing into the sea?"[25]

The conceits of immediacy and proximity are but the effects of technology. To that extent, in the confines of her secluded study Woolf was as much "immune" from war as was Austen. Favret does not address the scale of impact that technological innovations in each era enable, that is, the topological scaling up of the public experience of mediated war from Britain to Europe to Asia and the world at large as we move from the Napoleonic wars to World War II. This amplified topological reach of technology is what makes the experience of war *immanently global* in our digital era, even as, like

Woolf in her secluded study, many of us never really *hear* or *see* in person the devastation it causes.

The key issue here is not whether Woolf experienced war more palpably than Austen but that it was Austen's era that made it even possible to imagine wartime as a *shared* experience among vast sections of the civilian population, and that it was the growth of print technology and the subsequent emergence of the idea of a public sphere that were fundamental to this shift. Hence in literary and cultural history more broadly, the late eighteenth and early nineteenth centuries are critical to the emergence of modern wartime as a distinct experience in the public sphere, that is, wartime as it emerged explicitly as idea, sensorium, and aesthetic form.

The idea of war was no longer circumscribed by the actual scene of battle but encompassed realms of thought, imagination, and everyday life in ways unprecedented in previous eras. Not for nothing did Clausewitz refer to the Napoleonic wars as "total war," even if, as is well known, he did not quite mean it in the sense I invoke here, as an all-pervasive epistemological and affective experience. Two responses by major thinkers, one post-Napoleonic, the other pre-Napoleonic, illustrate this shift in the contemplation of war. For Hegel the many wars of the eighteenth century, culminating in the Napoleonic wars, enabled a philosophical formulation of a metahistorical idea of war that stood as the epistemological correlate of the Idea of History. Just as Napoleon sacrificed millions of lives for an ideal, the march of History as general Idea demonstrates a falling by the wayside of particular passions and ambitions, trials and tribulations of specific individuals: "It is not the general idea that is implicated in opposition and combat, and that is exposed to danger. It remains in the background, untouched, uninjured. This may be called *the cunning of reason*—that it sets the passions to work for itself while that which develops its existence through such impulsion pays the penalty, and suffers loss. . . . The particular is for the most part of too trifling value as compared to the general: individuals are sacrificed and abandoned."[26] For William Godwin, writing in 1793 on the eve of the French Revolution and at the end of a century that had already experienced massive war casualties, the evils of war could be countered only by the force of imagination. He urges his readers to conjure with every power of imaginative insight the most minute particulars of war-induced devastation. Nothing short of a novelistic imagination that recounts in painstaking detail the evils of war across the expanses of devastated humanscapes—the world of the maimed, the widowed, the orphaned, the abandoned—can allay the evils of war:

We can have no adequate idea of this evil unless we visit, at least in the imagination, a field of battle. Here men deliberately destroy each other by thousands, without resentment against, or even knowledge of, each other. The plain is strewed with death in all its forms. Anguish and wounds display the diversified modes in which they can torment the human frame. Towns are burned; ships are blown up in the air, while mangled limbs descend on every side; the fields are laid desolate; the wives of inhabitants exposed to brutal insult; and their children driven forth to hunger and nakedness.[27]

Jan Mieszkowski observes that for "the philosophers of [this] period, these bloody performances became paradigmatic objects of inquiry, as if viewing Austerlitz or Waterloo could help them decide whether the course of human affairs was governed by agency or chance, whether a given set of acts was an autonomous dynamic or a side effect of a broader process."[28] While wartime was experienced in the era of Romanticism as a shared sensibility beyond the confines of the actual scene of battle, the idea that war was more than the physical scene of battle originated before the era of Napoleonic wars. Hobbes and Rousseau both wrote about two distinct domains of war. In *Leviathan* Hobbes distinguished between the physical battleground and the virtual domain of will, planning, and explicit communication of intention to go to war.[29] The latter built on and in turn regenerated a field of proto-philosophical inquiry on the power and politics of state making, which for generations to come a mere focus on the actual happenings on the battlefield could hardly illuminate. In *Emile, or On Education*, Rousseau went a step further and explored the efficacy of historical writing as a theatrical stage on which conflicts of an era are played out. Ironically, for Rousseau graphic historical accounts of an actual battle were incapable of providing insights into the true causes of conflict. War was but the manifest outcome of a range of moral issues. A historian intent on giving an objective account of the spectacle of battle might entertain generations of readers and "show [people] in other times or other places and in such a way that the [student] can see the stage without ever being able to act on it." But a mere focus on the war spectacle could never offer insights into the larger determinants of conflict, could never offer the student a deep view of human motivations. Appearing as an end in itself, the war spectacle is the "least instructive thing in the world."[30]

This inability of historians to see war in its multifarious dimensions was already beginning to be radically overcome by the time of *Emile*'s publication in 1762. Transformations in media technology, changing notions of territorial protection, sovereignty, and sense of history, and the emergence of a new ethics of the market based on mutual dependencies and obligations across vast distances, all contributed to a radically new perceptual field within which wars in the long eighteenth century were publicly experienced in Europe and, more specifically, in Britain. By some accounts at least 194 battles were fought by the British during the eighteenth century. War became a pervasive horizon for political and moral deliberations in the public sphere. While the Seven Years War (1756–63) established Britain as an imperial power, the French Revolution and the subsequent Napoleonic wars brought home the importance of protecting the territorial integrity of Britain and consolidating a mode of cultural belonging that affirmed the superiority of the English over the French.

Two landmark legislative developments—the lapse of the Licensing Act in 1695 that removed government censorship on print publishing and a revised Copyright Law around 1774—had already led to a flourishing print culture that in turn fed off a revolutionary shift in the perception of British armed forces as the keepers of the nation's integrity.[31] Scholars have traced in substantial detail shifts in public perception of military personnel across the entire period. Far from being respectable figures in the early decades of the war-torn century, soldiers were perceived as licentious, violent, and immoral. An increasing sense of Britain's global importance, especially in a few successful military campaigns by the mid-eighteenth century, coupled with a flourishing print and performance culture, gradually turned the tide of public perception, so that military personnel were seen as men of honor and feeling. Russell notes that soldiers were a large part of the theatergoing audience, and a range of plays reinforced the noble theatricality of military action. The grandeur on the stage matched the display of military might in parades on land and sea, and both spectacles fed into an array of print genres—pamphlets, songbooks, and chapbooks—that circulated rapidly among the masses.[32] In the last decade of the eighteenth century, England witnessed a surge of patriotic feeling that was fed largely by the increasing velocity of print circulation. This phenomenon went hand in hand with a growing sensitivity to the horrors of warfare and recognition of the importance of the distinction between Britain as home, the domain of peace and stability, and the rest of Europe as a potential threat that only the patriotic armed forces could keep at bay. This sentiment was integral to an increasing clamor for an ever more powerful Britain that imperially entrenched its powers in faraway foreign shores. This fiction of brave soldiers battling to protect the home territory while Britain extended its economic and political might overseas through the work of its industrious citizens was the staple of much writing emanating from this era.[33]

In tandem with these transformative public imaginings of war, at least three significant themes emerged in what we would now consider literature proper of the eighteenth century. Each of these resonates with the novelistic preoccupations of our own war-saturated era.

One was the reconfiguration of the soldier as a man of feeling and aesthetic tastes whose hard physical exterior was offset by a capacity to imagine the pain of war through extended reenactment and reflection. The flip side of this was the concomitant abstraction of the soldier into a solid citizen and an alibi for patriotic pride. The character of Uncle Toby in Laurence Sterne's *Tristram Shandy* is a classic illustration of the soldier as a man of reflection. Toby's groin wound inflicted during the Siege of Namur does not begin to heal until he literally reconstructs a model of the siege in his back garden and can work through his war-induced trauma by reliving the significant moments of combat. In the process he confronts the moment of his injury and aesthetically transforms the ruins of war into an imaginative construct and a structure of feeling. Read retroactively in the contemporary register of trauma and healing, it is not implausible to conceive of Toby's hobbyhorse allegorically as a slow psychoanalytics of recovery from posttraumatic stress disorder. In the affective register of his times, however, a more plausible reading would cast Uncle Toby in a *sentimental* mode, by which one means, to cite James Chandler, "a circuit of reflections. . . . passion that has been mediated by a sympathetic passage through a virtual point of view."[34] This recasting of the soldier as a noble "man of feeling" who struggles to make sense of the sensorium of war through an imaginative projection is the prototypical literary contribution of the eighteenth-century war novel to our times. This empathetic projection across worlds of war through a mediated gaze is, as I argue throughout the book, the fundamental affective structure of the novel worlds of our time.

The second theme that finds substantial expression in the works of this era is the entanglement of the home and the trench and a pronounced sensitivity to the coextensiveness of war injury from battlefields to the privacy of the domestic space. The analogy of the wounded soldier and the weeping widow pervaded Romantic poetry around the time of the French Revolution.[35] Several poems published between 1798 and 1815 feature the war widow; these include the anonymously published "The Widow," Wordsworth's "The Female Vagrant," and poems such as "Anna's Complaint" and "The Widow's House." In an interesting twist to the given public rhetoric of the citizen-soldier (inevitably male) as the protector of the private domain made up of wives, mothers, and daughters, Favret sees the collapsing of this gendered public/private boundary in literary imaginings of the wounded or dying soldier. The public face of the soldier-protector works on the assumption of his omnipotence and invulnerability. It demands a level of abstraction of the might of the armed forces that is impossible to sustain if one turns to the battered and maimed body of the soldier. The unsustainable nature of this divide becomes even more acute when one considers the historical fact that it was often privates who actually fought in the battle fronts and were exposed to injury.[36] As an injured body, the soldier is interestingly transfigured into the *private* domain of vulnerability that defines the condition of those meant to be under his protection, namely, the hapless wife, mother, and daughter. In the poetic imaginings of the Romantic era, the violence of war not surprisingly is coded in graphically domestic and feminized terms and often transposed onto the body of the soldier's wife. A brief example illustrates this phenomenon. In a poem by Robert Merry titled "The Wounded Soldier," published in 1799, an injured and disfigured soldier returns home to experience the shock and horror of his family as they gaze at him. His mother faints, his father "look'd to heaven with streaming eyes," and his wife "sunk, alas! To rise no more."[37] The ravages of war that he narrowly managed to escape consume his home, and he is no longer recognizable as the public face of valorous citizenship. Romantic war poetry provided this radical opening to the conception of war as a mode of violence that cannot be contained within the public sphere of citizenship talk because of its repeated infliction on the private world of civilians. This conception of war resonated across literary worlds from that era to ours. In fact it is vastly amplified in our context for, as I noted earlier, after the cold war era civilian casualties massively outnumber the military's, more often than not as the result of direct hits. As for casualties from shock, dislocation, dispossession, and deprivation, one need only take their measure from the large-scale media coverage that now inevitably accompanies any war.

The third thematics of war literature in the Romantic age is the idea of wartime as a *condition* rather than an *event*. "War tears, rends. War rips open, eviscerates. War scorches. War dismembers. War *ruins.*" So runs Susan Sontag's grim inventory of the impact of war on civilian lifescapes in the wake of Sarajevo, Kabul, Jenin, and 9/11 Manhattan.[38] *Wartime* is the title of Paul Fussell's book on what he describes as the "psychological and emotional culture of Americans and Britons" during the Second World War.[39] Both Sontag and Fussell draw on yet another conceptual contribution from Romantic literature, one that envisions war less as a finite event with clearly demarcated agents than as a condition that affects the spirit of an age. In theorizing the contribution of Romantic writers as "architects of modern wartime," Favret identifies four sets of relations that these writers established to the physical wars waged in battlegrounds across Europe: the relations of distance, temporality, epistemology, and affect: "the felt distance from crucial events, the limits of knowledge in a mediated culture, the temporal gaps in the transmission of information, and finally, the difficulty of finding sounds or forms to which feelings can attach itself."[40]

Each of these, when mapped on the corpus of Romantic literature, produces an understanding of war as the shaper of a nation's everyday life. This Romanticist theorization of wartime as an overarching affective and aesthetic horizon has been critical to subsequent literary theorizations of war writing, from World War I to our time. Modernism is unthinkable without World War I, as is postmodernism without World War II and the Vietnam and Korean wars. The wars of decolonization are indelibly connected to the rise of the postcolonial rubric in literary studies. Likewise the global wars since the end of the cold war and the iconic mediatization of 9/11 overwhelmingly constitute the horizon of literary theorizations in our global era.

From the Dossier to the Spectacle

My schematic account signals the emergence in the eighteenth century of the idea of war as an experience that incorporates several things at once: the actual physical scene of battle, its mediation in the public sphere through technological advancement, its epistemological implications for ideas of governance and political community formation, its infiltration into everyday life, its affective structures, and its imaginative transfiguration in the hands of creative writers and artists. Each of these is a significant element in the orizations of global wars in our times. Actual physical battles are no longer delimited by real sites like Waterloo. The sites of contemporary war are indiscriminate and straddle civilian domains with impunity. Digital technological advancement likewise has made nonsense of the distance between physical war and its public mediation. If print technology in the late eighteenth century enabled the imagination of war at a distance, digital technology brings war physically into civilian homes. Technological innovations in our era *wage* war at the same time as they *mediate* it. They are both death-delivering and sensitizing. They both destroy and inform. Wars of our era also give rise to new philosophical reflections on the fragility of national borders, on the various nonstate agents that have become major actors in the global theaters of war, on the emergence of deterritorialized political communities, and on transformed notions of alliance and enmity. As for war's quiet infiltration into everyday lives, for vast swaths of people around the globe, there is nothing quiet or under the surface about this experience. War literally and materially circumscribes their every move and every breath, as these two entries in Riverbend's blog novel *Baghdad Burning* so graphically demonstrate:

Sunday. August 17, 2003.

WAKING UP

Waking up anywhere in Iraq these days is a trial. It happens in one of two ways: either slowly or with a jolt. The slow process works like this: you're hanging in a place on the edge of consciousness . . . something creeps up around. . . . A warm heavy fog. It's the heat . . . 120F on the cooler nights. Your eyes flutter open and they search the dark in dismay—electricity has gone off. The ceiling fan is slowing down and you are now fully awake. . . . The other way to wake up is to be jolted into reality with the sound of a gun-shot, explosion or yelling. You sit up, horrified and panicked. . . . An attack? A bomb? Or may be it's just an American midnight raid?

Monday. August 18, 2003.

ANOTHER DAY . . .

Normal day today. We are up at early morning, did the usual "around the house things," you know—check if the water tank is full, try to determine when the electricity will be off, checked if there was enough cooking gas. (7–8)

The mapping of the formal dimensions of warfare onto literary forms and genres in each era is uncanny. The revolutionary wars of the Romantic age found their literary correlate in some of the most elevating poetry of the time, while the display of military and patriotic pride found expression in the theaters of war. The novels subtly captured those quiet undulations of wartime that inevitably shaped the worlds of ordinary people. In writing about the historical novel, György Lukács notes that the "inner life of a nation is linked with the modern mass army in a way it could not have been" before the French Revolution.[41]

This novelistic depiction of the coextensiveness of the nation's inner life with its militarized persona takes fascinatingly new forms in the cold war era. The cold war was warfare by surveillance and intelligence rather than the hot fire of blitz and bombardment. The threefold polarization of the world—brilliantly allegorized in Orwell's *1984* as Eurasia, Eastasia, and Oceania—and an overwhelming focus on strategies of containment of the threat of nuclear war brought to the front line of war not armed soldiers but spies, those superlative agents of intelligence. Intelligence agencies became epicenters of the cold war, and the materiality of war itself was manifested in rows and rows of folders in boxes, drawers, and locked cabinets. Not surprisingly spy fiction became the most popular novelistic genre in that era, and as David Pascoe remarks, many of these books have titles that evoke the bureaucratic infrastructure of cold war intelligence: Kingsley Amis's *The James Bond Dossier* (1965), Adam Hunt's *The Berlin Memorandum* (1965), Frederick Forsyth's *The Odessa File* (1972). Len Deighton's *The Ipcress Files* (1962) is actually written in the form of a secret dossier.[42] Tales of treason and patriotically driven smart intelligence work that characterize so many of the plots of these novels go to the heart of the moral conundrum of the era: How does one preserve the dominance of the First World while averting nuclear annihilation? A character in Norman Mailer's magisterial fictional account of the cold war, *Harlot's Ghost* (1992), puts his finger on the dilemma of regulating espionage appointments: "In Intelligence we look to discover the compartmentalization of the heart. We made an in depth study once in the CIA and learned to our dismay (it was really horror!) that one-third of the men and women who could pass our security clearance were divided enough—handled properly—to be turned into agents of a foreign power."[43]

If the secret world of intelligence gathering served as the leitmotif of cold war fiction, its radical opposite—the all too visible spectacle of war—provides the leitmotif for novels written after 1989. But the transition to the spectacular has not been all that sudden. "The terrorists were the first to have waged an information war," Paul Virilio wrote with frightening prescience in 1982; "the explosion only existed because it was simultaneously coupled to a multimedia explosion."[44] Another anticipatory remark, this one by a character in Don DeLillo's *Underworld*, likens the terrorist act to a radically new kind of screen authorship. The technologized terror script began to be graphed onto our collective imaginations before the *ur*-event of 2001 actually occurred. The globally hypermediated 9/11 explosions and the subsequent wars in Iraq and Afghanistan were but the inevitable fulfillment of a technological momentum that has been gathering steady pace since the cold war. One remembers Hannah Arendt's wondrous yet tremulous thoughts in *The Human Condition* on the fragility of human habitation on earth after the *Sputnik* phenomenon. The atomic explosions in Japan and the phenomenon of automation in general had already exercised her anxieties about the annihilative potential of technology. While Arendt's dystopic vision in 1958 of an apocalyptic space and nuclear warfare did not quite materialize in her lifetime, the *Sputnik* moment of the opening up of the skies reverberates through many a literary work. It is experienced by DeLillo's character Erica Deming in *Underworld* as a symbolic frisson of the sky-high pyrotechnics to come: "It [*Sputnik*] flew at an amazing rate of speed over the North Pole, beep beep beep, passing just above us, evidently, at certain times. She could not understand how this could happen. *Were there other surprises coming, things we haven't been told about?* . . . All up and down the curving streets there were young trees and small new box shrubs and a sense of openness, a sense of seeing everything there is to see at a single glance, with nothing shrouded or walled or protected from the glare."[45] The sense of *everything there is to see in a single glance* foreshadows the digitized intensification of the visual regime of post-9/11 counterinsurgency and the increasing proliferation of visual technologies across the surface of the planet toward the latter half of the cold war era. Among the "other surprises coming," things that Erica wasn't "told about," was the visual unraveling, first through Vietnam, of the manic hubris of the bipolar cold war politics. The Vietnam War was the first televised war, and its explosive violence circulated in the global media with an obscene vividness never seen before. The war shattered all assumptions about the cold, systemic, and contained secretiveness of cold war maneuvers. The aesthetics and affect of the Vietnam misadventure were all too visible in literary and cultural spheres, in pop-art posters, antiwar songs, agit prop theater, artistic photography, blockbuster films, rock-n-roll music, novels, docufiction, and poetry. These forged a link with global eruptions in 1968 of various countercultural and political protests on the state of the world. They included widely televised spectacles of the black civil rights movement, the rise of the new left, the Prague Spring, the student protests on campuses in Berkeley, Mexico City, Paris, and Warsaw, and the radicalization of the feminist movement.

The high visibility of the Vietnam War in tandem with the televisuality of the 1968 uprisings can be seen as a critical transition point between the secret optics of cold war surveillance and the spectacular wars after 1989. It is not a coincidence that the key premises of Guy Debord's *The Society of the Spectacle* were formulated in the years leading up to Vietnam and 1968.

Nor is it surprising that the book gained such currency after the upheavals of 1968.[46] Published in 1967 and very much a product of the new left movement, Debord's Marxist classic defines the spectacle not as an array of images that flash before the eye but as "a social relationship among people, mediated by images." As a system the spectacle comes into being at the confluence of advanced capitalism, mass media, and governmentality. It is capital accumulated "to such a degree . . . that it becomes an image." By all accounts, the decade extending from the Cuban missile crisis in 1962 to the end of the Vietnam War in 1973 had seen the emergence of a global public sphere constituted primarily through televisual exposure of repeated crises in both capitalist and communist worlds. After a brief hiatus of six years, the spectacle of the cold war erupted once again in 1979 with the Soviet invasion of Afghanistan and the U.S. pushback through guerrilla insurgents, *mujahideens*, from the Muslim world. Exactly a decade later the world witnessed the end of the cold war in yet another spectacle: the fall of the Berlin Wall. In the 1994 preface to the third edition of his book Debord was in a position to differentiate the nature of the spectacle before and after 1989. If before—especially in the 1960s—spectacles alternated between the "concentrated" and "diffuse," the decade leading up to 1989 saw the emergence of the era of the "integrated" spectacle, that is, the ultimate virtualization of capital in the name of market democracy: "The spectacle has its roots in the fertile field of the economy, and it is the produce of this field which must in the end come to dominate the market. . . . This striving of the spectacle toward modernization and unification, together with all the other tendencies toward the simplification of society, was what in 1989 led the Russian bureaucracy, suddenly and as one man, to convert to the current ideology of democracy—in other words, to the dictatorial freedom of the Market, as tempered by the recognition of the rights of *Homo Spectator*."[47]

The triumph of the integrated spectacle had its imagistic correlate in the incessantly televised event of the fall of the Berlin Wall. Debord did not live to see the most spectacular "integration" of the spectacle at the turn of the century in the terrors of 9/11. However, unlike the spectacle of 1989, the world as *one* witnessed not the triumph of the market but its unraveling. What would he have made of this open theater of violence that paradoxically doubled as an *ur*-spectacle in the classic Debordian sense: the image as the ultimate commodity?[48] How might we interpret the relevance of this twenty-first-century spectacle? More specifically, how does the contemporary novel configure this act of war waged primarily as an ultimate media event?[49]

SIX
THE SKY IS FALLING:
THE NARRATIVE
SCREEN OF TERROR

Myriad iterations of Debord's society of the spectacle circulated as the visual horror of September 11 unraveled on screens around the world. Another auteur who was variously invoked as the world witnessed falling figures from the towers was Antonin Artaud, the celebrated exponent of the theater of cruelty. This chapter explores the ramifications for the world novel of the aesthetic excess of these visual and performative interpretations that came into play during this unprecedented act of terrorist warfare. How, I ask, does the contemporary novel constellate twenty-first-century warfare as sensorium, performance, and spectacle? What narrative and tropological strategies does it marshal? I begin with an exploration of the aesthetic and ethical conundrum that the performative model of the theater of cruelty poses in accounting for the 9/11 terrorist attack, and then explicate in some detail how the novel addresses this conundrum. The tense interplay between performance as trope and performance as terror is central to my explication.

Art Spiegelman's iconic graphic novel *In the Shadow of No Towers* begins with a preface entitled "The Sky Is Falling," where he vividly describes the prolonged temporality of the end-of-the-world kind of terror he experienced on seeing the burning towers; a "slow motion diary," he calls it. Tempered by his reflections on the radical transformation of the United States and the world and his desire to make sense of the immediate horror of the event and its long-term ramifications, the preface is a snapshot of a novelistic imagination at work. It promises a careful calibration of the event, points of view, plots, characters, tropes, and images—in other words, a mode of aesthetic meditation that is simultaneously sensitive to the incomprehensible horror of the event and distant from the visual noise of the spectacle. The object of his meditation is an image that haunted him for years after the tragedy, of the "looming north tower's glowing bones just before it vaporized" (see figure 6.1). As a counterimage to the infinitely mediatized falling towers in public broadcasts, Spiegelman brings into view this visual tableau that was firmly grafted in his mind's eye but not seen in any media coverage. In plate 4 of his book, itself bound in a rectangular frame, he graphs his experience in these words: "A roar. We turn to see the bones of the tower glow and shimmy in the sky. Ever so slowly it cascades into itself, awesome . . . sublime." The visual experience of this glowing tower becomes the leitmotif in this graphic novel, appearing on every page in various stages of vaporization. The slowly eviscerating glow of the North Tower captures the disintegration of the world as Spiegelman and countless New Yorkers experienced it on September 11, 2001.

While primarily referring to his own and the collective paranoia of New Yorkers about the imminent ending of their world after 9/11, Spiegelman was perhaps not unaware of the reference to the "falling sky" in the writings of one of the foremost proponents of the theater of cruelty in the 1930s, Antonin Artaud. In a 1938 piece entitled "No More Masterpieces," Artaud averred, "We are not free. And the sky can yet fall on our heads. And the theatre has been created to teach us that first of all."[1] One cannot but be struck by the resonance between Artaud's exposition on the theater of cruelty and the spectacle that was unleashed on the world that September morning: "The theatre of cruelty proposes to resort to a mass spectacle; to seek in the agitation of tremendous masses convulsed and hurled against each other, a little of that poetry of festivals and crowds when, all too rarely nowadays, the people pour out into the streets. The theatre must give us everything that is in crime, love, war or madness, if it wants to recover its necessity. . . . Hence this appeal to cruelty and terror . . . on a vast scale."[2]

FIGURE 6.1. From *In the Shadow of No Towers*, by Art Spiegelman.

Artaud's focus on sensory violence, on the power of the spectacle over dialogue, on the potential of pure theater to agitate the masses into spilling out into the streets in fear and terror not surprisingly found resonance among many performing artists, writers, and scholars who saw in the spectacle of 9/11 the realization of the most sublime form of art, a "one-time" spectacle of the purest kind.[3] Una Chaudhuri, for instance, cites a *New York Times* editorial that featured a child's exclamation to his teacher when he saw burning bodies falling off the towers: "Look, Teacher, the birds are on fire!" Chaudhuri comments, "It's a vision worthy of Artaud and a truth we might do well to contemplate."[4] Brian Singleton called the experience "catharsis seeped into Artaudian fear as the perpetrators were themselves sacrificed within their performance."[5]

As against these readings, I suggest that there is a different aesthetic temporality at work in the novel, one that fosters distance from the performative *presence* of an event and its immediate impact on our senses. The novel's mediation of the spectacular and the sensational intervenes in an act of aesthetic deliberation to allow us to experience the event's magnitude in a symbolic rather than an indexical manner, to borrow from Peirce. I will develop this argument further as the chapter unfolds; first I consider the ramifications of interpreting the terrorist act as an Artaudian theatrical performance.

Artaud specifically emphasized the *impossibility* of such theater through his idea of the "one-time" temporality of cruelty in performance. Such a formulation is, in effect, the very opposite of conventional theatrical performance, which calls for repeated rehearsal and staging. Pure theater for Artaud escaped the death of repetition and representation and ripped through our normalized temporalities and patterns of performative expectations. He used the term *cruel* in this sense of something that cuts through our being and whose death is written into its very *singularity* as an unrepeatable performance. "Artaud wanted to erase repetition in general," says Derrida. "For him repetition was evil. . . . Repetition separates force, presence, and life from themselves. . . . This power of repetition governed everything that Artaud wished to destroy, and it has several names: God, Being, Dialectics."[6] Caught in the aporia of not being able to resign himself to theater as repetition and not being able to renounce the impossible idea of theater as nonrepetition,[7] his theater of cruelty stayed in the domain of the metaphorical. Its impossibility operated as an analogue of his ideal of the nonrepresentative theater, a phenomenon that Susan Sontag referred to as the "failure of practice."[8] This is not a failure to be lamented but to be upheld as a distinct phenomenology of pain that is ever present in the horizon of pure theatricality. Artaud's reference to the proleptic temporality of the "falling sky"—*the sky can yet fall*—and its indefinite postponement ought to be read in conjunction with such a phenomenology of apprehension of the impossible ordeal of theater.

The gap between Artaud's hypothetical "can . . . yet" and Spiegelman's present continuous apprehension—"the sky is falling"—is often lost in the many extrapolations from the theater of cruelty to the spectacle of 9/11 horror. In all his extreme rhetoric about falling skies and convulsed masses, Artaud was not talking about real-world disaster scenarios but the impossible performativity of the singular, nonrepetitive event in the domain of theatrical art. A similar morbid flourish can be seen in the manifestoes of Dadaism and Surrealism. Tristan Tzara in the Second Dada Manifesto of 1918 wrote, "We are like a raging wind that rips up the clothes of clouds and prayers. We are preparing the great spectacle of disaster, conflagration and decomposition. Preparing to put an end to mourning and replace tears by sirens spreading from one continent to another."[9] To literalize the metaphoricity and rhetorical violence of avant-garde art is a fundamentalism of sorts, no different from the fundamentalisms of believers who take the word of god in religious texts literally.[10]

But another kind of reading is possible here, one that heralds the death of avant-garde radicalism itself when it is literalized in a spectacle like 9/11. To *hear* the language of avant-garde art even as its rhetoric is exposed for its inadequacy to grasp the enormity of the event is truly to announce its death. The world witnessed this phenomenon in one of the most notoriously celebrated interventions on 9/11 soon after its occurrence, by the German composer Karlheinz Stockhausen: "[The attacks of 9/11 were] the greatest work of art imaginable for the whole cosmos. Minds achieving something in an act that we couldn't even dream of in music, people rehearsing like mad for ten years, preparing fanatically for a concert, and then dying, just imagine what happened there. You have people who are that focused on a performance and then five thousand [*sic*] people are dispatched to the afterlife, in a single moment. I couldn't do that. By comparison, we composers are nothing." The outrage that Stockhausen's remarks generated led to the cancellation of his concerts across the North Atlantic. He was forced to retract by admitting that what he conceived as an *über*-aesthetic spectacle was in truth a heinous act: "It's a crime because those involved didn't consent. They didn't come to the 'concert.' That's obvious. And no one announced that they risked losing their lives."[11]

There is a world of difference between being aesthetically shaken from political and moral torpor and the morbid aestheticization of an act of spectacular crime. In collapsing the two, the Stockhausen incident exposes the void at the heart of avant-garde aestheticism. What remains of the rhetorical and aesthetic force of the Dada Manifesto or Artaud's theater of cruelty when real-world catastrophes truly make the sirens go viral?

Aesthetic Distance

The sensationalism of responses by performance artists and musicians like Stockhausen stands in sharp contrast to the more considered response one finds in novels on the ethical conundrum of seeing an act of war as art.[12] This is not to say that novelists are necessarily better attuned ethically than theater and performance artists. In fact, as I stated in chapter 1, more than one novelist was willing to cede the genre's imaginative capital to terrorism's narrative hijacking. It is rather that, as I suggested earlier, the novel is less invested in the visceral impact of staging than in abstracting phenomena for deliberate narrative configuration. This gives it a capacity for the contemplation and distancing required to generate aesthetically complex portrayals of war spectacles. Don DeLillo's *The Falling Man* (2007) demonstrates the painstaking novelistic labor involved in reckoning with the sublime theatricality of the mediated war spectacle I have been talking about. To aesthetically world such acts of war is to assume a responsibility to confront its full horror. As if anticipating the challenges to his own crafting of *Falling Man*, DeLillo writes in 2001, "The event itself has no purchase on the mercies of analogy or simile. We have to take the shock and horror as it is. But living language is not diminished. The writer wants to understand what this day has done to us. . . . The writer begins in the towers, trying to imagine the moment desperately. Before politics, before history and religion, there is the primal terror. People falling from the Towers hand in hand. . . . The writer tries to give memory, tenderness and meaning to all that howling space."[13]

It is significant that *Falling Man* begins and ends with scenes—*that howling space*—from the collapsing towers. The sequence, however, is reversed: the opening pages describe an ash-covered Keith Neudecker emerging from the rubble after failing to rescue his friend Rumsey, and the last pages take us to the moments before Keith's miraculous emergence, the last moments of those in the two towers just after the planes struck. The movements of the tower—that marvel of technology—become central to Keith's consciousness for a few seconds. All he can feel are its "lurching," its "long sway left," its "rolling back" into vertical position, and its gradual implosion. These experiences are "massive," "undreamed of," for they witness the sublime destruction of an avowedly indestructible structure enabled by the might of advanced technology. As DeLillo says in his essay "In the Ruins of the Future," "The World Trade towers were not only an emblem of advanced technology but a justification in a sense, for technology's irresistible will to realize in solid form whatever becomes technologically allowable."[14] The people caught in the "crush of meshed steel" experience the counterforce of their technological prowess turned against them.

In this lethal conjoining of terror and technology at the epicenter of American-style hypercapitalism, one has never felt more acutely the imagistic force of Bakhtin's idea of the chronotope as a spatiotemporal matrix in the novel, a narrative conjuncture of a specific space-time continuum that "takes on flesh," that makes "palpable and visible" particular worldviews.[15] The iconography of the falling man against the collapsing Twin Towers on 9/11, combined with a cataclysmic "time and space of falling ash and near night" that transforms the street into the "world," provide the chronotopical frame of DeLillo's *Falling Man*:

> He was walking north through rubble and mud and there were people running past holding towels to their faces or jackets over their heads. They had handkerchiefs pressed to their mouths. They had shoes in their hands.... They ran and fell, some of them, confused and ungainly, with debris coming down around them, and there were people taking shelter under cars.
>
> The roar was still in the air, the buckling rumble of the fall. This was the world now. Smoke and ash came rolling down streets and turning corners, busting around corners, seismic tides of smoke, with office paper flashing past. Standard sheets with cutting edge, skimming, whipping past, otherworldly things in the morning pall.[16]

That terror of this kind can literally take on flesh becomes evident to the survivor protagonist, Keith Neudecker, when he visits a makeshift clinic to have shards of glass extracted from his flesh. The doctor tells him that survivors of suicide bombings often come back months later with "bumps" under their skin that are actually "tiny fragments of the suicide bomber's body ... that come flying outward with such force and velocity that they get wedged ... in the body of anyone who's in striking range" (16). These are "organic shrapnels," pellets of flesh under the skin.

While the character of Keith—and through him his entire domestic universe—becomes the obvious conduit for DeLillo's capture of the political and psychological terror of the event,[17] the mediated nature of the spectacle itself is aesthetically configured through ekphrastic rhetorical devices that foreground with startling acuity the conjoining of art, mediation, and terror in our times. These enable contemplation of the simulacral nature of the *ur*-spectacle, its animated iconicity, and its viral reproducibility—all of which have been identified as features of the digital transformation of the erstwhile Debordian spectacle.[18] Three recurrent motifs woven into the narrative structure are significant in this regard: the still-life paintings of the Italian modernist Giorgio Morandi; the falling man who walks on tightropes suspended between the buildings of lower Manhattan; and the shadowy world of the German art dealer Martin Ridnour, who was once part of a German terrorist outfit in the 1960s, the death of whose members was the object of a series of paintings by Gerhard Richter.

The sequence with the Morandi paintings is ethically the least fraught of the three. Keith's wife, Lianne, visits her mother, Nina, one evening. Her mother is a distinguished art historian, and Martin Ridnour, her partner, is an art dealer. Together Lianne and Martin gaze at the two still-life paintings of Morandi on the walls of Nina's apartment. One painting in particular fills the living room with a hushed grimness; it features several objects of domestic use. DeLillo's ekphrastic gesture is evident here: "The painting in question showed seven or eight objects, the taller ones set against a brushy slate background. The other items were huddled boxes and biscuit tins, grouped before a darker background. The full array, in unfixed perspective and mostly muted colors, carried an odd spare power" (49).

Two objects in particular from this artwork—tall, dark, smoky glass bottles against the slate background—reproduce for Lianne and Martin the ominous iconicity of the Twin Towers. Like the Twin Towers that symbolized a power that transcended the localized architectural grandeur of the Manhattan skyline, these objects acquire a looming symbolism that make them appear autonomous from their immediate context. As Martin says, "I'm looking at these objects, kitchen objects, but removed from the kitchen, free of the kitchen, the house everything practical and functioning. And I must be back in another time zone. . . . Because I keep seeing the towers in this still life" (49).

Just before he makes this observation, he has a tense conversation with his partner, Nina, about the events of September 11. While Nina sees the event purely in ethical terms as an evil that kills the innocent, Martin is emphatic that the culpability of the West needs to be reckoned with in bringing the world to this perilous juncture. Nina's political views are clear: the attackers live in stagnant societies and wage war out of panic; theirs is an attack on civilization itself. How long can they continue to blame the West for their problems? Accordingly, for Nina the Morandi paintings actually resist visual extrapolation of the kind Martin claims: "These shapes are not translatable to modern towers, twin towers. It's a work that rejects that kind of extension or projection. It takes you inward, down and in. That's what I see here, half buried, something deeper than things or shapes of things" (111).

Martin's response, "We're all targets now," irrespective of where people stand in the political spectrum, is then symbolically projected onto the Morandi painting, where utterly innocuous objects of domestic use look like the doomed towers:

> They looked together.
> Two of the taller items were dark and somber, with smoky marks and smudges, and one of them partly concealed by a long-necked bottle. The bottle was a bottle, white. The two dark objects, too obscure to name, were the things that Martin was referring to.
> "What do you see?" he said.
> She saw what he saw. She saw the towers. (49)

Martin's statement, "We're all targets now," recalls Rey Chow's description of the period after the Atomic Age as the age of the world target. To see the world not just as a picture in the Heideggerian sense but as a target is to see it as an object of potential destruction. To accord a target maximal visibility through ever more sophisticated technology is simultaneously to prime it for destruction. W. J. Perry, a former U.S. undersecretary of defense, once said, "If I had to sum up current thinking on precision missiles and saturation weaponry in a single sentence, I'd put it like this: once you can see the target, you can expect to destroy it."[19]

While DeLillo does not directly address this convergence of hypervisualization and targeted warfare in his plot, he configures the mediated nature of what Baudrillard calls the "Absolute Event" through precisely such motifs as Morandi's tall glass bottles that figure as simulacra of the two towers as targets.[20] Lianne and Martin visualize the towers' destruction through their projected simulation in the painting. Neither was an eyewitness of the actual event, but like millions of others, they did witness the hypervisualization of the buildings in the decades preceding their destruction. As Martin says with some irritation, "Weren't the Towers built as fantasies of wealth and power that would one day become fantasies of destruction? You build a thing like that so you can see it coming down. The provocation is obvious. What other reason would there be to go so high and then double it, do it twice? It's a fantasy, so why not do it twice? You're saying, Here it is, bring it down" (116). His words recall Baudrillard's phrase "precession of simulacra," the idea that simulacra *precedes* the real in our mediated age. The destruction of the towers was written into their very iconicity, and the real destruction was but a realization of the destiny that awaited it. The Morandi painting in DeLillo's ekphrastic imagination accrues meaning as an intermedial space of evidence for this doubling of global capital's provocative fantasy that compels a destructive response from parts of the world that cannot partake of its promised plenitude. For those like Nina who resist such interpretations, the artwork is pure, self-referential materiality.

Falling as Performance

Another iconic animation of the 9/11 attacks that gives the novel its name is the figure of the falling man. It has several referents in DeLillo's text, real and fictional, and he deploys all of these brilliantly to capture the psychic projections of his characters as well as the anxieties surrounding the circulation of the original iconic image. The figure of the young man in a white shirt with his knee bent diving from the World Trade Center became one of the ubiquitous images of 9/11. Photographed by Richard Drew and named "Falling Man" by Tom Junod in an *Esquire* essay, the image inspired several journalistic searches for the identity of the man.[21] The image itself was removed from circulation on September 12, but it remained suspended in the digital realm, generating many documentaries and feature articles. In DeLillo's novel this mediated emblem of the catastrophe—its world-making power—features in its original only once, as Keith witnesses the fall:

> The *world was this as well*, figures in windows a thousand feet up, dropping into free space, and the stink of fuel fire, and the steady rip of sirens in the air. . . .
>
> There was something else then, outside all this, not belonging to this, aloft. He watched it coming down. A shirt came down out of the high smoke, a shirt lifted and drifting in the scant light and then falling again, down toward the river. (4)

The second reference is to the image and appears toward the end of the novel, when Lianne remembers the horror she felt on seeing its aesthetic perfection:

> It hit her hard when she first saw it, the day after, in the newspaper. The man headlong, the towers behind him. The mass of the towers filled the frame of the picture. The man falling, the towers contiguous . . . the enormous soaring lines, the vertical column stripes. The man with blood on his shirt, she thought, or burn marks, and the effect of the columns behind him, the composition, she thought, darker stripes for the nearer tower . . . lighter for the other, and the mass, the immensity of it, and the man set almost precisely between the rows of darker and lighter stripes. Headlong, free fall, she thought, and this picture burned a hole in her mind and heart, dear God, he was a falling angel and his beauty was horrific. (222)

For a novelist who in his other works has extensively transcribed the artifactual reality of media worlds in late modernity, DeLillo in *Falling Man* surprisingly does not directly plot the influence of the media in making 9/11 a world event.[22] Instead he experiments with the architectonics of mediation through the figure of another falling man, Janiak, an acrobat and performance artist. At various points in the novel, Janiak stages precarious acts of tightrope walking between tall buildings across Manhattan. The real-life shock of seeing figures falling from the World Trade Center is transposed onto the psychic projections of characters such as Lianne who are horrified at the precariousness of Janiak's performance and are made to relive their anguish at witnessing the falling figures from the Trade Center:

> A man dangling there, above the street, upside down. He wore his business suit, one leg bent up, arms at his sides. A safety harness was barely visible, emerging from his trousers at the straightened leg and fastened to the decorative rail of the viaduct. . . . He brought it back, of course, those stark moments in the burning towers when people fell or were forced to jump. . . .
>
> There were people shouting up at him, outraged at the spectacle, the puppetry of human desperation, a body's last fleet breath and what it held. It held the gaze of the world, she thought. There was the awful openness of it, the single falling figure that trails a collective dread, body coming down among us all. And, now . . . this little theatre piece. (33)

The uncanny doubling with the falling man of the Trade Center is all too obvious here, as is the evocation of the mediated nature of his symmetrical fall that "held the gaze of the world." Is DeLillo simply being gratuitous and aesthetically indulgent in his playfulness with this doomed figure? Before I answer, it is worth noting that there are at least two real-life referents to whom Janiak's acrobatic performance could correspond. One is a BASE jumper and skydiver named Jeb Corliss who was arrested in 2006 for trying to jump from the Empire State Building. He had previously attempted similar stunts from the Eiffel Tower, the Golden Gate Bridge, and the Petronas Towers.[23] Another is a performance artist, Kerry Skarbakka, who gained notoriety after 9/11 when he staged leaps from the Museum of Contemporary Art at Chicago.[24] He had previously photographed himself falling from treetops, scaffolding, billboards, rooftops, cliff edges, and staircases. His portfolio of many precarious acts of falling is framed by a serious contemplation of his art, which he sees as a struggle to "keep oneself from falling." Entitled "The Struggle to Right Oneself," the online catalogue of his performance art begins with an invocation of Heidegger's ruminations on the "thrown-ness" of *Dasein* and the implied precariousness of human existence. He goes on to add, "We live in a world that constantly tests our stability in various other forms. War and rumors of war, issues of security, effects of globalization, and the politics of identity are external gravities turned inward, serving to further threaten the precarious balance of self, exaggerating negative feelings of control. This photographic work is in response to this delicate state."[25]

That DeLillo noted the outrage that Skarbakka's post-9/11 Chicago performance evoked can be deduced from his wry, self-reflexive, fictive New School panel discussion on Janiak's acrobatics entitled "Heartless Exhibitionist or Brave New Chronicler of the Age of Terror?" (220). What does DeLillo intend in generating this composite fictional figure of the acrobat who "performs" the falling man? In the first instance he wishes to highlight the *artifice* of performance that cannot begin to be commensurate with the horror of the actual death leaps. Skarbakka, for instance, is clear about how *staged* his performance is, how very carefully he and his team calibrate risk in planning each jump: "Using myself as model with the aid of climbing gear and other rigging, I photograph the body as it dangles from dangerous precipices or tumbles down flights of stairs. . . . It is necessary to point out that I do not consider myself a glorified stuntman, nor do I wish to become a sacrifice to art. Therefore, safety is an important factor; however, the work does carry with it a potential risk of personal injury as I engage the moment."[26]

The novel also highlights the role played by Janiak's sibling, a software engineer, in helping the acrobat with the right equipment to perform his precarious acts. When Janiak does die at the age of thirty-nine, heart failure and low blood pressure are cited as reasons. In deploying the Janiak figure in an interventionist mode, much like the artists of the Situationist International in the 1970s, the novel quite explicitly refuses to conflate the performative precarity of this staged mode of falling with the actual experience of the hundreds of men and women leaping to their deaths that fatal morning.

At the same time, in conceiving the acrobatic figure of the falling man as a verisimilitude of the iconic image of the figure falling in perfect symmetry against the vertical lines of the two towers, DeLillo highlights both the lifelike quality that inheres in the very *artifice* of mediated images in our digital age and the real-life effects they have on our worlds. W. J. T. Mitchell uses the term *biopicture* to theorize this new symbolic conjoining of life and image, of the real and the virtual. The biopicture is the icon animated, "given motion and the appearance of life by means of the technologies of biology and information." With its origins in the popular domain of Steven Spielberg's *Jurassic Park*, this coming together of technology and the biosciences, argues Mitchell, has imbued images with a lifelike capacity to intervene in real-life events and to fundamentally transform our sense of engagement with the world. The following features make visible the biopicture's presence in our public spheres: "instantaneous reproduction and viral circulation; the irruption of twins, doubles and multiples in the sphere of public, mass consumed imagery; the reduction of human form to bare life or to mere image such as a corpse waiting to be mutilated, defaced or destroyed; the corresponding loss of identity, the proliferation of images of facelessness and heedlessness."[27] We recognize almost all of these qualities in the horrific iconicity of the falling man. In tandem with the planes crashing into the two towers, this image has symbolized for the world the impetus for the military misadventure that until recently went under the name "War on Terror." The real-life effects of this quintessentially twenty-first-century, biopictorial war continue to reverberate across the globe.

Shades of Richter

DeLillo's contemplative aesthetics of terror's biopictorial iconicity in *Falling Man* takes yet another interesting turn in his historical braiding of another corpus of artistic works, by the painter Gerhard Richter, on a postwar German terrorist group, the Baader-Meinhof Group. Richter's paintings were based on a rich personal archive of forensic photographs, police reports, newspaper articles, posters, and televisual images that he had collected over a decade.[28] His remediation through his art of this rich media archive of another period of terrorism finds a deep resonance in the novel. The character of Martin Ridnour is the conduit for this retrospective exploration. Martin's real name, we are told, is Ernst Hechinger, and he works as an art dealer with shady links to Europe. In her twenty years with Martin, all Nina knows is that he was a member of a group called Kommune 1 in Germany (the group that emerged from the German student movement in the 1960s) and that in his Berlin apartment he kept a poster of the nineteen wanted members of this group. This subplot is a fictionalization of the Baader-Meinhof episode in postwar German history. More particularly, the novel stages an exposé on the status of Richter's paintings of the dead members of this terrorist group, famously titled *October 18 1977*. The series was exhibited at MoMA most recently in 2002 as part of a Richter retrospective. Interestingly DeLillo himself published a short story in the *Guardian* in 2002 entitled "Looking at Meinhof" that depicts the impact of the paintings on two strangers as they walk around the MoMA exhibit. Before attending to the significance of DeLillo's crafting of this episode within the larger rubric of *Falling Man*, I will briefly revisit the details of the Baader-Meinhof case.

Despite its short existence from 1967 to 1969, the writings of Kommune 1 inspired Ulrike Meinhof and Andreas Baader to create their own antifascist, radical left outfit around the same time. Baader-Meinhof, as the outfit was called (and later called the Red Army Faction), initially began peaceful protests against the Vietnam War, nuclear proliferation, and, more significantly, against what they saw as the persistence of fascist tendencies in the German state and business enterprises. After the state cracked down on the group, they went underground and their activities purportedly became more violent. Meinhof, Baader, and other members of the group were arrested in 1972 and held without trial in isolated cells at Stammheim Prison. Between 1974 and 1977 five of the key members were found dead in the prison. The police claimed they all took their own lives, but suspicions of state complicity hovered for a long time. The death of the last three—Baader, Gudrun Ensslin, and Jan-Carl Raspe—on October 18, 1977, and a subsequent book by one of their sympathizers, Stefan Aust, entitled *The Baader-Meinhof Group: The Inside Story of a Phenomenon*, provided Richter with the impetus to embark on a series of fifteen black-and-white oil paintings on the incarceration and death of the Baader-Meinhof members.[29]

The paintings are blurred and anamorphic images of the dead inmates and their prison surroundings. The resemblance to forensic imaging and the simultaneous erasure of that mode's referential authority are both starkly evident in these works. Three images of heads, torsos, and prostrate bodies of Meinhof, Ensslin, and Baader appear thrice in the series. The repetition marks an impasse, gridlock, a refusal of representational transparency. Richter himself puts it thus: "What have I painted. Three times Baader, shot. Three times Ensslin, hanged. Three times the head of dead Meinhof after they cut her down. . . . Their presence is the horror and the hard-to-bear refusal to answer, to explain, to give an opinion."[30]

The arrest of meaning in the face of horror, the resistance to quick judgments projected outward, does not, however, preclude an ekphrastic mode of responding—that is, a mode that attends carefully to the details of the image as it confronts the viewer. In fact it urges such a response, as DeLillo recognizes all too well in his short story "Looking at Meinhof." The story features a man and a woman, strangers to each other, walking in silence through the MoMA exhibit of Richter's paintings. The woman experiences the sensation of being surrounded by the fifteen canvases as "keeping watch over the body of a relative or friend" in a mortuary chapel. Her viewing of the three paintings of Meinhof after she was brought down from her hanging rope and laid to rest is noticeably devoid of any quest after signification or affect:

> She was looking at Ulrike now, head and upper body, her neck rope-scorched, although she didn't know for certain what kind of implement had been used for hanging. . . . She stood before the picture of Ulrike, one of three related images, Ulrike dead in each, lying on the floor of her cell, head in profile. The canvases varied in size. The woman's reality, the head, the neck, the rope burn, the hair, the facial features, were painted, picture to picture, in nuances of obscurity and pall, a detail clearer here than there, the slurred mouth in one painting appearing nearly natural elsewhere, all of it unsystematic.

When the stranger asks her about the rationale for the oddness of the images—their opaque, out-of-focus, misshapen quality—she responds, "I don't know." Five years later DeLillo transcribes this sequence into *Falling Man*, with Lianne walking around a gallery staring into the multiform still-life paintings of Morandi. With their deep engagement with the materiality of shape and form in all their dimensions (partially erased, in shadow, blurred), the paintings of Richter and Morandi demand a visual attention that fundamentally resists the viral reproducibility of media images and their incessant circulation. Keeping watch over the dead demands a level of respectful alertness and humility unavailable to our everyday experience of bio-pictorial viewing.

DeLillo's inclusion of the Baader-Meinhof episode is significant in yet another regard. According to Linda Kauffman, he wishes to illuminate "the long history, hidden logic and deep structure" of terror. In bringing the history of German state repression and its heinous effects into play with the contemporary terrors unleashed by global forms of neoliberal governance, *Falling Man* challenges the rhetoric of exceptionality of the 9/11 catastrophe. Far from visualizing the terrorists as exemplars of an incomprehensible evil, he sees them as melancholic, albeit dangerous, symptoms of a much larger geopolitical malaise infecting the globe, one that is, in some senses, also a viral revisitation of past violence. Through his ekphrastic description of the 9/11 catastrophe via Morandi, Richter, and Janiak, DeLillo offers a somber novelistic counterpoint to the hypervisualization of this spectacular event and its instant aestheticization in the rhetoric of performance. Consequently aesthetic pleasure in *Falling Man* does not collapse into the sublime thrill of the annihilating spectacle; it segues into a mode of contemplation as it calibrates the continuities between the culture of spectacle and the culture of surveillance that mark the parameters of warfare in our times. Such an aesthetic also signals the ethical limits of instantaneous visualization. It suggests that the triumph of the eye in warfare is radically at odds with the melancholic act of keeping watch over the dead.

PART III
WITNESS

SEVEN

THIS I SAW:
GRAPHIC SUFFERING

From Goya to Abu Ghraib

The cover of Susan Sontag's book *Regarding the Pain of Others* reproduces an etching from the nineteenth-century Spanish artist Francisco Goya's series *The Disasters of War* (1810–20). The aquatint print is vertically divided into two approximately equal halves. On the left is a victim of war brutalized and hanged; on the right is a fully clothed mustachioed figure leaning back slightly, his left arm supporting his chin, and gazing intently at the dead man's bowed head. While not captioned as such, this etching captures the force of Goya's statement *"This I saw,"* a statement recorded in art history as acknowledging that he witnessed much of the horror of the 1808 Dos de Mayo Uprising and the subsequent Peninsular War of 1808–14, the subject of this series of eighty-two prints. Since the nineteenth century Goya's etchings of Napoleon's horrific invasion of Spain have become emblematic of the transformative power of witnessing extreme violence in a visual medium. As is well-known, the caption "Yo Lo Vi" was given to plate 44 in the series; it portrays a terrified mother with a baby in her arms and pulling the arm of her toddler as she tries to make him look away from the horror of a battle obviously close by. The Spanish phrase, which literally translates as "Me, I saw this," captures the force of Goya's declaration made a few years later: "I saw it myself, I was there, I saw unbearable, inhuman scenes such as these. I am a witness."[1] Since the public display of this series in 1863, thirty-five years after Goya's death, his uncompromising gesture of witnessing—one that affirms a moral obligation to record evidence of the horrors of war for posterity—has gained significant currency.

The caption of plate 44, in its subsequent rhetorical transformation to "*This* I saw," has today acquired an aesthetic and ethical charge unthinkable in Goya's time, for the witnesses of violence have multiplied a million times over in this age of saturated visual connectivity and exposure. Goya's acknowledgment of the sheer *singularity* of confronting violence through the decisive act of seeing and not turning away and his foregrounding of the *medium* through which such witnessing happens are foundational to the vast scholarship that has followed in the wake of the magnified scale of war and violence in the twentieth and twenty-first centuries. Sontag sees Goya's art as a "turning point in the history of moral feelings and of sorrow," for a "new standard of responsiveness to suffering enters art." Goya's etchings foreground the excesses of war in ways "fashioned as an assault on the sensibility of the viewer. . . . A voice, presumably the artist's, badgers the viewer: can you bear to look at this?"[2] In Sontag's meditation on the ethics of visualizing war, the charge of Goya's sketches, etchings, and paintings acquires cumulative power as she contemplates how witnessing is now mediated through the photograph and has become the very condition of living in our times.[3] Goya's etchings anticipate the photograph not by capturing the essence or wholeness of the violence witnessed—an allegorical gesture common to many conventional paintings before the photographic era—but by capturing the contingency of violence, its projective and retrospective temporality, a quality that nudges the viewer to imagine worlds of war beyond the immediate frame of reference.

Both the print of the hanged man and his spectator witness and the print of the terrified mother wrenching her child away from the scene of violence contain an iterative power that can be invoked at points in history well removed from Goya's early nineteenth-century prephotographic world.[4] They become part of an extended historical narrative as they propel us to identify two other critical moments in the twentieth century that transformed the relationship among the *agon* of suffering, the ethics of witnessing, and the medium of representation. Surprisingly these are not the two world wars but the Spanish Civil War of 1936–39 and the Vietnam War.[5] In the Spanish conflict *photographers* were embedded in the military lines for the first time in history, and their images evoked an immediacy and intimacy to the human experience of war that had previously been transmitted only by the written word or theatrical performances. The Vietnam War was waged amid the power of *televisual* intimacy, a medium that came closest to naturalizing the immediacy of what was previously only a trope of the everyday experience of distant suffering.[6] If the impact of war on people who have never been to war had previously been measured in terms of their exposure to literary and journalistic writing, or more generally to the labor of the human hand on canvas, it was now commonplace, as we saw in previous chapters, to measure such impact in terms of exposure to televisual and digital media. Digital image making in particular has had an exponential reach unimaginable even two decades ago.

Novelizing Witness

The theoretical spectrum on mediated suffering ranges across at least four critical coordinates: the transitive affectivity of mediation (how far it goes and who it touches and why), the cultural politics of spectatorship, the calibration of responsibility to the subject of suffering, and the presence or absence of the suffering body itself. These are the nodal points around which this part of the book revolves.

The larger frame of my argument that I develop in these three chapters is that world novels are not contiguous with contemporary cinematic or televisual or new media genres in representing the *immediacy* of violence; rather they are texts that register the sedimented and recursive history of such mediation. Their alternative way of documenting witness—that is, of abstracting the architectonics of testimonial work—enables me to focus not so much on the questions of visibility and its stock thematics of overexposure and desensitization as on the *legibility* of this new mode of witnessing. The distinction I make here between visibility and legibility amounts to calibrating differently the *work* of witnessing in novels, their textual and tropological play with multiple modalities of spectatorship and witnessing, and their distinctively different braiding of the factual and the affective in comparison with genres of the visual.

My argument here is quite different from the classic postcolonial one, as seen, for instance, in a recent essay by Robert Eaglestone on fiction in the age of war and terror.[7] Eaglestone's contention is that the novels of our time rhetorically enact their inability to capture the truth about war, terror, and suffering due to an entrenched Western sensibility that cannot bridge a cultural chasm—that terror is seen as simply evil in Jonathan Foer's *Extremely*

Loud and Incredibly Close or as illness in Ian McEwan's *Saturday* or something stemming from frustrated passion, as in Salman Rushdie's *Shalimar the Clown*. While Eaglestone is right about the thematic focus of these novels and the pathologies they graph, such an argument does little to highlight the contemporary conjunctures of postcolonial thought, our information era's spatiotemporal ruptures and what these mean for scale, distance, and sensibility, both materially and culturally. Turning the cultural chasm argument between Western and postcolonial worlds on its head, I contend that the turn to witnessing and (re)mediation in contemporary novels actually works across this chasm in that it is symptomatic of the foreshortening of the distance between the postcolonial world's violent spasms and the various forms of spectatorship that have been generated in the global West, which is the true site of the media apparatus. In other words, the saturations and reinflections of witnessing violence across multiple media, including the novel, are actually *prime world-making moments*, and they need to be read explicitly as products of both postcolonial planetary reconfigurations and the concomitant effects of hypermediation in our information era.

Fact and affect constitute the *topoi* of witnessing: one provides the objective ground for claiming that violence has occurred, and the other becomes a subjective measure of the human cost of experiencing violence. The two novels chosen as source texts for the chapters under "Witness," *Anil's Ghost* by Michael Ondaatje and *Orpheus Lost* by Janette Turner Hospital, configure this play of fact and affect and build their narratives around the allegorical power of their doubling. Witnesses and perpetrators in these fictional works cannot be easily disaggregated. One becomes the other depending on the narrative context. For reasons that will become clearer as the chapters progress, I read *Anil's Ghost* under the sign of fact and *Orpheus Lost* under the sign of affect. Telegraphically speaking, the witness in Ondaatje's novel is a Sri Lankan forensic anthropologist commissioned by an international human rights group to find out the truth about an organized massacre during the long years of civil conflict in her homeland. The skeletal remains of the victims become evidence in the hands of this scientist, and she soon discovers how dangerous her informed and factual witnessing is in a zone of war, especially one that implicates her culturally. The novel's forensic realism offers a telling contrast to the music-drenched terrors of *Orpheus Lost*. With a historical frame ranging from the Holocaust to the post-9/11 world, the novel is a passionate paean to the deathworlds of global terror, to the inhabitants of gray zones that limn victimhood and criminality. A lover unaware of her beloved's past is called upon to give witness under extreme duress to the beloved's terrorist activities. The terrorist lover in turn becomes a witness to his long-lost Lebanese father's extensive militant networks, when all he seeks is a musical connection with what he believed to be his most precious inheritance from an absent parent. Even perpetrators, mostly midlevel minions following security injunctions, morph into witnesses of unconscionable brutalities. Music, not bones, is the nonforensic trope of discovery, testimonial agency, and catharsis.

While this novelistic double graphing of the contemporary experience of witnessing constitutes the core of my analysis, I need also to reckon with at least some aspects of a literary and intellectual history of witnessing and spectatorship in modernity. The Holocaust itself, which haunts much of the literature on witnessing, cannot but be an important frame of reference. I come to it repeatedly not only through the narrative thread in *Orpheus Lost* but also through the works of Derrida and Agamben, who have given us a complex comparative frame from which to gauge the power, fallibility, and limits of witnessing. Art Spiegelman's graphic novels on the Holocaust and the 9/11 horrors, *Maus* and *In the Shadow of No Towers*, respectively, provide yet another point of reference for my discussion of the relationship between the literary and the imagistic in representing violence.

My analytical frame, however, is not limited to these postwar insights. The idea of the witness has a long literary and intellectual history that goes back to mid-eighteenth-century expositions on sympathy and spectatorship. These, as I noted earlier, were tremendously influential in theorizations of the sentimental novel, one of the earliest recognized prototypes of a quintessentially modern European novel. The conjoining of fact and feeling inhering in this genre also constituted the foundations of Adam Smith's theorization of the impartial spectator, except that he introduced a third element, reflection. The impartial spectator is neither the actual spectator nor the actor or agent but a third force that stands outside the two, the "demigod within the breast" that holds the fulcrum of judgment.[8] This notion of the spectatorial third inflected not just Hegel's phenomenological apprehension of the master-slave dialectic but both Derrida's and Agamben's theorizations of the witness in the wake of the Holocaust. I discuss this dimension of the third in detail later, weaving it into my analysis of Spiegelman's, Ondaatje's, and Turner Hospital's works. For now I simply note its importance in mediating the bifurcated reading of novelistic witnessing into the genres of speculative realism (the witness as objective spectator) and melancholic realism (the witness as engaged agent) that I discussed briefly at the start of this book. Impartial spectatorship in Smith does not preclude empathetic engagement, but it is first and foremost an act of the imagination, not one of total identification with the suffering agent. Further, it is fundamentally a social act imbued with reflection and moderation as it "extends the remit of sympathy to embrace what we would now see as mass society, the comfort of strangers."[9] This reins in irregular sentiment and modulates the flow of emotions between the real spectators and agents. The abstraction that happens here is not *devoid of* but *actually the work of* empathy through an imaginative foray into the situation of another. This triangulation of empathy-imagination-reflection is critical to Smith's formulation and is replete with possibilities to help us not only rethink the concept of melancholic witnessing as distinct from abstract spectatorship but also reconsider generic differences and overlays between literary and visual spectatorship. Particularly apposite for my purposes, especially in relation to my discussion of the power of visual witnessing, is Smith's recourse to the theatrical metaphor in elaborating the ideas of sympathy and spectatorship. One of the celebrated passages in *The Theory of Moral Sentiments* is his disparagement of Greek tragedies that attempt to solicit the audience's pity with spectacles of excessive emotion and graphic physical suffering. Sophocles's Philoctetes, "who cries out and faints from the extremity of his sufferings," is the particular object of his contempt: "We are disgusted with that clamorous grief which, without any delicacy, calls upon our compassion with sighs, tears and importune lamentations. But we reverence that reserved, that silent and majestic sorrow, which discovers itself only in the swelling of the eyes, in the quivering of the lips and cheeks, and in the distant, but affecting, coldness of the whole behaviour."[10]

It is telling that aesthetic witnessing here is coded in a visual frame in an era that was a predominantly print and literary society. Thus historically the visual has been central to any literary trope of witnessing—not just visual experience but the *framing* and *mediation* of that experience. Extrapolating from an eighteenth-century account of literary spectatorship, I ask how our contemporary experience of exorbitant visual witnessing through ever proliferating media inflects the world novel today. What indeed is the literary purchase in the twenty-first century of a global culture of witnessing dominated by the image?

Spiegelman's Comic Grids

In the work of the renowned graphic novelist Art Spiegelman we see the most explicit abstraction and remediation of the visual into narrative form and vice versa. Spiegelman's self-described "double-track disposition toward reading and looking" propelled him to create novelistic pictorials, two of which, *Maus* and *In the Shadow of No Towers*, have become classics of the genre.[11] Spiegelman's brilliant architectural interplay between the verbal and the pictorial in graphing the horrors of both the Holocaust and 9/11 is, for the purposes of my analysis, a generic tour de force. His works iconicize the conceptual kernel of my book in the way they graphically foreground the act of novelistic witnessing and world-making in our era of global wars and informational hyperconnectivity. He has repeatedly described the architecture of his comics as structurally witnessing the demolition of the "world grid"—a translation into aesthetic form of two momentous world historical events of our times, the Holocaust and 9/11. His comic grids architecturally *externalize* the complex intertwining of narrative and image in the act of witnessing catastrophic moments in human history. In doing so, I submit, they stage the history of the novelization of the complex relationship between human suffering and mediated spectatorship that I have traced thus far.

Spiegelman calls his art "novel graphics" rather than "graphic novels" to highlight precisely this feature; in fact he is explicit in naming the novel and not cinema or visual art as the medium that comes closest to his work. *Maus* was an attempt, he says, "to see what one could do as a structured thing that had the beats and rhythms of a novel."[12] While crafting *Maus* he even gave up his art supplies and instead worked with ordinary typing paper, a fountain pen, and typewriter correction fluid. In his book-length interview with Hillary Chute he talks extensively about the technicalities of his art:

> The process for doing *Maus* started with a thumbnail breakdown of my visual "paragraph," then a direct sketch draft of the page—just a first stab at making the page. Then I'd refine each of the panels, trying to find a zone somewhere between the casualness of handwriting and the precision of a typeface. I could only arrive at that by doing study after study, building up layers of tracing paper with coloured felt-tips. All these pages were drawn over a grid that could use either three tiers or four tiers—or a combination of the two—and panels were initially divided in halves, thirds or various increments in a relatively flexible but important-to-me set of possible layouts for each page.[13]

His execution of *Maus* "felt more like writing," he says, "like offering up a manuscript, something made by hand." Making even more explicit his affinity with narrative art, he observes, "I worked with the metaphor that each panel was analogous to a *word*, and each row of panels was a *sentence*, and each page was a *paragraph*."[14]

Further, in framing his elaborate sketches in ways that deliberately capture the shifting horizons of witnessing, Spiegelman bridges the architectonics of witnessing violence from Goya's time to ours. In fact he recently invoked the power of Goya's sketches in his interview with Chute. When asked about the significance of drawings by Holocaust survivors, and especially his use of them in *Maus*, Spiegelman urges us to see them not as expressive modes but as information about what really happened:

> The few collections of survivors' drawings and reproductions of surviving art that I could get my hands on were essential for me. Those drawings were a return to drawing not for its possibilities of imposing the self, as of finding a new role for art and drawing after the invention of the camera—*a kind of commemorating, witnessing, and recording of information—what Goya referred to when he says, "This I saw." The artists, like the memoirists and diarists of the time, are giving urgent information in the pictures*, information that could be transmitted in no other way, and often at great risk to their lives.[15]

This way of conceiving information imparts an ethical depth that information theorists of our hyperconnected and mass-mediated digital age are hard put to attribute to the constant flow of news stimulus around us. In his study *Critique of Information*, for instance, Scott Lash finds no symbolic or iconic value in televisual and digital media content, only indexical signification— something that flashes a signal but does not generate a substantial and sustained ethical response: "The sports, the news on television, the sending of electronic messages, playing computer games, is signification via signal and may be more or less *indexical*. . . . The sort of signification that is going on is neither predominantly *symbolic* nor *iconic*, but indexical through the signal."[16] Lash proposes a new form of sociality that he calls "informationality"—a mode of orientation to the world informed by an economy of signs. While he resists Baudrillard's thesis of the collapse of the real and the hyper-real into one depthless entity, he is skeptical of the capacity of the everyday, ephemeral visual stimuli to generate a field of meaning powerful enough to stir a collective moral response. He would, of course, have had to revise his thesis comprehensively since 9/11 and the 2011 Arab Spring political mobilizations. In both, the visual sign operated far beyond the indexical to take on massive symbolic and iconic value. Communication through digital media was critical to the mass uprisings against dictatorial regimes in the Middle East. The multiple forms of mediation and remediation that enabled the global flow of information of these world-historical events of our century—from the visual to the narrative, the digitally iconic, and the conventionally expressive arts of painting and music—give far more credence to Spiegelman's powerful formulation of informationality through the pictorial and other media, one that we are ethically compelled to respond to and one that his comic medium is well placed to re-present, that is, make present again. "Comics," he says, "lend themselves to direct communication and clarity. Their show-and-tell attributes are well suited to the task by inviting both halves of the brain to grapple with information."[17]

Excerpts from his comic strips help illustrate the thrust of this argument about visual and graphic informationality that records, witnesses, and commemorates traumatic events and that simultaneously appeals to our analytical and affective sides. One recurrent motif in Spiegelman's work is the intersection of what he calls "personal history" and "world history." The artist's presence as both survivor and witness is explicit in almost every plate of both *Maus* and *In the Shadow of No Towers*. Plate 6 of *In the Shadow of No Towers* is a particularly powerful example of the formal processes at work here. The skeletal frame of the glowing North Tower, this time ash-colored, looms across the left column of the entire page. We see five falling figures across the length of the tower, each of them resembling Spiegelman and no doubt commemorating one of the most iconically disturbing images of the 9/11 catastrophe (see figure 7.1). The rapidly distributed global images become the source of his witnessing. A text inserted halfway through the tower reads:

He is haunted now
by the images he *didn't* witness . . .

images of people
tumbling to the
streets below . . .

especially one man
(according to a
neighbor) who exe—
cuted a graceful
Olympic dive as his
last living act.

The falling figure symbolizes at once the history of Spiegelman's personal trauma as a child of Holocaust survivors, his own terrifying experience of the attack on the towers as a resident of Lower Manhattan, and his identifica-

FIGURE 7.1. From *In the Shadow of No Towers*, by Art Spiegelman.

tion with the fateful death leaps of the inhabitants of the towers. This vertical telescoping across the ashen frame of the burned North Tower of multiple temporalities of trauma, both personal and historical, is then replicated horizontally in a series of violent palimpsests across eleven other panels more conventionally associated with a comic book. Holocaust history, the history of Arab anti-Semitism, and 9/11 smash into each other in these panels. The key encounter here is between Spiegelman and a homeless Russian woman who daily hurls anti-Semitic abuse at him in her native tongue as he walks down the street. On the afternoon of 9/11 she disappears from the street, only to reappear as a demonic specter right at the center of the plate. The reader is confronted by a flaming rectangular panel featuring her devilish profile, framed by Nazi iconography, the biblical Hell, and the familiar glowing skeletal frames of the Twin Towers. The boxed caption reads, "Her inner demons had broken loose and taken over our shared reality." Interestingly she is back on the street after the fatal day; this time she spouts her anti-Semitic venom in English, not Russian, in a series of three panels. The panels become charged with her hate-filled invectives. "You damn Kikes, you did it!" she screams. This dangerous coalescing of the histories of Nazi and Arab hatred of the Jews in the figure of this woman shakes Spiegelman out of his stupor. In his preface to the book, memorably entitled "The Sky Is Falling!," he admits his own predilection for conspiracy theories and his realization of their limits during 9/11: "In those first few days after 9/11 I got lost constructing conspiracy theories about my government's complicity in what happened that would have done a Frenchman proud. (My own susceptibility for conspiracy goes back a long way but had reached its previous peak after the 2000 elections.) Only when I heard paranoid Arab Americans blaming it all on the Jews did I reel myself back in."[18] We see this position graphically hypostatized in panel 9, where the homeless Russian woman is physically thrown back by the force of his retaliation: "Damn it, Lady! If you don't stop blaming everything on the Jews, people are gonna think you're CRAZY!" Panel 10 shows him striding off after his successful knockdown of the specter of conspiracy, except the sequence ends recursively with a throwback to his figuration as the little son in *Maus*, suffering a nightmare and being consoled by his mother, "Hush, you fell out of bed sweetie." In the space of a single plate with twelve panels in all—*windows*, he calls them—Spiegelman manages brilliantly to compress multiple histories of personal trauma and political catastrophes.

Much like the world novels discussed in this study, both *Maus* and *In the Shadow of No Towers* remediate experiences formerly mediated in other forms. The second book, though, was also the product of the artist's first-hand experience: seeing the collapse of the North Tower, inhaling the toxic dust clouds as he ran to rescue his son, then attending the United Nations School. To that extent it is less remediated than *Maus*. "It took a long time to put the burning towers behind me," Spiegelman says in the preface. One image in particular iconicizes his eyewitness experience and recurs throughout the book: the glowing skeletal remnants of the North Tower. September 11 is by far the most photographed and televised of world catastrophes, but there are no public images of the "glowing bones" of the North Tower that Spiegelman captures in his comic book: "The pivotal image from my 9/11 morning—one that didn't get photographed or videotaped into public memory but still remains burned onto the inside of my eyelids several years later—was the image of the looming north tower's glowing bones just before it vaporized. I repeatedly tried to paint this with humiliating results but eventually came close to capturing the vision of disintegration digitally on my computer. I managed to place some sequences of my most vivid memories around that central image but never got to draw others." Apart from this iconic original, most other instances of remediation in *In the Shadow of No Towers* occurs through an interweaving of textual material: newspaper clips from one hundred years earlier of the capture of an anarchist accused of murdering President McKinley, cartoon strips from the 1920s to the postwar period, the official 9/11 report, news coverage of the wars in Afghanistan and Iraq, and even *Maus*.

Maus in turn draws extensively on interviews with his parents, sketches, booklets, documents, documentaries, photographs, family memorabilia, and even Hollywood sets of the Nazi death camps. An anecdote about the film set and its role in helping Spiegelman reconstruct the wooden barracks of Birkenau is particularly bizarre, but also uncannily apposite for my argument about the complex novelistic relationship among imagination, visualization, remediation, and narration in witnessing extreme violence. Spiegelman mentions a visit to Birkenau in the late 1970s, when he looked in vain for the wooden barracks that housed prisoners. All he found was rubble, for the local residents had taken the planks for heating in the winter after the war. The barracks were originally horse stables into which the Nazis crammed eight hundred prisoners per stall. The only way he could identify the location of the barracks was by the chimneys that remained from the skeletal structure. On his second visit, in 1987, however, he was amazed to find a fully built complex of wooden barracks on the same spot. His discovery that this was a film set that the Polish authorities had since preserved for its verisimilitude outraged him at first: "The idea of a Hollywood reconstruction of a death camp eventually replacing the haunted ruins just seemed deeply wrong."[19] But he did end up photographing it from every angle so he could transform the images into sketches for *Maus*. The informational potential of this mediated reality mattered far more to him than its lack of authenticity.

What does one make of these second- and third-order modes of mediation in relation to the ethics of witnessing and, especially, novelistic witnessing? What happens to the sanctity of original witnessing? To the testimony of survivors such as Spiegelman's father, Vladek, whose experience in the Nazi death camps provides the bulwark of *Maus*? Before answering these questions, I wish to recount another anecdote from *MetaMaus* that further complicates the role of memory, narrative, visualization, and mediation in witnessing. If the episode about the film set illuminates the relationship between an atrocity site, its inadvertent erasure, and its architecturally re-created simulacra, the episode I am about to narrate is about an atrocity event, its inexplicable forgetting, and its painstaking narrative and visual reconstruction.

Readers of *Maus* may recall a set of four panels on page 214, in the first of which Vladek remembers marching with other prisoners to their work sites. He says he looked forward to these marches for he often encountered someone called Manice who occasionally gave him news about his wife, Anja, from another camp. In the next panel Art tells his father, "I just read about the camp orchestra that played as you marched out of the gate." The following two panels present a sharp disjunction between memory and documentation, with Vladek emphatic that he never heard any orchestral music during his marches and Art gently affirming that "it's very well documented." In *MetaMaus* Spiegelman talks at length about this episode and especially his role not just in actively witnessing the fragility of his father's memory but also in consciously undertaking to re-create *all* the events of the camp for the sake of posterity: subsuming his father's memory into a "grander memory," as he puts it.[20] This act of what one may call holistic witnessing involves supplementing his father's narratives with extensive research into other sources, an epistemological act that Spiegelman considered prima facie ethical in its saturation with factual evidence:

Memory is a very fugitive thing. . . . It was obvious to me doing my homework, that Vladek's memory didn't jibe with everything I read. I knew I had to allude to that somewhere. And for a while that was troublesome to me. And as is often the case, the things that are troublesome lead to the more profound solutions. So, I specifically asked Vladek about the orchestras in Auschwitz in order to have the sequence at the top of page 214 happen. . . . The Auschwitz orchestra is about as well documented as anything in Auschwitz might have been. Enough of those musicians survived, wrote memoirs. There are photographs of the orchestra taken by Nazis. There are so many different descriptions of it happening that I knew I wasn't veering off into Holocaust-denier Heaven: "Oh, he's just making this stuff up, spreading the big lie!" So, when I asked Vladek about the orchestra and he didn't remember one, I thought: "Ok, that's the moment!"[21]

Spiegelman highlights here an aspect of artistic witnessing that is critically in *excess* of one's experience, one that Alain Badiou calls the experience of "linking my component elements via that *excess beyond myself* induced by the passing through me of a truth."[22]

We can now go back to the questions I posed about the sanctity of first-hand witnessing and the legitimacy of the various orders of mediation that distance the viewer from the actual event. Vladek's eyewitness testimony is, no doubt, central to the crafting of *Maus*, Spiegelman asserts. But he also encounters facts about the Holocaust that signal the limits of his father's experience, not just of his memory. The integrity of his own narrative visualization of his parents' life in the camps, Spiegelman avers, lies precisely in attending very carefully to this *passing through him* of this larger *truth* in the sense Badiou talks of, in opening himself up to a profound process of historical mediation for the sake of future generations. It is an experience simultaneously epistemological, ethical, and aesthetic. It compels him to double as both witness and medium, as empathetic observer and scribe of a truth beyond the personal. The creative act that follows brings to light a form of truth that is never *not* mediated, but that is no less powerful for being relayed through accumulated historical data and desiderata. This way of conceptualizing the recursive relationship among witnessing, mediation, and further witnessing, not just through words, images, and technology but also through the very person and consciousness of the writer and artist at a particular point in history—through history's "third party," so to say—is also paradoxically to depersonalize the act of spectatorship and witnessing, a gesture that is of significant import in novel writing and which, as we have seen, has a genealogy that goes back to philosophical and literary debates on sympathy and impartial spectatorship in the eighteenth century.

In order to develop this point further and to consider the implications for my argument about novelistic modes of witnessing through a model of composite spectatorship and narrative visualization, it may be useful to consider some of Derrida's recent philological work on witnessing. "A Self-Unsealing Poetic Text: Poetics and Politics of Witnessing," begins with a puzzle posed by the poet Celan in these enigmatic lines about incineration at the Nazi camps:

Aschenglorie . . .
No one
bears witness for the
witness

An obvious and essential reading of these lines is the total absence of any trace when everything and everyone has been put through an incinerator. Not only are there no witnesses, but there is nothing left to witness except the glory of ash. As Derrida says, "Ashes are the figure of annihilation without remains, or without a readable or decodable archive."[23] What charge does the term *witness* have in the poem? Why does the image of the third recur either as a hand or as a forked road? Derrida offers two translations of the same German verse:

Aschen—glorie hinter
euch Dreiweg
Handen

Ash—glory behind
your three-forked
hands

Glory
of ashes behind
your hands
of the triple road

In order to decipher the poetic connection between the witness and the third hand or road, Derrida attends carefully to the multiple etymological strands of the term *witness* in Latin, unearthing three equivalents: *testis*, *terstis*, and *superstes*. The first is "witness" as such. It is, however, coextensive with *terstis*, one who is present as a third party to observe an exchange between two agents. *Superstes* is witness as "survivor," one who persists beyond the event and holds onto the truth of the event for the future. The source of this fine distinction that Derrida posits and then undoes between witness as the third party and as survivor is Emile Benveniste's philological tract on the institutions of the Indo-European period of civilization, *Vocabulaire des institutions europeenness* (Dictionary of European Institutions). Benveniste cites a Sanskrit allusion to the third in his chapter "Religion and Superstition" and goes on to distinguish it from the idea of witness as *superstes*, or survivor: "As the Sanskrit text says: 'Every time two persons are present, Mitra is there as a third.' Thus the God Mitra is by nature the 'witness.' But *superstes* describes the 'witness' either as the one who 'subsists beyond,' witness at the same time as a survivor, or as 'the one who holds himself to the thing,' who is present there. We now see what can and must be meant theoretically by 'superstitio,' the function of the *superstes*. This will be the 'property of being present' as a 'witness.'"[24]

In funneling his reading of Celan on the aporia of Holocaust witnessing through Benveniste's philological tract, Derrida foregrounds the unworkability of the opposition between observer and survivor and also ascribes to the act of poetic witnessing a power to prolong the temporality of the event by making present the *perceptible* dimension of witnessing as something seen, heard, and felt, not merely something that can be proven in a court of law: "'Bearing witness' is heterogeneous to the administration of a legal proof or the display of an object produced in evidence. 'I bear witness' means not 'I prove,' but 'I swear that I have seen, I have heard, I have touched, I have felt, I have been *present*.'"[25] His point about Celan is that even when the ashes signify the impossibility of witnessing—"No one bears witness for the witness"—the poetic sensibility can still stand for the only condition of bearing witness. The poem observes, holds, and survives *beyond* the potential witness who has perished and becomes the vehicle of legible transmission for future acts of witnessing—a testamentary promise. This notion of witnessing as a role ascribed to a third party, but also to someone or something that survives the event while holding on to its truth—being *perceptibly present* while undertaking to prolong its temporality—is a powerful way to conceive the role of Spiegelman the author and of *Maus* as textual evidence. At first glance Vladek appears to come closest to this etymological reading of witnessing: as a third (someone present at multiple scenes of interaction between the condemned Jews and the Nazi perpetrators) and as a survivor. But it is in Art Spiegelman that we see a far more powerful actualization of this dual role. We have already seen his resolve to embed his father's story in a larger narrative and thus become an authorial witness precisely with the full force of a third-party arbiter of truth about one of history's most horrific moments. Interestingly Spiegelman also invokes the power of the third in the eighteenth-century sense of Adam Smith's impersonal spectator. In reflecting on his role as a comic artist, he says, "The story of Maus isn't just the story of a son having problems with his father, and it's not just the story of what a father lived through. *It is about a cartoonist trying to envision what his father went through.*"[26] This experience of putting himself in his father's situation and imagining what it would feel like—this triangulation of empathy-imagination-reflection—could not be more akin to what Smith himself envisioned as the role of the sympathetic spectator. Further, in his painstaking thirteen-year labor of creating *Maus*, he not only *survives* the experience of transcribing his parents' firsthand witnessing of life in the camps but also transmits to posterity the power of this authorial act of surviving beyond the event, of *making perceptibly present*, in the extrajudicial, Derridean sense, that which would have perished with his parents' generation. The temporality of such witnessing is prolonged and eventually telescoped into yet another traumatic world historical event, of which he himself becomes a firsthand witness: the September 11 attacks on the Twin Towers.

SPIEGELMAN'S CASE IS A powerful exemplar and template for my analysis of the modes of novelistic witnessing in the two following chapters. Here I must gather the various strands of the argument thus far about witnessing, visibility, legibility, and mediation. I began with an extrapolation from Goya's *Disasters of War* series to talk about the architectonics of witnessing violence in our photographic, televisual, and digital ages. I then posited an argument about the distinction between visually mediated and novelistic witnessing and suggested that the latter was not contiguous with our everyday experience of televisual and electronic witnessing after 1989. Rather it could be seen as a legible record and creative transmutation of our very experience of mediated witnessing through history, and also one that conjoins the factual and affective in ways that prolong the temporality of witnessing a traumatic event. I also plumbed the philological depth and complexity of the term *witness* and noted the significance of the figuration of the third as a role ascribed not just to legal judgment but to the act of elongating the temporality and perceptual reach of a traumatic event, to an ability to patiently, empathetically transcribe for future generations what really happened. This triangulated argument about visual witnessing, novelistic legibility, and the philologically configured third offers a powerful frame within which to situate my analysis of Ondaatje's *Anil's Ghost* and Turner Hospital's *Orpheus Lost*.

EIGHT
FORENSIC WITNESSING:
THE (NON)EVIDENCE
OF BONES

An Epistemic Turn

Art Spiegelman makes a case for why his panel drawings are not merely expressive but also *informational*, that they are a form of witnessing and recording of firsthand information for posterity in the spirit of Goya's "Yo Lo Vi" (I saw this). This emphasis on the truth-telling or documentary function of art appears to have made a phenomenal comeback in the novels of our time. One sees this in what many literary critics have called the "realism explosion" in fictional works and also in the shift in the epistemological lexicon of the contemporary novel, where one quite clearly discerns the emergence of new understandings of the factual and the evidentiary in relation to trauma and witnessing. Michael Ondaatje's novel *Anil's Ghost* offers an exemplary case study in this regard. The novel displays an intimate if tortuous traction with truth-telling genres. War, violence, and trauma often throw these genres into crisis, a process that Michael Rothberg has called "traumatic realism."[1] Ondaatje's novel allows us to trace a shift in the epistemological purchase of the contemporary war novel where the legibility of witnessing appears to be inextricable from the braiding of two kinds of evidentiary truth: the forensic and the testimonial—forensic because zones of war and genocide double as massive crime scenes, and testimonial because truth here is also the product of many eyewitnesses, so excavating it entails a complex remediation of genres of evidence.

This generic interplay between forensic truth and testimonial truth is brought to crisis in Ondaatje's novel. This novel does not explicitly thematize the exorbitant impact of media and imagistic witnessing; it powerfully abstracts the conundrum of truth-making in our era of proliferating genres of evidence. The witness in Ondaatje's novel is a Sri Lankan forensic scientist and anthropologist, Anil Tissera, commissioned by an international human rights group to find out the truth about a series of extrajudicial massacres in 1988–90, during the long years of civil conflict in her homeland. The remains of the victims—bones—become evidence in the hands of this scientist, and she soon discovers how dangerous her informed and factual witnessing is in a zone of war, especially one that implicates her culturally. *Anil's Ghost* was published barely twelve years after the Sri Lankan massacres of 1988–89 in which at least two militant groups, the Liberation Tigers of Tamil Elam from the North and the People's Liberation Front from the South, were engaged in repeated bouts of high-intensity civil conflict with the government. The ominous scale of the killings is noted early on in the novel by the archaeologist Sarath Diyasena in his briefing to Anil. Significantly he also warns her that in this triangulated warfare culpability is difficult to apportion: "The bodies turn up weekly now. The height of the terror was eighty-eight and eighty-nine, but it was going on long before that. Every side was killing and hiding evidence. *Every side.* . . . The government is not the only one doing the killing. . . . A couple of years ago people just started disappearing. Or bodies kept being found burned beyond recognition. There's no hope of affixing blame. And no one can tell who the victims are."[2] In a text saturated with such dark, inscrutable, and illegible deaths, excavating truth and providing witness—making scorched bones speak, as it were—are herculean tasks. My argument is that it is precisely this conundrum—this necessity *and* impossibility of finding the truth about extreme human violence—that *Anil's Ghost* primarily sets out to delineate, and it does so with astonishing aesthetic flair.

To recast this point in terms of the architectonics of novelistic witnessing (as distinguished from witnessing in visual media), Ondaatje's novel *makes legible* the work of witnessing by drawing into its narrative ambit a range of fact-finding genres—the case, journalistic pieces, human rights reports, forensic records—many of which constituted the prehistory of the English novel as it evolved in the eighteenth century.[3] To that extent it experiments with the novel's epistemological purchase in the history of what counts (and has counted) as fact in modernity. Rather than represent a singular truth about what happened in Sri Lanka during the years 1988–90, *Anil's Ghost* journeys through the monumental hurdles that confront anyone who sets out to find such truths. Tropes of the factual, the case, evidence, light, and sight proliferate through the text. Much to the disappointment and even dismay of its many politically informed readers, the novel is not an epic rendering of the many dimensions of Sri Lanka's prolonged civil conflict with the Tamil Tigers.[4] It is not a realist historical novel staking its merit on crafting a literary verisimilitude of the conflict, even if Ondaatje's matter-of-fact prefatory note does appear to partly encourage such expectations: "From the mid-1980s to the early 1990s, Sri Lanka was in a crisis that involved three essential groups: the government, antigovernment insurgents in the south and separatist guerillas in the north. Both the insurgents and the separatists had declared war on the government. Eventually, in response, legal and illegal government squads were known to have been sent out to hunt down the separatists and the insurgents. . . . *Anil's Ghost* is a fictional work set during this political time and historical moment" (n.p.). Interestingly there is no hint in this note about the novel's epistemic orientation, its stunningly creative transfiguration of notions of evidence, the factual, the empirical, and the case in the operation of human witnessing, both legal and historical. What, then, prompts me to read *Anil's Ghost* under the sign of fact? Why do I see Ondaatje's novel first and foremost as a powerful statement on the novel's capacity to explore the vagaries of the factual in witnessing human experience in extremis? There are three reasons.

First, the novel plunges us right away into the worlds of a forensic anthropologist and an archaeologist. Both are professional seekers of evidentiary truth, and almost every dimension of the conflict is refracted through their gaze. Second, rather than flesh out the historical and political coordinates of the civil conflict as a background to their quest, *Anil's Ghost* shifts the narrative to an alternative historiographical and archaeological world where the quest for evidence through the dissection of bones continues in a nonscientific register through the agency of Palipana, an old Buddhist monk and a retired and disgraced former teacher of the archaeologist. Much of the novel in fact plays out this epistemological battle between true and false evidence. Third, the forensic quest does not culminate in a political denouement with a categorical impugning of the truths internationally avowed by the Sri Lankan political establishment. In fact both Anil and Sarath become casualties of their quest and depart from the novel prematurely and precipitously. We are left with an allegorical opening up and prolonging of the perceptual reach of witnessing beyond the immediate site of violence. This happens through the archetypal Buddhist figure of Ananda, who, in a sequence reminiscent of the shell-shocked aftermath of the Taliban's exploding of the Bamiyan Buddhas, is shown reconstructing a shattered statue of Buddha while leaving all the cracks visible. The sequence is metaphorically enriched by motifs of sight and illumination—obvious markers of knowledge worlds—not of wounding and death.

There is one caveat to the three points just outlined. *Anil's Ghost* does not simply romance the scientism of bones or the archives. The epistemological purchase of evidence as a product of modern science is never taken for granted. There is in fact almost a pre-Enlightenment reading of empiricism as the evidence of the senses, not simply that of scientific reasoning. Each of the main characters—Anil, Sarath, Palipana, and Ananda—allegorizes a distinctly different modality of getting to the truth of the massacres: Anil believes in the indubitable nature of forensic evidence; Sarath in the "archaeological surround of a fact"; Palipana in tactile exploration reaching back to ancient nontextual practices when the natural and human were not clearly disaggregated; and Ananda in the aesthetics of vision. Each is transformed in the end by the force of the other three. To advance this argument about an expansive notion of empirical truth as "evidence of the senses" that questions the dominance of scientific reason,[5] I read Anil's and Sarath's witnessing under the sign of "bones," Palipana's under the idea of "hand," and Ananda's under the term "eye."

Bones

One of the prevalent visual memories of massacres and genocides in our modern era—Auschwitz, Cambodia, Rwanda, Somalia—is that of bones, either a pile of skeletal faces or shards of charred bones. In the killing fields of Cambodia piles of skulls eventually incriminated the Khmer Rouge. In the aftermath of the Rwandan genocide the Tutsi-led Rwanda Patriotic Front took the astonishing decision to leave the corpses where they lay, between the church pews, beneath the school desks, in the yard outside. In the words of Michael Ignatieff, who witnessed the grim memorialization a year later in the company of the UN Secretary-General Boutros Boutros-Ghali, "The survivors turned the church compound at Nyarubuye into the Yad Vashem of African genocide." This is how Ignatieff describes the scene: "Stretched out on the floor are row upon row of dust-coloured skeletons in rags. A dirty light slants across femurs, ankles, hipbones, shoulderjoints, teeth, skulls. No flesh remains. There's no smell of putrefaction. The clothing has faded to the colour of ash. Boutros-Ghali shuts his eyes and quietly mutters, 'Everywhere we work, we are struggling against a culture of death.'"[6]

Bones are often the only remnants of hard scientific evidence to demonstrate crimes against humanity. Not surprisingly forensic scientists and anthropologists have been at the heart of international human rights investigations of such killings. Their intimate knowledge of bones and their knowledge of cultures of killing make them increasingly sought after, more so since the digital revolution, which has radically transformed the science of crime detection. Scholars in recent years have noted a spike in the publication of histories of forensic science.[7] In fact it would not be an exaggeration to say that the scholarly world as well as the global popular imaginary has been saturated with the world of forensic crime detection since the late 1990s. Television crime dramas like CSI and *Bones* have forensic experts as central characters. The history of the production of *Bones* is particularly fascinating in its entanglement of real-life and televisual characters. Its lead character is Dr. Temperance Brennan (called "Bones" in the series), who is loosely based on a real-life forensic anthropologist and author, Kathy Reichs, also the producer of the show. Brennan is also the name of the detective in Reich's crime novel series, even though the TV show is not based on the series. Interestingly, however, the TV character of Brennan writes crime mysteries in her spare time, which feature a detective named Kathy Reich! It is beyond the scope of this chapter to examine what this late modern obsession with forensic evidence says about the importance of the factual in the wake of three decades of postmodern problematization of positivist knowledge making. What I can say in the context of the discussion of Ondaatje's novel is that the composite figure of Temperance-Kathy—and the gender is not incidental—becomes emblematic of the importance of witnessing objectively yet compassionately, qualities that Ondaatje's forensic anthropologist, Anil, demonstrates in equal measure.

There is one other critical point to be made here. Forensics works by building *cases* from bodies, corporal fragments, or bones of victims. If one recasts this fact in relation to the importance of the case study in understanding the evolution of the novel form, one can say that central to the act of novelistic witnessing in our violent times is the construction of *cases* that combine the force of *juridical, individuating,* and *sentimental* forms—forms that were seen as distinctly different in earlier eras and on which scholars such as Michel Foucault, John Forrester, Paul Hunter, and James Chandler have written extensively. Briefly, the earliest secular cases in seventeenth-century England were predominantly juridical in that they constituted a set of circumstances around a particular act that could modify or confirm an existing set of rules. With medicine and forensics, the case began to operate with an individuating force, foregrounding the specific constitution or body of the patient or victim as the locus of knowledge. Hunter also notes that the individuating register of casuistry gained increasing prominence in an evolving culture of beliefs in the significance of "individual temperament," which he dates to the seventeenth-century Interregnum in England, "when [England] had to confront what individuation had made of tradition and authority."[8] The sentimental case follows from this process of individuation and, as Chandler has forcefully argued, is the precursor to one of the most critical features of the novel form: the point of view.[9] Chandler dates its emergence to the mid-eighteenth century with the publication of Adam Smith's *The Theory of Moral Sentiments* and Laurence Sterne's *The Sentimental Journey*. The sentimental case is a "specific description of a person's experiential situation, as what had befallen that person." It is anticasuistic in that it is less concerned with a set of rules than with enabling what Chandler calls "sentimental mobility," that is, "a capacity to put oneself in the place of another—a mobility made possible by the sympathetic imagination."[10] When the sentimental case is extrapolated to the novel form, the very structure of the novel hinges on the reader's ability to move from one point of view to another. Through rhetorical and narrative strategies, in other words, the novelist *makes a case* for directing our sympathetic imagination from one character to another, which in turn advances the plot. In making a case for empathetic witnessing in our era of global civil wars through the forensic realism of Ondaatje's novel, I draw on the force of all three readings of casuistry—juridical, individuating, and the sentimental—and demonstrate their limits and possibilities in situations of terror and trauma. The forensic anthropologist in the novel not only makes a juridical case to be presented before a tribunal but also seeks to individuate each case medically through painstaking research on the nature of the victim's death. Further, her sympathetic imagination urges her to seek help from unconventional sources to reconstruct the terror and pathos of the extinguishing of lives in the civil conflict; that is, she goes beyond her scientific training and finds complementary pathways to research and present a sentimental case.

Apart from manifesting the continuing relevance of casuistry to the development of the novel form, *Anil's Ghost* is also an exemplary *world* novel in the way I have been using the term. It gestures repeatedly to the post-1989 world of civil wars and state terror—in Congo, Kurdistan, Guatemala, and China—and situates the forensic expert's role in Sri Lanka within this larger global awareness of crimes against humanity. Inhabiting violent deathworlds is the very condition of her everyday belonging in this world: "They heard the rhetoric of death over the intercom; 'vaporization' or 'microfragmentation' meant the customer in question had been blown to bits. They couldn't miss death, it was in every texture and cell around them. No one changed the radio dial in a morgue without a glove on" (147). This is the world that Anil Tissera, a Sri Lankan expatriate, has lived in for most of her adult life in the West. And a deathworld is what she walks into as soon as she lands in Sri Lanka: "The country existed in a rocking, self-burying motion. The disappearance of schoolboys, the death of lawyers by torture, the abduction of bodies from the Hokandara mass grave. Murders in the Muthurajawela marsh" (157).

We see her passion for bones early in the novel. She boasts to her American lover, Cullis, that she knows "the names of several bones in Spanish . . . *Maxilar . . . Cubito, Omoplato, Occipital*" (34). As a forensic anthropologist attached to the United Nations Commission on Human Rights she is an active seeker of truth about crimes against humanity. We are told that she has previously worked on massacre sites in Guatemala; in fact the novel begins with a page of her thoughts while in South America on the significance of keeping "vigil over the dead" so as to "ensure that the evidence would not be lost again" (5). When the Sri Lankan government decided to set up a war tribunal with the help of the UN to stem the damage to its international reputation on human rights, Anil volunteered to represent the global body in the country of her origins. She wrote to the Centre for Human Rights in Geneva in response to their call for applicants. For years she did not have any hope that human rights organizations would be allowed into the country: "Over the years complaints from Amnesty International and other civil rights groups had been sent to Switzerland and resided there, glacierlike. President Katugala claimed no knowledge of organized campaigns of murder on the island. But under pressure, and to placate trading partners in the West, the government eventually made the gesture of an offer to pair local officials with outside consultants" (16).

Anil had not visited Sri Lanka for fifteen years. Her entry into the country is low key, and she displays none of the nostalgia of the returning expatriate. She appears single-minded in her mission: to verify on behalf of the international human rights community that the Sri Lankan government was not involved in extrajudicial killings. Her firm commitment to a global juridico-political framework is conjoined with her scientific zeal in "tunnelling towards [the] discovery" of facts (69). Together they propel her into a forensic quest for truth in her ravaged native land that she believes will "set one free" (102). She has not contacted a single relative in Colombo; she pleads with the driver that he not talk during their ride from the airport to her hotel; and all she asks for, much to the bemusement of the chauffeur, is a drink of toddy before she retires for the night. She "had read documents and news reports full of tragedy," but "she had now lived abroad long enough to interpret Sri Lanka with a long-distance gaze" (11). Not that the long-distance reports left her with any illusions about the scale of the massacres. But she had hereto-fore managed to process the horror through either statistical or literary allu-sion, both ultimately abstracting: "Yet the darkest Greek tragedies were in-nocent compared with what was happening here. Head on stakes. Skeletons dug out of a cocoa pit in Matale. At university Anil had translated lines from Archilocus—*In the hospitality of war we left them with their dead to remember us by*. But here there was no such gesture to the families of the dead, not even the information of who the enemy was" (11).

This luxury is no longer afforded her from her very first day at the local hospital. She agrees to meet some forensic students and encounters her first potential case, a man killed since her arrival. Despite her long years of train-ing she feels a frisson as she tests the time of death. It coincides, she realizes, with her early evening walk the day before. "She never usually translated the time of a death into personal time" (13). We see her struggle to appear pro-fessional and distant as she takes stock of her first case and, soon after, her second, a body thrown into the sea from a helicopter. Her partner investi-gator, the local archaeologist Sarath Diyasena, arrives soon after and whisks her off to their lab space, the abandoned passenger liner *Oronsay*. Apart from bodies wrapped in plastic sheets, the space, Anil notices, is also used to store Sarath's archaeological findings, mainly rock and bone fragments. Anil's pro-fessional instincts inexorably draw her to the bone fragments. Sarath tells her they are from a sixth-century dig, a graveyard for Buddhist monks. Her sharp forensic eye soon notices a fragment that does not belong to that era, that is, in fact, more recent. When she points this out to the archaeologist, he freezes: "He had stopped what he was doing and was watching her" (21). Did he know about this? Is he part of a government conspiracy to hide bodies of the recently killed in this ancient site? At this stage we as readers and Anil as an outsider have no way of knowing. This signals the start of her quest. She urges Sarath to make arrangements for them to visit the ancient site. His response is full of ambivalence about his actual role in these findings: "It's a government-protected zone. The skeletons were interred in natural hollows near the Bandarawela caves. Skeletons and loose bones. It's unlikely you'd find anything from another era" (21).

As a narrative reinforcement to Anil's commitment to the evidence of bones, two digressions appear right after this incident. Both appear in italics, and each serves as an epistemological metaphor for Anil's single-minded quest for unequivocal truth: a map and an inventory. The map sequence is a narrative of the seventy-three versions of the natural landscape of Sri Lanka found in *The National Atlas of Sri Lanka*. Each template reveals "only one aspect, one obsession: rainfall, water, winds, surface waters of lakes, rarer bodies of water locked deep within the earth" (39–40). The inventory documents in barest detail the names of persons missing from November 1989 to January 1990. This is the period referred to by both the novelist and the archaeologist character as one of the darkest in Sri Lanka's civil war history. The details provided are minimal and exactly the same for each case: name, age, date and time of disappearance, and the site on which the missing person was last seen.

Kumara Wijetunga, 17. 6th November 1989. At about 11.30 p.m. from his house.

Prabath Kumara, 16. 17th November 1989. At 3.20 a.m. from the home of a friend.

Kumara Arachchi, 16. 17th November 1989. At about midnight from his house.

Manelka da Silva, 17. 1st December 1989. While playing cricket, Embilipitiya Central College playground.

Jatunga Gunasena, 23. 11th December 1989. At 10.30 a.m. near his house while talking to a friend.

Prasantha Handuwela, 17. 17th December 1989. At about 10.15 a.m. close to the tyre centre, Embilipitiya.

Prasanna Jayawarna, 17. 18th December 1989. At 3.30 p.m. near Chandrika reservoir.

Podi Wickramage, 49. 19th December 1989. At 7.30 a.m. while walking along the road to the centre of Embilipitiya town.

Narlin Gooneratne, 17. 26th December 1989. At about 5.00 p.m. at a tea-shop 15 yards from Serena army camp.

Weeratunga Samaraweera, 30. 7th January 1990. At 5.00 p.m. while going for a bath at Hulandawa Panamura. (4)[11]

In foregrounding the skeletal outlines of *landscapes* and *deathworlds*, respectively, these two narrative sequences presage Anil's discovery of actual skeletons soon afterward, on the Bandarawela visit. The rest of the novel is a delineation of her efforts to determine the life history and cause of death of these skeletons. Much like the natural historian and the crime detection squad who work their way through the bare details of a map's outline and a police inventory, Anil devotes her time in Sri Lanka to making a case for the extrajudicial killings of the skeletons. Her journey is fraught with cultural, political, and intellectual challenges, and the narrative is challenged by the irruption of cases, characters, and conjunctures that thoroughly complicate the idea of witnessing.

When Sarath and Anil proceed to Bandarawela on the basis of the news that three other skeletons had been found on that ancient site, Sarath cautions Anil against jumping to conclusions about their antiquity or lack of it. Interestingly his warning has both epistemological and cultural overtones. "I want you to understand," he says, "the *archaeological surround of a fact.*" Elsewhere in the book archaeological practice is compared to the reading of a complex historical novel (151). Forensics, Sarath suggests, is too abstracting; it is incapable of working through the layers of deep history in the way archaeology can. Anil's disciplinary training is seen as an extension of her diasporic status—both are ultimately distancing. "You know," Sarath tells her, "I'd believe you more if you lived here. You can't just slip in, make a discovery and leave" (44). He is dismissive too of the power of the global humanitarian gaze: "International investigations don't mean a lot" (45). This thematic interplay between the polarities of an abstract versus a culturally informed pursuit of knowledge both informs and complicates the ethics of witnessing war crimes. For instance, Anil's forensic commitment to get to the bottom of the truth of these extrajudicial killings does not necessarily make her a disinterested, objective, and detached witness in the way Sarath seems to suggest. We see her in turns anxious, angry, outraged, dismayed, and fatalistic about the situation in Sri Lanka. At several points we see also her sympathetic imagination as she contemplates the emotional toll of these violent, inexplicable deaths on the families of the victims. They lose language and logic; fragments of clothing are often their only source of connection with the loved one they have lost: "They held on to just the coloured and patterned sarong a missing relative last slept in, which in normal times would have become a household rag but now was sacred" (56).

In an effort to individuate each of the three modern skeletons at the Bandarawela site, in order to bring them back into the realm of language and meaning, Anil starts by giving them names: Tinker, Tailor, Soldier. Ondaatje's play on the popular detective novel genre is evident here. John le Carré's novel of the same title (with the addition of *Spy*) is the obvious referent here. This playful rhetorical gesture is a sure sign that Ondaatje, while crafting this novel, was mindful of the popular cultural impact of forensic crime fiction and its resonance with the experience of mediated witnessing of real-world massacres. The invocation of le Carré does not take away from the seriousness of Anil's nominalist gesture. She talks repeatedly of the importance of *naming* the skeletons because to her they "become representative of all those lost voices," the voices of those reported missing in that long inventory of names, voices of those "who were slammed and stained by violence" (55–56). We see the significance of *naming* early in the novel in the very way Anil gets her name. She was not born with it but had to "buy" this masculine-sounding name from her brother because she was so unhappy with the name given her by her parents. We never hear what her original name was, but it is clear that it violated her sense of what constituted her essential being. There is no doubt that the thematics of naming in this novel is intricately woven with that of individuation, sympathetic recognition, and testimonial plenitude. Extrapolated onto the deathworlds of post-1989 Sri Lanka, *naming* appears to be the only antidote to annihilation. If death is "vaporization" and "microfragmentation" in Anil's forensic world, life is making the flesh whole and singularly sovereign with the power of naming.

Anil's discovery of a fourth skeleton, which she names Sailor, reinforces her conviction that this ancient burial site was used by government officials to bury their more recent killings. "Something not prehistoric" about this skeleton, she tells Sarath, as her forensic training affirms that it belongs to a badly burned body. In defiance of his caution not to rush into conclusive truths, she draws on her training to build a clear case for murder in this instance: "*Listen* . . . there are trace elements you can find in bones—mercury, lead, arsenic, even gold—that don't belong to them, they seep in from the surrounding soil. . . . In this skeleton there are traces of lead. . . . But there is no lead in this cave where we found him, the soil samples show none. Do you see? He must have been buried somewhere else before. Someone took precautions to make sure the skeleton was not discovered. This is no ordinary murder or burial. They buried him, then later moved him to an older gravesite" (51).

The implication she draws from this discovery is that only a government official could have had access to a protected archaeological site to rebury the body. So the skeleton is evidence of a state crime. In Anil's eyes, Bandarawela is now both an ancient site of burials and *a crime scene*, and much like Dr. Temperance Brennan from the television series *Bones*, she is intent on getting to the heart of the truth. From this point on the novel appears to give her an edge over her native investigator. Sarath is compelled to acknowledge that she may have stumbled on an indubitable, if unpalatable, truth. She, however, continues to be suspicious about the extent of his complicity in this cover-up and wonders if there are any veiled threats to her life in his cautioning her against knowing too much. She expresses her intention to guard the skeletons at all cost and confronts him with her suspicion:

> She thought she'd say it right out. At once. "I don't really know, you see, which side you are on—if I can trust you."
>
> He began to speak, stopped, then spoke slowly. "What would I do?"
>
> "You could make him disappear." (53)

And again later, "Can I trust you?," to which he replies, "You have to trust me" (64). Her masterful knowledge of bones surfaces right afterward—"permanent truths same for Colombo as for Troy"—as she accurately reconstructs the circumstances of Sailor's death: "She could read Sailor's last actions by knowing the wounds on the bone. He put his arms up over his face to protect himself from the blow. He is shot with a rifle, the bullet going through his arm, then into the neck. While he's on the ground, they come up and kill him. . . . The smallest, cheapest bullet. A .22's path that her ballpoint pen could slide through. Then they attempt to set fire to him and begin to dig his grave in this burning light" (65).

As if converted by her forensic zeal, Sarath becomes determined to excavate the identities of the skeletons. Only one of them, Sailor, has a skull, which Sarath separates from the skeleton and brings to his desk. He is aware that they have reached an impasse in their investigations unless they find a way to reconstruct the face around the skull. Seeking such expertise openly is dangerous in a political context that openly implicates the Sri Lankan government in a murder case. Rather than go back to the murky world of Colombo's bureaucracy—medical and political—they turn to his old teacher, Palipana, an epigraphist and archaeologist, now blind and living an ascetic life amid sixth-century ruins in faraway Anuradhapura. In this turn of the plot the novel opens up to an epistemological world that is distinctly different from forensic science. It would be simplistic to call it an Asian knowledge world and mark it as culturally specific in the way that forensic science is not. That would primordialize knowledge worlds in Asia that are otherwise congruent with the universal claims of modern science. Rather, to use a psychoanalytic term heuristically, this is the Unconscious of the scientific world, science's disavowed predilection toward the imagined, the sublime, the trace of the ancient or the prehistoric beyond the obvious reach of the evidentiary but not beyond the reach of a finely attuned perception using all available senses. What does such a world have to offer to the novel's thematics of witnessing in our era of humanitarian civil wars? Why does Ondaatje direct his novelistic energies toward an apparently antiquated and institutionally disavowed mode of knowledge making? I pursue these questions through the metaphor of the hand. In my reading the hand connotes the obverse of scientific abstraction (bones), not its antinomy. It represents the force of a now disenfranchised mode of pursuing truth, a proto-scientific empiricism dependent on a variety of sense perceptions. I use the term *obverse* here to mean counterpart or complement, in the way it is used in formal logic. The counterpart or obverse of a proposition exchanges the affirmative for the negative quality of the whole proposition and then negates the predicate. Thus a hypothetical statement representing Anil's categorical commitment to abstract scientific truth, "All evidence points to the fact that I am right," would, in the logic used by Palipana to describe his commitment to the epistemological power of sense perception, including the tactile, read, "No evidence points to the fact that I am not right."

Hand

Palipana's brother, Narada, also a Buddhist monk, was found murdered one evening during the civil war. Despite his habitation outside the bounds of civilization, Palipana is haunted by the mystery of his brother's death. But his nonforensic knowledge world cannot directly assist in investigating either Narada's death or crimes against humanity. Before retreating from the scholarly domain, he was a celebrated epigraphist known for his ability to translate ancient Pali scripts and also rock graffiti from the pre-Christian era. In middle age he turned to archaeology and transformed that field in South Asia by integrating into a conventional archaeological scientism his knowledge of the deep history of the subcontinent in all its expressive forms: oral, written, and inscribed in rock and other discernible geological manifestations of human habitation. Ondaatje takes great pains to delineate Palipana's protean and unorthodox knowledge world to us. We learn that, despite being feted globally for his rare achievements, he shunned the limelight. A man of spare habits with a manic dedication to his work, he made a formidable teacher and researcher. Students rarely lived up to his exacting standards, but a few of them, Sarath included, became renowned scholars in their field. Despite feeling alienated from him due to his repeated intellectual brutality, they were compelled to acknowledge that "he was the best archaeological theorist in the country, that he was nearly always right, and that even with his fame and success he continued to live a life-style more minimal than any of them" (80–81).

Palipana's hands and fingers were critical to his talents as a scholar even before he lost his eyesight. He thrilled at theorizing parallels between the expertise of stonemasons and his own work translating Pali texts. He needed to *feel* the texture of rocks and ancient inscriptions and spent more time in *tactile* contact with his sites than with scholarly books. His need to experience these sites as places of everyday dwelling, of continuous human activity was also a critical aspect of his scholarly orientation: "As a historian and a scientist he approached every problem with many hands. He was more likely to work beside a stonemason or listen to a *dhobi* woman washing clothes at a newly discovered rock pool than with a professor from the University of Peradeniya. He approached runes not with a historical text but with the pragmatic awareness of locally inherited skills" (82).

In Palipana's predilection toward finding uncanny resemblances between apparently nonproximate phenomena—epigraphy and the sound of washing in a rock pool, for instance—one is tempted to read a mode of knowledge making that Foucault in *The Order of Things* called "pre-classical." Readers will remember Foucault's account of the evolution of knowledge in terms of ruptures in the three epistemes he named the preclassical, the classical, and the modern. The preclassical episteme was characterized by four types of similitude: *convenientia*, or the tendency to find hidden resemblances due to plain proximity in space; *aemulatio*, or the tendency to see two things imitate each other over a great distance; *analogy*, or "subtle resemblances of relations"; and *sympathy*, or the power to assimilate likeness into identity or sameness. The classical rupture, which he dates from the seventeenth century with the works of Francis Bacon and René Descartes, moved away from this system of resemblances and directed the comparative enterprise toward discrimination, measurement, and ordering of phenomena. In the eighteenth century, broadly considered the apogee of the classical age, enumeration and taxonomy became the dominant modes of accumulating, sifting, and categorizing information on wealth, nature, and languages, the three recognized sites of knowledge making. Resemblance was to be "contained" by rigorous comparative schemas that emphasized difference over similitude. The classical episteme was ruptured by the modern in the nineteenth century. It witnessed the total disenfranchisement of resemblance as the foundation of knowledge and the transformation of "order into history." Succession in time replaced contiguity in space: "The contemporaneous and the simultaneously observable resemblances in space [were] simply the fixed forms of a succession."[12] The impact of this rupture on positivist comparativists was enormous. Comparison was no longer, writes Natalie Melas, "primarily a procedure for analyzing similarity and difference in order to determine individual units suitable to evaluation, but rather a means of determining the general laws of development ascertainable beyond objects of analysis."[13] In other words, the modern episteme was responsible for relegating the preclassical and classical epistemes into the past as less developed modes of knowledge making.

No doubt Foucault's analysis of knowledge systems had Europe at its center, and an immediate postcolonial response would be to say that Palipana's epistemological orientation ought not to be read within this paradigm. But given the robust intellectual history of postcolonialism in provincializing Europe, we can read Palipana's approach to the historical and archaeological past of Sri Lanka not as an abjuration of European modes of knowledge making altogether but as a resistance to the temporal advantage accorded to positivist approaches to historical studies within the modern episteme. In an analogous reading Antoinette Burton interestingly aligns Palipana's orientation with that of the subaltern studies historians who did not reject disciplinary history but sought to rearticulate its procedural parameters: "Palipana is an anti-colonialist who does not reject history, but seeks to re-imagine it on new procedural grounds: a kind of fictional Subaltern Studies hero, albeit a fallen one. In an echo of the 'small histories' which scholars like Ranajit Guha have called for as the bases for new historical knowledges, Palipana's contribution, we are told, lay not simply in a rejection of evidentiary procedures or even in a rejection of 'History per se,' but rather in a more imaginative and less text-driven archive."[14]

Postcolonial historians are not the only ones who have questioned the positivist and textual bias of disciplinary history. The interpretive turn in the discipline—with oral, literary, linguistic, ethnographic, and visual inflections—has had a long run and has not been restricted to the writing of non-

European histories. The metonymic and metaphoric power of the hand in my analysis of Palipana thus does not fetishize a culturally distinct mode of understanding the past, one that is somehow "backward" in the global scheme of things. What it does is complicate the novel's graphing of what constitutes the factual and the evidentiary in witnessing violence and trauma.

One of Sarath's most memorable expeditions with Palipana, for which Sarath claims he could trade his entire subsequent life, was to a newly discovered rock site where Palipana made him miraculously *see* through the labor of his *hands* the outlines of a woman trying to protect her child from danger. Visible to the naked eye were mere blotches of faded color and shadowy outlines of human form. Palipana's fingers discovered an entire narrative as he patiently, meticulously traced every inscription, every line on the inside of the rock: "He [Sarath] would, he knew ... give his life for the rock carving from another century of the woman bending over her child. He remembered how they had stood before it in the flickering light, Palipana's arm following the line of the mother's back bowed in affection or grief. An unseen child. All the gestures of her motherhood harnessed. A muffled scream in her posture" (157).

Palipana eventually squandered his reputation by taking his unorthodox approach too far. In open defiance of the acceptable standards of both legibility and credibility in the academic world, he wrote a conjectural treatise about hitherto undiscovered rock graffiti that he claimed contained a priceless historical narrative about the political intrigues of a sixth-century royal kingdom on the island. He published a translation of the verses he had purportedly discovered, which ranged from the soliloquies of dying warriors to social manifestoes by kings and erotic verse by courtiers. All of these persons were named, and their historical existence, Palipana claimed, could be confirmed in existing Pali tracts such as the *Culavamsa*. The logic of doing so was impeccable to him:

> In the last few years he had found hidden histories, intentionally lost, that altered the perspective and knowledge of earlier times. It was how one hid or wrote the truth when it was necessary to lie. . . . The dialogue between old and hidden lines, the back-and-forth between what was official and unofficial during solitary field trips, when he spoke to no one for weeks, so that these became his only conversations—an epigraphist studying the specific style of a chisel-cut from the fourth century, the coming across an illegal story, one banned by kings and state and priests, in the interlinear texts. These verses contained the darker proof. (105)

For a while the academic world was enthralled by his publications. Soon enough, one of his own protégés challenged Palipana's discovery and exposed his tracts as fictional. There was no visible evidence of the runes he talked of, nor were any of the ancient characters he named found in *Culavamsa*. The distinction between the decipherable and the indecipherable, which had blurred in his mind, was one that the academic establishment fastened onto with an authoritative grip. What followed was unequivocal condemnation and academic shaming. His name was struck off the national register of archaeologists. Palipana, undeterred by his downfall, scornfully turned his back once more on conventional academia.

What did this formidable master of archaeological theory and epigraphy set out to prove with this last defiant act of worldly scholarly engagement? The limits of the factual and the evidentiary? The lamentable disenfranchisement of a holistic epistemology that ought to incorporate all human faculties, not just reason and visual evidence? The impasse his defiance signals is this: "The point was not that he could ever be proved wrong in his theories, but that he could not prove he was right" (83). The motif of the hand in my analysis stands for this aporia of the provable and the demonstrable as much as it stands as a counterpart—obverse, I called it earlier—of scientific knowledge, one that begins where forensic science, the science of bones, reaches its limits. "We use the bones to search for truth," Anil tells him, even as she is forced to admit she does not know where that will lead unless he is willing to help them. She and Sarath have come to him for help reconstructing Sailor's skull. Given his extensive connections in the nonscholarly world of artisans and stonemasons—the reconstructors of his archaeological findings—they are hopeful he will be able to direct them discreetly to a nonprofessional reconstruction specialist. By reconstructing Sailor's face they hope to individuate him, to bring him back to the realm of human belonging. The reconstructed head is also, of course, meant to be presented as a juridical case against the government in the presence of a UN tribunal.

Despite his infamy in the world of knowledge, Palipana becomes for them an indispensable medium through which to channel their forensic witnessing of the civil war massacres. There are a couple of memorable sequences worth recounting in this encounter between two discrete knowledge worlds. In one, Palipana's *hand* confronts the evidence of the *bones* and does a thorough reading of the skull in the way the former master is accustomed to reading ancient rock carvings. Anil is spellbound: "Anil watched his fingers, beautiful and thin, moving over the outlines of the skull Sarath had given him, his long fingernails at the supraorbital ridge, within the orbital cavities, then cupping the shape as if warming his palms on the skull, as if it were a stone from some old fire. He was testing the jaw's angle, the blunt ridge of its teeth" (87). Palipana's tactile exploration is in a continuum with his general orientation toward archaeological and epigraphic truth. He reads the skull as he would read an ancient Pali inscription or rock graffiti: noting the texture, undulations, curvature, indentation, density, and fragility.

The second sequence is an intellectual exchange between Anil and Palipana about their respective approaches to the factual and temporal divide that spans their search for truth. Sarath sets the stage for the epistemological discussion by starkly differentiating the science of forensics from archaeology and epigraphy: "Sir, you and I work on ancient rocks, fossils, rebuild dried-up water gardens, concern ourselves with why an army moved into the dry zone. We can identify an architect by his habit of building winter and summer palaces. But Anil lives in contemporary times. She uses contemporary methods. She can cut a cross-section of bone with a fine saw and determine the skeleton's exact age at death that way" (95). Palipana is not uninterested. He can sense that their approaches are not as sharply differentiated as Sarath makes them out to be. Both probe deep and long into their object of investigation, but their instruments in this pursuit of truth are different. He uses his fingers and those of the artisans he hires to re-create scenes from paint fragments, which helps him reconstruct eras from the runes he explores. Anil uses her microscope and her power of visual observation. He is willing to be disarmed by her smartness, and this is exactly what happens. Anil's confident response about how her scientific training enables her to determine the age of a skeleton at the time of death leads to a discussion on probability and certainty. She asserts that her observation under a microscope of a cross-section of bone that is one-tenth of a millimeter thick gives her conclusion far more certainty than his tactile study of every aspect of the skull. The margin of error in her microscopic study is a bare 5 percent, an acceptable margin in science. He appears ready to concede this point and playfully challenges her to guess his age by looking at his bone structure. She names an accurate number, and once again the old teacher is charmed, until she abruptly points out the limits of conjecture and the importance of checking facts from the right sources:

"I suppose you can tell how old a geezer like me is too, with a piece of bone."

"You're seventy-six."

"How?" Palipana was disarmed. "My skin? Nails?"

"I checked the Sinhala encyclopaedia before we left Colombo." (97)

Convinced that he has an able intellectual counterpart in Anil despite their different approaches to the truth, Palipana offers to help reconstruct the skull. In doing so he directs the conversation to Sri Lanka's history and warns her of the political muddying of veracity through the long history of this unfortunate island: "'Well, kings also caused trouble in those days,' he said. 'Even then there was nothing to believe in with certainty. They still didn't know what truth was. We have never had the truth. Not even with your work on bones'" (102). He directs them to an artist, Ananda, a dissolute soul who stumbles through his work in the gem mines, inebriated and bereft. His wife disappeared one night during the height of the civil war, and the trauma made him renounce the world of art. But Palipana has complete faith in his talent. In his view Ananda is not just an accomplished artist; he is the best eye painter of three generations in a family that specializes in the auspicious ritual of eye painting, an ancient practice on the island called Netra Mangala, painting the eyes on a sculpted holy figure without looking directly at the face. With his back to the statue, the artist holds his brush over his shoulder and paints the eyes by looking in a mirror. The aura attached to this artifice is immense. The statue acquires divine life only after the eyes are painted on it.

From this point on the novel turns to a third modality of engagement with truth, for which I use the term *eye*, not in the sense of direct and demonstrable visible evidence but as a metaphor for insight into the truth of the abyssal and sublime beyond the horror of the event. It connotes a mode of witnessing that transcends the temporal logic of justice and retribution. In terms of the Derridean reading of the tripartite etymological import of witness, Anil functions in the novel as *terstis*, the third-party observer whose primary role is to provide impartial evidence in a juridical setting. Her role exhausts itself as soon as she does that. She has no power to prolong the temporality of the event. Even her sympathetic imagination, which often impels her to exchange places imaginatively with Sailor in the manner theorized by Adam Smith as constituting the essence of impartial spectatorship, does not extend beyond her role as a third-party witness. Ananda, on the other hand, functions as the *superstes*, the survivor of trauma who persists beyond the traumatic event and holds onto its truth, makes *present* its terror for generations to come through his artistic labor, much like Spiegelman in *Maus*.

Anil and Sarath first encounter Ananda, "the eye-painter turned gem-pit worker, turned head-restorer," in an obscure, decrepit town. The entire exchange is described rather hurriedly in the third person to signal the distance these scholars feel from Ananda's world and also to manage this sequence spatially, as something taking place surreptitiously, away from the zones of governance and politics. Narratively Ananda is kept incognito and is referred to as just "the man":

> When they locate him, it appeared that he had just woken up from an early-evening sleep. . . . Sarath explained what they wanted him to do, mentioned Palipana, and that he would be paid. The man, who wore thick spectacles, said he would need certain things—erasers, the kind on the end of small pencils, small needles. And he said he needed to see the skeleton. They opened the back of the jeep. The man used their squat flashlight to study the skeleton, running it up and down the ribs, the arcs and curves. Anil felt there was little he could learn from such a viewing. . . . Sarath persuaded the man to come to them. After a slight shake of the head, he went into the room he was living in and came out with his belongings in a small cardboard box. (162)

They move to the abandoned house of a deceased artist in the remote town of Ekneligoda and work away at the skeleton. They are quite close to the area where Sailor may have been buried the first time. Ananda labors over the head while Anil examines the skeleton for multiple markers of identity, including occupation. Much like Palipana's, Ananda's artistry emerges from his immersion in the local landscape. On the morning after his arrival, he walks to the local market and eventually settles himself by the public well. There he talks to the locals who happen to pass by. His "anthropomorphic" research is coextensive with this immersive experience: "He watched the village move around him, with its distinct behaviour, its local body postures and facial characteristics. He wanted to discover what the people drank here, whether there was a specific diet that would puff up cheeks more than usual, whether lips would be fuller than in Batticaloa. Also the varieties of hairstyle, the quality of eyesight. Did they walk or cycle. Was coconut oil used in food and hair" (166–67). At the end of the day he is ready to start working on his project. He walks to a local field and looks closely at the soil. His paint is locally derived from three varieties of mud, one black and two browns, which he mixes in various proportions to get the right shade for the skin. He also brings back large quantities of the local alcohol, arrack. His days oscillate between artistry and drunken stupor, without so much as a word being exchanged with either Anil or Sarath. The gaps in his life narrative are progressively filled in parallel with his reconstruction of the skeleton's face. His silences and alcoholism begin to make sense as we learn that his young wife, Sirissa, disappeared one morning on her way to work at a local school. This was the same morning in 1989 when forty-six school students and staff from Ratnapura district—thought to be insurgents or sympathizers of the insurgency—were rounded up and led away to an unknown destination. Their severed heads were later found strung up on poles near their school. Ananda's reconstruction of the head takes on monumental significance against the backdrop of this horrific train of events.

The completed artifact stuns Anil and Sarath. The face they encounter is not an approximation arrived at by a rigorous and abstracted forensic calculation, the type of face that is a plausible fleshing out of the coordinates of the skull. It is too individuated, too singular, and too vividly emblematic of the creator's *agon*. While they were aiming at an aggregated similitude, Ananda created a likeness that bears the weight of his personal and collective loss. The face shakes the objective equanimity of the archaeologist and the forensic scientist. In looking at it Anil feels "she was finally meeting a person who had been described to her in letters, or someone she had once lifted up as a child who was now an adult" (185). She and Sarath are struck by two things: the youthfulness of the face and its serene expression, which defies Anil's conclusion that Sailor was a plumbago mineworker. They know that "the face was in no way a portrait of Sailor but showed a calm that Ananda had known in his wife, a peacefulness he wanted for any victim" (187). The face Ananda creates is a projection of his unfathomable, unspeakable sense of loss, his melancholia that refuses to let go of the dead, that seeks to bestow on the severed heads but also on the unfound body of his young wife a sense of peace and dignity after death. Instinctively Anil and Sarath recognize in this gesture the defeat of their epistemological and legalistic assumptions about forensic witnessing. In fact Anil, unable to reconcile the staggering incommensurability between their mode of witnessing and Ananda's, breaks down and cries inconsolably. Her effort to construct a sentimental case, that is, a case that brings to the fore the experience of what has befallen a person, is completely defeated by the sublimity of Ananda's witnessing. She is the Smithian impartial spectator and the Derridean terstes: abstractly speculative with an empathetic imagination that enables her to trade places with the subject of suffering. Her aspiration is to eventually transcend both positions and occupy a third one that is legible in a court of law. Unlike Smith's spectator, however, she opens herself to risk and momentarily abandons the safety of her spectatorial position.[15] Nevertheless she ultimately cannot transcend her spectatorial status. Sailor's skeleton remains a piece of *evidence* for her; without it she has no agency. Ananda is the quintessential *superstes*, the witness as the survivor of trauma who through a melancholic encryption of the dead prolongs the affective temporality of the occurrence beyond that of distributive justice.

This aporia between two modes of witnessing—the speculative and the melancholic, or what I called the forensic and the testimonial—could well have been the ending of the novel. However, Ondaatje takes the narrative further and chooses to arrest the novel at three distinct junctures. Each constitutes an ending of sorts, and each is a powerful tableau of witnessing. The first is Anil's appearance before a tribunal and her subsequent hasty departure from Colombo for fear of her life. The second is Sarath's murder and his brother's discovery of his body. The third is Ananda's metamorphosis from a drunk and derelict miner to an eye painter who reconstructs a shattered Buddha statue. Let us take a brief look at the implications of all three for the overarching thematics of witnessing.

Despite Ananda's failure to reconstruct Sailor's face, Sarath and Anil are able to trace the skeleton's identity. His name was Ruwan Kumara. He worked as a toddy tapper before breaking his ankle in a fall, then, as Anil surmised, he worked in a mine. Sarath's and Anil's meticulous adherence to the protocols of their respective disciplines combined with their detective zeal enable them to come up with fairly conclusive evidence of the circumstances of Ruwan Kumara's murder. That it was an extrajudicial murder they are sure of. Sarath, not content with their findings, decides to go back to Colombo to check if the man's name appeared on the government's "wanted" list. When he doesn't return after six days, Anil's suspicions about his complicity in a government cover-up come to the fore and she decides to act alone. She calls a Colombo doctor, a family friend, and decides to face the tribunal alone with Sailor's skeleton as her evidence.

The trial turns out to be a farce. The skeleton is stolen from her as soon as she arrives in Colombo. She continues undeterred with another skeleton, one of the three they found in Bandarawela. Her confidence in her forensic conclusions enables her to work with a substitute, but she draws the right conclusions from the wrong evidence. Her dilemma is identical to Palipana's: "The point was not that he could ever be proved wrong in his theories, but that he could not prove he was right" (83). Her *juridical* case falls flat for she violates the rule of evidence in a court of law. She has no way to demonstrate the truth of her *individuating* case either; in the absence of the right skeleton her meticulous research into the circumstances of Sailor's life and death has no merit in the eyes of the forensic establishment. Her only recourse is to make a *sentimental* case: to project a relay of evidence of extreme suffering, that is, to make Sailor's evidence transferrable to all other cases of extrajudicial killings. "The skeleton I had was evidence of a certain kind of a crime. That is what is important here. . . . *One victim can speak for many victims,*" she bravely, desperately avers (275). Significantly her projective imagination does not stop at that. In a gesture that typically marks the sentimental as a *social* and not a *personal* passion, she includes all citizens of Sri Lanka in her empathetic circuitry.[16] She is no longer the foreign-returned UN representative but a citizen giving evidence: "I think you murdered hundreds of *us,*" she thunders at an audience full of government officials and counterterrorism experts (272).

The denouement is not what she anticipates. Sarath, of all people in that powerful audience, emerges from hiding and questions her claims. They duel researcher to researcher, and she eventually loses this epistemic and juridical battle. He then arranges for her to be stripped of all incriminating paperwork and quietly leave the country. She is not to know for another few hours that he feared for her life, that his actions at the trial were an attempt to save both of them, that there was no space for the heroics of truth and justice in the necropolitical world of this doomed island.

She is also not to know one other tragic outcome of her attempt at forensic witnessing. Soon after her departure, Sarath's doctor brother, Gamini, another traumatized and dissolute soul, discovers the horrific murder of his older brother in an avalanche of bodies that arrive at the hospital after yet another bout of violence. This constitutes the second culminating moment of the novel. Hitherto left out of the novel's epistemic circuit, Gamini, in these final moments, becomes the medical witness par excellence of his brother's gruesome death. His close attendance to his dead brother's wounded body is soon elevated into a communion with his estranged sibling's soul, an act of healing that connects both their wounded beings:

> He could see the acid burns, the twisted leg. He unlocked the cupboard that held bandages, splints, disinfectant. He began washing the body's dark-brown markings with scrub lotion. He could heal his brother, set the left leg, deal with every wound as if he were alive, as if treating the hundred small traumas would eventually bring him back into his life.

The gash of scar on the side of your elbow you got crashing a bike on the Kandy Hill. This scar I gave you hitting you with a cricket stump. . . . You were always too much of an older brother, Sarath. Still, if I had been a doctor then, I could have sewn the stitches up more carefully than Dr. Piachaud. It's thirty years later, Sarath. It's late afternoon—with everyone gone home except me, your least favourite relative. The one you can never relax with or feel secure with. Your unhappy shadow. (287–88)

The novel now well and truly abandons its forensic and speculative registers of witnessing. The secular tropes of the evidentiary and the factual—the universal grammar of knowledge—give way to the dialogic, nonsecular, and sublime language of reconciliation, remembrance, and transcendence. Gamini's simultaneous acts of witnessing, mourning, and healing are conceived as a *pietà*, the sublime, nonsecular act of gazing at the dead with pity and melancholy. As he leans across to dress the wounds on his brother's prostrate body,

the horizontal afternoon light held the two of them in a wide spoke. . . . This was a pieta between brothers. And all Gamini knew in his slowed, scrambled state was that this would be the end or it could be the beginning of a permanent conversation with Sarath. If he did not talk to him in this moment . . . his brother would disappear from his life. . . . He opened his brother's shirt so the chest was revealed. A gentle chest. Not hard and feral like his own. . . . Sarath's chest said everything. . . . There seemed to be a mark like that made with a spear. A small wound, not deep in his chest, and Gamini bathed it and taped it up.

He had seen cases where every tooth had been removed, the nose cut apart, the eyes humiliated with liquids, the ears entered. He had been, as he ran down that hospital hallway, most frightened of seeing his brother's face. It was the face they went for in some cases. They could in their hideous skills sniff out vanity. But they had not touched Sarath's face. (288–90)

The original *Pietà* was, of course, immortalized by Michelangelo in his Renaissance masterpiece in St. Peter's Basilica in Vatican City. The sublime marble sculpture of Mary holding the dead Jesus in her arms has become the very emblem of grief in the Christian world. Gamini's holding his dead brother's body also brings to mind Adam Smith's fevered reflections on sympathy for the dead, which he conceives of in the language of the sublime as *transport* of "our own living souls in their inanimated bodies, and thence conceiving what would be our emotions in this case." "It is miserable," he continues, "to be deprived of the light of the sun; to be shut out from life and conversation; to be laid in the cold grave, a prey to corruption and the reptiles of the earth. . . . The idea of that dreary and endless melancholy, which the fancy naturally ascribes to their condition, arises altogether from our joining to the change which has been produced upon them, on our consciousness of that change; from our putting ourselves in that situation, and from lodging . . . our own living souls in their inanimated bodies."[17] This idea of *transporting* one's soul into the dead and inanimate is the language of the sublime, not that of the reflective, sympathetic spectator that Smith otherwise is at pains to theorize.

Trauma, the novel ultimately suggests, occupies an epistemic and affective domain beyond the evidentiary and the sentimental. A theoretical framing of trauma in terms of the sublime has characterized much postwar and Holocaust scholarly literature on witnessing. Cathy Caruth's psychoanalytical formulation of the "blocked encounter" at the heart of the traumatic experience, and more specifically its unrepresentability, is central to this literature.[18] We also saw Derrida's reading of Celan's poem "Aschenglory" as the ultimate conundrum of the unrepresentable: the ashes as the "unreadable, undecodable archive." A slightly different approach to the idea of the unrepresentable and, in effect, the sublime appears in Agamben's *Remnants of Auschwitz*. Agamben reminds us that etymologically the term *holocaust*, from the Greek *holocaustus*, means something totally burned, something that leaves no trace. In its subsequent semantic migration to biblical narratives, the term undergoes a euphemistic transformation into "supreme sacrifice in the sphere of complete devotion to sacred and superior motives." It is a shift Agamben comprehensively rejects: "In the case of the term 'holocaust' . . . the attempt to establish a connection, however distant, between Auschwitz and the Biblical *olah* and between death in the gas chamber and the 'complete devotion to sacred and superior motives' cannot but sound like a jest. Not only does the term imply an unacceptable equation between crematoria and altars; it also continues a semantic heredity that is from its inception anti-Semitic. That is why we will never make use of this term." Agamben's rejection of the term's biblical mystification parallels his outrage at being accused by a French newspaper of "ruining the unique and unsayable character of Auschwitz." *Euphemism*, he points out, has its origins in the Greek *euphemein*, "to observe in religious silence." "Why confer on extermination the prestige of the mystical? . . . To say that Auschwitz is 'unsayable' or 'incomprehensible' is equivalent to *euphemein*, to adoring in silence, as one does with a God. Regardless of one's intention, this contributes to its glory."[19] Much like Derrida, he turns to the idea of witnessing to overcome this impasse at the heart of Holocaust representation.

In the final chapter of *Anil's Ghost*, in a different theological register, but in a spirit not unlike Agamben's rejection of the "unsayable" and the "mystical," Ondaatje transforms Ananda from a bit player in a juridical case into a superhuman sculptor who is called in to repair the face of a shattered Buddha statue damaged by vandals. The discovery that the Buddha's stomach was prized open in search of jewels prompts the authorial voice to intervene and direct the reader away from an overdetermined reading of this incident as sacrilegious and as indelibly stained by the civil war: "This was for once not a political act or an act perpetrated by one belief against another. The men were trying to find a solution for hunger or a way to get out of their disintegrating lives" (300). There is also scarcely anything sacred about the field in which the statue is located. The obscurity and desolation of this area make it an ideal location for trucks to dump bodies, to "burn and hide victims who had been picked up" (300). The politicotheological overtones of the civil war manifested in the ominous chasm between Sinhalese Buddhists and Tamil Hindus are here metamorphosed into a materialist reading by the very way Ananda undertakes the reconstruction of the Buddha statue. He approaches it as an artificer, not as a devotee. He labors for months, sifting through rocks and stones in volatile weather to find just the right texture and color. He gathers around him as many village workers as he can, for "it was safer to be seen working for a project like this . . . otherwise you could be pulled into the army or you might be rounded up as a suspect" (301–2). Most significantly, in his reconstruction of the Buddha's face he makes no attempt to smooth the cracked contours. The reader is compelled to confront a close-up of the face in which "one hundred chips and splinters of stone" are brought together with just a shadowy bamboo strand visible across the cheek. Ananda sees this as the "human shadow" on the Buddha's face, a shadow that had hitherto never fallen on this towering sacral form. This gesture of de-sanctification is sublime, but it is not outside the realm of human expressivity. It bespeaks resistance, reconciliation, and transcendence all at once. His artificer self, Ananda admits, helps exorcise the demon of retribution within him. He becomes the witness par excellence, one who has a glimpse of life beyond the blood-soaked quagmire of war even as he dons Sarath Diyasena's cotton shirt under his elaborate costume and holds forever in his mind's eye his young wife's calm visage. The novel ends with Ananda walking toward the horizon hand in hand with his young nephew, who served as his apprentice during the long months of reconstruction.

Ananda is the quintessential *superstes*, the witness as the survivor of trauma who helps prolong the temporality of the occurrence beyond distributive justice. His reconstruction of the Buddha statue allegorizes the impasse between the two modes of witnessing—the forensic and the testimonial—that frame the novel. The truth of Ananda's shattered life, like that of countless other victims of the civil war, resides forever in the cracked visage of the reconstructed Buddha, less as mystical metaphor than as material evidence. In ending the novel thus, Ondaatje makes chronotopically legible the vicissitudes of what counts as evidence in the history of violence in our times. The novelization process here, while not explicitly allegorizing the impact of exorbitant media witnessing, nevertheless abstracts from the political surround of our precarious time the power of such witnessing in times of endemic war and violence.

NINE
AFFECTIVE WITNESSING:
ORPHIC NETHERWORLDS

Proleptic Terror

I have traced at quite some length Ondaatje's novelistic abstraction of what I have called the chronotopical braiding of forensic and testimonial witnessing. What, then, of novelistic work on its affective counterpart, the relay of intensities that permeate the everyday world of terror, marked by "unactualized threat," by "an unconsummated surplus of danger"?[1] While the zeal for justice consumes the humanitarian activist or the immediate kin of those killed, the distributive intensities across the general population are overwhelmingly marked by constant anxiety and fear about the imminence of violence. There is a proleptic shift widely acknowledged in the temporality of fear, whereby the terror unleashed by one deadly bomb attack triggers a collective pathology about ever more violence to come. The mirror image of this affective insecurity can be found in the political management of such threat. The governmental language of preemptive strike, of enhancing security for the general populace through an incremental erosion of individual liberty—these are familiar narratives that have resulted in a gratuitous amplification of the very sense of threat the political apparatus sets out to alleviate. How might one calibrate the power and salience of witnessing through such an affective lens in the corpus of world novels? What indeed constitutes the novel's tropological work of witnessing at the threshold of dissolving evidence?

Janette Turner Hospital's *Orpheus Lost* (2007) offers a powerful case study for precisely such an investigation. This novel is a tragic ode to the fear-saturated worlds of ordinary people who live in the shadow of precisely this proleptic temporality of terror. As everyday witnesses to events that have the force of both the actual and the imminent, they are compelled to embark on extraordinary journeys through underworlds dark with unspoken traumas from the past that are folded into the acrid horrors of the present. Much like the way Spiegelman's 9/11 graphic novel, *In the Shadow of No Towers*, is punctuated by episodes from the Holocaust and other catastrophic moments in world history, *Orpheus Lost* telescopes journeys from Auschwitz to Guantánamo Bay and the arid brutalities of refugee detention centers in the wilderness of the South Australian desert. Music—at once affect, mood, passion, and event—informs the novel's overarching tonal and rhythmic patterning. The plot loops through the Orpheus and Eurydice myth in recursive movements that are also retroactive in their impact. Entwined with the novel's narrative, characterological, and tropological work, music constitutes the affective script of *Orpheus Lost*.

A brief reflection on my use of the term *affect* is, perhaps, not out of place at this juncture, especially since the term has been understood and deployed in such diverse critical registers—neurological, physiological, psychoanalytical, cultural, phenomenological, empirical, and historical.[2] For all its protean weight in the world of critical theory, I find it productive for the purposes of my analysis to recuperate two primary ways in which the term has circulated in recent years: as ontological and as contextual. The ontological sees affect as intrinsic to *being* in the world. Derived from the thought of Spinoza and later Deleuze, affect is broadly understood as a terrain of nonsymbolic, psychophysiological intensities generated by but also generating moods, emotions, orientations, will, and a range of bodily reactions, including movement and activity. Such intensities are not owned and individualized. They are a noncognitive registering of the being's coextensiveness with the world—a philosophical cognate almost of the Heideggerian *Dasein*. They exist as potential until they are manifested as what we might call emotions or feelings. These we then drag into the symbolic domain to make sense of, and they become indexed to conventional meaning and subject making. Affective intensity, understood ontologically, is autonomous from the processes of sense making and individuating.[3] At its most radical, such intensity is theorized at a remove from all forms of even physiological consciousness, not just the symbolic and the cognitive. An instance of this is Brian Massumi's foundational essay on affect theory, "The Autonomy of Affect." He writes, "Modulations of heartbeat and breathing mark a reflux of consciousness into the autonomic depths, coterminous with a rise of the autonomic into consciousness. They are a conscious-autonomic mix, a measure of their participation in one another. *Intensity is beside that loop, a nonconscious, never-to-be-conscious autonomic remainder. It is outside expectation and adaptation, as disconnected from meaningful sequencing, from narration, as it is from vital function.* It is narratively de-localized, spreading over the generalized body surface, like a lateral backwash from the function-meaning interloops traveling the vertical path between head and heart."[4]

Massumi's formulation emerges from his analysis of a set of experiments conducted by a group of scientists to test bodily reactions to images. The scientists found little correlation between the content of an image and its immediate effect on the body, which was measured in terms of heartbeat, eye and pupil movement, brain waves, and galvanic skin response. In one experiment there was evidence of brain activity half a second before the participant consciously registered a reaction. In another, a galvanic skin response registered a sad image as pleasant, which was at odds with the heartbeat.[5] Massumi theorizes this disjunction as the difference between the *quality* of an image and its *intensity*. The quality of an image emerges when its content is indexed to conventional meanings that emerge in intersubjective contexts. The intensity of an image, on the other hand, is the strength and duration of impact, the visceral remainder that escapes the subsequent coding of the physiological response in conventional meaning patterns. The philosophical import for Massumi of this "never-to-be-conscious autonomic remainder" lies in the opening up to the indeterminacy of affect, its virtual potentiality before it is captured, differentiated, and made to "fit conscious requirements of continuity and linear causality." Such indeterminacy and virtuality are not presocial but "open-endedly social . . . in a manner 'prior to' the separating out of individuals."[6] In sum, the *autonomy* of affect is the *escape* of affect from the particular thing or body that particularizes it.

The second reading of affect, the *contextual*, rejects this autonomy thesis as too focused on the body and urges instead a scrupulous attention to assemblages and discursive regimes that produce affective fields. Here the body functions as a distributive interface rather than a biophysiological locus of affect. Lawrence Grossberg, one of the more strident critics of the autonomy thesis, talks of the importance of attending to historical ontology, that is, to the "various culturally and phenomenologically constituted emotional economies" that organize affect.[7] Another iteration of this position is found in the work of Lauren Berlant. In her recent study of "cruel optimism" as an affective form, she is at pains to theorize a structure of desire in our late capitalist lifeworlds in which the objects of our attachment, those that promise a good life and are essential to our sense of flourishing, are simultaneously the source of our attrition. In undertaking such an archaeology of affect—to get at the deep structure of the conditions of possibility of contemporary pathologies—Berlant seeks out what she calls a "historical sensorium" through cultural work between the 1990s and the present that "has developed belatedly since the fantasmatic part of the optimism about structural transformation realized less and less traction in the world." What are these frayed and failed fantasies? "Upward mobility, job security, political and social equality, and lively, durable intimacy. This set of dissolving assurances also included meritocracy, the sense that liberal-capitalist society will reliably provide opportunities for individuals to carve out relations of reciprocity that seem fair and that foster life as a project adding up to something and constructing cushions for enjoyment."[8] The force of the affective in Berlant's formulation lies not in our individualized experience of the neuroses and pathologies of the present but in the conjunctures—political, social, cultural, economic—that constellate our collective energies and intensities in the era of neoliberal capitalism. These are the conditions of possibility that structure our desires, orientations, and acts of will.

It is clear that while the *contextual* theorization of affect does not and, in fact, cannot preclude the *ontological*, it resists the primacy and autonomy accorded to biophysiological fields by the ontological. Interestingly in "The Future Birth of Affective Threat" even Massumi, with whom the autonomy thesis is most associated, shifts to a contextual reading wherein he constructs a political ontology of affective fields produced by the discourse on the war on terror and pandemic scares such as the SARS virus and the avian flu. In a reading deep with resonance for my analysis of *Orpheus Lost*, Massumi highlights two critical aspects of this ontology of threat. One is the *felt* reality of a menace that *will have happened* no matter what the nature of the evidence one has in the present. The experience is not an individualized one of conscious threat perception but rather a distributed feeling simmering under the surface of the everyday. An illustration of this appears in the following passage from *Orpheus Lost*: "People had begun to speak of incidents the way they spoke of accidents on the pike: the frequency was distressing, but such things always happened to someone else. There was a certain *frisson*, a low-level hum of anxiety that was more or less constant, especially in crowds, especially at sporting events, or in concert halls, or in the subway."[9] This "menace-potential" is aggravated by the commanding logic of a preemptive politics that has nothing to do with the materialization of threat. A *felt* threat is judged to be as real as an actualized one. This is illustrated in the way Leela, a postdoctoral fellow at MIT working on the mathematics of music, is picked up for interrogation without a warrant because her boyfriend, a musical genius and a Harvard graduate student, visits a mosque frequently. Afterward she is returned home as abruptly with a warning: "'When your boyfriend asks where you've been,' he said, 'remember we'll be listening in.' He got back into the car. 'Now that you've followed your boyfriend to the mosque, you are radioactive. Every Boston incident, from last year's Prudential bombing to this week's big bang at Park Street, has been traced to that mosque. Think about it. We've got you both under surveillance'" (84).

The second aspect of the political ontology of threat is the performative dimension of the *sign* of menace on which the operative logic of preemption critically depends: the mosque, for instance. Such a sign is indexed not to *facts* but to *affects* and to the body's becoming alert. Hints, instincts, unaccountable apprehension, set off by a single sign of threat, all mark the performative semiosis of preemption. Coextensive with the body's perpetual state of alertness, such semiosis dissolves the distinction between agent and patient. Drawing on Peirce's work on the indexical force of the sign, Massumi highlights the critical force of this zone of indistinction "between the body reactivating and the action of the sign," which then extends to the surrounding environment. The indexical for Peirce is the sign's force on the body before the body's conscious awakening to signification. Massumi works with Peirce to philosophically foreground an affective field of surplus danger that operates with such indexical force, one that is always already felt as *real* before being consciously experienced as such, "a world of infinitely seriating menace-potential made actual experience . . . [through] sign's formative performance."[10]

The fallout of the foundational threat event in *Orpheus Lost*, a bomb blast in Prudential Tower, and its recursive patterning through the semiosis of both preemption and the sentient world of music to which the protagonists belong, are classic manifestations of this twofold affective ontology of political threat. The novel's structure is telling in this regard. Five chapters are eponymous, marking the worlds of Leela, Mishka, and Cobb. Four of these alternate between Leela (the witness) and Cobb (the interrogator and her childhood friend). The centerpiece, chapter 5, is on Mishka, the novel's Orpheus, at once victim, witness, and the accused. He is the fulcrum of this work's menace-ridden affective world. The remaining four chapters are titled "Promised Land" (which appears twice), "Underworld," and "Unheard Music." Read in conjunction, they oscillate between the *topoi* of hellish incarceration and emancipation. All nine chapters are saturated with the distributive intensities of threat and preemption. An elaborate musical ensemble carries the affective load; it oscillates between the East and the West, the analytic and the sentient, the perpetrator and the law enforcer, the witness and the interrogator. As this ensemble emerges into the domain of the symbolic, it becomes a twenty-first-century iteration of the Orpheus-Eurydice myth, where Hades is now a series of underground networks of sanctioned torture, and, in a reversal of the Orphic legend, it is Leela as Eurydice who undertakes a journey to the netherworlds of torture to rescue Mishka, her Orpheus. The modalities of witnessing here are wrenched from the epistemic infrastructure of forensic fact and graphic visual evidence that constituted the bulwark of witnessing in Ondaatje's *Anil's Ghost*. The experience of witnessing in *Orpheus Lost* is coextensive with its affective script. It nestles in the novel's musical layering; it cowers in horror from its terrifying shadows; it stumbles through its historical nightmares and oftentimes revels in the novel's promissory vision of emancipation.

Melodic Assemblages

The force of the novel's affective field is evident from the very start. It opens with a flow of subliminal sequences, beginning with Leela's nonplussed murmurings about misreading the code of mystery that surrounds Mishka, though she is a mathematical genius in the making and is obsessed with code cracking and problem solving. This quickly segues into a recurring dream sequence in which Leela follows Mishka into the dark fog as he walks away from her while playing his violin. He resists her entreaties to stop, and when he turns around one last time, she confronts a skeletal face draped in a shroud, a face that warns her not to follow him. This vision from hell soon morphs into Leela's euphoric immersion in Mishka's music from their very first encounter. She hears him before she sees him. The setting is an underground station in Harvard Square, and he is immersed in playing Gluck's "Che faro senza Euridice," the lament of Orpheus as he descends into the underworld to bring Eurydice back. The violin, Leela immediately recognizes from its sound, is a rare Renaissance-era instrument. A scholar of the "math of music" of the High Baroque era, she finds herself transported to a symphonic realm so rarefied—something that she had hitherto only contemplated in her conceptual work—that she is transfixed, much like the listeners of yore, in the Orphic legend: "She could feel the music graphing itself against her skin, her body calculating the frequencies and intervals of the whole subway symphony: bass throb of trains, tenor voice, soft lament of the strings, a pleasing ratio of vibration. Mathematical perfection made her weak at the knees" (5).

Propelled by a euphoric storm surge that cuts through the clanging sound of inbound trains and the rush of feet, she finds herself in Mishka's presence and sees an Orpheus-like figure who lives inside his music, just as music seems to emanate from "inside his blood vessels, from the underside of his skin" (157). He appears oblivious to the enthralled crowds gathering around him as he plays on with his eyes closed and a lock of hair falling across his forehead. When their eyes eventually meet, she realizes that his convey a deep sadness, as if he has already lost his Eurydice to the snake bite and is preparing for his long journey to Hades to bring her back. The frisson that Leela experiences even before she sees Mishka is replicated in Mishka's experience of her. But we learn of this nearly two hundred pages later, when the novel shifts its point of view:

> Long minutes before he and Leela stood face to face for the first time, he sensed her presence. He sensed her as the pressure of air ahead of a subway car. He sensed her as he used to sense Uncle Otto waiting in the closed upper room when his mother climbed the stairs in Chateau Daintree. All his nerves stood on tiptoe. His skin read barometric changes in the air. He knew a major disturbance was moving in.
>
> When she was there, in front of him, speaking to him, all he heard was static. His pressure gauges went wild. (203)

Mishka's life, as it unfolds through his passionate liaison with Leela, appears structured around key motifs of the Orphic legend. These include the magnetic magic of his musical genius, his travels across many seas, his many pain-ridden quests for his transcontinental musical lineage, his lament for his lost love, his journey into the underworld in quest of a terrorist father, and his eventual torture and mutilation at the hands of privatized military personnel. They parallel Ovid's tale of this archmusician whose lute transfixes man, beast, plant, bird, and god and whose horrific end at the hands of the Thracian women Ovid documents in *Metamorphoses*. Mishka has never lived without music and never not enthralled his listeners with his playing.

Having grown up in a home steeped in traditions of Western classical music from the early Renaissance to the eighteenth-century German geniuses, by the age of five he could identify a performer by hearing the first five notes played. Leela tells her interrogator in the counterterrorism squad, "Music is Mishka's passion. It's his whole life. I have never known anyone less political. I have never known anyone less connected to the real world at all. *Mishka's not like ordinary mortals*" (73).

Much like Orpheus's victorious sojourn with the Argonauts, Mishka's musical genius takes him from a remote North Queensland town to Harvard after a series of painful trials: his estrangement from his family, his sense of isolation in Brisbane despite his brilliant academic performance, his discovery of a teacher who can teach him to play the Persian *oud*, his departure to North America without saying goodbye to his mother. By the time he appears in Leela's life at the Harvard Square subway station, he has left behind a past of personal and historical catastrophes and is about to find the truth he has been searching for all his life: his father's true identity.

For much of his childhood and adolescence his two biggest musical influences, his uncle Otto and his Lebanese father, are spectral presences. Mishka's father, a Lebanese student and a talented player of the Persian lute, the *oud*, was dead to the family before Mishka was born until Mishka discovers otherwise. Each represents a catastrophic moment in world history: the Holocaust and the post-1989 transformation of Islamic mujahideens into terrorists who created the 9/11 world of threat and preemptive politics. Much like Spiegelman's creative journey in the shadow of these catastrophes, Mishka's musical sojourn straddles both, and his compositions become testamentary performances, witnessing through music the brutal ravages of history.

Mishka grew up in a family of Hungarian refugees from Nazi Germany that fled to Australia. Their northern Queensland home in a region where "the rainforests meet the reefs" became their refuge. All they carried from their erstwhile European abode was their musical ensemble, ranging from Renaissance masters to Bartok's early twentieth-century masterpieces. This became their emotional mainstay such that their "after-dinner menu rotated from Gluck to Monteverdi, from Beethoven to Mendelssohn and Bartok and back" (159). Talking of his hard times under Nazi persecution, his grandfather Mordecai tells Mishka, "When I was your age . . . we thought music was much more important than food. . . . When we didn't have enough to eat, our mother would say: let's eat music. And she would sit at the piano and Otto would play his violin and we all would sing. And our mother would say: think of the notes as *pirogi* and fill yourself up. And we did" (163). Otto, Mishka's granduncle and the musical genius in his mother's family, was killed by the Nazis, but his family kept him alive in their transplanted home through his music. For the child Mishka he was a real presence in the attic room to which access was forbidden. Every evening of Mishka's childhood his mother, Devorah, climbed up to the attic and asked Uncle Otto to play. Riches from Gluck, Beethoven, Mendelssohn, and Bartok would waft down and encircle them in an enchanting family bond. A visit from an inquisitive and persistent schoolmate who made a dash to the sanctified attic room in order to see Mishka's genius relative revealed for Mishka the true horror of Uncle Otto's death. The attic room was empty; his grandparents had remediated the horror of the past by keeping Otto's music alive. Much like Spiegelman's graphic grids and Celan's poem, music for the Bartok family becomes their testamentary promise to hold onto the truth of Otto's perishing, to keep alive the *presence* of a horror they had only been indirect witnesses to. To his bereaved grandparents Mishka is Otto restored. Also like Spiegelman's graphic novels and Ananda's reconstruction of the Buddha in *Anil's Ghost*, Mishka's music later becomes the medium through which this truth is extended beyond its immediate historical ambit.

Through his acts of mediated and melancholic witnessing at the liminal edge of music, Mishka serves as an affective bridge between multiple world histories of the Holocaust and the post-9/11 politics of terror and preemption. He grew up with the story that his father had died before Mishka was born. A single surviving photograph and scattered bits of information from his mother about how well he played the oud enabled the son to conjure a paternal heritage of musical alterity that he embraced with as much passion as he did his Western classical inheritance from his Jewish family. This is Orpheus's music folded into other worlds, strange and culturally different worlds like Vanessa Agnew's extrapolation of the myth to eighteenth-century encounter narratives.[11] From his early years Mishka palpably felt both the spectral presence and the real absence of Uncle Otto and his father: "During his early years at Mossman State School, Mishka thought of his father the way he thought of Uncle Otto, except that his father was in a different closed room in a different house" (175–76).

Inadvertently his mother creates for him a world of music that stretches from Daintree to Beirut and spans centuries of cultural history. Talking about her relationship with his father, Marwan Rahal Abukir, a Lebanese student at the University of Sydney, she says, "I told him about the rainforest. He told me about Beirut. And we both loved music. He took me to a concert that some Middle Eastern students put on. He was one of the performers.

He played the oud. . . . It's the ancestor of the lute. It came to Spain with the Moors, though not to the rest of Europe until the Crusades. His oud was a beautiful thing, a deep-bellied wooden instrument inlaid with ivory. And he sang. He had a beautiful voice" (189).

Mishka then learns that his father was killed in Beirut three months after his mother wrote him about her pregnancy. His sense of loss seeps into his musical compositions. Gluck's "Che faro senza Euridice" becomes a lament about his lost father:

> When Grandpa Mordecai put Gluck on the record player, Mishka suddenly knew what the aria meant: *What shall I do without my father?* It seemed to Mishka that the great bruise inside him, the hole where his father should have been, crept into the music like a wounded creature from its cave and cried piteously: *Look at me. How shall I live without my father?*
>
> Mishka could no longer hear Gluck without weeping. (175)

The rest of the novel unfolds as the story of his Orphic quest for his paternal roots. It begins with a complete break from his mother's family and a move to Brisbane to undertake a university degree in music. One of the first things he does there is insert an advertisement in the newspaper for a teacher who can teach him to play the oud and help him buy one. He gets a response from Mr. Hajj, who offers him both services. A refugee from Damascus, Mr. Hajj shares a startlingly similar family history. Like Mishka's grandfather, he escaped from Syria to Australia after his brother was tortured and executed by the regime. A professor of music in Damascus, Mr. Hajj works as a greengrocer by day and teaches Persian music by night. This is Mishka's second encounter with the narrative of a traumatic world historical journey. Much like the recurring motifs in the tale of Orpheus and Eurydice, both are mediated through music and are tales of overwhelming loss. Mishka's own transcontinental journey—the third in the novel's scheme—in search of his Middle Eastern musical lineage plunges him into the dark heart of a contemporary world malaise: the specter of Islamic terrorism. The layering of each of these traumatic histories into the folds of his own signals a magnitude of responsibility he has never hitherto borne. As his experiences of melancholic witnessing accrue, so does his sense of being swallowed by an abyss. Significantly, at his last meeting with his mother right after she tells him about his father, he has a viscerally powerful experience of descending into a blackness from which there is no return. The imagery fuses the Daintree seascape and fauna with the viscosity of oil, thus presaging a murky and tortuous descent into a hell of violently entangled world histories: "Mishka leaned on the railing of the seawall. He had the sensation that he was falling, falling right through the day when Tony Cavalari opened the door to Uncle Otto's room, falling again like a shot parrot down a black hole with no bottom to it. And then something stirred in the black nothingness below and came rushing up to meet him like an oil gush coming in" (192).

By the time Mishka encounters Leela in Harvard Square, this experience of being swallowed by waves of filial loss and cultural accrual has become second nature to him. He leads a double life as a doctoral student of Western classical music by day and a Persian musician at the local Café Marrakesh by night. A chance encounter with another music student, Jamil Haddad, gives him clues about his father's family in Beirut. Jamil is a hotheaded radical convinced of the superiority of Islam. He frequently disrupts Dr. Siddiqi's Persian music classes by claiming that there is no place for music in pure Islam. Jamil confronts Mishka one day about his physical similarity to a family in Beirut named Abukir. He especially extols the virtues of Marwan Abukir, a radical Islamist who had trained in Afghanistan and was one of the leaders of the Islamic jihad movement in that part of the world. Music again appears as a trope, but this time to demonstrate Marwan's metamorphosis into a terrorist. Witness Mishka's exchange with Jamil:

"My Uncle Marwan plays the oud," Mishka said. "He is a singer and a musician."

"That is a lie. Marwan Rahal Abukir abhors music." . . .

"There must be two people with the same name. The Marwan Abukir who is my uncle plays the oud. He sings. He loves music."

And Jamil had spat on the sidewalk. "Marwan Abukir," he said, "testified in the blasphemy trial of Marcel Khalifa in Beirut."

"Who is Marcel Khalifa?"

"A musician, a singer, a darling of the degenerates. He performed a song that included words from the Quran. We demanded his death." (207, 215)

Drawn fatally into Jamil's network at the local mosque, Mishka does not rest until he finds a way to travel to Beirut to confirm that Marwan is indeed his lost father. How could his musician father have become a terrorist? Maybe his son can revive in him a knowledge of his past life as an oud player?

In her reading of eighteenth-century histories of Anglo-German musical encounters with the Pacific, Agnew finds that the Orpheus myth has an ontological and epistemological relationship to travel and voyaging:

Orpheus was always an artful traveler. . . . It was his music that rendered travel possible by overcoming natural obstacles, negotiating forbidden boundaries, taming beasts, and persuading gods. His singing and lyre playing also made possible what thence followed—power, knowledge, prizes won, and losses recovered. . . . The relationship of music to travel was thus an ontological one: Orpheus traveled with music and through it, for he went where music enabled him to go. Music's relationship to travel was also epistemological: The musical journey produced knowledge about unfamiliar places and peoples, whose playing, singing, listening, and silence would suggest something about both their music and the strange new practitioners themselves.[12]

We have already seen Mishka's embrace of the unfamiliar in his musical travels. As the heir to a cross-cultural union, he holds himself to both inheritances and is determined to transform familial losses into stunningly beautiful musical scores. In his quest for his father, music again becomes both his way of *being* in the world and a means of *knowing* the truth about his father—both ontological and epistemological, in Agnew's construction. Like Orpheus, again, it is this one primordial loss that propels him toward Hades. While in Beirut looking for his father he is captured in a raid by special counterterrorism forces and vanishes into the netherworld of a high-security prison. Caught between the venomous hatred of radical Islamists toward one half of his inheritance and the paranoid machinery of post-9/11 global counterterrorism against the other half, Mishka vanishes into the abyss that he feared throughout his many journeys.

Networks through Hades

Mishka's Orphic Hades takes the spectacularly twenty-first-century form of the network. His journey through Hades in search of his father consists of secret meetings in mosques, questioning in interrogation rooms, capture in prison, torture in rendition chambers, and finally release into a refugee detention center. Each is part of a global mesh of interconnected nodes—a network, in the language of informatics. While the idea of the network has always had a metaphorical charge in descriptions of social and political morphologies—as in kinship, friendship, professional, citizen, or governmental networks—its material and spatial ubiquity today owes overwhelmingly to the rise of computational informatics with its nodal infrastructure. The Internet and the World Wide Web have enabled simultaneous interconnectivity that has revolutionized the way we produce, govern, manage, socialize, entertain, fantasize, make war, and preempt enemies. Each mode of interconnectivity, in fact, resembles the other. The term *network aesthetics* has been proposed by Patrick Jagoda as a way of understanding the narrative, formal, and material entanglements that make up the network infrastructure: "Network aesthetics are not merely an analytic that informs a wide range of contemporary theory, fiction, film, and digital media, but a necessary corollary to an era in which interconnection has become a dominant architectural mode, a multivalent metaphor, and even a weapon. Such aesthetics both render and influence the way we interface with computer webs, economic systems, disease ecologies, and . . . terrorist networks."[13]

The architecture of both terrorism and counterterrorism in our information age is the network, as analysts of twenty-first-century warfare note.[14] Marc Sagemen in *Understanding Terror Networks* observes the uncanny similarity of the Al Qaeda operations and other global jihadi formations with both corporate networks and social media networks. He calls them "social enterprises" because they are bottom-up structures based on kinship and the affiliate bonds of friendship and mentorship.[15] Their corporate features are manifest in their entrepreneurial activities wherein they constantly seek out new sources of funding and new avenues of expansion. The charismatic leadership of these enterprises may imply that they are hierarchically governed, but in reality they operate more as assemblages that are wired across the globe and that function with a high degree of flexibility and adaptability. The ubiquity of information technology to their proliferation has been documented extensively.

Terrorist and counterterrorist networks are often mirror images of each other. The security functions of the state themselves proliferate through privatized networks that are only loosely connected and are by no means fully accountable to a state-controlled center of command. According to a report by the British Muslim human rights group Cageprisoners, *Beyond the Law: The War on Terror's Secret Network of Detentions*, by 2006 there were at least a hundred detention facilities established across thirty-four countries as part of the global counterterrorism strategy.[16] More than seventy of these had some support from the U.S. government and most operated as extrajudicial sites, those spectral geographies of the carceral that exist at the "vanishing point of the law of war," to quote Lt. Col. William Lietzau, special adviser to the general counsel of the U.S. Department of Defense in 2001.[17] Cageprisoners was set up in 2003 to raise awareness of the plight of detainees held at the Guantánamo Bay facility. Its report was published within a month of the UN General Assembly adopting the UN Convention against Enforced Disappearance. In his foreword to the Cageprisoners report, the UN special rapporteur on torture Manfred Nowak writes, "The use of secret places of detention and the practice of enforced disappearance are among the worst human rights violations of our time. . . . In order to eradicate such practices, the newly created Human Rights Council in June 2006 agreed on the text of a United Nations Convention on Enforced Disappearances. . . . It is ironic that in the very same year, Cageprisoners publishes a comprehensive report which reveals the systematic practice of enforced disappearances in a *global network of secret places of detention.*"[18]

After the outbreak of the Iraq War, the Bush administration outsourced the "most sensitive and core functions of government—from providing health care to soldiers, to interrogating prisoners, to gathering and 'data mining' information." The documentation on this is extensive and shows that by 2006 homeland security was a $200 billion global industry.[19] Often special intelligence officers who had worked in defense departments branched out into the private security industry. They helped provide cover for operations carried out in foreign countries, especially those that involved significant diplomatic risk.

The character Cobb in the novel embodies this duplication and delegation of state sovereignty. A decorated U.S. officer who fought the Taliban in Afghanistan and was subsequently posted to Iraq, Cobb established his own security firm that specialized in domestic surveillance after 9/11. Turner Hospital novelizes firms such as these as the *performative* face of preemptive politics, reacting to the minutest signs of alert, tapping phones and email, maintaining secret photographic and video evidence, and interrogating citizens without warrant. *Orpheus Lost* captures brilliantly the affective foundation of such an enterprise. The specialist on alert is not someone trained in forensics, who primarily recognizes the referential value of hard evidence. What is valued instead is intuition, a somatic orientation to even the barest whiff of threat. It is a "gift" that Cobb possesses:

> He had a sixth sense. Before the first wiretap, he felt vibrations. He had never been wrong.
>
> Hugo, Switch-flow. Ferment. An excess of white heat was rampaging through the highways and the byways of his blood. He felt intoxicated. Every time, it was like this. He had never been wrong. (229)

Cobb's firm is part of a network of complementary outfits loosely wired across the United States and the Middle East. Given that Mishka and his father are not U.S. citizens, the U.S. armed forces must outsource their capture to Cobb's firm. Cobb is clear about his mission: he has to capture Mishka and his father in a covert operation in Beirut and ensure their secure handover to the U.S. forces in Baghdad:

> It was clear to Cobb that kidnapping and detention of both men in Beirut, on the grounds of forestalling major threats, was the only safe option. There was a risk that the Australian government would lodge a protest—international protocol frowned on the kidnapping of citizens by a foreign power, especially since Lebanon was not a combat zone—and this was why it was essential that no official unit, encumbered with national identity and sanction, be involved.
> The action would be officially disowned.
> It would be due to rogue elements. (239)

The precarious nature of this networked operation becomes evident when the outfit Cobb depends on to carry out the capture of Mishka and his father is intercepted by the Iraqi militia, and he ends up losing track of Mishka:

> "THOSE FUCKING BANDITS," Cobb fumed. "What do you mean, you don't know where he is." . . .
> "Special Forces barged in and took over, sir. They took both men."
> Cobb punched the desktop with his fist. "They wouldn't have either men if it weren't for us. Find out where they are."
> "I tried, sir, but they were ghosted. There's no paper trail. There's no way to trace them." (241)

Earlier I discussed the semiosis of security politics and its preemptive *rightness* irrespective of the actualization of threat. Semiosis, Massumi explains, is "sign-induced becoming," the dynamic act of a sign on the body that impels it to react and that in turn generates an affective field.[20] In *Orpheus Lost*, as in the post-9/11 world at large, networks constitute the matrix of these flows of indexical signification and affect. The *sense* of the ubiquity of terror has much to do with the networked nature of insurgent groups around the world. Multinodal, distributive, and nimble in their operations, they are, as many military strategists have found, notoriously difficult to track down and destroy in their totality. This loss of a "reliable enemy," or what Derrida has called the "structuring enemy," from the other side of the bipolar divide of the erstwhile cold war has unleashed a phobia that "projects a mobile multiplicity of potentially interchangeable metonymic enemies in secret alliance with each other."[21] This post–cold war change in the idea of the enemy from measurable and identifiable to immeasurable and irrepressibly fractured has irrevocably shifted the ground of traditional warfare, both rhetorically and strategically. Not only has the language shifted from "facing" the enemy to "interfacing" with an enemy network, but adapting to constantly evolving enemy networks requires "a shift from viewing actors as independent to viewing them as part of a continuously adapting ecosystem."[22]

The blurring of lines between citizens and terrorists, perpetrators and victims, law enforcers and human rights abusers in our era of networked wars blurs as well the juridical lines between the accused, the prosecutor, and the witness. The agonistic triangulation of these roles among Mishka, Cobb, and Leela makes the novel a powerful literary artifact of the conundrum of witnessing in our era of perpetual wars. Mishka is witness to his father's transformation from an oud-playing student in Sydney to the leader of an Islamic insurgent group in Beirut. But in the process of his own discovery he becomes marked as a terrorist in the eyes of Cobb, who runs a private security firm. After the bomb blast in which Mishka's Harvard friend Jamil Haddad's remains were found, he becomes a suspect. This impels Cobb to haul Leela into his interrogation room as a potential witness to Mishka's dark dealings with terrorists in the local mosque. In the absence of any hard evidence of Leela's complicity in Mishka's nocturnal trysts, or, for that matter, of Mishka's complicity in the suicide bombing plot, all the interrogator has at his disposal is his belief in the rightness of his intuition and his commitment to preemptive action. It is this *performance* of the future anteriority of his convictions ("I am acting in the belief that what I am interrogating you about will have happened") that Leela is forced to witness. Unlike the forensic charge of interrogation scenes in Ondaatje's *Anil's Ghost*, where excavation of an impersonal, objective truth is paramount, Cobb's interrogation of Leela is motivated by a pure desire to punish her, to make her confront the fear that saturates an entire population and that inhabits the everyday life of thousands of people around the globe due to the murderous acts of suicide bombers like Haddad:

> Cobb had legitimate reasons for wanting Leela to know the wet suck of fear. . . . He believed this. There were two kinds of people in the world: those who took safety for granted and those who never could because they knew on a visceral level that safety was a rare and capricious thing. . . . Survival lay in forcing the careless ones to understand. Cobb wanted to hold Leela's head under water (metaphorically speaking), let her gasp for breath, let her splutter, hold her under again. This is what

abjection does to people, he wanted to say. Now you know, now you can begin to understand. (40)

That his motivation in putting Leela through a tortuous cross-examination is entangled with his lifelong resentment of her erotic hold over him adds another twist to the thematics of witnessing, which I will discuss later. For now I wish to note two things. One is the novel's careful crafting of the parallelism between Cobb's security-obsessed private outfit and the torture chambers in detention complexes located at the edges of human habitation. Only the nature and degree of intimidation are different. The other is the novel's remediation—that is, rendering into another form—of real-life eyewitness accounts, both narrative and photographic, of horrific experiences at these sites of interrogation and imprisonment. The novel's affective horizon is always already saturated with years of high-velocity exposure—primarily through information technology networks—of the excesses of the global counterterrorism regime. By the time readers encounter this novel—in 2007 at the earliest—they have mostly traversed the gamut of shock, horror, rage, outrage, and shame at the exposés on Abu Ghraib and Guantánamo Bay. What makes *Orpheus Lost* a world novel in the way I have formulated throughout the book is precisely this graphing of the global experience of hypermediated witnessing in a form that is instantly legible to the reader irrespective of her location on the globe. But for now let us go back to the previous point about the torture spectrum that runs from interrogation rooms to high-security prisons in no-man's land, called "black sites" because their legal jurisdiction is dubious.

Cobb's prolonged mind game in an enclosed room away from the battle front is in a continuum with practices of torture to which terror suspects like Mishka are subjected in such prisons. This is the substance of a chapter entitled "Underground," which contains scenes of Mishka's torture in a prison that closely resembles Guantánamo Bay. Both the fictional and the actual prison aim for extreme sensory and affective disorientation. Leela is kept waiting for hours in a claustrophobic and brightly lit interrogation room with one-way mirrors. The interrogator appears in a ski mask, his concealment a deliberate inversion of her exposed state. Cobb's entire performance is aimed at breaking down her composure and sense of control. He explicitly admits so at one point: "I want to know what happens when other people believe they have done nothing wrong, but sense they'll be penalized anyway. When they realize deep down they are powerless" (68).

Once he has the satisfaction of seeing her trembling fingers, his probing cuts deeper; it becomes invasive and obscene as he thrusts intimate photographs of her and Mishka under her eyes. The novel brilliantly captures the incremental shift in the flow of power until it accumulates at the interrogator's end. This is when he reveals his identity by removing his mask. The scene culminates in Leela's total exposure and humiliation:

> Cobb placed one more photograph in front of her: two young men were talking in front of the mosque. The sign at the street corner was Prospect Street. "You'll recognize your lover, Mikael Abukir," Cobb said pointing. "The other one is Jamil Haddad, yesterday's subway bomber. Which would make your lover, at the very least, material witness for an atrocity and possibly accessory to mass murder. Which, in turn, makes your mathematical transcriptions of your lover's musical compositions of interest to us."
>
> He smiled and walked out of the room and locked the door behind him and left her there. (79)

Interrogating Leela without advance intimation, stripping her of the certitudes that make up her world, violating her spaces of intimacy at will, and reducing her to a state of helplessness are acts of cruel and overweening control. They constitute a form of psychological torture to the extent that they breach a fundamental social contract that Leela has hitherto taken for granted, a trust that the other person will spare her pain and that help will arrive. This violation of the social contract is, of course, absolute in the case of extreme physical torture of the kind Mishka experiences in his dungeon after his capture in Beirut.

The violation of the social contract in coerced interrogation and torture appears in several accounts of persecution. Marianne Hirsch, for instance, locates it in the writings of an Auschwitz survivor, Jean Amery. A Viennese of German Jewish and Catholic origin, he survived incarceration in two concentration camps before being liberated from Auschwitz in 1945. Until his suicide in 1977 he wrote on the impact of that "first blow," which for him carried the weight of "the loss of the world" and an annihilation of "trust in the world" (*Weltvertrauen*). He also writes of the absurd epidermal intimacy imprinted on both the torturer and the victim with the tearing open of the latter's skin and flesh during physical torture. The victim oftentimes literally bleeds into the torturer's fist and feels the full corporeal hand of absolute sovereignty. Such brutalized intimacy paradoxically only reinforces the truth that the chasm between their worlds is absolute. "No bridge leads from the former to the latter," writes Amery.[23] This chasm is manifested in Mishka's third-degree torture in one of the infamous black sites of global counterterrorism at the hands of Cerberus-like monsters. This is no Plutoesque Hades where his music still enthralls. He is a "ghost detainee," a prisoner of war unlike any other who is vanished into a nonplace where no law ever works. The operation of power is here so absolute that Orpheus is truly lost. Music here works neither as charm nor as lure. Its affective function as a bridge between life and death reaches its limits in these dungeons:

> Sometimes he said, "My name is Orpheus," and then he realized that the snarling shapes in the room were Cerberus and his fierce brood of pups.
> He tried to explain that he had not descended into the dark world of Cerberus to steal secrets. Love had brought him. He wanted to know if he could love his father and if his father could love him. He had come to call love to himself with his oud, if he could be permitted to play for Cerberus.
> His answers were always wrong and brought punishment. (253)

In a mythical leap to motifs from Ovid's *Metamorphoses*, the torturers here morph into monstrous hybrids of Cerberus and the wild Thracian women, the Maenads, who "set their bloody hands on Orpheus" and with every weapon at their disposal—plows, branches, ox horns—tear his limbs apart. His limbs are scattered, his lyre lies broken, and his severed head floats down the River Hebrus until it reaches the shore of Lesbos.[24] At each response that Mishka gave to their barking queries, "Cerberus snarled and growled and continued to tear at [his] flesh" (253). He is hung upside down, his shoulder blades, ribs, and wrists are broken, and his neck feels the suffocating tightness of the hood. Through his pain he often sees his oud being smashed, sometimes by Cerberus, sometimes by his father. When the pain sears through his entire body, he imagines being sliced head to toe by a scimitar.

Extreme pain of the kind Mishka encounters, scores of torture narratives tell us, renders language inadequate to the experience. The victim is reduced to pure flesh and abdicates all cognitive and communication agency. The only operational linguistic zone is that of the torturer, and when the pain crosses a particular threshold, every utterance by the victim is a mimic-phrase from the torturer's linguistic repertoire. "I talked," writes Amery, "I accused myself of invented absurd political crimes, and even now I don't know at all how they could have occurred to me, dangling bundle that I was."[25] Hung upside down with every limb broken, Mishka too confesses to knowing the secrets that led to the Boston bombing. He talks of Jamil Haddad's links to Professor Siddiqi; he even confesses that his Brisbane music teacher, Mr. Hajj, imported ouds from Syria to convert them into booby traps, that his music school was a cover for a terrorist network that extended from Brisbane to Damascus and Beirut.

There appears to be a disjunction between the ethical apprehension of the limits of language in the portrayal of such torture scenarios and the actual aesthetic modes of witnessing torture that we find in *Orpheus Lost*. Far from being lost for words, the novelist remediates Mishka's experience (and, through it, those of countless other detainees) through vivid metaphors of crashing and flight. The extremity of pain is sometimes compared to a body being hit by vehicles from all directions and at other times as transcendence from his corporeal self into a realm of pure music. Graphic descriptions of his beatings are interspersed with psychic journeys to his childhood home, his mother's rescue of his head, and his fantasies about a sweet reunion with his musician father. Marwan Rahal Abukir remains a spectral paternal presence throughout, and the reader is unsure of the result of Mishka's Beirut quest. The mythical and the mystical converge toward the end of this black site scene as the Orphic legend segues into the ultimate Judaic narrative of rescue: the parting of the Red Sea: "I am the messenger of the Lord of Music, proclaimed the Radiant Oud. Cerberus has lain meek at my feet and has licked my ankles. I have parted the Red Sea and led captivity captive and my power is so great that none can resist me and I cannot, cannot be destroyed. Do not weep by the rivers of Babylon, but seize my power" (257).

Translated into the register of mediated witnessing, such metaphorics of liberation and transcendence can be read as the remediation of human rights work into novelistic discourse. While not exactly Moses-like rendering "captivity captive," extensive research and interviews by numerous human rights groups have broken the linguistic impasse of torture by excavating horrific truths about prisoner experience across these networks of unlawful detention. From 2002 to 2006, a period that marked a seismic spike in counterterrorism detentions, publics across the globe, and more so in democracies with open media access, were daily witnesses of these exposures.

These truths and their mediation through an exorbitant mode of global witnessing have acquired narrative form in televisual documentaries, short films, digital memoirs, war blogs, and life narratives.[26] Spectral sites of carceral power and detainees *ghosted* by such power acquire flesh and visibility in these real-life testimonies in visual and narrative genres. In turn these genres have transformed the twenty-first-century humanitarian novel.

Witnessing in such novels is simultaneously trope, plot, and mise-en-scène. Witness: the novelist, the character, and the reader.

The archaeology of such witnessing can be traced to the work of truth commissions and nongovernmental human rights organizations. Anna Lucia Pighizzini's testimony on the disappearance, rendition, and torture of her husband, Abou Elkassim Britel, is a case in point. One of the first ghost detainees of the war on terror, Britel, an Italian citizen, was captured in Pakistan on March 10, 2002, and handed over to U.S. authorities. Here is his wife's description of his experience of rendition from Pakistan to Morocco to the human rights group Cageprisoners:

> 24 May 2002. He was taken to the airport by car, travelling hand-cuffed and with a hood on his head. After about half-an-hour waiting, someone grabbed him abruptly, having come onto him very quietly. He seized his neck with powerful strength, so much so that Kassim thought he was going to die. He was taken to a place that turned out to be a bathroom. Everything happened very fast. Brandishing a knife, they cut his clothes and took them all off. He was then able to see four or five men all dressed in black, with only the eyes showing, all around him.
>
> They searched him all over, also in the intimate parts, took a picture and quickly put his clothes back on cutting most of his t-shirt off. They put a sort of nappy [diaper] on him and blindfolded him again. They made him wear what felt like metallic underpants to which they attached chains connected to his handcuffs and legs.
>
> They took him to the aeroplane and forced him to lie down on his back; another passenger got on the plane after him. He was forbidden from moving from that position and every movement was punished by being hit, may be with a stick, may be with a shoe. . . . His back was in great pain, when he asked to be allowed to turn they covered his mouth with tape.
>
> When the plane was landing, they managed to swap his metal hand-cuffs with some plastic ones. After hearing the Moroccan dialect he understood where he had arrived. Some Temara policemen were waiting for him and transported him to the town.[27]

Working valiantly against the tide of public opinion in the United States in the aftermath of 9/11 and the Iraq War, when most were in favor of extraordinary detention measures, a civilian lawyer, Clive Stafford Smith, represented several Guantánamo Bay prisoners. In an interview in 2004 he said, "When we first brought litigation against the Bush administration two and a half years ago ... ninety-nine percent of Americans were against us. ... While we may have made some gains in terms of the notion that everyone should be accorded basic human rights, we have made very little headway on convincing Americans that a large proportion of those at Guantanamo are not guilty. It's hardly surprising."[28] Two celebrated not-guilty cases are those of the Australians Mamdouh Habib and David Hicks. Both spent years at the extrajudicial detention facility without being proven guilty of any association with Al Qaeda. Despite repeated appeals by human rights lawyers, the Australian government did nothing to protect their rights during their incarceration and torture. On January 11, 2005, just after the publication of a *Washington Post* article on Habib's rendition and torture over five years, the U.S. government announced that it would not be charging him after all and that he could be repatriated to Australia.[29] From 2001 until his release in 2005 Habib experienced horrific torture.[30] Causing the most outrage was the cultural violence against him, such as being threatened with rape by a prison guard wearing a condom with "Allah u Akbar" written on it and being shackled to the floor while a prostitute menstruated over him. On his return to Australia his passport was revoked and he was placed under constant surveillance by the Australian intelligence services. His interviews on *Dateline* and *60 Minutes* were edited and packaged in such a way as to leave open the question of his innocence, even though the interviewers appeared to listen to his side of the story. In fact media scholars have noted the similarity between the interviewers' method of questioning and the interrogation techniques Habib would have encountered during his detention. For example, on *60 Minutes* he was asked, "Do you or have you ever supported a jihad, a holy war against the West? Do you think that there is any justification in killing in the name of Allah? Do you admire Osama bin Laden?"[31]

Graphic testimony of torture techniques deployed at several extrajuridical sites of detention is now available. Here is the account of Babar Ahmad, who was arrested in London on December 2, 2003, by the Metropolitan Police Counter-Terrorism Command:

> I was subjected to physical, verbal, racial and sexual abuse by the police officers. I had nothing to hide when I was arrested so I made no attempt to struggle or resist.
>
> The police officers smashed my head through ... the window and punched me all over the body. They pulled my genitals and stamped

on my bare feet with their boots. They forced me into the prostration position of prayer and mocked my religious rituals by asking me, sarcastically, "Where is your God now?"

The officers tortured me by deliberately scraping metal handcuffs along my forearm bones and applying tight pressure to my neck so that I had difficulty breathing. I sustained over seventy-three medically recorded injuries including bleeding in my ears and urine.[32]

Anna Lucia Pighizzini testified on behalf of her husband:

Kassim still finds it difficult to relate what he has been through. Even though he does speak about it now, he is not up to telling the whole story.

My husband was psychologically tortured with death threats against him and threats of violence against the female members of his family. They told him that the Italian Ambassador was not interested in him "because he was a terrorist."

As for the physical torture, I know he was beaten severely, with a cricket bat at times. The handcuffs he wore around his wrists were tied behind his back with chains and he would be hung from the prison bars or off the ceiling for a long time. He would be blindfolded and his hands and feet would be chained so that he couldn't defend himself nor predict where he was going to be hit. The cell did not include a toilet and he was not allowed to relieve himself except once every twenty-four hours, when he was given a bucket. For three days he was sleep deprived while being tied to a gate.[33]

Frequently the family and extended kinship network of the detainees describe the ordeal from their perspective. Especially poignant are narratives of the trauma the detainee's children experience. These generate a field of witnessing I have been calling the affective. Their appeals are directed not to the law and governance but to the humanitarian imagination of global publics. The anguish of Nadia, the wife of another Guantánamo Bay detainee, Boudella Haji, is evident in her words:

My children are not children, they are grown up persons. Instead of cartoons and movies, they are watching news, and political stories. My son Abdul Aziz said to me . . . I will go in front of the US Embassy and make some trouble, so they send me to Guantanamo to be with my Baba. . . . Once the teacher of my daughter Iman she called me and said she did not have the necessary things for mathematics so she cannot concentrate on this subject.... [My daughter] told me, well I know that you will buy for me all that I need, but I do not want to make it hard for you to release our Baba.[34]

Close kin of detainees often make it their life's mission to free their loved ones, to file cases of unlawful detention against governments, or to litigate against media networks that attempt to defame their spouse or parent. Celebrated instances include Maha and Mamdouh Habib's successful defamation case against the Sydney radio stations Radio 2UE and Radio 2GB, for which they were awarded over US$170,000.[35] The Habibs were also paid an undisclosed sum by the Australian government in 2011, in return for which they signed a confidentiality agreement and dropped their six-year case. In Britain Anas El-Banna, the son of Guantánamo detainee Jamil El-Banna, was named the *New Statesman* Person of the Year in 2007 for his campaign to free his father.

Orphic Reversal

Orpheus Lost constellates this affective terrain of familial and erotic solidarity into a narrative of search, rescue, and redemption through the characters of Leela, Mishka's mother, Devorah, and, in an unexpected plot twist, Cobb himself. Their transcontinental journeys to bring Mishka back from the underworld reverse the mythical emplotment of Ovid's epic. In a novelistic world where gods have fled and the natural order of things is no longer available to humans, vulnerable heroes morph into spectral creatures secreted away by unfathomable evils and the Eurydices of the world are transformed into hapless seekers forever wandering from one black site to another in search of their beloveds. Leela's exchange with her MIT mentor, Berg, evokes this counterepical world:

"I'm in a strange underworld loop with Orpheus."

"Orpheus. Right."

"I mean Mishka. He's a musician. He's gone into the underworld and hasn't come back. It's not supposed to happen that way."

Berg looked away. He had to be careful. He did not want her to disappear. "Orpheus in the underworld," he repeated, neutral. What was it with mathematicians? Did it help to be crazy? From Newton onwards a case could be made.

Could he seriously consider himself unscathed?

"I'm the one who's been trying to rescue him," Leela said. "It's supposed to be the other way around." (303)

A crazed lover's relinquishment of all structures of intellectual and emotional flourishing in search of her *ghosted* beloved saturates the quest with the power of the superstes: a witness who extends the perceptual reach of loss and trauma beyond everyday temporal and spatial barriers. On hearing that Mishka may have been released and repatriated to Australia, Leela makes the long transcontinental journey to meet his mother in northern Queensland. There she encounters the long arm of the counterterrorism regime that incarcerates repatriated terrorists in desert prisons meant for illegal refugees. Together Mishka's mother and his beloved journey into the heart of Australia's barrenness, the South Australian desert, in the midst of which is situated the detention facility modeled on the infamous Woomera Centre. Their encounter with prison authorities is layered with Kafkaesque motifs, complete with a character called "K." Needless to say their quest is futile. The Mishka they are led to turns out to be someone else. But the sequence allows the novelist to constellate for global reading publics yet another dimension of the war on terror, the shameful conflation of refugees and terrorists in the history of refugee detention in Australia.

Woomera Immigration Reception and Processing Centre in South Australia is notorious. Its management was outsourced to Australasian Correctional Management, an arm of the private security corporation Wackenhut in 2000. Flooded with refugees from Iraq and Afghanistan since 2001, it was chronically understaffed and poorly equipped and shamefully housed over forty unaccompanied minors out of a national count of fifty-three in various other detention centers. For over a year since the start of its operations in 1999, no human rights group or lawyer was allowed within its precincts. Lawyers had to go to court to get access rights. Nurses and mental health workers who were allowed in later reported widespread psychological trauma among the inmates. One Adelaide lawyer, Julie Redman, reported in an interview with *Green Left Weekly*:

> As I approached the centre I couldn't help but feel sick at the stark contrast between the pleasant township of Woomera and the stark treeless compound of the detention centre. Millions of dollars have been spent at Woomera to make this one of the most high security prisons that I have ever seen. Double steel fences surround the compound with two layers of razor wire glistening in the sun. Outside the perimeter is a bright blue water canon ready for action, with another inside.

Children wandered aimlessly behind the huge compound fences with not one ball or play thing evident. I saw no children laughing or playing freely, ... The contrast between the way we now provide for animals in our own zoo in Adelaide is far superior to the facilities provided to these families. There is not a blade of grass in sight, the children wander slowly through the dust. The only time that whole day I saw children smiling was when they came with their mothers to see us and had a degree of freedom without the ever-watchful eye of the ACM [Australasian Correctional Management] guards. . . .

The only detainees who were allowed to see us were those who requested legal advice. I was able to see four unaccompanied minors, aged 10 and 11. What struck me most was how flat, lacking in life and depressed they obviously were.

One 11-year-old Afghan boy told me he was an orphan and had travelled from Afghanistan via Indonesia. His extended family had raised the money to send him to a safe place. He felt safe in the detention centre, it was so much better than the way he had observed at home. He did not know what was to become of him. He believed he's been in the detention centre for six months. He could not tell me who the migration agent was that was assisting the processing of his application for refugee status. He told me he spent most of his day sleeping.[36]

Redman also reports meeting two teenage Iraqi boys, one of whom attempted suicide while the other sewed his lips together. This act of self-mutilation was emulated by at least seventy inmates according to a January 2002 report in the Sydney *Sun-Herald*. The cultural racism of Minister of Immigration Philip Ruddock's response turned the episode into a national crisis of conscience. "Lip sewing," he averred, "is a practice unknown in our culture. It's something that offends the sensitivities of Australians. The protesters believe it might influence the way we respond. It can't and it won't."[37] This episode, among the saddest in Australia's bleak history of punishing asylum seekers, became the limit case that transformed public perception about the government's role in the war on terror. The official script conflating asylum seekers with terrorists could no longer run without counterscripts in the court of public opinion. In May 2012 the *Age* in Melbourne published a poem, "Asylum," by the Arab Australian poet Mehmet al Assad:

Will you please observe through the wire
I am sewing my feet together
They have walked about as far as they ever need to go.

Will you further observe through the wire
I am sewing my heart together
It is now so full of
The ashes of my days
It will not hold any more.
Through the wire
one last time
please observe
I am sewing my lips together
that which you are denying us
we should never have
had to ask for.[38]

Such writing "relayed affect" by mediating modes of humanitarian bond-
ing among complete strangers and, in effect, created the conditions of possibility for the proliferation of several refugee support networks—paralegal,
social, cultural, academic—throughout Australia.[39] In grafting a fictional narrative on the war on terror onto the Orpheus myth, Turner Hospital transfig-
ures humanitarian witnessing in the twenty-first century into a quest, less for
truth than for affective projection. One mother's loss of her son reverberates
across anguished war zones in Iraq and Europe, in Palestine and the United
States. Leela's desperation is shared by countless spouses of ghost detainees
across the globe.

The novelist takes this affective projection to its limit by transforming the
perpetrator himself into archwitness and liberator. Cobb, Leela's tormentor,
is also her childhood friend. Thwarted desire for her in his adolescent years is
sublimated into a fierce patriotism that is honed in turn by the conservative
ethos of the American South and the catastrophe of 9/11. We saw his exulta-
tion at being able to exert his power over Leela as the enforcer of the counterterrorism doctrine. His patriotic certitudes begin to unravel with Leela's
final pleading after her failure to find Mishka in Australia:

> "*Please*, Cobb. . . . I understand the surveillance. I don't hold any
> of that against you. I know you have to do what you have to do. But
> you're *decent*, Cobb, and he's innocent. All I'm asking is if you know
> where he is. . . . Please, Cobb, I'm begging you. It's not knowing that's
> so unbearable. I think I could handle any kind of news, but I need to
> know."
>
> Cobb could not get air into his lungs. . . . He was gasping. He was
> blue in the face. (338)

The ghosting of Mishka in Iraq had already subliminally shocked Cobb into confronting the anarchic impenetrability of networked warfare. We also see him unable to contain his outrage when his father, a Vietnam War veteran, declares, "It's total fucking lottery, war. No one knows what the hell they're doing, and afterwards no one can remember what happened, and what does it matter?" "It matters," Cobb says fiercely. "In war *there's right and there's wrong*" (323). Hearing Leela's pleading, he eventually acknowledges his complicity in leaning too far to the *wrong* side. He decides to atone by going to Baghdad and rescuing Mishka. "I'll bring him back," he promises Leela. In this transformed Cobb the novelist vests the full affective force of humanitarian witnessing taken to its radical end. Such force liberates as it annihilates. The novel's postmythic emplotment culminates in two dark scenes: one is Cobb's nightmare of the battered shapes of tortured bodies in the dungeons of an Iraqi prison; the other is a news report of his death in a daring prison raid that rescued Mishka and other prisoners. The bodies Cobb encounters in his search for Mishka are but lumps of flesh made to hang upside down. In their hooded state they "resemble a body hanged in effigy, more a parody of itself than an actual human form" (319). His is the act of primal, unmediated witnessing. The broken, misshapen, hooded, bleeding bodies that he jostles against as he walks through the dark tunnels are the ultimate evidence of the depredations of this war. It is hard not to see in them the ubiquitous icon of the Abu Ghraib tortures: the hooded figure suspended from a ceiling with electric nodes attached to its fingers and feet. In dying in their stead Cobb changes places with these abject forms of living dead and so fulfills his role as the first and most authentic witness, who enters into and inhabits their traumatic world but does not survive to tell their story. What survives is a report on the condition of the bodies found:

whistle-blower killed in baghdad
military maverick redeemed
secret torture chamber exposed
Associated Press reports that a former Ba'ath-party prison used by rogue militia groups has been discovered. One room in the prison was found to be piled with decayed and mutilated bodies. Scores of prisoners in malnourished condition, often with severe injuries due to torture, have been found. Among them are American businessmen and contractors who have been kidnapped and held for ransom. There are also many Iraqis and foreign nationals.

The prison was liberated in a daring and carefully planned pre-dawn raid by a small force of former members of the US military who took heavy fire from rogue troops. Among those killed was military maverick and former major in the US army, Cobb Slaughter, leader of the raiding party. (356)

The folding over of Cobb's act of primal and authentic witnessing into newspaper and digital reportage, which Leela and the rest of the world then witness at a distance of a few thousand miles, is a powerful tableau of what I have called the *legibility* of novelistic witnessing, that is, the novel's capacity to graph the transmedial layers of humanitarian witnessing in our era of perpetual wars.

Coda

In recent years we have witnessed a hypertrophy of concepts around the idea of the *human*, especially in literary and cultural theory. The three most prominent of these are human rights, humanitarianism, and the posthuman. These transdisciplinary rubrics, with their origins in law, moral philosophy, and critical theory, respectively, have significantly shaped recent debates on the moral purchase of literary genres.

The posthuman rubric questions the limits of the human in the wake of late twentieth-century developments in gene technology, artificial intelligence, robotics, reproductive cloning, and animal rights, not to mention the imminent threat from anthropogenic climate change. Far from being the natural sibling of the early modern idea of natural rights, and despite its UN enshrinement in 1948, the idea of *human rights*, as I discussed specifically in my engagement with Samuel Moyn's work in the introduction, actually became a force in world history in the 1970s as late modernity's "last utopia," when all other emancipatory models—nationalism, postcolonialism, communism—appeared to be fraying. I also discussed the emergence of the postliberal horizon of human rights that has fundamentally challenged our understanding of the human as an inalienable subject of rights in modernity. The gap between the "institutional invisibility of the human race as a political actor" and the global visibility of a human rights culture is all too evident in our time.[1] Radically different from the revolutionary model of rights in liberal thought and its proactive inscription in the novels of the eighteenth and nineteenth centuries, human rights offers a new challenge to the grammar of self-making, sovereignty, and the sympathetic imagination in contemporary novels. Humanitarianism, at least in its modern form, was honed in eighteenth-century debates on abolitionism and the early commercial society's moral infrastructure that included the capacity to envision the remote consequences of one's actions. Devalued throughout the nineteenth and twentieth centuries for being a soft, ineffective, and often exploitative mode of response to human suffering, the language of humanitarianism has now become an indelible part of the global lexicon of war and violence. Three factors, visited in much detail in this book, have contributed to the robust resurgence of humanitarianism since the end of the cold war: the escalation in genocidal violence, endemic ethnic conflicts, and global wars on terror as a result of the post–cold war realignment of the world order; the stupendous growth of the global humanitarian industry in the form of NGOs as a result of the magnitude of civilian carnage these wars have caused; and the global networks of information and communication technologies that incessantly mediate these sites of violence for witnessing publics around the world.

Now routinely conjoined with the discourse of human rights, the humanitarian imaginary has become one of the novel's most visible shaping forces. Not humanitarianism as largesse at a distance but as a sensorial and affective substrate that transforms the sovereignty-sympathy dyadic grammar of the erstwhile eighteenth-century novel into a hypervisible and globally immanent triage of rightlessness, vulnerability, and grievability. It is immanent because the exposure to injury is now experienced as an existential condition of planetary proportions, whose inevitability is heightened by the massive mediatization of violence. Since this is a humanitarianism that is tractable to digital connectivity, it is an ubiquitous global narrative and can be found in multiple genres across the globe: the blog, the docufiction, the graphic novel, and the memoir. I have explored the transitive nature of this creative humanitarian ensemble as it shapes the novel in our era.

In concluding this book I revisit a couple of key questions I raised at the start. How might we track the intensification and modulations of the sovereignty-sympathy dyad from its eighteenth-century manifestation to the world novel of today in light of the fact that the information technology revolution has radically transformed our threshold of responsibility to our distant others and has perforce brought worlds of untold suffering into our intimate spaces on a scale unthinkable in Adam Smith's time? More specifically I asked whether the classic Smithian moral infrastructure of sympathy, conceived as a vicarious exchange of places, as imagining oneself in the place of the suffering other, could be sustained on a world scale.[2] No less significant was the question about the aesthetic remit of the humanitarian gaze that is already mediated by a vastly amplified network of witnesses to human suffering. How are ideas about moral spectatorship and sympathetic recognition configured when we confront a relay of gazes virtualized in all too many media forms and not just on the printed page or the cinema screen?[3]

In these final pages I offer some brief reflections starting with a consideration of the Rwanda genocide as a paradigmatic contemporary case study that sutures extreme violence to a globalized trauma aesthetic that, in turn, is generated within a remediated field of visual and narrative excess. The genocidal horror in this central African republic in 1994, the year of the dismantling of apartheid in South Africa, witnessed an outpouring of creative responses across the world. Fiction, memoirs, feature films, documentaries, performances, and art exhibitions—scarcely any genre missed representing the genocide. For me the Rwanda case is a classic manifestation of the *kairos* of 1989 as a world-making site for it makes visible the proliferation of modes of aesthetic engagement with distant suffering on a truly global scale. There is no question that the panoptic apparatus of new communication technologies enabled the proliferation of creative responses to this genocide. How does one read such creative excess beyond the trope of voyeurism and the classic liberal outrage at the pornography of visible violence? What does such aesthetic proliferation mean for the narrative configuration of the human in our time? Finally, I turn to the novel with which I began this book, Ian McEwan's *Saturday*. As I noted then, I see this work as emblematic of the novel after 1989 in its spectatorial apprehension of a global humanitarian horizon in the wake of 9/11 and on the eve of the Iraq occupation. Here I conclude by tracing the makings of a postliberal imaginary in the novel's agonistic capture of a realm of human belonging beyond the certitudes of positive rights and a cognitive aesthetics of bourgeois self-making.

Trauma Aesthetics and the Humanitarian Gaze: The Case of Rwanda

In April 1994, when South Africa was celebrating the end of apartheid with the election of Nelson Mandela and the African National Congress, Rwanda, a tiny central African state, was awash with the blood of one of its ethnic minorities, the Tutsis. In one hundred days, from April to early July 1994, the country's Hutu paramilitary, Interahamwe [We who strike together], fattened and armed by its deceased president, Juvénal Habyarimana, butchered about a million Tutsis. The world chose to look the other way. As the Reuters photojournalist Corinne Dufka put it in her address to the UCLA International Institute on the tenth anniversary of the genocide, "There were thousands of journalists on the African continent during the genocide, but they were almost all in South Africa covering the elections."[4] The United States, already suffering from Somalia fatigue, refused to name the massacres "genocide" for fear it would be urged to intervene once again. The UN peacekeeping force present in Rwanda at the time refused to exceed its brief of keeping peace and engage in armed conflict with the genocidal Hutu paramilitary. The fictional UN general in Gil Courtemanche's novel *A Sunday at the Pool in Kigali*, says, "I would like to protect civilians, but I do not want to risk losing soldiers, even one, without written authorization. I am not here to save Rwandans. I'm here to respect the Arusha accord."[5]

When Dufka implored her editors to allow her to cover the Rwandan massacre, they told her the public had little appetite for seeing dead bodies in the morning newspaper. They finally allowed her to travel to Rwanda after seeing a particular photograph that caught their interest. The photograph was not of the genocide but of a massive exodus of refugees from Rwanda into neighboring Tanzania. "They finally said, 'This looks impressive. You can go.'" Dufka and her team chose a route to Rwanda from the southeast, passing through Tanzania and Burundi. Their assignment was to cover the refugee story. Dufka describes the gruesome tableau that lay before them: "There was a river that flowed between Tanzania and Rwanda. There was a large waterfall and there were bodies flowing over it. On the one hand there were refugees going into Tanzania and on the other hand we had these bloated bodies every couple of minutes flowing over this waterfall. It was horrific." She also writes about visiting churches and schools where many Tutsis sought refuge and were killed: "You could see the story of the chase in the ways the bodies fell. In one of them I remember seeing a dead mother and her two dead children. You could see she was trying to protect her children and you could see she was huddled over these children—they'd been dead for a number of weeks and you could see the machete marks on her body where the bone was shattered."

The decade after the genocide witnessed a proliferation of creative representations of this meticulously choreographed genocide, including Terry George's feature film *Hotel Rwanda*; Courtemanche's docufiction, *A Sunday at the Pool in Kigali*; Andrew Miller's novel *The Optimists*; Véronique Tadjo's memoir, *The Shadow of Imana: Travels in the Heart of Rwanda*; and many powerful documentaries, two of the most memorable being Roméo Dallaire's *Shake Hands with the Devil* and Michael Caton-Jones and David Belton's *Shooting Dogs*. There was also a sculpture exhibition at the Ecumen-

ical Centre in Geneva to commemorate the tenth anniversary of the genocide, in which an artist from Ghana, Kofi Setordji, displayed his wooden
sculpture and terracotta masks. The exhibition later traveled to Kigali.

In October 2005 the Sydney Opera House staged a Senegalese dance performance entitled *Fagaala* ("genocide" in Senegalese), choreographed by the
acclaimed Senegalese performer Germaine Acogny and the Japanese butoh
master Kota Yamazaki. A leading performer in the African art world, Acogny
was inspired to create this dance ensemble after reading a fictional account
of the genocide by the Senegalese writer Boubacar Boris Diop. In contrast to
the mediatized byte-sized coverage of the killings on television, Diop's novella *Murambi: The Book of Remains* humanized the genocide for Acogny to
such an extent that she could not rest until she enacted the horror through
dance and used her art to converse with the world. "This fiction," she said,
"was more real than reality. I saw myself in the story. I was the killer and
the victim. As a black African woman and artist, I took the responsibility to
speak."[6]

Acogny here addresses a critical link between trauma aesthetics and sympathetic projection that has been of prime concern to this book. A trauma
aesthetic connotes a creative uptake on human pain and suffering of extreme
magnitude. Entwined with this is the responsibility of such an aesthetic to
convey both the immediacy and the truth of such suffering—to make some
sense of senseless suffering—to diverse audiences that do not necessarily
share the same aesthetic and humanitarian values. Acogny's performative en-
actment of Diop's novella by exchanging places with both the victims and the
killers generates a substratum of sympathy as a visual and virtual mode that
allegorizes the conjoining of mediated violence and a remediated humanitarian imagination that constitutes the bulwark of the world novel as I have
theorized it throughout this book.

Let us now turn to a few responses to this proliferation of creative works
on Rwanda. A journalist from the London *Observer*, Jason Cowley, called
such quick creative reproductions "indecent" for they promoted "atrocity tourism," especially when Rwanda was far from healed: "What is one to
make of all this western interest in the unhappy central African state? Is there
not something indecent in the haste with which non-African [artists] and
film-makers are competing with each other to be the first with the . . . news
about the events of 1994? Is there not an element of atrocity tourism at work
here—as well as a kind of stylized poetics of misery? After all it took the
long perspective of many decades before novelists and Hollywood felt able
to represent, in fiction, the Jewish Holocaust." Cowley goes on to weave into

this ethical conundrum of a trauma aesthetic (the obscenity of art feeding off macabre killings) two contrasting scenarios that capture the dilemma of creative reenactments of genocidal violence. In the first, Terry George recounts why he chose to shoot his film *Hotel Rwanda* in Johannesburg rather than in Kigali: "I was afraid of recreating those scenes of murder on the streets of Kigali." Contrasted with this is the decision of the filmmakers Michael Caton-Jones and David Belton to film *Shooting Dogs* on the streets of Kigali. While this commitment to "real" location is understandable in terms of genre (the film is a documentary), a bystander and a resident of Kigali who occasionally witnessed the filming thought "there was something indulgent and wrong about the circus of activity created by a western film crew in the midst of such dire poverty." He added, "Some of us felt upset about the filming of the scenes of violence and mayhem. Perhaps *Hotel Rwanda*'s approach of having the violence in the background is the right one."[7] Such responses echo the reaction of Elizabeth Costello, the eponymous character in J. M. Coetzee's novel, to the gratuitous depiction of Nazi death camps in a novel by Paul West: she felt "sick with the spectacle, sick with herself, sick with a world in which such things took place, until at last she pushed the book away and sat with her head in her hands. *Obscene!* . . . She chooses to believe that *obscene* means *off-stage*. To save our humanity certain things that we may want to see (*may want to see because we are human!*) must remain offstage."[8] This paradox of our all-too-human voyeuristic fascination with traumatic spectacle and of our simultaneous impulse to turn our eyes away from it, to wish it offstage, as it were—the theatrical metaphor is pertinent in light of the overarching focus on spectacle and spectatorship in this book— is highly pertinent to my reading of the myriad aesthetic mediations of the Rwanda genocide.

Do creative representations of the Rwandan massacre only put non-Rwandan viewers in a position to stare, to look without consequence at sights from which, in practical life, we might turn away in horror? In other words, can our responses to these representations only be read as morally anaesthetizing and voyeuristic? Can we not also argue that they bring home the importance of narrating and hence naming the evil from which the world had once turned away its gaze? In this era of the global immanence of war and terror, can we really afford the luxury of adopting the classic liberal cosmopolitan stance of protecting the sanctity of the violated by keeping it *offstage* and away from our collective gaze, as Elizabeth Costello would want? In this regard the words of Rwanda's minister of culture Joseph Habineza are pertinent. When asked if these creative depictions troubled ordinary Rwandans, he replied, "In 1994, the world ran away from us. The world didn't want to know. These works, because they have a sense of history and a powerful message, are coming out at the right time because the world is starting to forget what happened. And we don't want people ever to forget what happened in 1994. Will ordinary Rwandans see these films and read these books? Many probably won't. But they know they are out there, they know they've been made. That is a source of consolation—and it stops them feeling abandoned all over again."[9] These sentiments counter the voyeurism argument and bring to the fore the urgent need for the genocide to stay in the public gaze as a reminder of the world's abdication of its responsibility. What we see in the global media aesthetics around Rwanda and its world-scale multidirectional relay of gazes, I would argue, is a real virtualization of a moral universal built on the idea of crime against humanity, where the interlocutor of the victim is a stranger and not her or his kith and kin. Judith Butler calls this the "'impingement by the Other's address' . . . a comportment towards the other only after the Other has made a demand upon me, accused me of a failing, or asked me to assume a responsibility."[10]

To index this impingement by the "other's address" is also to acknowledge the reality of the global scale of human suffering, no longer restricted, especially since 9/11, to the backwaters of the world: sub-Saharan Africa, Latin America, and impoverished parts of Asia. To recognize the global immanence of human insecurity and dread amid terror is to acknowledge that trauma aesthetics in late modernity does more than just feed off the misery of the less fortunate residing in distant parts of the world. This is an aesthetic indexed not to the timeless normativity of the human in rights discourse but to its melancholic temporal horizon: the ever-present future anteriority of the condition of absolute rightlessness that now pervades the world. Such an aesthetic makes visible the fact that the rights-bearing human has faced its most severe test in the latter half of the twentieth century and into the new millennium, when human beings have had to live through catastrophes that have destroyed entire social networks that define our moral universe. "The way stations on the road to this new internationalism," writes Michael Ignatieff, "are Armenia, Verdun, the Russian front, Auschwitz, Hiroshima, Vietnam, Cambodia, Lebanon, Rwanda and Bosnia."[11] Genocidal acts in particular create victims who are bereft of kinship and social networks. They thus make an ethics of care toward vulnerable and rightless strangers imperative for future life on the planet. If the proliferating creative responses to the Rwanda genocide enable the virtualization of such an ethics through the global media infrastructure, can we turn our eyes away?

This is precisely the kind of agonistic apprehension that pervades *Saturday* by McEwan. I trace the novel's staging of the conundrum of moral spectatorship and sympathetic recognition in our postliberal, hypermediated era. *Saturday* also captures three oscillating conceptions of the human that the cultural horizon of human rights confronts in our time. We have seen their interplay in the foregoing chapters. The first is based on a liberal worldview of the condition of the human as the possibility of freedom and transcendence from the immanence of the social, and the concomitant alienation produced by barriers to achieving its full potential. The second is based on the figure of the human in states of exception such as civil wars and genocide that conjoin both a condition of absolute rightlessness and sovereign exception. The third is the idea of the inhuman as immanent in the human—that is, the human as the product of the instrumentalities of global capital and its political coordinates that, in their extreme forms, transmogrify into "war machines," a state that Achille Mbembe has called necropolitics.[12] In foregrounding the simultaneity of these three discursive registers of the human, the world novels of our time are more than just agents of the normalization of the international human rights person. In them we see *both* a resistance to an actuarial economy that annexes the human to either the narrative of contract or the narrative of right *and* a desire to stay open to the aporia of human rights thinking that highlights the actuarial and melancholic dimensions of being human.

Toward a Postliberal Imaginary: Reading *Saturday*

Saturday's main protagonist, Henry Perowne, appears at first to embody the liberal fantasy of the transcendence of the inhuman through the exercise of a moral imagination grounded in reason, ethical care, and respect for the other. Witness, for instance, his measured reflections on the parameters of a sympathetic imagination when he sets out on his completely mundane errand of buying fish for the stew he plans to cook for dinner. His scientific knowledge about the capacity of fish to feel pain is up to date, and this sets off a train of thoughts: "Now it turns out that even fish feel pain. This is the growing complication of the modern condition, the expanding circle of moral sympathy. Not only distant people are our brothers and sisters, but foxes too, and laboratory mice, and now the fish." Carefully calibrating the reach of his own compassion, he admits he would eat a cooked lobster but draw a line at dropping a live lobster in a pot of boiling water. "The trick, as always," he muses, much in the manner of Hume, "the key to human success and domination, is to be selective in your mercies. . . . It's the close at hand, the visible that exerts the overpowering force."[13]

And yet, just a little while earlier, we see him unable to orient his sympathetic imagination toward a very visible trio of burkha-clad women struggling to cross the road with an infirm relative. His distaste at the sight is "visceral": "How dismal, that anyone should be obliged to walk around so entirely obliterated" (124). The chasm is not just cultural. He has enough Saudi male clients to know that the emblematic darkness of the burkha is but one facet of an otherwise highly modernized and consumerist lifestyle among these people.

It soon becomes clear that his reaction is an extension of his ambivalence about the Iraq War and his own anxieties about living in an era of spiraling violence, often catalyzed in his view by medieval political passions. The ubiquitous television screen that he watches in fragments throughout his Saturday perambulations becomes the novel's leitmotif. It frames for him in bits and pieces the news of the buildup to the Iraq War as he catches glimpses of protest marches in London and around the globe. His subliminal sense of being under siege is compounded by exposure to the twenty-four-hour news cycle. The information excess appears to be turning him into a docile citizen of a security-obsessed Leviathan of a state: "He suspects he is becoming a dupe, the willing, febrile consumer of news fodder, opinion, speculation and of all the crumbs the authorities let fall" (180).

While acknowledging the tremulous force of our intrinsic vulnerability in an era of globalized violence, McEwan's novel also enacts the vagaries of faith in the liberal power of a cognitive aesthetics to shape our anamorphic human condition. The term *cognitive aesthetics* refers to the power to generate images of beauty through a reflective self-consciousness "in the face of a disorienting and alien external world that fundamentally challenged individual autonomy."[14] *Saturday* depicts a traumatic experience, but its creative transmutation could not be more different from confronting the immanence of the inhuman in the human in sites of genocide like Rwanda. Violence here is anaesthetized by the surgical genius of the neurosurgeon Henry Perowne. The novel is set in London and depicts a series of events in the life of a single day of the neurosurgeon on the eve of the Iraq War. As we have seen throughout this book, this 2003 geopolitical crisis, along with 9/11 and the invasion of Afghanistan, has globalized the experience of a very particular kind of post–cold war terror and violence that is mediatized incessantly around the world. Due to such mediatization, terror now appears, as Derrida put it, "less a past event than a future possibility."[15] This anticipatory temporality of terror is graphically evoked in *Saturday*. To reprise the opening scene of the novel that I analyzed in chapter 1, Henry wakes up before dawn and sees a plane on fire descending on London. His first instinct is to read it as yet another post-9/11 nightmare. He lingers at the window for a few tense minutes, but soon the sense of imminent catastrophe is tempered with the political ambivalence of a privileged, self-reflecting, liberal mind-set that oscillates between giving in to this sense of dread and resisting it: "How foolishly apocalyptic these apprehensions seem by daylight, when the self-evident fact of the streets and the people on them are their own justification, their own insurance. The world has not fundamentally changed. . . . There are always crises, and Islamic terrorism will settle into place, alongside recent wars, climate change, the politics of international trade, land and fresh water shortages, hunger, poverty and the rest" (76). When terror does ambush Henry's comfort zone, it comes not in an apocalyptic form but in the figure of a deranged and angry resident of London named Baxter. A polymorphous depiction of the city's underclass, Baxter invades Henry's home with a knife purportedly to take revenge for a car collision that morning and, allegorically of course, to tear into the privileged fabric of Henry's world. He threatens to rape Henry's daughter, Daisy, a poet and a vociferous opponent of the Iraq invasion, and kill the rest of the family. How is he disarmed and made human? Not by the inhuman instrumentalities of a neoliberal world but, incredibly, by the humanizing power of poetry. After stripping out of her clothes on Baxter's demand, Daisy begins reciting Matthew Arnold's "Dover Beach," and Baxter is awestruck by its beauty even as he is Daisy's dupe, for he thinks she has written it. In a bizarre reprisal of a fantasy of agency of the Victorian liberal self and a belief in the capacity of art to humanize the Baxters of our day, the novel ends with Henry and his daughter deciding to attend with precision and care to Baxter's deranged corporeality. Daisy has now regained her composure and is full of sympathy for Baxter. Henry is no longer the vulnerable witness of unfolding terror but the objective and brilliant neurosurgeon who diagnoses Baxter's condition as Huntington's disease and offers to treat him. The final moments of the narrative are replete with images of Henry's domestic stasis, his grateful retreat into professional and marital fulfillment.

This narrative conjuncture can quite plausibly be read as the return of a characteristically liberal aesthetic of the self: a combination of thought and thoughtfulness, "a cognitive formalism that makes beautiful thought about humanity taken as a social whole."[16] In light of my discussion about the novelistic grammar of the human, on one level *Saturday* appears to return to a configuration of sovereignty that is disciplinary in the liberal sense of restoring the rational order of things, recognizing individual autonomy and dignity per se, recognizing also the power of human will and consciousness to transfigure a threatening reality into a more humane and manageable reality. On this level the novel's figuration of the human could not be more different from conceptions of the (in)human and sovereignty as the right to kill.

Yet does not Henry's intervention with his surgical knife to take care of Baxter's injuries parallel the surgical strike metaphor of the two Gulf wars? The imminence of the Iraq War, after all, looms large in the backdrop of the novel. We are only too familiar with the Pentagon's boast of its precision bombing techniques that it claimed would achieve the "world" objective of freeing Iraq of tyranny with minimum battle scars. Can one, then, read this novel as a pro–Iraq War manifesto? Not if one takes into consideration the subtlety with which McEwan distributes responses to the Iraq War. But *Saturday* can certainly be read as allegorizing the grammar of sovereignty as a site of tension between the fantasy of liberal agency and the actualization of the same agency into a political force that makes decisions about the life and death of multitudes in "disorderly" parts of the world. Henry's vacillations about the war capture this tension brilliantly. During his Saturday sojourn through London, he encounters protest marches against the war, and yet his bourgeois liberal mind-set at first appears to support the war. Better to rid the world of its tyrants, he tells his irate daughter when she charges him with political naïveté and even conservatism. "Here's a chance to turn one country around. Plant a seed. See if it flourishes and spreads," he says (192). His daughter retorts, "You don't plant seeds with cruise missiles" (192). Daisy represents a postliberal mind-set that has lost faith in the capacity of the state to restore order and that sees through the neoliberal rhetoric of "just war." "You know very well," she rages at her father's obtuseness, "these extremists, the Neo-cons, have taken over America. Cheney, Rumsfeld, Wolfovitz [*sic*]. Iraq was always their pet project. Nine eleven was their big chance to talk Bush round. . . . There's nothing linking Iraq to nine eleven, or to Al-Qaeda generally, and no really scary evidence of WMD [weapons of mass destruction]. . . . And doesn't it ever occur to you that in attacking Iraq we're doing the very thing that the New York bombers wanted us to do—lash out, make more enemies in Arab countries and radicalize Islam" (190–91).

After he counters her comeback with an even more hawkish wager about a transformed democratic Iraq in three months, he reflects bleakly on the truth of his vacillation on the issue, on the luxury he has of taking different points of view about the war with different interlocutors, "a dove with Jay Strauss and a hawk with his daughter," as he wryly muses (193). None of his conviction about the rightness of the war persists as the novel progresses. The vacuous and timid nature of his abstract desire to see the world freed of tyrants is exposed when he acknowledges that his agency means nothing in the larger scheme of things. "What sense is he making? And how luxurious to work it all out at home in the kitchen, the geopolitical moves and military strategy, and not to be held to account, by voters, newspapers, friends, history" (193).

It appears there is no real transcendence of the human from inhuman post–cold war circuits of violence, only a retreat into a hypermediated sensibility that can but endlessly reflect on its incapacity to bring some semblance of order to the world. "Will he revive his hopes for firm action in the morning? All he feels now is fear. He's weak and ignorant, scared of the way consequences of an action leap away from your control and breed new events, new consequences, until you're led to a place you never dreamed of and would never choose—a knife at the throat" (277). Toward the end of the novel Henry's liberal fantasy of sovereign agency retreats further and further as he contemplates the ubiquity of necropolitical power: "Perhaps a bomb in the cause of jihad will drive them out with all the other faint-hearts into the suburbs, or deeper into the country, or to the chateau—their Saturday will become a Sunday" (276).

Notes

INTRODUCTION

1. McEwan, *Saturday*, 176, emphasis added.

2. Castells, *The Rise of Network Society*, 101.

3. Autonomy and empathy are the correlates of these categories in cultural practice in the era of early industrial capitalism. See Hunt, *Inventing Human Rights*, 29.

4. On the importance of memory, memorialization, and musealization in the late twentieth century, see Huyssen, "Present Pasts."

5. See also Appadurai, *Globalization*, especially essays by Anna Tsing and Leo Chin.

6. Bakhtin, *The Dialogic Imagination*, 7.

7. Lukács, *The Theory of the Novel*; McKeon, *The Origins of the English Novel*; Watt, *The Rise of the Novel*; Moretti, *The Way of the World*; Armstrong, *Desire and Domestic Fiction*; Baucom, *Specters of the Atlantic*.

8. Hungerford, "On the Period Formerly Known as the Contemporary," 410.

9. Hungerford, "On the Period Formerly Known as the Contemporary," 410.

10. Eshel, *Futurity*, 14.

11. Kermode, *The Sense of an Ending*, 46–47.

12. See, for instance, Rabinow, *Marking Time*.

13. See Manovich, *The Language of New Media*; Bolter and Grusin, *Remediation*.

14. Wallerstein, *After Liberalism*, especially chapter 13, "The Collapse of Liberalism," 232–51. See also Wallerstein, "The World System after the Cold War."

15. Wallerstein, *After Liberalism*.

16. Latour, *We Have Never Been Modern*, 8.

17. Derrida, *Specters of Marx*, 46.

18. Here are Derrida's words: "Instead of singing the advent of the ideal of democracy and the capitalist market in the euphoria of the end of history, instead of celebrating the 'end of ideologies' and the end of the great emancipatory discourses, let us never neglect this obvious macroscopic fact, made up of innumerable singular sites of suffering:

no degree of progress allows one to ignore that never before, in absolute figures, have so many men, women and children been subjugated, starved or exterminated on earth" (*Specters of Marx*, 97).

19. Derrida, *Specters of Marx*, 100–104.

20. See Kaldor, *New and Old Wars*; Hansen and Heurlin, *The New World Order*; Burke, *The 9/11 Wars*; Robbins, *Perpetual War*; Butler, *Precarious Life*; Butler, *Frames of War*; Gregory, *The Colonial Present*.

21. Cox, "Who Won the Cold War in Europe?," 18.

22. See Robbins, *Perpetual War*; Gregory, "The Everywhere War."

23. Kaldor, *New and Old Wars*.

24. Baudrillard, *The Gulf War Did Not Take Place*; Singer, *Wired for War*; Virilio and Lotringer, *Pure War*.

25. Mbembe, "Necropolitics," 14.

26. Cited in Devji, *The Terrorist in Search of Humanity*, 201.

27. Moyn, *The Last Utopia*.

28. Hunt, *Inventing Human Rights*.

29. Moyn writes, "In the realm of thinking, as in that of social action, human rights are best understood as survivors: the god that did not fail while all other political ideologies did. If they avoided failure, it was most of all because they were widely understood as a moral alternative to bankrupt political utopias" (*The Last Utopia*, 5).

30. Moyn, *The Last Utopia*, 8.

31. Cited in Elizabeth Drew, "A Reporter at Large: Human Rights," *New Yorker*, July 18, 1977.

32. Moyn, *The Last Utopia*, 172.

33. See Lévy, *Barbarism with a Human Face*.

34. Action Contre la Faim, "History," http://www.actioncontrelafaim.org/en/content/history.

35. Action Contre la Faim, "What We Do," http://www.actioncontrelafaim.org/en/our-countries-around-the-world.

36. Fassin, *Humanitarian Reason*, 206.

37. ICTJ, "What Is Transitional Justice?," http://ictj.org/about/transitional-justice.

38. See Mieszkowski, *Watching War*, for an elaboration of this argument.

39. See Mitchell, *Cloning Terror*; Mieszkowski, "Watching War"; Peebles, "Lines of Sight"; Wright, "The Desert of Experience." See also Mirzoeff, *The Right to Look*; Flynn and Salek, *Screening Torture*.

40. Given that visuality was a technique for waging war appropriated as a means to justify authority as the imagining of history, the end of the cold war in 1989 might have been expected to create an era of postvisuality. Instead, the global revolution in military affairs, usually considered to have commenced at roughly the same moment, has extended and transformed visuality using digital technology to pursue nineteenth-century tactical goals, creating what Derek Gregory has called the "visual economy [of the] . . . American military imaginary" (Mirzoeff, "The Right to Look," 485).

41. Mirzoeff, "The Right to Look," 489.

42. Gregory, "Vanishing Points," 61.

43. Baudrillard, *The Gulf War Did Not Take Place*.

44. Mitchell, *Ghostwritten*, 316.

45. A relevant study is Berlant, *Compassion*. See also Boltanski, *Distant Suffering*.

46. See Sontag, *Regarding the Pain of Others*; Butler, *Frames of War*.

47. Sontag, *Regarding the Pain of Others*, 108.

48. Feldman, "The Structuring Enemy and Archival War," 1706.

49. A recent work is Trotter, *Literature in the First Media Age*.

50. Cited in Baucom, *Specters of the Atlantic*, 219.

51. Other sources include Davis, *The Problems of Slavery in the Western World*; Aravamudan, *Slavery, Abolition and Emancipation*; Baucom, *Specters of the Atlantic*.

52. Cited in Baucom, *Specters of the Atlantic*, 210.

53. Baucom, *Specters of the Atlantic*, 215–16.

54. Hayot mentions the "rhetorically unmatched prestige" of the concept of "world" in literary criticism of the twenty-first century (*On Literary Worlds*, 30).

55. Said, *Culture and Imperialism*, 69.

56. Gandhi, *Affective Communities*, 152.

57. Lukács, *The Theory of the Novel*, 71.

58. Timothy Bewes does an excellent reading of Lukács in "The Novel Problematic."

59. On the operation of set logic in literary theory, see Ronen, *Possible Worlds in Literary Theory*; Pavel, *Fictional Worlds*.

60. Hayot, *On Literary Worlds*, 32.

61. Heidegger, "The Age of the World Picture."

62. DeLillo, *Cosmopolis*, 206–7.

63. Nancy, *The Creation of the World*, 95, 28.

64. See Harvey, *The Condition of Postmodernity*.

65. Nancy, *The Creation of the World*, 39.

66. Urquhart, "Learning from the Gulf," 17.

67. Albright, "International Law Approaches in the Twenty-First Century," 1597.

68. Simma, "NATO, the UN and the Use of Force," 1.

69. Antonio Cassese, cited in Orford, "Muscular Humanitarianism," 695.

70. Cassese, cited in Orford, "Muscular Humanitarianism," 699.

71. Bloomfield, "Collective Security and US Interests," 190.

72. For a powerful exposition of this point, see Downes, "Melville's *Benito Cereno* and the Politics of Humanitarian Intervention," 472.

73. Slaughter, *Human Rights, Inc.*, 328.

74. Watt, *The Rise of the Novel*; McKeon, *The Origins of the English Novel*; Cohen, "Sentimental Communities"; Hunt, *Inventing Human Rights*.

75. Haskell, "Capitalism and the Origins of Humanitarian Sensibility," part 2, 551–52.

76. Aravamudan, *Slavery, Abolition and Emancipation*; Cohen, *The Sentimental Education of the Novel*; Baucom, *Specters of the Atlantic*; Chandler, "*Lord Jim* and the Sentimental Novel"; Hunt, *Inventing Human Rights*. While not mentioning any explicit links with the abolitionist movement, Chandler notes that the term *sentimental* in relation to the novel did not appear until the 1750s and clearly demarcated a new narrative mode. However, he establishes a connection between the emergence of the sentimental novel and the publication of Smith's *The Theory of Moral Sentiments* in 1759: "Though Smith neither employs the term *sentimental* nor concerns himself at length with the novel, his

arguments about the processes of character formation by way of sympathetic exchange of positions in modern commercial society do seem to resonate later in the first examples of the self-consciously identified sentimental novel. The connection seems especially strong in relation to the then-fashionable epistolary method of fiction, an exercise in the alternation of views that, one might say, is very much at the centre of what Smith is describing" ("The Face of the Case," 840).

77. Cohen, "Sentimental Communities," 108.

78. Slaughter, *Human Rights, Inc.*, 17; Festa, "Sentimental Bonds and Revolutionary Character," 73.

79. An oft-cited anecdote concerns the novelist Jane Austen, who famously declared after the British victories in the Peninsular Wars, "How horrible it is to have so many killed. And what a mercy that one cares for none of them!" This was an expression of her relief that her two brothers in the navy were safe. Cited in Laqueur, "Bodies, Details and the Humanitarian Narrative," 203.

80. Chandler, *An Archaeology of Sympathy*, 13, 12.

81. Laqueur, "Bodies, Details and the Humanitarian Narrative."

82. For critical analysis of these works, see details in Aravamudan, *Slavery, Abolition and Emancipation*.

83. Watt, *The Rise of the Novel*; Jameson, *The Political Unconscious*.

84. See Cohen, *The Sentimental Education of the Novel*, for a detailed account of the sentimental narrative contexts in which nineteenth-century realism arose in France. She writes of the rise of Balzac and Stendhal, "Realist novels were not unequivocally celebrated masterpieces in their own time nor was the realist aesthetic the inevitable teleology of the modern novel when it first appeared. Rather, Balzac and Stendhal made bids for their market shares in a hostile takeover of the dominant practice of the novel when both started writing: sentimental works by women writers" (6).

85. Cohen, *The Sentimental Education of the Novel*, chapter 2; Moretti, *The Way of the World*.

86. Cited in Slaughter, *Human Rights, Inc.*, 325.

87. President George W. Bush's speech to the Afghan people on March 1, 2006, cited in Slaughter, *Human Rights, Inc.*, 317.

88. Slaughter, *Human Rights, Inc.*, 324–25.

89. See Mbembe, "Necropolitics."

90. Tim Parks, "The Dull New Global Novel," *New York Review of Books*, blog, February 9, 2010, http://www.nybooks.com/blogs/nyrblog/2010/feb/09/the-dull-new -global-novel/.

91. The scholarship on world-making consulted here includes Goodman, *Ways of World Making*; Pavel, *Fictional Worlds*; Lubonir, *Heterocosmica*; Nancy, *The Creation of the World*; Karagiannis and Wagner, *Varieties of World Making*. Contemporary scholarship on world literature includes Damrosch, *What Is World Literature?*; Dimock, "Literature for the Planet"; Cooppan, "Ghosts in the Disciplinary Machine"; Cheah, "World Literature as World-Making Activity."

92. Brennan, "The Subtlety of Caesar"; Kadir, "Comparative Literature in an Age of Terrorism."

93. Rancière, "Who Is the Subject of the Rights of Man?," 307.

94. Mitchell, "Ekphrasis and the Other," 161, 162.

95. Arendt, *The Human Condition*.

96. Baucom, *Specters of the Atlantic*, 244, emphasis added.

97. See Derrida, "A Self-Unsealing Poetic Text." Agamben's reflections on the ethics and politics of witnessing in our era can be found in *Remnants of Auschwitz*.

98. Moretti, "Conjectures on World Literature," 55.

ONE. Real Virtualities and the Undead Genre

1. Cited in McKeon, *Theory of the Novel*, 58.

2. See Arac, "This Will Kill That," 7. Arac does not so much categorically propound this as his own position as comment on the widespread perception of the novel's growing irrelevance with the rise of the media industry.

3. Vince Passaro, "Dangerous Don DeLillo," *New York Times*, May 19, 1991.

4. *Mao II*, 157. In a feature on DeLillo published in 1991, right after the publication of *Mao II*, DeLillo's editor Gerald Howard said this about the character Bill Gray: "I think this is a book about Salman Rushdie in a way. Don was very upset about the Rushdie business, and I think you can sense that feeling of threat all the way through *Mao II*" (cited in Passaro, "Dangerous Don DeLillo").

5. Don DeLillo, "In the Ruins of the Future," *Harper's*, December 2001, 39, http://harpers.org/archive/2001/12/in-the-ruins-of-the-future/.

6. Bakhtin, *The Dialogic Imagination*, 324. For a powerful explication of both Bakhtin's and Lukács's theorizations of the novelistic, see Bewes, "The Novel Problematic."

7. My position here is at significant variance from the novelization thesis articulated by Timothy Bewes, John Plotz, and Srinivas Aravamudan in the special issue "Futures of the Novel." I am more interested in seeing the interplay of other genres with the novel as a form in print fiction rather than the novelization of other cultural media, which is what these scholars address. Plotz metaphorizes the transitive nature of the novel—its relay effect from one cultural form to another—as a lack, a negative capability, as he calls it, a universal blood donor with the blood type O positive: a genre that serves many purposes but lacks substance on its own, for it has spread itself too thin. Toward the end of his essay this purported lack acquires a malign form, "a virus poised always to pass on its genetic information to others." And what is the nature of the information? Merely "a stripped down, endlessly replicable set of instructions" ("No Future," 26). Aravamudan takes this negative capability argument to yet another malign figural realm, that of the gothic: "Just as an alien creature, say Dracula, materially occupies and completes all finite bodies/victims that he takes over and surpasses, the novel absorbs its predecessors into a self-perpetuating network, making them 'undead.' Temporality is important: before the novel all other genres lived; after the novel's takeover, other genres have an afterlife as 'creatures' ventriloquized by the monstrous novel as meta-organism" ("Refusing the Death of the Novel," 20–21). Aravamudan's witty provocation inverts the mortality thesis to confer the status of the undead not on the novel but on genres that it has inhabited in its endless hunger for new forms. Bewes usefully moderates some of this provocative dialectic between the novel as an ubiquitous star and as a malign has-been. His statement is qualified by neither enthusiasm nor deprecation but

is a solid if arguable proposition: "If there is to be an expansion in the range of the possible objects of study beyond the novel, its basis is *not any historical redundancy of the novel or the obsolescence of forms of thought made available by the novel*, but the opposite: the recognition that the novel is a logic, a structure of problematicity that is not limited to works conventionally understood to be novels; that, insofar as we think critically about the forms of the contemporary world, we do so within, through, and alongside the novel" ("The Novel Problematic," 18).

8. Bazin, "In Defense of Mixed Cinema," 726.

9. Amis subsequently wrote *Yellow Dog*, a satire on the post-9/11 world order that received a scathing reception from reviewers. The novel did not feature the collapse of the towers or the violence that subsequently followed, but reviewers universally commented on the sense of doom that prevailed throughout the book. Amis also edited a collection of essays on 9/11, *The Second Plane: September 11. Terror and Boredom*. His subsequent comments on Muslims after 9/11 caused worldwide offense. See Ronan Bennett, "Shame on Us," *Guardian*, November 18, 2007, http://www.theguardian.com/uk/2007/nov/19/race.bookscomment.

10. Martin Amis, "The Last Days of Muhammad Atta," *Observer*, September 3, 2006, emphasis added.

11. See Lund, *Text as Picture*; Mitchell, *Picture Theory*.

12. Bal, "Over-Writing as Un-Writing," 597.

13. For some important responses, see Baer, *110 Stories*.

14. DeLillo, *Mao II*, 157.

15. See Asad, *On Suicide Bombing*; Hage, "Comes a Time We Are All Enthusiasm."

16. Palumbo-Liu, *The Deliverance of Others*, xi.

17. Asad, *On Suicide Bombing*.

18. McEwan, *Saturday*, 15. Subsequent quotations are cited parenthetically in the text.

19. A few readings of McEwan's *Saturday* have put forward this thesis of retreat into the aesthetics of an advanced capitalist middle-class lifeworld as an antidote to the travails of viewing war online. See, for instance, Sphar, "Prolonged Suspension."

20. Keenan, "Publicity and Indifference," 107, 105, emphasis added.

21. Sontag, *Regarding the Pain of Others*, 85.

22. In the context of my work this system is the global military-industrial-information complex that has gained such ascendancy since 1989.

23. Baucom's *Specters of the Atlantic* offers one of the richest analyses to date of the technologies of self-making—both actuarial and melancholic—under finance capitalism and of the debates on the abolition of slavery. I extrapolate from his conceptual framework to talk of melancholic and actuarial modes of self-making in novels of the post–cold war era. The comparative frame works to great advantage, for Baucom and other scholars such as Giovanni Arrighi have seen in our contemporary speculative mode of finance and information capitalism an intensification of the speculative cycles of finance capital in the era of transatlantic slavery.

24. For the political and psychoanalytical charge of the idea of disposability, see Khanna, "Disposability."

25. Aslam, *The Wasted Vigil*, 191.

26. Baucom, *Specters of the Atlantic*, 217.

27. The Second Intifada, also referred to as the Al-Aqsa Intifada, is the Palestinian uprising against Israeli occupation that lasted from September 2000 to 2005. The First Intifada lasted from December 1987 to 1993.

28. Sacco, *Footnotes in Gaza*, ix.

29. The "right to look" that challenges the "right of the [official] gaze" is Mirzoeff's idea ("The Right to Look").

30. Rancière, *The Politics of Aesthetics*, 13.

31. Rancière, "Introducing Disagreement," 6.

32. Mirzoeff, "The Right to Look." Also see Mirzoeff, *The Right to Look*.

33. Cited in Baucom, *Specters of the Atlantic*, 219.

34. Mirzoeff, "War Is Culture," 492.

35. Mirzoeff, "War Is Culture," 492.

36. The words are attributed to Col. Daniel S. Roper, director of the U.S. Army and Marine Corps Counterinsurgency Center, cited in Mirzoeff, *The Right to Look*, 486.

37. Powers, *The Yellow Birds*, 22.

38. Powers, *The Yellow Birds*, 24.

39. Riverbend, *Baghdad Burning*, 105.

40. Riverbend, *Baghdad Burning*, vol. 2, http://riverbendblog.blogspot.com.au/.

41. Sacco, *Footnotes in Gaza*, 168.

42. Cited in Mirzoeff, *The Right to Look*, 303.

43. Sacco, *Footnotes in Gaza*, 169.

T W O. World-Making and Possible Worlds

1. Auerbach, "Philology and *Weltliteratur*," 2.

2. Whitman, *Song of Myself*, verse 52, 75.

3. Pollock, *The Language of Gods in the World of Men*, 203.

4. In a recent analysis of modernism's relation to the idea of world-making, Eric Hayot puts forward the notion of the modern itself as a cosmographical social form that "constitutes an attempt to grasp the wholeness of the world as the function of the arrival of the universal in it" (*On Literary Worlds*, 104).

5. The term *philological-lexigraphic revolution* is used by Pascale Casanova in her reading of Anderson to describe the expansion of literary horizons in the late eighteenth and early nineteenth centuries. See her chapter "The Invention of Literature," in *The World Republic of Letters*, 48.

6. Strich, *Goethe and World Literature*; Mufti, "Orientalism and the Institution of World Literatures."

7. Marx and Engels, *The Communist Manifesto*, 98.

8. Marno, "The Monstrosity of Literature"; Damrosch, "Hugo Meltzl and the Principle of Polyglottism"; Guillen, *Literature as System*; Guillen, *The Challenge of Comparative Literature*; Villanueva, "Claudio Guillen"; Schmitz-Emans, "Richard Meyer's Concept of World Literature"; Auerbach, "Philology and *Weltliteratur*"; Apter, "Global Translation"; Mufti, "Auerbach in Istanbul"; Mufti, "Orientalism and the Institution of

World Literatures"; Said, *The World, the Text and the Critic*; Said, *Humanism and Democratic Criticism*; Ganguly, "Edward Said, World Literature and Global Comparatism."

9. Meltzl, "Present Tasks of Comparative Literature," 46.

10. Said, *Humanism and Democratic Criticism*, 58, 68, 69.

11. All quotations from Tagore's "World-Literature" are translated by S. Chakravorty and appear in *Rabindranath Tagore*, 179, emphasis added.

12. Tagore, *Nationalism*, 74, 126.

13. See Ganguly, "The Language Question in India."

14. With the exception of Said, who talked relentlessly about the "worldliness" of literature. But Said's interventions were less a meditation on world literature than a critique of the insulation of canonical texts of English literature from the world historical imperatives of their times. His historical frame was the period of high European imperialism, from the mid-eighteenth century until the end of the Second World War. At the time of Said's writing, the category world in relation to literature did not quite circulate with the charge it does today. The emergence of globalization as a powerful intellectual rubric was still a decade away, as were ways of imagining the world as maximal connectivity through information technology—all of which give the idea of world literature and the world in literature today an inflection not exactly available to Said's protean intellect and imagination in the late 1970s and early 1980s.

15. See, among others, Damrosch, *What Is World Literature?*; Damrosch, *How to Read World Literature*; Prendergast, *Debating World Literature*; Dimock, *Through Other Continents*; Damrosch et al., *The Routledge Companion to World Literature*.

16. Brennan, "The Subtlety of Caesar," 202.

17. Moretti, *Graphs, Maps, Trees*; Casanova, *The World Republic of Letters*.

18. See especially Franco, "Globalization and Literary History," 445.

19. See Gaston, "Derrida and the End of the World," 506.

20. Derrida, *The Problem of Genesis in Husserl's Philosophy*, 110.

21. Nancy, *The Creation of the World*, 34–35, 54.

22. Pavel, "Literary Genres as Norms and Good Habits."

23. For an elaboration of this point, see Ronen, *Possible Worlds in Literary Theory*, 6–7.

24. Ronen, *Possible Worlds in Literary Theory*, 9.

25. Ronen, *Possible Worlds in Literary Theory*, 21–23.

26. Adams, "Theories of Actuality"; Plantinga, "Actualism and Possible Worlds"; Kripke, *Naming and Necessity*.

27. See Brennan's statement in "The Subtlety of Caesar," 202, for instance: "Through various channels of quiet influence and unacknowledged inspiration, cultural theory echoes often with slavish regularity and in a variety of idioms that central self image of American globalization: 'the global ecumene,' 'single world culture,' the 'multitude.'" Or Andrew McCann's remark in "The International of Excreta," 21: "Today the notion of world literature is an abstraction implying old forms of cultural capital that embody the residue of old imperial hierarchies . . . and modes of distribution that embody the coercive pressure of a contemporary, neo-imperial culture industry."

28. Anderson, *Imagined Communities*.

1. Mitchell, *Ghostwritten*, 172. Subsequent quotations are cited parenthetically in the text.

2. Anderson, *Imagined Communities*.

3. Culler, "Anderson and the Novel."

4. Anderson, *The Specters of Comparison*, 33–34.

5. See Lanier, *You Are Not a Gadget*.

6. See Barnard, "Fictions of the Global," 210.

7. http://www.amazon.com/253-Geoff-Ryman/dp/0006550789, accessed September 2015.

8. See Gane's reading of Friedrich Kittler, "Radical Post-Humanism." The reference to "information materialism" is on 39. IM is a body of cybernetic theory that sees digital agency as a confluence of the human and the machine. This strand of posthuman information theory is not one that ultimately prioritizes the human, but rather decenters the human by urging scholars to pay attention to the physical and material infrastructure of information and communication technology—a close study of machines, programs, and codes. Kittler maintains that these are the drivers of what will count as human and social intelligence in the near future. The Zookeeper in the novel is an apt figuration of this humanoid-cyborgian agency.

9. Bakhtin, "Forms of Time and Chronotope in the Novel," 84.

10. See Anderson, *Imagined Communities*, 7.

11. Castells, *The Rise of Network Society*. See also Jagoda, "Terror Networks and the Aesthetics of Interconnection."

12. See especially Harvey, *The Conditions of Postmodernity*; Harvey, *Spaces of Hope*.

13. Castells, *The Rise of Network Society*, 408–9.

14. By "real virtuality" Castells means the world of electronic mediation of real-life experiences. It is a world that appears experientially as real as any physical world. This is how he explicates the idea: "What is, then, a communication system that, in contrast to earlier historical experience, generates real virtuality? It is a system in which reality itself (that is, people's material/symbolic existence) is entirely captured, fully immersed in a virtual image setting, in the world of make believe, in which appearances are not just on the screen through which experience is communicated, but they become the experience" (*The Rise of Network Society*, 404, emphasis in original).

15. Derrida, *Specters of Marx*; Žižek, *The Ticklish Subject*.

16. Žižek, *The Ticklish Subject*, 137–38.

17. The allusion to *The Satanic Verses* is clear when Marco writes, "Gibreel got his rocks off with one once by pretending to *spik no Eenglish* and be just off the boat from Lebanon" (282, emphasis added).

18. Anderson, *The Specters of Comparison*, 334.

19. See, for instance, Giles, *Virtual Americas*; Cooppan, *Worlds Within*; Bode, *Reading by Numbers*.

20. Moretti, *Atlas of the European Novel*, 53, 45.

21. See Beck, *Cosmopolitan Vision*, for an articulation of the future as the horizon of a global cosmopolitical mobilization.

1. John Updike, "Paradises Lost: Rushdie's *Shalimar the Clown*," *New Yorker*, September 5, 2005, http://www.newyorker.com/archive/2005/09/05/050905crbo_books ?printable=true&currentPage=all.

2. Ginny Dougary, "The Incredible Lightness of Salman," *Times* (London), August 20, 2005, http://www.thetimes.co.uk/tto/arts/books/article2450494.ece.

3. See Brennan, "The Subtlety of Caesar"; Kadir, "To World, to Globalize."

4. Desmond, "The Insurgency in Kashmir"; Rai, *Hindu Rulers, Muslim Subjects.*

5. Salman Rushdie, "Double Standards Make Enemies," *Washington Post*, August 28, 2002.

6. See, for instance, Devji, *The Terrorist in Search of Humanity*; Mamdani, *Good Muslim, Bad Muslim.*

7. Updike, "Paradises Lost."

8. Chaudhuri, "Translating Loss," 270.

9. Mishra, *Bollywood Cinema*; Rajadhyaksha, *Indian Cinema in the Time of Celluloid.*

10. Ellison, *Cato's Tears and the Making of Anglo-American Emotion*, 101.

11. Rushdie dedicates the novel to his "Kashmiri grandparents Dr Ataullah and Amir un nissa Butt (Babajan and Ammaji)."

12. Rushdie, *Midnight's Children*, 10.

13. Rushdie, *Shalimar the Clown*, 83, 71. Subsequent quotations will be cited parenthetically in the text.

14. Produced in 1953 and directed by Nandlal Jaswantlal, *Anarkali* starred the celebrated film couple Pradip Kumar and Bina Rai. The songs, set to music by C. Ramchandra, immortalized this epic love story of Salim and Anarkali. Directed by K. Asif and released in 1960, *Mughal-e-Azam* continues to be rated one of India's most successful films. The glamorous cast, featuring Dilip Kumar, Madhubala, and Prithviraj Kapoor, combined with Naushad's sublime music based on Indian classical ragas, elevated the love story of Salim and Anarkali to an epic realm.

15. Several Urdu versions of this lore—novelistic, theatrical, and cinematic—were produced in the early years of the twentieth century. These include Imtiyaz Ali Taaj's 1922 novel *Anarkali* and Ardeshir Irani's silent film of the same title produced in 1928.

16. See Rushdie, "Inside the Mind of Jihadists."

17. Cited in Stuchtey and Fuchs, *Writing World History*, 44.

18. Livings, "Salman Rushdie," 110–11.

19. Herwitz, *Heritage, Culture and Politics in the Postcolony*, 4.

20. I borrow the phrase *live-action heritage* from Herwitz, *Heritage, Culture and Politics in the Postcolony*, 11–12.

21. See Morton's argument in this regard in "There Were Collisions and Explosions."

22. Rushdie, "Inside the Mind of Jihadists," 9.

23. See Faisal Devji's fine study on this global face of Islam as a humanitarian project, *The Terrorist in Search of Humanity.*

24. Devji, *The Terrorist in Search of Humanity*, 171–72, emphasis added.

25. Rushdie, "Inside the Mind of Jihadists," 7.

26. Devji, *The Terrorist in Search of Humanity*, 55.

1. Dunya Mikhail, "The War Works Hard," translated by Elizabeth Winslow, Poets
.org, accessed August 12, 2012, http://www.poets.org/viewmedia.php/prmMID/16991.

2. See Favret, *War at a Distance*; Russell, "The Eighteenth Century and the Romantics on War."

3. A recent powerful exposition of the phenomenon is W. J. T. Mitchell's *Cloning Terror*.

4. Roger Cohen, "#StopKONY Now!!!," *New York Times*, March 12, 2012, http://www
.nytimes.com/2012/03/13/opinion/cohen-stop-kony-now.html, accessed August 16,
2012.

5. Jeffrey Gettleman, "In Vast Jungle, US Troops Aid Search for Kony," *New York
Times*, April 29, 2012, http://www.nytimes.com/2012/04/30/world/africa/kony
-tracked-by-us-forces-in-central-africa.html?ref=josephkony.

6. http://www.nytimes.com/2012/04/30/world/africa/kony-tracked-by-us
-forces-in-central-afr, accessed August 16, 2012; http://www.nytimes.com/2014
/03/24/world/africa/obama-is-sending-more-resources-for-joseph-kony-search
.html?rref=collection%2Ftimestopic%2FKony%2C%20Joseph&action=click&
contentCollection=timestopics&region=stream&module=stream_unit&version=latest
&contentPlacement=9&pgtype=collection.

7. See Favret, *War at a Distance*; Mieszkowski, *Watching War*.

8. Virilio and Lotringer, *Crepuscular Dawn*, 11.

9. http://www.kony2012.com/, accessed August 15, 2012; https://plus.google.com
/101936568183489575979/posts/T2g7z7Fmvay.

10. Not surprisingly the *Kony 2012* media phenomenon did not maintain its momentum beyond the year. Many controversies dogged its maker, Jason Russell, including a story that he had a traumatic breakdown. See the article by Polly Curtis
and Tom McCarthy in *The Guardian* for an account of these developments; http://
www.theguardian.com/politics/reality-check-with-polly-curtis/2012/mar/08/kony
-2012-what-s-the-story, accessed August 2012.

11. McLagan, "Principles, Publicity and Politics."

12. Agamben, *Homo Sacer* and *Remnants of Auschwitz*.

13. See the chapter "Witness" in Agamben, *Remnants of Auschwitz*, 15–39.

14. In fact Didier Fassin calls the 1970s the "Second Age of Humanitarianism," characterized by the "emergence of the witness," thus emphasizing the overlap between the
two domains of politics that Agamben talks of (*Humanitarian Reason*, 206).

15. In *An Archaeology of Sympathy*, Chandler defines *sensorium* as a threefold apparatus consisting of *sensibility*, "the capacity for fine grained sensory experience" to feel;
mobility that specifically "registers the relation between motion and emotion, that is our
capacity to move and be moved both in body and spirit"; and *virtuality*, the "capacity of
an embodied sensorium to undergo circulation among a range of imagined locations"
(xviii). My use of the term *sensorium* in the context of our hypermediated age carries
the charge of all three components.

16. Kaldor, *New and Old Wars*, 9.

17. According to Kaldor, "The number of UN Peacekeeping operations increased dramatically in the 1990s as did the range of tasks they were asked to perform including the

delivery of humanitarian aid, the protection of people in safe havens, disarmament and demobilization, creating a secure environment for elections and reporting violations of international humanitarian law in addition to the traditional tasks of monitoring and maintaining ceasefires" (*New and Old Wars*, 119).

18. https://witness.org/, accessed September 2012.

19. Cited in Keenan, "Publicity and Indifference," 108.

20. Gregory, "Transnational Story-telling," 201.

21. Avni, "Mobilizing Hope," 206. "If Israeli Jews regard themselves to be on the brink of perpetual extermination, then it is unlikely that naming and shaming alone will succeed in curbing what they consider to be defensive and thus necessary or legitimate behaviour. Similarly, if Palestinians determine that they have limited options in the face of bulldozers, settler violence and an Israeli army with far superior resources and military capabilities, they are unlikely to mobilize *en masse* against guerilla tactics or suicide bombings" (208).

22. Avni, "Mobilizing Hope," 210.

23. Russell, "The Eighteenth Century and the Romantics on War," 115.

24. Woolf, "The Leaning Tower," 130–31.

25. Favret, *War at a Distance*, 46–47.

26. Hegel, *The Philosophy of History*, 33.

27. Godwin, *Enquiry concerning Political Justice and Its Influence on Modern Morals and Happiness*, 510.

28. Mieszkowski, "Watching War," 1651.

29. Hobbes declared that war was constituted "not of Battle only, or the act of fighting, but in a tract of time, wherein the Will to contend by Battle is sufficiently known. . . . The nature of War consists not in actual fighting, but in the known disposition thereto. . . . All other time Is Peace" (*Leviathan*, 88–89).

30. Rousseau, *Emile*, 237, 239.

31. See Russell, *Theatres of War*; St. Clair, *The Reading Nation in the Romantic Period*; Bainbridge, *Napoleon and English Romanticism*; Shaw, *Waterloo and the Romantic Imagination*.

32. Russell, *Theatres of War*.

33. Some of the early writings of Wordsworth, such as his poem "To the Men of Kent" (1803), are good illustrations of these public imaginings of war amid an expanding British imperium: "No parleying now! In Britain is one breath; / We all are with you now from shore to shore:—/ Ye men of Kent, tis victory or death!"—Hayden, *William Wordsworth*, 594.

34. Chandler, *An Archaeology of Sympathy*, xix, 12.

35. See Favret, "Coming Home," for an account of the pathos of the war widow in Romantic poetry.

36. "It is worth remembering that most of the privates fighting in romantic wars did not have the capacities for consent and speech that define Habermas' citizen" (Favret, "Coming Home," 544).

37. Cited in Favret, "Coming Home," 546.

38. Sontag, *Regarding the Pain of Others*, 8.

39. Fussell, *Wartime*, 1.

40. Favret, "Coming Home," 11.

41. Lukács, *The Historical Novel*, 24.

42. See Pascoe, "The Cold War and the War on Terror," 240.

43. Mailer, *Harlot's Ghost*, 13.

44. Virilio, *Pure War*, 174.

45. DeLillo, *Underworld*, 514–18, emphasis added.

46. The history of Debord's involvement with the Situationist International (1957–72) is well documented, as is the role of the Situationists in the May 1968 uprising in France.

47. Debord, *Society of the Spectacle*, thesis 4, thesis 34, thesis 58.

48. Schechner notes that barely four days after the event, outlets in the Chinese town of Yueging stocked videos of the attacks on the same shelves as Hollywood movies: "Often the 9/11 videos were located in the cheaper sections alongside dozens of American films. . . . All of the 9/11 videos had been packaged to look like Hollywood movies. There was a DVD entitled 'The Century's Greatest Catastrophe.' The box front featured photographs of Osama Bin Laden, George W. Bush and the burning twin towers. On the back, a small icon noted that it had been rated R for violence and language" ("9/11 as Avante-Garde Art?," 1822).

49. Numerous novels have been published in the aftermath of 9/11, and there are independent studies of these works. Rather than rehearse the story of the emergence of this corpus, I propose to look at two emblematic publications to focus specifically on the architectonics of twenty-first-century war as both spectacle and intimate witnessing.

SIX. The Sky Is Falling

1. Artaud, "No More Masterpieces," 76.

2. Artaud, "The Theatre of Cruelty," 85–86.

3. For detailed discussions of such comparisons, see Román, "A Forum on Theatre and Tragedy in the Wake of September 11."

4. Una Chaudhuri, in Román, "A Forum on Theatre and Tragedy in the Wake of September 11," 98–99.

5. Brian Singleton, in Román, "A Forum on Theatre and Tragedy in the Wake of September 11," 119.

6. Derrida, "The Theatre of Cruelty and the Closure of Representation," 14.

7. This is a paraphrase of Derrida's reading.

8. Susan Sontag, "Approaching Artaud," *New Yorker*, May 9, 1973.

9. Tristan Tzara, "Second Dada Manifesto," March 23, 1918, http://www.391.org/manifestos/1918-dada-manifesto-tristan-tzara.html#.VfmX3M9RFok.

10. For an extensive commentary on this kind of avant-garde fundamentalism, see Bharucha, *Terror and Performance*.

11. Stockhausen's comments at a press conference six days after the event have been variously reported over the years. One of the most cited versions is Osborne, "Documentation of Stockhausen's Comments re: 9/11."

12. This is not to say that there were no nuanced or ethically sensitive responses to

9/11 as spectacle among performance scholars. See the special issue of *Theatre Journal* 54, no. 1 (2002).

13. Don DeLillo, "In the Ruins of the Future," *Harper's*, December 2001, 39, http://harpers.org/archive/2001/12/in-the-ruins-of-the-future/; http://www.theguardian.com/books/2001/dec/22/fiction.dondelillo, accessed November 10, 2015.

14. DeLillo, "In the Ruins of the Future," 38.

15. Bakhtin, "Forms of Time and the Chronotope in the Novel," 250.

16. DeLillo, *Falling Man*, 3. Subsequent quotations are cited parenthetically in the text.

17. Robbins, "The Worlding of the American Novel."

18. See Mitchell, *Cloning Terror*; Baudrillard, *Simulacra and Simulation*.

19. Cited in Chow, *The Age of the World Target*, 31.

20. Jean Baudrillard, "The Spirit of Terrorism," translated by Chris Turner. Originally published in *Le Monde*, November 3, 2001; insomnia.ac/essays/the_spirit_of_terrorism/, accessed on November 10, 2015.

21. Tom Junod, "The Falling Man," *Esquire*, September 2003; also available at E Classic, http://www.esquire.com/features/ESQ0903-SEP_FALLINGMAN. Junod writes of the quest of a Canadian journalist, Peter Cheney, to find out who the falling man truly was. Cheney got some initial confirmation from the man's brother and sister that he was a pastry chef at Windows on the World, the restaurant on the top floor of the North Tower that lost many employees that day; however, his wife and daughters vehemently denied that the man in Drew's photograph was Norberto Hernandez.

22. A similar though less elaborated point is made by Frost, "Falling Man's Precarious Balance."

23. See details on Corliss's website, http://jebcorliss.net/. The reference to Corliss appears in Kauffman's essay on DeLillo, "The Wake of Terror."

24. The New York *Daily News* headline was "Kick Him in the Arts." Mayor Michael Bloomberg referred to Skarbakka's work as "nauseatingly offensive."

25. Kerry Skarbakka, "The Struggle to Right Oneself," http://www.skarbakka.com/portfolios/struggle_statement.htm.

26. Skarbakka, "The Struggle to Right Oneself."

27. Mitchell, *Cloning Terror*, 70, 99.

28. See Storr, *Gerhard Richter*.

29. I am indebted to Kauffman's fine essay in MFS, "The Wake of Terror," for details on Baader-Meinhof and its links to DeLillo's novel. See also Houen, *Terrorism and Modern Literature*.

30. Richter, "Notes for a Press Conference," 175.

SEVEN. This I Saw

1. Renouart de Bussierre, "Rembrandt-Goya," 63.

2. Sontag, *On Photography*, 44–45.

3. Sontag, *Regarding the Pain of Others*.

4. See, for instance, the appeal of Goya to global discourses on humanitarianism in

an article written by a senior medical adviser of the International Committee of the Red Cross, Bouvier, "*Yo Lo Vi.*"

5. Sontag, *Regarding the Pain of Others*, 21.

6. Favret, *War at a Distance*.

7. Eaglestone, "'The Age of Reason Was Over.'"

8. Or as Smith writes in *The Theory of Moral Sentiments*, "The impartial spectator evaluates the situation neither from our own place, not yet from his [the agent's], neither with our own eyes not yet with his, but from the place and with the eyes of the third person, who has no particular connexion with either and who judges with impartiality between us" (3).

9. Gibbons, *Edmund Burke and Ireland*, 96.

10. Smith, *The Theory of Moral Sentiments*, 38, 31.

11. Spiegelman, *MetaMaus*, 52.

12. Spiegelman, *MetaMaus*, 170.

13. Spiegelman, *MetaMaus*, 174.

14. Spiegelman, *MetaMaus*, 174, 175, emphasis added.

15. Spiegelman, *MetaMaus*, 49–50, emphasis added.

16. Lash, *Critique of Information*, xx, emphasis added.

17. Spiegelman, *MetaMaus*, 171.

18. Spiegelman, *In the Shadow of No Towers*, preface, n.p.

19. Spiegelman, *MetaMaus*, 56.

20. Spiegelman, *MetaMaus*, 30.

21. Spiegelman, *MetaMaus*, 30.

22. Badiou, *Ethics*, 50.

23. Derrida, "A Self-Unsealing Poetic Text," 182.

24. Derrida, "A Self-Unsealing Poetic Text," 187, emphasis added. Interestingly *mitra* in Sanskrit means "friend," a literal allusion that Benveniste does not mention.

25. Derrida, "A Self-Unsealing Poetic Text," 188–89.

26. Spiegelman, *MetaMaus*, 73, emphasis added.

EIGHT. Forensic Witnessing

1. Rothberg, *Traumatic Realism*.

2. Ondaatje, *Anil's Ghost*, 17. Subsequent quotations are cited parenthetically in the text.

3. See Davis, *Factual Fictions*; Hunter, *Before Novels*; Poovey, *The History of the Modern Fact*.

4. See, for instance, the hostile reviews of the novel by two Sri Lankan scholars: Qadri, "A Flippant Gesture towards Sri Lanka"; Mendis, "A Review of *Anil's Ghost.*"

5. I borrow the phrase *evidence of the senses* from McKeon, *Origins of the English Novel*, chapter 2.

6. Ignatieff, *The Warrior's Honour*, 76, 75.

7. See Burton, "Archive of Bones," 39; Roy Porter, "Body of Evidence," *Guardian Weekly*, February 7–13, 2002, 16.

8. See Hunter, *Before Novels*, 291.

9. Chandler, "The Face of the Case: *Lord Jim* and the Sentimental Novel." See also Chandler, *An Archaeology of Sympathy*.

10. Chandler, "The Face of the Case: *Lord Jim* and the Sentimental Novel," 841, 842.

11. Ondaatje draws this inventory of missing persons from a report produced by Human Rights Watch.

12. Foucault, *The Order of Things*, 29–30, 219.

13. Melas, *All the Difference in the World*, 25.

14. Burton, "Archive of Bones," 45.

15. Baucom calibrates the level of risk involved in Smith's formulation of the sentimental as a sympathetic and imaginative exchange of places with the sufferer. According to Baucom, Smith's spectator in his use of the imagination "permits the self . . . to make a purely speculative investment in the suffering of another without ever having to abandon the safety of its purely spectatorial position" (*Specters of the Atlantic*, 249).

16. See Chandler's *An Archaeology of Sympathy* for a theorization of the sentimental as a social passion.

17. Smith, *The Theory of Moral Sentiments*, 18, 8–9.

18. Caruth, *Unclaimed Experience*.

19. Agamben, *Remnants of Auschwitz*, 28, 31, 32–33.

NINE. Affective Witnessing

1. Massumi, "The Future Birth of Affective Fact," 53.

2. See Gregg and Seigworth, "An Inventory of Shimmers," 6–9, for their seven-fold typology of affect theory.

3. See Massumi's "The Autonomy Affect," for an elaboration of this ontological theorization of affect.

4. Massumi, "The Autonomy Affect," 85, emphasis added.

5. Massumi, "The Autonomy Affect," 84.

6. Massumi, *Parables for the Virtual*, 9.

7. Grossberg, "Interview with Seigworth and Gregg," 316.

8. Berlant, *Cruel Optimism*, 3.

9. Turner Hospital, *Orpheus Lost*, 92–93. Subsequent quotations are cited parenthetically in the text.

10. Massumi, "The Future Birth of the Affective Fact," 65–66.

11. Agnew, *Enlightenment Orpheus*.

12. Agnew, *Enlightenment Orpheus*, 11–12.

13. Jagoda, "Terror Networks and the Aesthetics of Interconnection," 66.

14. Galloway and Thacker, *The Exploit*; Sageman, *Understanding Terror Networks*; Arquilla and Ronfeldt, *Networks and Netwars*.

15. Sageman, *Understanding Terror Networks*, 119.

16. http://www.cageuk.org/article/beyond-law-war-terror%E2%80%99s-secret -network-global-detentions.

17. See Lietzau, "Combating Terrorism."

18. Cited in Qureshi, *Rules of the Game*, 138, emphasis added.

19. Klein, *The Shock Doctrine*, 12.

20. Massumi, "The Future Birth of Affective Fact," 65.

21. Derrida, *The Politics of Friendship*, 84.

22. Patrick Jagoda, "Terror Networks and the Aesthetics of Interconnection," 67; Arthur Cebrowski and John Garstka, "Network-Centric Warfare: Its Origin and Future," in *Proceedings* (Annapolis, MD: U.S. Naval Institute, 1998), cited in Jagoda, "Terror Networks and the Aesthetics of Interconnection," 66.

23. Cited in Hirsch, "The First Blow," 365.

24. See Ovid's *Metamorphosis*.

25. Cited in Hirsch, "The First Blow," 366.

26. Documentaries and short films include *Ghosts of Abu Ghraib*, directed by Rory Kennedy, 2007; *Standard Operating Procedure*, directed by Errol Morris, 2008; *Torture Question*, directed by Frontline Collective, 2005; *The Road to Guantánamo*, directed by Mat Whitecross and Michael Winterbottom, 2006. War blogs include *Baghdad Burning* by Riverbend, 2003–6; *My War: Killing Time in Iraq* by Colby Buzzell, 2005. Memoirs include Marcus Luttrell, *Lone Survivor* (Boston: Little, Brown, 2007); Byran A. Wood, *Unspoken Abandonment* (Amazon: CreateSpace, 2012).

27. Cited in Qureshi, *Rules of the Game*, 148.

28. Interview with Cageprisoners, September 28, 2004, cited in Qureshi, *Rules of the Game*, 120.

29. See Mayer, *The Dark Side*, 125.

30. Details appear in Habib and Collingwood, *My Story*. His interviews with a few Australian broadcasting media from 2005 onward also testify to the torture techniques he was subjected to.

31. See Osuri, "Media Necropower," paragraph 19.

32. Cited in Qureshi, *Rules of the Game*, 168.

33. Cited in Qureshi, *Rules of the Game*, 173.

34. Cited in Qureshi, *Rules of the Game*, 124.

35. http://www.news.com.au/national/habibs-win-over-radios-big-guns/story -e6frfkwi-1226281655746.

36. Sarah Stephen, "Inside Woomera Asylum Seekers Treated Like Animals," *Green Left*, December 12, 2001, http://www.greenleft.org.au/node/23704.

37. Andrew West, "Asylum-Seeker Teenagers Join Lip Sewing Protest," *Sun-Herald* (Sydney), January 20, 2002.

38. Republished online in several outlets. The academic e-journal *Borderlands* published this poem in its inaugural issue, "Borderphobias: The Politics of Insecurity post 9/11," 1, no. 1 (2002).

39. The phrase *to relay affect* is Butler's. She uses it in her discussion of Susan Sontag's writing on the power of photographs in *Frames of War*, 68. Examples of refugee support networks include the South Australian Coalition for Refugee Children; the Refugee Action Committee, with branches in all major cities; Sydney PEN's publication of an anthology of refugee writing, *Another Country*; academic forums at universities around Sydney, such as "Imprison and Detain: Racialised Punishment in Australia Today" at the University of Technology, Sydney, May 24, 2001, and "Regimes of Terror" at Macquarie University, December 2005.

1. Devji, *The Terrorist in Search of Humanity*, 213.

2. See Chandler, *An Archaeology of Sympathy*, 241.

3. This is an extrapolation from Chandler's formulation of the architecture of the sentimental as "a relay of regards virtualized in a medium" (*An Archaeology of Sympathy*, 13).

4. All Dufka quotes are from Musselman, "Remembering Rwanda."

5. Courtemanche, *Sunday at the Pool in Kigali*, 109. The Arusha Accord was a pact on power-sharing agreements signed in Arusha, Tanzania, by the Hutu-dominated Rwandan government and the Tutsi-led Rwandan Patriotic Front. The signing took place in two stages, on October 30, 1992, and January 9, 1993. But the agreement did not include power sharing with the Hutu extremist Coalition pour la Défense de la République. Further, the cabinet's role was enhanced, but the president's was cut down. It entitled President Habyarimana to stay in office until the transition to a coalition government fully materialized. The power-sharing clause of the Arusha Accord was, not surprisingly, strongly opposed by Hutu extremists, including members of Habyarimana's entourage. See Klinghoffer, *The International Dimension of Genocide in Rwanda* for complete details of the accord and its failure, which led to the genocide.

6. Cited in Jennifer de Poyen, "Art from Genocide—Two Paths to Understanding," *San Diego Union Tribune*, October 30, 2005, http://www.utsandiego.com/uniontrib/20051030/news_1a30rwanda.html.

7. Jason Cowley, "Rebirth of a Nation," *Observer* (London), February 27, 2005, http://observer.guardian.co.uk/review/story/0,6903,1425995,00.html.

8. Coetzee, *Elizabeth Costello*, 158–69.

9. Cowley, "Rebirth of a Nation."

10. Butler, *Precarious Life*, 129–30.

11. Ignatieff, *The Warrior's Honor*, 18–19.

12. Mbembe, "Necropolitics." See also Cheah, *Inhuman Conditions* for an extensive analysis of the immanence of the inhuman in the human in later modernity.

13. McEwan, *Saturday*, 127. Subsequent quotations are cited parenthetically in the text.

14. Hadley, "On a Darkling Plain," 94.

15. Borradori, *Philosophy in a Time of Terror*, xiii.

16. Hadley, "On a Darkling Plain," 95.

Bibliography

Adams, Robert. "Theories of Actuality." In *The Possible and the Actual: Readings in the Metaphysics of Modality*, edited by M. J. Loux, 190–209. Ithaca, NY: Cornell University Press, 1979.

Agamben, Giorgio. *Homo Sacer: Sovereign Power and Bare Life*. Translated by Daniel Heller-Roazen. Stanford, CA: Stanford University Press, 1998.

Agamben, Giorgio. *Remnants of Auschwitz: The Witness and the Archive*. Translated by Daniel Heller-Roazen. London: Zone Books, 2002.

Agnew, Vanessa. *Enlightenment Orpheus: The Power of Music in Other Worlds*. New York: Oxford University Press, 2008.

al Assad, Mehmet. "Asylum." *Borderlands* 1, no. 1 (2002). Accessed January 22, 2016. http://www.borderlands.net.au/vo11no1_2002/alassad_asylum.html.

Albright, Madeleine. "International Law Approaches in the Twenty-First Century: A U.S. Perspective on Enforcement." *Fordham International Law Journal* 18 (1994–95): 1595–606.

Alston, Philip. "The Myopia of the Handmaidens: International Lawyers and Globalization." *European Journal of International Law* 8, no. 3 (1997): 435–48.

Amery, Jean. *At the Mind's Limits: Contemplations by a Survivor on Auschwitz*. Translated by Sidney Rosenfeld and Stella P. Rosenfeld. Bloomington: Indiana University Press, 1980.

Amis, Martin. *The Second Plane: September 11. Terror and Boredom*. London: Vintage, 2009.

Amis, Martin. *Yellow Dog*. London: Vintage, 2003.

Anarkali. Directed by Nandlal Jaswantlal. Bombay: Filmistan, 1953.

Anderson, Benedict. *Imagined Communities: Reflections on the Origin and Spread of Nationalism*. Rev. ed. London: Verso, 1991.

Anderson, Benedict. *The Spectre of Comparisons: Nationalism, Southeast Asia and the World*. London: Verso, 1998.

Appadurai, Arjun, ed. *Globalization*. Durham, NC: Duke University Press, 2001.

Apter, Emily. "Global Translation: The Invention of Comparative Literature, Istanbul, 1933." *Critical Inquiry* 29, no. 2 (2003): 253–81.

Arac, Jonathan. "This Will Kill That: A Provocation on the Novel in Media History." In "Futures of the Novel." Special issue, *Novel: A Forum on Fiction* 44, no. 1 (2011): 6–7.

Aravamudan, Srinivas. "Refusing the Death of the Novel." In "Futures of the Novel." Special issue, *Novel: A Forum on Fiction* 44, no. 1 (2011): 20–21.

Aravamudan, Srinivas, ed. *Slavery, Abolition and Emancipation: Writings in the British Romantic Period*. Vol. 6. London: Pickering and Chatto, 1999.

Arendt, Hannah. *The Human Condition*. Chicago: University of Chicago Press, 1958.

Armstrong, Nancy. *Desire and Domestic Fiction: A Political History of the Novel*. Oxford: Oxford University Press, 1987.

Arquilla, John, and David Ronfeldt, eds. *Networks and Netwars: The Future of Terror, Crimes and Militancy*. Santa Monica, CA: RAND, 2001.

Arrighi, Giovanni. *Adam Smith in Beijing: Lineages of the Twenty-First Century*. London: Verso, 2007.

Artaud, Antonin. "No More Masterpieces." In *The Theatre and Its Double*, translated by Mary Richard, 74–83. New York: Grove, 1958.

Artaud, Antonin. "The Theatre of Cruelty." In *The Theatre and Its Double*, translated by Mary Richard, 85–86. New York: Grove, 1958.

Asad, Talal. *On Suicide Bombing*. New York: Columbia University Press, 2007.

Asif, K., dir. *Mughal-e-Azam*. Produced by Shapoorji Pallonji. Delhi, 1960.

Aslam, Nadeem. *The Wasted Vigil*. London: Vintage, 2008.

Auerbach, Eric. "Philology and *Weltliteratur*." Translated by E. Said and M. Said. *Centennial Review* 13, no. 1 (1969): 1–17.

Avni, Ronit. "Mobilizing Hope: Beyond the Shame-Based Model in the Israeli-Palestinian Conflict." *American Anthropologist* 108, no. 1 (2006): 205–14.

Badiou, Alain. *Ethics: An Essay on the Understanding of Evil*. Translated by Peter Hallward. New York: Verso, 2001.

Baer, Ulrich. *110 Stories: New York Writes after September 11*. New York: New York University Press, 2002.

Bainbridge, Simon. *Napoleon and English Romanticism*. Cambridge: Cambridge University Press, 2006.

Bakhtin, Mikhail. *The Dialogic Imagination*. Edited by Michael Holquist. Translated by Caryl Emerson and Michael Holquist. Austin: University of Texas Press, 1981.

Bakhtin, Mikhail, "Forms of Time and Chronotope in the Novel." In *The Dialogic Imagination*, edited by Michael Holquist. Translated by Caryl Emerson and Michael Holquist, 84–258. Austin: University of Texas Press, 1981.

Bal, Mieke. "Over-Writing as Un-Writing: Descriptions, World-Making, and Novelistic Time." In *The Novel: Forms and Themes*, vol. 2, edited by Franco Moretti, 571–610. Princeton, NJ: Princeton University Press, 2007.

Barnard, Rita. "Fictions of the Global." *Novel: A Forum on Fiction* 42, no. 2 (2009): 207–15.

Baucom, Ian. *Specters of the Atlantic: Finance Capital, Slavery, and the Philosophy of History*. Durham, NC: Duke University Press, 2005.

Baudrillard, Jean. *The Gulf War Did Not Take Place*. Bloomington: Indiana University Press, 1995.

Baudrillard, Jean. *Simulacra and Simulation*. Translated by Sheila Faria Glaser. Ann Arbor: University of Michigan Press, 1994.

Bazin, André. "In Defense of Mixed Cinema." In *Theory of the Novel: A Historical Approach*, edited by Michael McKeon, 719–32. Baltimore: Johns Hopkins University Press, 2000.

Beck, Ulrich. "Cosmopolitan Society and Its Enemies." *Theory, Culture and Society* 19, nos. 1–2 (2002): 17–44.

Beck, Ulrich. *Cosmopolitan Vision*. Cambridge: Polity Press, 2006.

Bellamy, C. *Knights in White Armour: The New Art of War and Peace*. London: Pimlico, 1997.

Berlant, Lauren, ed. *Compassion: The Culture and Politics of an Emotion*. New York: Routledge, 2004.

Berlant, Lauren. *Cruel Optimism*. Durham, NC: Duke University Press, 2011.

Bewes, Timothy. "The Novel Problematic." In "Futures of the Novel." Special issue, *Novel: A Forum on Fiction* 44, no. 1 (2011): 17–19.

Bharucha, Rustom. *Terror and Performance*. London: Routledge, 2014.

Bloomfield, Lincoln P. "Collective Security and US Interests." In *Collective Security in a Changing World*, edited by T. G. Weiss, 189–208. Boulder, CO: Lynne Rienner, 1993.

Bode, Katherine. *Reading by Numbers: Recalibrating the Literary Field*. London: Anthem Press, 2012.

Boltanski, Luc. *Distant Suffering*. Translated by Graham Burchell. Cambridge: Cambridge University Press, 1999. Originally published in French, 1993.

Bolter, Jay David, and Richard Grusin. *Remediation: Understanding New Media*. Cambridge, MA: MIT Press, 1999.

Borradori, Giovanna, ed. *Philosophy in a Time of Terror: Dialogues with Jürgen Habermas and J. Derrida*. Chicago: University of Chicago Press, 2003.

Bouvier, Paul. "*Yo Lo Vi*, Goya Witnessing the Disasters of War: An Appeal to the Sentiment of Humanity." *International Review of the Red Cross* 93, no. 884 (2011): 1107–33.

Brennan, Timothy. "The Subtlety of Caesar." *Interventions* 5, no. 2 (2003): 200–206.

Burke, Jason. *The 9/11 Wars*. London: Allen Lane, 2011.

Burton, Antoinette. "Archive of Bones: *Anil's Ghost* and the Ends of History." *Journal of Commonwealth Literature* 38, no. 1 (2003): 39–56.

Butler, Judith. *Frames of War: When Is Life Grievable?* London: Verso, 2009.

Butler, Judith. *Precarious Life: The Powers of Mourning and Violence*. London: Verso, 2004.

Carter, Jimmy. "University of Notre Dame: Address at Commencement Exercises at the University," May 22, 1977. The American Presidency Project, by John Woolley and Gerhard Peters. http://www.presidency.ucsb.edu/ws/?pid=7552.

Caruth, Cathy. *Unclaimed Experience: Trauma, Narrative and History*. Baltimore: Johns Hopkins University Press, 1996.

Casanova, Pascale. *The World Republic of Letters*. Translated by M. B. De Bevoise. Cambridge, MA: Harvard University Press, 2004.

Castells, Manuel. *Communication Power*. Oxford: Oxford University Press, 2009.

Castells, Manuel. *The Rise of Network Society*. 2nd ed. Sussex, UK: Wiley-Blackwell, 2010.

Chandler, James. *An Archaeology of Sympathy: The Sentimental Mode in Literature and Cinema*. Chicago: University of Chicago Press, 2013.

Chandler, James. "The Face of the Case: *Lord Jim* and the Sentimental Novel." *Critical Inquiry* 33, no. 4 (2007): 837–64.

Chaudhuri, Supriya. "Translating Loss: Place and Language in Amitav Ghosh and Salman Rushdie." *Etudes Anglaises* 62, no. 3 (2009): 266–79.

Cheah, Pheng. *Inhuman Conditions: On Cosmopolitanism and Human Rights*. Cambridge, MA: Harvard University Press, 2006.

Cheah, Pheng. "World Literature as World-Making Activity." *Daedalus* 137, no. 3 (2008): 26–38.

Chow, Rey. *The Age of the World Target: Self-Referentiality in War, Theory and Comparative Work*. Durham, NC: Duke University Press, 2006.

Clausewitz, Carl von. *On War*. Translated by James John Graham. London: N. Trübner, 1873.

Coetzee, J. M. *Elizabeth Costello*. New York: Penguin, 2003.

Cohen, Margaret. "Sentimental Communities." In *The Literary Channel: The International Invention of the Novel*, edited by Margaret Cohen and Carolyn Dever, 106–32. Princeton, NJ: Princeton University Press, 2002.

Cohen, Margaret. *The Sentimental Education of the Novel*. Princeton, NJ: Princeton University Press, 1999.

Cooppan, Vilashini. "Ghosts in the Disciplinary Machine: The Uncanny Life of World Literature." *Comparative Literature Studies* 41, no. 1 (2004): 10–36.

Cooppan, Vilashini. *Worlds Within: National Narratives and Global Connections*. Stanford, CA: Stanford University Press, 2009.

Courtemanche, Gil. *A Sunday at the Pool in Kigali*. Melbourne: Text, 2003.

Cox, Michael. "Who Won the Cold War in Europe? A Historiographical Overview." In *Europe and the End of the Cold War*, edited by Frederic Bozo, Marie-Pierre Rey, N. Piers Ludlow, and Leopoldo Nuti, 9–19. New York: Routledge, 2008.

Culler, Jonathan. "Anderson and the Novel." *Diacritics* 29, no. 4 (1999): 19–39.

Curtis, Polly, and Tom McCarthy. "Kony 2012: What's the Real Story?" *The Guardian*, March 9, 2012.

Cushman, Thomas, and Stjepan G. Mestrovic, eds. *This Time We Knew: Western Responses to Genocide in Bosnia*. New York: New York University Press, 1996.

Damrosch, David. *How to Read World Literature*. Oxford: Wiley-Blackwell, 2008.

Damrosch, David. "Hugo Meltzel and the Principle of Polyglottism." In *The Routledge Companion to World Literature*, edited by Theo D'haen, David Damrosch, and Djelal Kadir, 12–20. London: Routledge, 2011.

Damrosch, David. *What Is World Literature?* Princeton, NJ: Princeton University Press, 2003.

Damrosch, David, Theo D'haen, and Djelal Kadir, eds. *The Routledge Companion to World Literature*. London: Routledge, 2013.

Davis, David Brion. *The Problems of Slavery in the Western World*. Oxford: Oxford University Press, 1966.

Davis, Lennard. *Factual Fictions: The Origins of the English Novel*. Philadelphia: University of Pennsylvania Press, 1983.

Debord, Guy. *Society of the Spectacle*. Detroit: Black and Red, 1983.

DeLillo, Don. *Cosmopolis*. London: Picador, 2003.

DeLillo, Don. *Falling Man*. London: Picador, 2007.

DeLillo, Don. *Mao II*. New York: Viking, 1991.

DeLillo, Don. *Underworld*. New York: Scribner, 1997.

Derrida, Jacques. *The Politics of Friendship*. Translated by George Collins. New York: Verso, 1997.

Derrida, Jacques. *The Problem of Genesis in Husserl's Philosophy*. Translated by Marian Hobson. Chicago: University of Chicago Press, 2003. Originally published in French, 1954.

Derrida, Jacques. "A Self-Unsealing Poetic Text." In *Revenge of the Aesthetic: The Place of Literature in Theory Today*, edited by Michael Clarke, 180–207. Berkeley: University of California Press, 2000.

Derrida, Jacques. *Specters of Marx: The State of Debt, the Work of Mourning and the New International*. Translated by Peggy Kamuf. London: Routledge, 1994. Originally published in French, 1993.

Derrida, Jacques. "The Theatre of Cruelty and the Closure of Representation." In *Writing and Difference*, 292–316. Translated by Alan Bass. Chicago: University of Chicago Press, 1978.

Desmond, Edward. "The Insurgency in Kashmir (1989–1991)." *Contemporary South Asia* 4, no. 1 (1995): 5–16.

Devji, Faisal. *The Terrorist in Search of Humanity: Militant Islam and Global Politics*. London: Hurst, 2008.

Dimock, Wai Chee. "Literature for the Planet." *PMLA* 116, no. 1 (2001): 173–88.

Dimock, Wai Chee. *Through Other Continents: American Literature across Deep Time*. Princeton, NJ: Princeton University Press, 2008.

Downes, Paul. "Melville's *Benito Cereno* and the Politics of Humanitarian Intervention." *South Atlantic Quarterly* 103, nos. 2–3 (2004): 465–88.

Drew, Elizabeth. "A Reporter at Large: Human Rights." *New Yorker*, July 18, 1977.

Eaglestone, Robert. "'The Age of Reason Was Over . . . an Age of Fury Was Dawning': Contemporary Fiction and Terror." In *Terror and the Postcolonial*, edited by Elleke Boehmer and Stephen Morton, 361–69. Oxford: Wiley-Blackwell, 2010.

Ellison, Julie. *Cato's Tears and the Making of Anglo-American Emotion*. Chicago: University of Chicago Press, 1999.

Eshel, Amir. *Futurity: Contemporary Literature and the Quest for the Past*. Chicago: University of Chicago Press, 2012.

Fassin, Didier. *Humanitarian Reason: A Moral History of the Present*. Translated by Rachel Gomme. Berkeley: University of California Press, 2011.

Favret, Mary. "Coming Home: The Public Spaces of Romantic War." *Studies in Romanticism* 33, no. 4 (1994): 539–48.

Favret, Mary. *War at a Distance: Romanticism and the Making of Modern Wartime*. Princeton, NJ: Princeton University Press, 2009.

Feldman, Allen. "The Structuring Enemy and Archival War." PMLA 124, no. 5 (2009): 1704–13.

Festa, Lynn. "Sentimental Bonds and Revolutionary Character: Richardson's *Pamela* in England and France." In *The Literary Channel: The Inter-National Invention of the Novel*, edited by Margaret Cohen and Carolyn Dever, 73–105. Princeton, NJ: Princeton University Press, 2002.

Flanagan, Richard. *The Unknown Terrorist*. London: Random House, 2006.

Flynn, Michael, and Fabiola Salek, eds. *Screening Torture: Media Representations of State Terror*. New York: Columbia University Press, 2012.

Foucault, Michel. *The Order of Things*. London: Routledge, 2002. Originally published in French, 1966.

Franco, Jean. "Globalization and Literary History." *Bulletin of Latin American Research* 25, no. 4 (2006): 441–52.

Frost, Laura. "Falling Man's Precarious Balance." *American Prospect*, May 11, 2007.

Fussell, Paul. *Wartime: Understanding and Behaviour in the Second World War*. New York: Oxford University Press, 1989.

Galloway, Alexander, and Eugene Thacker. *The Exploit: A Theory of Networks*. Minneapolis: University of Minnesota Press, 2007.

Gandhi, Leela. *Affective Communities: Anticolonial Thought, Fin-de-Siècle Radicalism and the Politics of Friendship*. Durham, NC: Duke University Press, 2006.

Gane, Nicholas. "Radical Post-Humanism: Friedrich Kittler and the Primacy of Technology." *Theory, Culture and Society* 22, no. 3 (2005): 25–41.

Ganguly, Debjani. "Edward Said, World Literature and Global Comparatism." In *Edward Said: The Legacy of a Public Intellectual*, edited by Ned Curthoys and Debjani Ganguly, 176–202. Melbourne: Melbourne University Press, 2007.

Ganguly, Debjani. "The Language Question in India." In *The Cambridge History of Postcolonial Literature*, vol. 2, edited by Ato Quayson, 649–80. Cambridge: Cambridge University Press, 2011.

Gaston, Sean. "Derrida and the End of the World." *New Literary History* 42, no. 3 (2011): 499–517.

Gibbons, Luke. *Edmund Burke and Ireland*. Cambridge: Cambridge University Press, 2003.

Giles, Paul. *Virtual Americas: Transnational Fictions and Transatlantic Imaginary*. Durham, NC: Duke University Press, 2002.

Godwin, William. *Enquiry Concerning Political Justice and Its Influence on Modern Morals and Happiness*. Edited by Isaac Kramnick. London: Penguin, 1985.

Goodman, Nelson. *Ways of World Making*. New York: Hackett, 1978.

Gregg, Melissa, and Gregory J. Seigworth. "An Inventory of Shimmers." In *The Affect Theory Reader*, edited by Melissa Gregg and Gregory J. Seigworth, 1–26. Durham, NC: Duke University Press, 2010.

Gregory, Derek. *The Colonial Present: Afghanistan, Palestine, Iraq*. Oxford: Blackwell, 2004.

Gregory, Derek. "The Everywhere War." *Geographical Journal* 177, no. 3 (2011): 238–50.

Gregory, Derek. "Vanishing Points: Law, Violence, and Exception in the Global War Prison." *Terror and the Postcolonial*, edited by Elleke Boehmer and Stephen Morton, 55–98. London: Routledge, 2011.

Gregory, Sam. "Transnational Story-telling: Human Rights, WITNESS and Advocacy." *American Anthropologist* 108, no. 1 (2006): 191–220.

Grossberg, Lawrence. "Interview with Seigworth and Gregg." In *The Affect Theory Reader*, edited by Melissa Gregg and Gregory J. Seigworth, 309–38. Durham, NC: Duke University Press, 2010.

Guillen, Claudio. *The Challenge of Comparative Literature*. Cambridge, MA: Harvard University Press, 1993.

Guillen, Claudio. *Literature as System: Towards the Theory of Literary History*. Princeton, NJ: Princeton University Press, 1971.

Habib, Mamdouh, with Julia Collingwood. *My Story: The Tale of a Terrorist Who Wasn't*. Melbourne: Scribe, 2008.

Hadley, Elaine. "On a Darkling Plain: Victorian Liberalism and the Fantasy of Agency." *Victorian Studies* 48, no. 1 (2005): 92–102.

Hage, Ghassan. "Comes a Time We Are All Enthusiasm: Understanding Palestinian Suicide Bombing in Times of Exighophobia." *Public Culture* 15, no. 1 (2003): 65–89.

Hamid, Mohsin. *The Reluctant Fundamentalist*. London: Harcourt, 2007.

Hansen, Birthe, and Bertel Heurlin, eds. *The New World Order: Contrasting Theories*. London: Palgrave Macmillan, 2000.

Hardt, Michael, and Antonio Negri. *Multitude*. New York: Penguin, 2004.

Harvey, David. *The Condition of Postmodernity: An Inquiry into the Origins of Cultural Change*. Oxford: Wiley-Blackwell, 1989.

Harvey, David. *Spaces of Hope*. Berkeley: University of California Press, 2000.

Haskell, Thomas. "Capitalism and the Origins of Humanitarian Sensibility." Part 1. *American Historical Review* 90, no. 2 (1985): 339–61.

Haskell, Thomas. "Capitalism and the Origins of Humanitarian Sensibility." Part 2. *American Historical Review* 90, no. 3 (1985): 547–66.

Hayden, John O., ed. *William Wordsworth: The Poems*. Vol. 1. New Haven, CT: Yale University Press, 1981.

Hayot, Eric. *On Literary Worlds*. Oxford: Oxford University Press, 2012.

Hegel, G. W. F. *The Philosophy of History*. New York: Dover, 1956.

Heidegger, Martin. "The Age of the World Picture." In *Questions Concerning Technology and Other Essays*, translated by William Lovitt, 115–54. New York: Harper and Row, 1977.

Herwitz, Daniel. *Heritage, Culture and Politics in the Postcolony*. New York: Columbia University Press, 2012.

Hirsch, Marianne. "The First Blow: Torture and Close Reading." PMLA 121, no. 2 (2006): 361–70.

Hobbes, Thomas. *Leviathan*. New York: Cambridge University Press, 1991.

Houen, Alex. *Terrorism and Modern Literature: From Joseph Conrad to Ciaran Carson*. Oxford: Oxford University Press, 2002.

Hungerford, Amy. "On the Period Formerly Known as the Contemporary." *American Literary History* 20, nos. 1–2 (2008): 410–19.

Hunt, Lynn. *Inventing Human Rights: A History*. New York: W. W. Norton, 2007.

Hunter, J. Paul. *Before Novels: The Cultural Contexts of Eighteenth-Century English Fiction*. New York: W. W. Norton, 1990.

Huyssen, Andreas. "Present Pasts: Media, Politics and Amnesia." In *Globalization*, edited by Arjun Appadurai, 57–77. Durham, NC: Duke University Press, 2001.

Ignatieff, Michael. *The Warrior's Honor: Ethnic War and the Modern Conscience*. New York: Henry Holt, 1998.

Jagoda, Patrick. "Terror Networks and the Aesthetics of Interconnection." *Social Text* 28, no. 4 (2010): 65–89.

Jameson, Fredric. *The Political Unconscious: Narrative as a Socially Symbolic Act*. Ithaca, NY: Cornell University Press, 1982.

Kadir, Djelal. "Comparative Literature in an Age of Terrorism." In *Comparative Literature in an Age of Globalization*, edited by Haun Saussy, 68–77. Baltimore: Johns Hopkins University Press, 2006.

Kadir, Djelal. "To World, to Globalize—Comparative Literature's Crossroads." *Comparative Literature Studies* 41, no. 1 (2004): 1–9.

Kaldor, Mary. *New and Old Wars: Organized Violence in a Global Era*. 2nd ed. Cambridge: Polity Press, 2006.

Karagiannis, Nathalie, and Peter Wagner. *Varieties of World Making*. Liverpool: Liverpool University Press, 2007.

Kauffman, Linda. "The Wake of Terror." *Modern Fiction Studies* 54, no. 2 (summer 2008): 353–77.

Keenan, Thomas. "Publicity and Indifference (Sarajevo on Television)." *PMLA* 117, no. 1 (2002): 104–16.

Keneally, Thomas. *The Tyrant's Novel*. New York: Random House, 2004.

Kermode, Frank. *The Sense of an Ending: Studies in the Theory of Fiction*. Oxford: Oxford University Press, 1967.

Khanna, Ranjana. "Disposability." *differences* 20, no. 1 (2009): 181–98.

Klein, Naomi. *The Shock Doctrine*. New York: Metropolitan Books, 2007.

Klinghoffer, Arthur Jay. *The International Dimension of Genocide in Rwanda*. New York: New York University Press, 1998.

Kripke, Saul. *Naming and Necessity*. Cambridge, MA: Harvard University Press, 1980.

Lanier, Jaron. *You Are Not a Gadget: A Manifesto*. New York: Vintage, 2010.

Laqueur, Thomas W. "Bodies, Details and the Humanitarian Narrative." In *The Cultural History*, edited by Lynn Hunt, 177–204. Berkeley: University of California Press, 1989.

Lash, Scott. *Critique of Information*. London: Sage, 2002.

Latour, Bruno. *We Have Never Been Modern*. Translated by Catherine Porter. Cambridge, MA: Harvard University Press, 1993. Originally published in French, 1991.

Lévy, Bernard-Henri. *Barbarism with a Human Face*. Translated by George Holoch. New York: Harper and Row, 1979. Originally published in French, 1977.

Lévy, Bernard-Henri. *Who Killed Daniel Pearl?* London: Gerald Duckworth, 2004.

Lewis, David. *Counterfactuals*. Oxford: Blackwell, 1973.

Lietzau, William K. "Combating Terrorism: Law Enforcement of War?" In *Terrorism and International Law: Challenges and Responses*, 75–84. San Remo, Italy: International Institute of Humanitarian Law, 2002. http://www.iihl.org/iihl/Album/terrorism-law .pdf.

Livings, Jack. "Salman Rushdie: The Art of Fiction No. 186." *Paris Review* 174 (2005): 107–43.

Lubonir, Dolezol. *Heterocosmica: Fiction and Possible Worlds.* Baltimore: Johns Hopkins University Press, 1998.

Lukács, Georg. *The Historical Novel.* Translated by Hannah Mitchell and Stanley Mitchell. Lincoln: University of Nebraska Press, 1983. Originally published 1937.

Lukács, Georg. *The Theory of the Novel.* Translated by Anna Bostock. Cambridge, MA: MIT Press, 1971. Originally published 1920.

Lund, Hans. *Text as Picture: Studies in Literary Transformation of Pictures.* New York: E. Ellen Press, 1992.

Mailer, Norman. *Harlot's Ghost.* London: Abacus, 1992.

Mamdani, Mahmood. *Good Muslim, Bad Muslim: America, the Cold War and the Roots of Terror.* New York: Doubleday, 2004.

Manovich, Lev. *The Language of New Media.* Cambridge, MA: MIT Press, 2001.

Marno, D. "The Monstrosity of Literature: Hugo Meltzl's World Literature and Its Legacies." In *World Literature and World Culture,* edited by K. M. Simonsen and J. Stougaard-Nielsen, 37–50. Aarhus, Denmark: Aarhus University Press, 2008.

Marx, Karl, and Friedrich Engels. *The Communist Manifesto.* In *Marx/Engels Selected Works,* vol. 1, 89–137. Translated by Samuel Moore. Moscow: Progressive, 1969.

Massumi, Brian. "The Autonomy Affect." *Cultural Critique* 35 (1995): 83–109.

Massumi, Brian. "The Future Birth of Affective Fact." In *The Affect Theory Reader,* edited by Melissa Gregg and Gregory J. Seigworth, 52–70. Durham, NC: Duke University Press, 2010.

Massumi, Brian. *Parables for the Virtual: Movement, Affect, Sensation.* Durham, NC: Duke University Press, 2002.

Mayer, Jane. *The Dark Side: The Inside Story of How the War on Terror Turned into a War on American Ideals.* New York: Doubleday, 2008.

Mbembe, Achille. "Necropolitics." *Public Culture* 15, no. 1 (2003): 11–40.

McCann, Andrew. "The International of Excreta: World Literature and Its Other." *Overland* 186 (2007): 20–24.

McEwan, Ian. *Saturday.* London: Vintage, 2006.

McKeon, Michael. *The Origins of the English Novel: 1600–1740.* Baltimore: Johns Hopkins University Press, 2002. Originally published 1987.

McKeon, Michael, ed. *The Theory of the Novel: A Historical Approach.* Baltimore: Johns Hopkins University Press, 2000.

McLagan, Meg. "Principles, Publicity and Politics: Notes on Human Rights Media." *American Anthropologist* 105, no. 3 (2003): 605–12.

Melas, Natalie. *All the Difference in the World.* Stanford, CA: Stanford University Press, 2007.

Meltzl, Hugo. "Present Tasks of Comparative Literature." Translated by H. J. Schulz. In *The Princeton Sourcebook in Comparative Literature,* edited by D. Damrosch, N. Melas, and M. Buthelezi, 41–49. Princeton, NJ: Princeton University Press, 2009.

Mendis, Ranjini. "A Review of *Anil's Ghost.*" *Chimo* (2000): 7–12.

Mieszkowski, Jan. "Watching War." *PMLA* 124, no. 5 (2009): 1648–61.

Mieszkowski, Jan. *Watching War.* Stanford, CA: Stanford University Press, 2012.

Miller, Andrew. *The Optimists.* London: Hodder and Stoughton, 2005.

Mishra, Vijay. *Bollywood Cinema: Temples of Desire.* London: Routledge, 2001.

Mitchell, David. *Ghostwritten*. London: Vintage, 1999.

Mitchell, W. J. T. *Cloning Terror: The War of Images, 9/11 to the Present*. Chicago: University of Chicago Press, 2011.

Mitchell, W. J. T. "Ekphrasis and the Other." *Picture Theory: Essays on Verbal and Visual Representation*, 151–82. Chicago: University of Chicago Press, 1994.

Mitchell, W. J. T. *Picture Theory: Essays on Verbal and Visual Representation*. Chicago: University of Chicago Press, 1994.

Mirzoeff, Nicholas. "The Right to Look." *Critical Inquiry* 37, no. 3 (2011): 473–96.

Mirzoeff, Nicholas. *The Right to Look: A Counterhistory of Visuality*. Durham, NC: Duke University Press, 2011.

Mirzoeff, Nicholas. "War Is Culture: Global Counterinsurgency, Visuality and the Petraeus Doctrine." PMLA 124, no. 5 (2009): 1737–46.

Moretti, Franco. *Atlas of the European Novel*. London: Verso, 1998.

Moretti, Franco. "Conjectures on World Literature." *New Left Review* 1 (2000): 54–68.

Moretti, Franco. *Graphs, Maps, Trees: Abstract Models for a Literary History*. London: Verso, 2007.

Moretti, Franco. *The Way of the World: Bildungsroman in European Culture*. London: Verso, 1987.

Morton, Stephen. "'There Were Collisions and Explosions: The World Was No Longer Calm': Terror and Precarious Life in Salman Rushdie's *Shalimar the Clown*." *Textual Practice* 22, no. 2 (2008): 337–55.

Moyn, Samuel. *The Last Utopia: Human Rights in History*. Cambridge, MA: Harvard University Press, 2010.

Mufti, Aamir. "Auerbach in Istanbul: Edward Said, Secular Criticism and the Question of Minority Culture." *Critical Inquiry* 25, no. 1 (1998): 95–125.

Mufti, Aamir. "Orientalism and the Institution of World Literatures." *Critical Inquiry* 36, no. 3 (2010): 458–93.

Murray, John. *A Few Short Notes on Tropical Butterflies*. New York: HarperCollins, 2003.

Musselman, Anson. "Remembering Rwanda: Ten Years after the Massacres." UCLA African Studies Center, May 11, 2004. http://www.international.ucla.edu/africa/article/11069.

Nancy, Jean-Luc. *The Creation of the World or Globalization*. Translated by François Raffoul and David Pettigrew. Albany: State University of New York Press, 2007.

Ondaatje, Michael. *Anil's Ghost*. New York: Vintage, 2000.

Orford, Anne. "Muscular Humanitarianism: Reading the Narratives of New Interventionism." *European Journal of International Law* 10, no. 4 (1999): 679–711.

Osborne, William. "Documentation of Stockhausen's Comments re: 9/11." September 22, 2001. http://www.osborne-conant.org/documentation_stockhausen.htm.

Osuri, Goldie. "Media Necropower: Australian Media Reception and Somatechnics of Mamdouh Habib." *Borderlands e-Journal* 5, no. 1 (2006). http://www.borderlands.net.au/vol5no1_2006/osuri_necropower.htm.

Palumbo-Liu, David. *The Deliverance of Others: Reading Literature in a Global Age*. Durham, NC: Duke University Press, 2012.

Pascoe, David. "The Cold War and the War on Terror." In *The Cambridge Companion to*

War Writing, edited by Kate McLoughlin, 239–49. Cambridge: Cambridge University Press, 2010.

Pavel, Thomas. *Fictional Worlds*. Cambridge, MA: Harvard University Press, 1986.

Pavel, Thomas. "Literary Genres as Norms and Good Habits." *New Literary History* 34, no. 2 (2003): 201–10.

Peebles, Stacey. "Lines of Sight: Watching War in *Jarhead* and *My War: Killing Time in Iraq*." PMLA 124, no. 5 (2009): 1662–76.

Plantinga, Alvin. "Actualism and Possible Worlds." *Theoria* 42 (1976): 139–60.

Plotz, John. "No Future." In "Futures of the Novel." Special issue, *Novel: A Forum on Fiction* 44, no. 1 (2011): 23–26.

Pollock, Sheldon. *The Language of Gods in the World of Men: Sanskrit, Culture and Power in Premodern India*. Berkeley: University of California Press, 2006.

Poovey, Mary. *The History of the Modern Fact*. Chicago: University of Chicago Press, 1998.

Powers, Kevin. *The Yellow Birds*. London: Sceptre Books, 2012.

Prendergast, Christopher, ed. *Debating World Literature*. London: Verso, 2004.

Qadri, Ismail. "A Flippant Gesture towards Sri Lanka: A Review of Michael Ondaatje's *Anil's Ghost*." *Pravada* 6, no. 9 (2000): 24–29.

Qureshi, Asim. *Rules of the Game*. New York: Columbia University Press, 2009.

Rabinow, Paul. *Marking Time: On the Anthropology of the Contemporary*. Princeton, NJ: Princeton University Press, 2008.

Rai, M. *Hindu Rulers, Muslim Subjects: Islam, Rights and the History of Kashmir*. Princeton, NJ: Princeton University Press, 2004.

Rajadhyaksha, Ashish. *Indian Cinema in the Time of Celluloid*. Bloomington: Indiana University Press, 2009.

Rajasekhara. *Kavyamimansa*. Edited and translated by A. N. Jani. New Delhi: D. K. Print World, 2000.

Rancière, Jacques. "Introducing Disagreement." Translated by Steven Corcoran. *Angelaki* 9, no. 3 (2004): 3–9.

Rancière, Jacques. *The Politics of Aesthetics: The Distribution of the Sensible*. Translated by Gabriel Rockhill. New York: Continuum, 2004.

Rancière, Jacques. "Who Is the Subject of the Rights of Man?" *South Atlantic Quarterly* 103, nos. 2–3 (2004): 297–310.

Renouart de Bussierre, Sophie. "Rembrandt-Goya." In *Goya: Graveur*, edited by Maryline Assante di Panzillo and Simon André-Deconcha, 10–16. Paris: Paris-Musée et Nicolas Chaudun, 2008.

Ricci, Ronit. *Islam Translated: Literature, Conversion and the Arabic Cosmopolis of South and Southeast Asia*. Chicago: University of Chicago Press, 2011.

Richter, Gerhard. "Notes for a Press Conference, November–December 1988." In *The Daily Practice of Painting: Writings and Interviews 1962–1993*, edited by Hans-Ulrich Obrist, translated by David Britt, 173–83. Cambridge, MA: MIT Press, 1995.

Riverbend. *Baghdad Burning: Girl Blog from Iraq*. New York: Feminist Press of the City University of New York, 2005.

Robbins, Bruce. *Perpetual War: Cosmopolitanism from the Viewpoint of Violence*. Durham, NC: Duke University Press, 2012.

Robbins, Bruce. "The Worlding of the American Novel." Bruce Robbins Papers. http://www.columbia.edu/~bwr2001/papers/Robbins%20Worlding%20w%20xrefs%205.25.09.pdf.

Román, David, ed. "A Forum on Theatre and Tragedy in the Wake of September 11." *Theatre Journal* 54, no. 1 (2002): 1–17.

Ronen, Ruth. *Possible Worlds in Literary Theory*. Cambridge: Cambridge University Press, 1994.

Rothberg, Michael. *Traumatic Realism: The Demands of Holocaust Representation*. Minneapolis: University of Minnesota Press, 2000.

Rousseau, Jean-Jacques. *Emile: Or on Education*. Translated by Allan Bloom. New York: Harper and Row, 1979.

Rushdie, Salman. "Inside the Mind of Jihadists." *New Perspectives Quarterly* 23, no. 1 (2006): 7–11.

Rushdie, Salman. *Midnight's Children*. London: Jonathan Cape, 1981.

Rushdie, Salman. *The Satanic Verses*. London: Jonathan Cape, 1988.

Rushdie, Salman. *Shalimar the Clown*. London: Jonathan Cape, 2005.

Russell, Gillian. "The Eighteenth Century and the Romantics on War." In *The Cambridge Companion to War Writing*, edited by Kate McLoughlin, 112–25. Cambridge: Cambridge University Press, 2009.

Russell, Gillian. *Theatres of War*. Oxford: Clarendon Press, 1995.

Sacco, Joe. *Footnotes in Gaza*. New York: Metropolitan Books, 2009.

Sageman, Marc. *Understanding Terror Networks*. Philadelphia: University of Pennsylvania Press, 2004.

Said, Edward. *Culture and Imperialism*. New York: Vintage, 1993.

Said, Edward. *Humanism and Democratic Criticism*. New York: Columbia University Press, 2003.

Said, Edward. *The World, the Text and the Critic*. Cambridge, MA: Harvard University Press, 1983.

Scarry, Elaine. *The Body in Pain: The Making and Unmaking of the World*. New York: Oxford University Press, 1985.

Schechner, Richard. "9/11 as Avante-Garde Art?" PMLA 124, no. 5 (2009): 1820–29.

Scherrer, Christian. *Genocide and Crisis in Central Africa*. London: Praeger, 2002.

Schmitz-Emans, Monika. "Richard Meyer's Concept of World Literature." In *The Routledge Companion to World Literature*, edited by Theo D'haen, David Damrosch, and Djelal Kadir, 49–61. London: Routledge, 2011.

Scott, Rosie, and Thomas Keneally, eds. "Another Country." Special issue of *Southerly* 64, no. 1 (2004).

Shaw, Phillip. *Waterloo and the Romantic Imagination*. New York: Macmillan, 2002.

Simma, Bruno. "NATO, the UN and the Use of Force: Legal Aspects." *European Journal of International Law* 10, no. 1 (1999): 1–22.

Singer, P. W. *Wired for War: The Robotics Revolution and Conflict in the 21st Century*. London: Penguin, 2009.

Slaughter, Joseph. *Human Rights, Inc.: The World Novel, Narrative Form and International Law*. New York: Fordham University Press, 2007.

Smith, Adam. *The Theory of Moral Sentiments*. London: Penguin, 2009. Originally published 1759.

Sontag, Susan. *On Photography*. New York: Picador, 1977.

Sontag, Susan. *Regarding the Pain of Others*. New York: Farrar, Straus and Giroux, 2003.

Sphar, Clemens, "Prolonged Suspension: Don DeLillo, Ian McEwan and the Literary Imagination after 9/11." *Novel: A Forum on Fiction* 45, no. 2 (2012): 221–37.

Spiegelman, Art. *In the Shadow of No Towers*. New York: Pantheon Books, 2004.

Spiegelman, Art. *MetaMaus*. Edited by Hillary Chute. New York: Pantheon Books, 2011.

St. Clair, William. *The Reading Nation in the Romantic Period*. Cambridge: Cambridge University Press, 2004.

Sterne, Laurence. *The Life and Opinions of Tristram Shandy, a Gentleman*. London: Wordsworth, 1996. Originally published 1759.

Storr, Robert, ed. *Gerhard Richter: October 18, 1977*. New York: Museum of Modern Art, 2000.

Strich, Fritz. *Goethe and World Literature*. London: Routledge and Kegan Paul, 1946.

Stuchtey, Benedikt, and Eckhardt Fuchs, eds. *Writing World History 1800–2000*. Oxford: Oxford University Press, 2003.

Tagore, Rabindranath. *Nationalism*. 2nd ed. New Delhi: Rupa Paperback, 1994. Originally published 1917.

Tagore, Rabindranath. "World-Literature." Translated by S. Chakravorty. In *Rabindranath Tagore: Selected Writings on Literature and Language*, edited by Sisir Kumar Das and Sukanta Chaudhuri, 138–50. New Delhi: Oxford University Press, 2001.

Taylor, Christopher. "The Hamitic Hypothesis in Rwanda and Burundi." In *Sacrifice as Terror: The Rwandan Genocide of 1994*, 55–98. Oxford: Berg, 1999.

Trotter, David. *Literature in the First Media Age*. Cambridge, MA: Harvard University Press, 2013.

Turner Hospital, Janette. *Orpheus Lost*. Sydney: Fourth Estate, 2007.

Updike, John. *Terrorist*. New York: Random House, 2006.

Urquhart, Brian. "Learning from the Gulf." In *Whose New World Order? What Role for the United Nations?*, edited by M. R. Bustelo and P. Alston. Sydney: Federation Press, 1991.

Villanueva, Dario. "Claudio Guillen." In *The Routledge Companion to World Literature*, edited by Theo D'haen, David Damrosch, and Djelal Kadir, 108–16. London: Routledge, 2011.

Virilio, Paul, and Sylvère Lotringer. *Crepuscular Dawn*. Translated by Mike Taormina. New York: Semiotext(e), 2002.

Virilio, Paul, and Sylvère Lotringer. *Pure War*. Los Angeles: Semiotexte, 2008.

Wallerstein, Immanuel. *After Liberalism*. New York: New Press, 1995.

Wallerstein, Immanuel. "The World System after the Cold War." *Journal of Peace Research* 30, no. 1 (1993): 1–6.

Watt, Ian. *The Rise of the Novel: Studies in Defoe, Richardson and Fielding*. Berkeley: University of California Press, 1962.

Whitman, Walt. *Song of Myself*. In *Leaves of Grass*. New Delhi: Eurasia, 1971.

Woolf, Virginia. "The Leaning Tower." In *The Moment and Other Essays*, 130–31. New York: Harcourt Brace, 1948.

Wright, Geoffrey A. "The Desert of Experience: *Jarhead* and the Geography of the Persian Gulf War." PMLA 124, no. 5 (2009): 1677–89.

Žižek, Slavoj. *The Ticklish Subject: The Absent Centre of Political Ontology*. London: Verso, 1999.

Index

Page numbers followed by *f* indicate figures.